STRATEGIC STUDIES INSTITUTE

The Strategic Studies Institute (SSI) is part of the U.S. Army War College and is the strategic-level study agent for issues related to national security and military strategy with emphasis on geostrategic analysis.

The mission of SSI is to use independent analysis to conduct strategic studies that develop policy recommendations on:

- Strategy, planning, and policy for joint and combined employment of military forces;

- Regional strategic appraisals;

- The nature of land warfare;

- Matters affecting the Army's fu   ,

- The concepts, philosophy, and theory of strategy; and,

- Other issues of importance to the leadership of the Army.

Studies produced by civilian and military analysts concern topics having strategic implications for the Army, the Department of Defense, and the larger national security community.

In addition to its studies, SSI publishes special reports on topics of special or immediate interest. These include edited proceedings of conferences and topically oriented roundtables, expanded trip reports, and quick-reaction responses to senior Army leaders.

The Institute provides a valuable analytical capability within the Army to address strategic and other issues in support of Army participation in national security policy formulation.

Strategic Studies Institute
and
U.S. Army War College Press

AMERICAN GRAND STRATEGY AND THE FUTURE OF U.S. LANDPOWER

Joseph Da Silva
Hugh Liebert
Isaiah Wilson III
Editors

December 2014

*****

Comments pertaining to this report are invited and should be forwarded to: Director, Strategic Studies Institute and U.S. Army War College Press, U.S. Army War College, 47 Ashburn Drive, Carlisle, PA 17013-5010.

*****

All Strategic Studies Institute (SSI) and U.S. Army War College (USAWC) Press publications may be downloaded free of charge from the SSI website. Hard copies of this report may also be obtained free of charge while supplies last by placing an order on the SSI website. SSI publications may be quoted or reprinted in part or in full with permission and appropriate credit given to the U.S. Army Strategic Studies Institute and U.S. Army War College Press, U.S. Army War College, Carlisle, PA. Contact SSI by visiting our website at the following address: *www.StrategicStudiesInstitute.army.mil.*

*****

The Strategic Studies Institute and U.S. Army War College Press publishes a monthly email newsletter to update the national security community on the research of our analysts, recent and forthcoming publications, and upcoming conferences sponsored by the Institute. Each newsletter also provides a strategic commentary by one of our research analysts. If you are interested in receiving this newsletter, please subscribe on the SSI website at *www.StrategicStudiesInstitute.army.mil/newsletter.*

ISBN 1-58487-645-X

CONTENTS

FOREWORD

The current international security environment is characterized by unprecedented uncertainty. In the Asia-Pacific, our allies adjust to China's rise and hedge against instability coming from North Korea. In the greater Middle East, the Syrian civil war draws in powerful state and nonstate actors, Iran's weapons program worries its neighbors, the Arab Spring continues its uncertain course, and we see a growing Sunni-Shia split throughout the region. In Europe, the need for a strong North Atlantic Treaty Organization alliance has become clear as nations along Russia's periphery reevaluate their strategic alignments in the wake of the situation in Crimea. In Africa, weak states with ethnic and religious tensions set conditions for terrorist groups to operate with near impunity. It is in this uncertain and unstable world that U.S. military forces will operate for the foreseeable future.

These security challenges require us to remain the most highly-trained and professional All-Volunteer land force in the world, uniquely organized with the capability and capacity to provide expeditionary, decisive Landpower to the Joint Force, and ready to perform the range of military operations in support of combatant commanders to defend the Nation and its interests at home and abroad, both today and against emerging threats.

In order to ensure our Army is postured for the future, we must continue to look forward. We know that the pace of change is accelerating. The number of connections between people and societies has increased exponentially. Media can elevate local actions instantly to strategic importance. Technology and weapons once reserved to states now find their way into the hands of disaffected individuals and disruptive groups. These conditions suggest it will become increasingly more difficult for the United States to act independently. Thus, developing a global network of unified Landpower will be an essential element of our Nation's future security.

However, before we can develop a global Landpower network, we must first fully understand where the intersection of Landpower occurs with the human domain. Our experiences in Iraq and Afghanistan clearly reinforced that lasting strategic results are only achieved by influencing people effectively. Conflict, in all its forms, remains a fundamentally human endeavor. Destroying infrastructure and weaponry offers a physical approach to shaping an adversary's decisions, but by itself is rarely sufficient and can occasionally be counterproductive. Success depends as much on understanding the social and political fabric of the surroundings as it does on the ability to physically dominate them. A security strategy that does not adequately take into account human factors and the need for Landpower to take and hold terrain in a future conflict will be fundamentally flawed.

This volume takes a hard look at the many challenges our Nation and our Army will face and the grand strategy we need for the future. More importantly, it poses tough questions and looks forward at what our future missions may be and how our Army should be organized to accomplish those missions. Additionally, it examines the way in which we grow and manage our talent, our most important resource, and whether that is sufficient to meet our future needs. As a profession, we must always be willing to take a hard look at ourselves and ask these tough questions. It is the best way to ensure that we do not just focus on today, but think and prepare for tomorrow.

RAYMOND T. ODIERNO
General, 38th Chief of Staff
U.S. Army

FOREWORD

THE ARMY'S MIRACLE MOMENT

In 1980, the United States defeated the Soviet Union in an Olympic hockey game. The victory was surprising and dramatic; in short order, it became the "Miracle on Ice," and in 2004, it became the subject of a feature film, *Miracle*. But what was happening off the ice on February 22, 1980, was as significant as what happened on it. As the victorious American team left the rink in Lake Placid, NY, other Americans began their 110th day of captivity in Tehran, Iran. As the Soviet team hung their heads, Soviet troops surged into Afghanistan. The American victory was a sensation in part because it seemed an aberration.

The events surrounding the "Miracle on Ice" foreshadowed our current threat environment. How do we better anticipate second- and third-order effects of events? Did the Cold War lens narrow our understanding of possibilities? Are our current lenses, whether they be post-9/11 or post-Iraq/Afghanistan wars, as clear as they should be? One may argue that the forces of globalization have made many threats more proximate both in space and time. Failing to fully comprehend global complexities often results in repercussions right around the corner. We cannot afford an Army that can't see around the corner, which is why officer education is a security imperative.

I assumed the role of Superintendent of the United States Military Academy after spending much of the last decade in combat. I can guarantee that America's Army will always respond to our Nation's call, but to be most effective, we must always be preparing for what lies around the corner. The Army not only provides the country with an essential element of its strategic hedge, but right now it is also providing the enablers to prevent conflict and shape conditions that support our national interests. This is the perfect moment to aggressively focus on our leader development through education. The complexity of the security environment is such that how we fight wars may not adequately address many of the threats that put our Nation's interests at risk, and we need leaders who can think strategically to address proactively these emerging security challenges.

What impact do these complex regional security issues have on tomorrow's regional security environments, and how should we approach them? This is a real question faced by many Army units that are now regionally aligned. At first glance, this complexity in a regional context may seem daunting to a division or a brigade. If we just look at the Middle East, there is no doubt that major states in the region suffer from demographic pressures, resource scarcity, economic deprivation, rampant urbanization, and other human security issues that would place enormous stress on any state, much less illegitimate and underdeveloped ones. Moreover, many of these states have been in existence only since the last century, were carved out artificially by Western powers, and have depended on outside powers for both legitimacy and aid. For example, Syria's Hafiz al-Assad was able to maintain power through the Cold War by relying on Soviet aid, while Egypt received a tremendous amount of aid through its bold realignment with the West. In truth, these leaders, among others, derived much of their legitimacy from the international community, not necessarily from their own people.

The United States favorably viewed this situation because these states remained "stable." What September 11, 2001, demonstrated, however, is that this stability came with a price, and the forces of globalization facilitated the emerging trends of human security issues. These issues feed directly into the messy concept of legitimacy that once only entered into academic discourse, not practical applications of military power. Over time, the legitimacy formulas have changed, and people have become a potent political force that cannot be ignored.

The Army, whether in the Pacific, the Middle East, Africa, or anywhere else in the world, will always be engaged with the indigenous population, other U.S. Government departments and agencies, international and regional organizations, nongovernmental organizations, other Department of Defense Services, and host nation leaders and informal leaders. It is within this regional context that Army leaders will face increasing challenges from dynamics as varied as environmental changes, cyber effects, new technologies, and extremist ideas. How does one learn to lead in such a fast-changing world? How do leaders learn not just how to solve problems but to have the agility to anticipate new problem sets and lead others to do the same?

First, leaders must begin their strategic thinking and develop essential habits of mind at the undergraduate level. These habits—that is, thinking critically, creatively, holistically, and empathetically—must be continually nurtured because they are the foundation for the intellectual curiosity that ensures the health of the Army as a learning organization.[1] Such thinking does not automatically occur just because someone is promoted to colonel.

Second, leaders need to immerse themselves in broadening opportunities, whether it be serving an assignment with interagency partners, a posting abroad with key allies, or attending graduate school and serving on West Point's faculty, which offer an opportunity to study in depth, learn from civilian counterparts in all walks of life, and develop the humility necessary to know what they do not know. Broadening of officers is also invaluable to developing the civil-military relationships and mutual trust so essential to our democracy and our profession. A key part of my job here is to ensure we resource faculty so they can continually deepen their studies and conduct important research so that we can continually look around corners across all domains.

Third, a values-based education is imperative, to include valuing intellectual courage: the courage to ask the hard questions, to reevaluate long-held assumptions, and to know when it is time to embrace new traditions. It also inculcates professionals with the moral courage to ensure that our words and deeds are aligned with our values.

Educated officers, guided by the Chief of Staff of the Army's "Prevent, Shape, and Win" framework, can translate this framework into tangible roles and missions with impactful results. The Army already is contributing to the joint force in terms of enablers, such as its intelligence, logistics, civil affairs, weapons of mass destruction security, train and assist, and other military-to-military roles and missions. Such leaders are not produced overnight. The Army must invest in its junior leaders now to ensure we grow strategically-minded senior leaders who are unafraid to think differently in our changing world, who value diverse talents, who know how to work collaboratively with other enablers throughout our government and international communities, and who have the right empathy required to truly empower people on the ground to make good choices.

The country requires Army leaders of great courage to stay the course without seeing immediate effects. This is particularly hard for an Army culture and a political process that crave immediate effects. We are committed to invest in our people to produce servants to the Nation who can look around corners and decisively set strategic conditions that best support our national interests, while keeping combat teams ready. The Army has always been the Nation's strategic hedge, and embracing leader education as its key component of leader development has been an essential element of being this hedge. To paraphrase the coach of the 1980 U.S. hockey team, "great moments come from great opportunities." We cannot let this moment pass.

ROBERT L. CASLEN, JR.
Lieutenant General, U.S. Army
Superintendent
U.S. Army Military Academy

ENDNOTE

1. For this description of strategic thinking, see Gregory D. Foster, "Teaching Strategic Thinking to Strategic Leaders," *The World & I Online*, November 2005, online edition.

CHAPTER 1

INTRODUCTION

Hugh Liebert

Hugh Liebert is the lead author of this chapter. Contributing authors include Robert Chamberlain, Jessica Grassetti, John Griswold, Todd Hertling, Michael Rosol, and Scott Smitson.

Since men live upon the land and not upon the sea, great issues between nations at war have always been decided—except in the rarest cases—either by what your army can do against your enemy's territory and national life, or else by the fear of what the fleet makes it possible for your army to do.

> Julian Corbett,
> *Some Principles of Maritime Strategy* (1911)[1]

The decade following September 11, 2001, witnessed a strategic anomaly: an island nation playing the part of a Landpower. For U.S. leaders worried about terrorism, weapons of mass destruction, and the frightful prospect of their convergence, the oceans on the nation's flanks, and the friendly neighbors along its borders seemed suddenly immaterial. As the United States sought to reconstruct the region that had sent suicide bombers to its shores, the American military instrument tilted toward the large land forces deployed into Afghanistan and Iraq. But now these wars have waned. Strategies for countering terrorism have evolved from nation-building to targeted strikes. An era of austerity has emerged. In grand strategic debates, the United States has again drifted "offshore." As a result, the U.S. military faces a dramatic rebalancing among its services. The absence of an existential

1

threat leaves the U.S. land services—the Army, Marines, and Special Operations—facing an existential question.[2] For a born-again island, just what is Landpower for?

One can attempt an answer in one of two ways. First, one can start from the tool—Landpower—and consider the range of missions it might be used for. But this assumes that we know the tool we have at hand, which is by no means evident. Landpower is divided **internally** into a tangle of branches—infantry, armor, and so on—each of which claims to be the trunk, while **externally** it is separated from not only sea and air power, but from diplomacy, economics, and other instruments of national power.[3] Individuals within each division act (and often think) as if their department, service, or branch reflected nature carved at its joints. But they do not—or at least not necessarily. It is therefore preferable to take a second line of approach, and to start from the task rather than the tool. The tasks that come immediately to view, however, themselves issue from these very divisions among the nation's tools, such that core national interests can appear distinct when approached militarily, economically, or diplomatically. What is more, it is not clear that one can consider national interests apart from the means a nation has to pursue them, since some ends might exceed a nation's grasp. Both task and tool, then, deserve a say. What is needed is some starting point that allows one to think outside of the boundaries that structure the nation's policy instrument (and give rise to the parochial preferences of each part), while allowing means to have their proper say in the determination of ends.

It is this starting point that grand strategy provides. Grand strategy entails the calculated relation of means to large ends.[4] In foreign policy debates, it signifies the overarching objective orienting all the means at a nation's disposal—diplomatic, economic, and military. The grand strategist views the military as one tool among others and Landpower as merely one of its facets; the lines dividing the military from diplomacy, land from sea, infantry from intelligence, blur in the eye of the grand strategist, who looks on disciplinary barriers like Joshua looked on Jericho's walls. In the formulation of grand strategy the primary fact is the nation's broad objectives in the world at large; everything else might inform, but should ultimately follow from, those objectives. It is from this perspective that one can consider most profitably the place of Landpower among the nation's policy instruments.

When Corbett pioneered the maritime angle of strategic vision in opposition to the then-dominant divisions of Britain's services, he looked on military force as a grand strategist would. This perspective enabled him to discover that so long as humans "live upon the land and not the sea" landpower will remain an essential instrument of national power. The following volume stands on the shoulders of Corbett and others like him in posing this question: What is the future of landpower in U.S. grand strategy? We begin by considering U.S. grand strategy, past and present, and the place of the military within it. We then consider the nature of landpower and the missions appropriate to it—particularly when means are constrained by austerity. We conclude by considering how the landpower of the United States and its allies might help to address foreign policy challenges in regions vital (Asia and the Middle East) and peripheral (Africa and Latin America) to national interests. This chapter will map the main questions that arise from each of these topics.

GRAND STRATEGY

At present, U.S. grand strategy represents a set of questions and a method of deliberating upon them rather than a set of definitive answers, for it is not clear that the United States has a grand strategy. Some lament this fact and suggest that were a single purpose to animate the myriad tools at American policymakers' disposal—as containment did during the Cold War—American foreign policy would be more successful than it is.[5] Others say that the United States, in fact, pursues a grand strategy—"global domination" to its detractors, "liberal internationalism" or "the freedom agenda" to its promoters—albeit surreptitiously (and perhaps foolishly).[6] Still others claim that the problem is not a deficiency of grand strategy but an excess: according to one account, the Barack Obama administration has two grand strategies; on another account, the United States has consistently pursued four.[7] In light of such deep uncertainty regarding what end might possibly coordinate U.S. diplomatic, economic, and military means, it is not surprising that the proper balance among the military services seems so elusive. Perhaps it is so hard to know what Landpower is for because we hardly know what American power is for.

Past as Prologue.

It is in moments of uncertainty regarding future American grand strategy that American history is most instructive. Its most general lesson is perhaps the most important: we have been here before. To those who worry that the United States has grown weak relative to rising powers, American history offers up moments of far greater weakness, such as when the United States was constrained to be merely the "**well-wisher** to freedom and independence of all" and "the champion and vindicator only of her own."[8] To those content with the present U.S. position but worried about downward trends, American history offers its own moments of darkness — post-War of 1812, post-Civil War (especially in the South), post-Vietnam — each of which ushered in soul-searching, followed by reform and, eventually, another dawn.[9] If nothing else, then, one learns from the American past that each nation in its time plays many parts.

Alongside moments of profound strategic uncertainty, the history of American grand strategy holds moments of deep ambivalence regarding the place of Landpower within the nation's military. When the frontier closed in the 1890s and the United States first became an island, Army leaders responded to their prospective diminishment by professionalizing the force.[10] Nearly a century later, U.S. victory in the Cold War, rapid advances in missile technology, and an awesome display of land dominance combined to make Landpower seem, once again, all but obsolete. In the 1890s and the 1990s, the balance of military power shifted away from the land — only to be restored within a generation. Is the proper lesson from these episodes that Landpower should not be diminished since at some point it will be needed again, or that the nation can raise Landpower to meet a future crisis, just as it has in the past?

Goals and Challenges.

Since the close of its frontier, American grand strategy has been animated by two broad goals: preventing the rise of a European or Asian power capable of

5

overcoming U.S. oceanic defenses, and making the international political order more nearly resemble U.S. domestic political order. Both goals pertain to national security, but they conceive of the nation differently. The first considers the American nation one discrete group among many; the second considers the American nation a potentially universal set of ideas. The first goal includes issues in American nationalism and the second in American liberalism. The identity and grand strategy of the United States, a liberal nation, has been defined by the tension between the two.[11]

As a result of these competing traditions, identifying true U.S. national interests at any given time has been challenging—and the present day is no different. Today, those who start from American nationalism tend to locate the overriding national interest in forestalling the rise of China to regional hegemony, and to a lesser degree in countering the threats of terrorism and nuclear proliferation.[12] Those who start from American liberalism also worry about the rise of China, though more for its illiberalism than for its sheer power, and they worry, too, about the health of the international economy and international institutions.[13] How do these two sets of interests converge and diverge? What **are** the U.S. core national interests—enduring, particularly to the present, and going forward into the 21st century?

Strategy and Force Planning in Times of Austerity.

American policymakers' understanding of U.S. national interests informs their force planning decisions. Which of the military services are built up and which drawn down, which weapons systems are invested in and which cancelled, what sort of officers are cultivated and promoted and which are not—all of these decisions depend in large part on the national goals the military is meant to serve. As of this writing, the national goal of "rebalancing" (or "pivoting") to Asia in order to manage China's rise has become most prominent, and concomitantly an operational concept known as Air-Sea Battle has shaped much of the debate over force planning.[14]

Theorists of Air-Sea Battle hold that potential U.S. adversaries in Asia and the Middle East may not soon be able to confront the United States in a "great power war," but they are not for that reason strategically negligible.[15] Indeed, China and Iran are quite close to limiting American power in certain select circumstances—particularly in choke points of global commerce like the Straits of Malacca and Hormuz. These states are investing heavily in the weapons necessary to achieve this goal. The result could be catastrophic for U.S. interests, with a view to both preventing the rise of regional hegemons and maintaining global commerce. The United States should therefore invest in military means to counter these threats; since they are threats in the first instance to our navy, i.e., our ability to project power close to our adversaries' shores, they are best met with sea and air power. Landpower is a tertiary concern.

This doctrine has won widespread assent for a number of reasons. In part, it operationalizes widespread American anxieties; in part, it speaks to an age of austerity in which manpower has become increasingly costly; in part, it reflects long-standing U.S. preferences for anesthetic technology over messier forms of military power. But Air-Sea Battle also raises a host of as yet unanswered questions: How should austerity influence our force planning—is investing in capital-

intensive military hardware and decreasing investment in human capital, in fact, the optimal balance?
Can Air-Sea Battle alone deliver what it promises?
What *is* the role of Landpower in Air-Sea Battle and in
future force planning more generally?

LANDPOWER

To answer this question, we must know what
Landpower is. This is not a straightforward matter, because it is of Landpower's essence that it is not a whole
unto itself, but a component of national military force,
which itself is a component of national power. Landpower, then, is a part of a part. Like each of its sister
services, it embodies a partial insight into geopolitics.
Proponents of sea power know both that the world is
divided into two large islands — four if one cuts at the
isthmuses — and that modern nations struggle to sustain themselves when unable to interact by sea. Proponents of air power know that the complex systems
characteristic of modern states, including populations
and economies, tend to organize themselves into
spokes and potentially vulnerable hubs. Proponents
of Landpower, by contrast, know that human beings
trade and travel by sea and air — but they live on land.

The Future of U.S. Landpower.

Landpower's potential roles within grand strategy
flow from this foundational fact. Because humans live
on land and modern states monopolize coercive force
in order to protect them where they live, Landpower
has the potential to displace foreign states by controlling inhabited terrain. Because modern states aspire
to protect their populations, decisions to deploy pop-

8

ulations-in-arms are a costly sign of resolve. Because humans have the potential to interact face-to-face and eye-to-eye on land, Landpower has a unique capacity to acquire intelligence, exercise immediate judgment, and foster relationships; on land, modern war comes closest to conflict on a human scale. In short, because humans live on land, Landpower has a unique potential to deter aggression, signal commitment, and shape allies and enemies' intentions.

If, however, the balance of U.S. national interests has shifted toward maritime regions, in what ways are Landpower's latent traits to manifest themselves? How might an extended period of fiscal austerity influence the grand strategic roles that Landpower might assume?

The Army in Times of Austerity.

As ours is not the first moment of strategic uncertainty in the nation's history, so it is not the first time that the U.S. Army has encountered austerity. Nevertheless, there is a widespread reluctance to learn the lessons that these past encounters might offer the present. As prior periods of budget stringency have approached, academic and professional journals have been quick to advise the military what cuts to make, but slower to develop systematic theories based on past cases.[16] This has been true of the current period of budget stringency as well. Once a period of stringency has passed and resources again become plentiful, there is little incentive to review previous policy choices.[17] So we have a responsibility — now, in particular — to ask what we might learn of the Army's history under austerity.

9

Perhaps the most comprehensive study of austerity's impact on the U.S. Army as a whole is Michael Meese's "Defense Decision Making Under Budget Stringency: Explaining Downsizing in the United States Army."[18] Meese argues that, when faced with limited funding, the Army has shown consistent cultural and institutional biases. It has prioritized people over modernization, short-term readiness, and doctrine. It has preferred a large, hollow, but expandable force to a smaller, better-manned force. It has opted for equitable allocations of resources between commands and branches, even when the threat environment suggested that some commands and branches were more important than others.[19] These inclinations did not have entirely negative results. The Army's focus on personnel and leadership during the interwar years, for instance, expanded its professional education system, which figured prominently in producing a generation of Dwight Eisenhowers and George Marshalls in the next war. Nevertheless, the intentional neglect of technological modernization and readiness assumed that the nation would have significant time to react to new threats, while lagging technology, the hollow force, and reluctance to prioritize spending made development and testing of new doctrine difficult.[20] There are exceptions to Meese's model (one might consider in particular Maxwell Taylor's post-Korean War Pentomic Army[21]), but there have also been confirmations of it subsequent to the cases he examined. The post-Vietnam Army, for instance, was an example of success that worked within the broad limits of the model, but also recognized the importance of readiness, modernization, sustainability, and doctrine. The Army's success in Operation DESERT STORM arose from just these post-Vietnam structural reforms.[22]

What are we today to make of prior efforts at reform under the strictures of austerity? While the existing literature on this theme agrees on the importance of balancing personnel, leadership, doctrine, readiness, and equipment, a number of questions still remain.[23] To what degree does the Army accurately identify national threats and create a force to deal with them, particularly since such choices may lay outside of the Army's bureaucratic interests in autonomy, funding, and organizational prestige? How should the Army inform national strategy and grand strategy in these periods? Is the Army capable of providing reliable and candid feedback to political leaders about its full capabilities (and lack of capabilities) under austerity? To what degree have recent examples of senior officer misconduct damaged the Army's ability to advise senior civilians? How can senior political and military leaders incorporate changes in capabilities into revised and possibly more limited visions of U.S. grand strategy?

Landpower as a Strategic Means.

As useful as historical cases are, a number of important factors separate contemporary debates over Landpower from their predecessors. Among these factors is the prominence of the Reserve Components. Over the past decade, the U.S. Army Reserve and Army National Guard have made indispensible contributions to national security—at home and, especially, abroad. As senior Army leaders look ahead to challenges beyond 2014, the implications of the past decade's experience for the future relationship of Active and Reserve Components are unclear. Creighton Abrams originated the "total force" concept in order to ensure that the All Volunteer Force would not sever the Army's connection to American society. As the modern day Army looks to the future, it once again must revisit the question of what balance it wants and needs to maintain between Reserve, Guard, and Active Components. Ultimately, the Army has considerable say in determining how it relates to the nation it serves. However, the nation's fiscal reality will weigh heavily on this question.

Senior leaders inside and outside the Army must not view moving force structure into the Reserve Component as a panacea for budget woes. Overreliance on Reservists prevents these Soldiers from pursuing meaningful civilian careers; it therefore disrupts the Reserve's traditional balance between citizen and Soldier. To avoid this, leaders of both the Active and Reserve Components must work assiduously with Department of Defense (DoD) and congressional leaders to find that narrow fulcrum point between overusing the Reserve Component and allowing its hard-earned warfighting prowess to atrophy.

Upsetting the Citizen-Soldier identity of the Reserve is undesirable not only because it violates tradition; it is also strategically unwise. As the Army leaves Afghanistan, senior Army leaders face the challenge of translating national strategy into coherently-defined demands on the total force. Some of these demands are likely to be qualitatively different from the Army's traditional roles. They will include such varied requirements as defending computer networks, combating terrorist organizations, combined operations with foreign militaries for training and operations, and disaster relief, both at home and abroad. Senior leaders should consider ways to meet these demands in terms of capabilities to employ rather than existing organizational structures to deploy. By virtue of their Citizen-Soldier makeup, Reserve Component units possess a unique and wide-ranging set of skills, and this expertise is not always apparent, at present, to planners outside the reserve itself. Army leaders have a rare opportunity to rebalance capabilities across the Total Force to maximize the advantages that the Reserve Component can best provide, while retaining the rapid-deployment capabilities that the nation needs in the Active Component.

What, then, is the proper role for the Reserve Components in the post-Afghanistan U.S. Army? How can the Army's leadership best employ Reserve Component capabilities to pursue our nation's strategic imperatives? How should the Army align its Active and Reserve Component force mix to meet these challenges?

The Human Domain: Leader Development.

Another factor that sets current debates over Landpower apart from earlier iterations is the U.S. land forces' abundance — overabundance, in fact — of talented and tested leaders. These commissioned and noncommissioned officers are not only battle-tested, but tested in a particularly demanding and potentially damaging sort of battle. The generation preceding theirs had fought in Operation DESERT STORM, where conventional lines were clearly drawn, and the strategic objective of defeating the Iraqi Army and restoring Kuwaiti sovereignty was achieved in a mere 89 hours. All of this had the dangerous effect of suggesting that, from that point forward, war would be quick and easy. How different the experiences of the succeeding generation have been.[24] The sons and daughters of Gulf War veterans found war to be grisly and intense, a test of combat and diplomatic skills alike. They have endured long periods of boredom and anxiety; they have become by turns humanitarians and killers. Above all, their experiences have reinforced the enduring truth that war is not a matter of mere machines. Rather, war is an all too human endeavor — as Clausewitz put it, a matter of compulsion and will.

This truth will continue to endure. The debates that usher in the post-war period, however, focus not on securing hard-won insights into war, but on each service's parochial preferences. Which service can best assert its relevance? Which one can produce the most convincing narrative? These are practically consequential questions, of course, but in a more fundamental sense, they are profoundly unserious. They neither reflect nor engage the wide range of capabilities, experience, and flexibility that this generation of military men and women offers.

Above all, these questions do not reflect the lessons that this generation learned first-hand. A range of current Army leaders remember viscerally that the necessity of counterinsurgency came unanticipated, and many draw from that memory the following conclusions: events dictating U.S. involvement in regional and world conflicts have and will continue to surprise us;[25] effective strategy requires that war be understood as a tool of policy; and the United States must maintain in its kit the potential to shape political situations on land, particularly for the sake of reconciliation once the killing is done. If we doubt any of this, and choose instead to focus on the sorts of war we would prefer to wage, we will likely be reminded of another lesson the past decade taught: the enemy has a vote. U.S. enemies watch it closely and trace its vulnerabilities carefully. The Army's struggles to pacify Afghanistan and Iraq in particular have not gone unnoticed. Future hybrid threats will likely pool the military resources of host nation-states and employ them in an asymmetric manner that removes association—and thus the possibility of clear, satisfying retaliation by U.S. instruments of power. How will the United States employ joint task forces to keep states accountable and counter a quickly proliferating hybrid threat? How will it approach regimes that are failing institutionally and ripe for such nonattributed fighters? How will it shape these political conditions to avoid these precarious situations in the first place?

A generation of experienced leaders must shape the answers to these questions. The challenge is to resist the temptation to define the nation's problems according to each agency's preferences. Strategy is in part a function of the terms dictated by the nature of a threat, which does not usually comply with what we would like that threat to be. The nation requires leaders who are agile, flexible, and sharp; thanks to the peculiarly trying war it has waged for the past decade, it has them, by and large. How, then, can the United States retain and continue to develop leadership suited both to the nation's wars and to the nation's thinking about war?[26]

Applying Lessons of the Past: Prevent, Shape, Win.

American thinking about war traditionally has rested on a strong distinction between war and peace. The American military, by contrast, uses peace to prepare for war and so has always approached this distinction differently.[27] Recent Army doctrine has deepened this characteristic military approach by viewing peace as a time not only to prepare for war, but to prevent it on terms favorable to the United States—i.e., to make the military in peacetime as effective an instrument of policy as it is during war.

At the foundation of this doctrine is recognition that the Army can signal and shape as well as fight. Maintaining the Army as a force more than equal to any other nation's, for instance, serves as a powerful deterrent to war. This is particularly so when the Army's strategic positioning enhances its power as a signal of resolve, as it does when troops are stationed in critical regions abroad and when they are "regionally aligned" at home. The Army's peacetime interactions with foreign militaries—and particularly those of allied nations—has also been reconceived along these lines, as a means for shaping vital regions and nurturing partnerships in a manner favorable to national interests. Regionally acculturated talent—leaders as fluent in foreign languages as they are expert in the capabilities of foreign arms—facilitates Landpower's shaping role. With prevention and shaping, emerging Army doctrine holds, the United States stands to win wars as the most reflective warriors have historically done. "Ultimate excellence [in war]," wrote Sun Tzu, "lies not in winning every battle, but in defeating the enemy without ever fighting."[28]

But without fighting, how does one know when one has subdued an enemy? It is easier to show territory conquered and trophies seized than it is to prove what is by nature a negative case—**but for** a set of strategies, the war would have come (or the enemy would remain). As a result, even if it is true that prevention and shaping deserve scarce resources, it is still a difficult case to make persuasively. An officer who speaks Korean has a less viscerally-felt value than an Abrams tank positioned along the demilitarized zone.

The notion of prevention and shaping as a core Army mission raises other questions as well: Is it, in fact, possible to scale-up some of the skills traditionally associated with the relatively small Special Forces? Can the Army afford the time it takes to cultivate leaders who specialize in regions, as well as units whose regional alignment is a meaningful indicator of a shared skill (not only a shared slot on deployment lists)—how might these goals alter the Army's present systems of recruitment and promotion? Could such officers and units in fact maintain their regional alignment, given the Army's identity as both a global power and an all-purpose force?

APPLICATIONS

Having taken stock of task and tool, we turn to consider concrete cases—the strategic decisions that American leaders will face in coming years. Austerity and a renewed appreciation of Landpower's peacetime role in shaping allied forces have combined to heighten American leaders' sense of the world's multipolarity (or as others have put the point, its **post-American** character). This has opened an unparalleled opportunity for creative strategic thought. What new structures and practices can bond the United States to its allies, allowing each to efficiently rely on the others' strength? What opportunities do regions of vital interest afford the United States? What aside from distraction and entanglement do regions of peripheral interest offer American grand strategists?

Rebalancing Land Forces in the United Kingdom and Australia.

The United States is not alone in its efforts to re-shape its force structure for the demands of the 21st century. The United Kingdom (UK) and Australia have engaged in 5 years of intense introspection on their future strategy and the place of Landpower in it. To be sure, their strategic constraints, opportunities, and worldviews are their own; they cannot be translated immediately into American English. It is nevertheless worthwhile to consider what American strategists might learn from the thoughts and deeds of two of their closest allies.

The most recent appraisal of the UK's strategic direction culminated in the 2010 *Strategic Defence and Security Review* (SDSR), the first review of its kind in British history. The SDSR set out new priorities for the defense establishment and mapped out significant cuts in defense budgeting, especially within the British Army. When these cuts are finally finished in 2020 (and British involvement in Iraq and Afghanistan has drawn down) the total force will shrink from 150,000 to 82,000 troops. This Army is much smaller than it has been, but it is intended nevertheless to remain relevant on the battlefield and to conduct seamless allied and coalition operations with the United States. Subsequent development of the 2010 SDSR has stressed that it is in the UK's interests to address instability and conflict overseas when possible. To this end, the British government intends to amplify the power of its small land force through both whole-of-government approaches to foreign policy (e.g., closer integration of diplomatic and military efforts) and reform of the Army's organizational structure.[29] Britain's *Army 2020* concept divides its Landpower into (1) a **reaction force** capable of conducting no-notice crisis response missions; (2) an **adaptable force**, composed of a mix of regulars and reserves, to build other nations' military capacity, oversee homeland resilience, and support the long-term efforts of the reaction force; and (3) a **force troops** organization to carry out myriad combat service support missions.[30] Taken together, these reforms aim to generate a force tailored to Britain's strategic goals.[31]

While Britain's Landpower reforms have responded first and foremost to austerity, Australia's have had shifting geostrategic realities in view — particularly the rise of China and the United States' recent "rebalancing" (or "pivot") to Asia. Like their British counterparts, Australian strategists emphasize whole-of-government approaches to security challenges; they accordingly present the Army as just one component in Landpower, and they construe "Landpower" broadly to include other government agencies, nonprofits, contractors, and coalition partners.[32] The Australian Army is intended to be a highly flexible and responsive force capable of performing missions across the spectrum of conflict. Above all, the Army is expected to pursue what the Australian Defence Force calls "adaptive campaigning," the attempt:

> to influence and shape the overall environment to facilitate peaceful discourse and stabilise the situation, noting that there may be no end state to an operation but rather an enduring set of conditions conducive to Australia's national interests.[33]

The Australian Army's commitment to adaptive campaigning has been further elaborated in the new Plan BEERSHEEBA initiative.[34] This plan integrates regular and reserve components into an expeditionary force adept at both traditional Landpower and amphibious operations. The Australian Army is accordingly organized into three "Multi-Role Combat Brigades," three other combat enabler brigades, and a well-integrated special operations command. Like the British Army, then, the Australian Army is beginning to organize its forces along dedicated functional lines. Unlike the British Army, the Australian Army sees less of a distinction between Landpower and sea power, and instead considers itself to play a role distinct from both — that of a land-based, amphibious-capable force able to support a broader national maritime strategy.

Both British and Australian efforts to transform their Landpower should be of great interest to the United States. Although the three nations face distinct security challenges, the similarity of their regimes and the long precedent of collaboration among their armed forces suggest that the United States might learn from their examples. But what lessons are American strategists to take? Do British and Australian reforms suggest how U.S. Landpower should be organized in order to "prevent, shape, and win"? How will these deep changes in the forces of U.S. allies impact multinational plans and operations? Can shared interests enable closer collaboration and coproduction between the three armies? Austerity measures and new strategic challenges may have the unintended consequence of encouraging new levels of collaboration within the "Anglosphere," but it will require farsighted leadership on the part of all three governments to realize this potentially attractive possibility.

Prevent, Shape, Win in Context:
The Asia Pacific and the Middle East.

Collaboration among allied land forces and innovative approaches to U.S. Landpower are particularly important in light of emerging challenges in regions of vital strategic interest: Europe, Asia, and the Middle East. The Pacific Rim and Middle East present oddly similar challenges with a view to the American application of Landpower. Both regions pose significant logistical difficulties; both include American allies that may not prefer large-scale permanent deployments; both contain American adversaries with significant ballistic and cyber capabilities; both give rise to dangerous state-collapse scenarios that would demand a land-based response; and both present American strategists with the dilemma of supporting vulnerable allies to maintain a regional balance of power, while preventing wealthy free-riders from passing the buck to the United States. This last challenge is particularly complex when it is hard, as it often is, to distinguish between "vulnerable ally" and "wealthy free-rider." Prevention requires land forces capable of responding decisively across the spectrum of operations; threats to American interests in oil and global trade require additional deterrent capacity from missile defense and defensive cyber. Should the United States fail to prevent contingencies from arising in either Asia or the Middle East, partner capacity, prepositioned logistics, and, most importantly, the relationships formed, rehearsed, and strengthened through shaping operations, will all factor in the success of the American response.[35]

What are the tools that generate prevent, shape, and win capabilities in these regions? Air-Sea Battle proposes that the United States ought to focus its contribution to regional security on highly mobile and lethal off-shore platforms. In the Middle East, Air-Sea Battle would likely entail the closure of many, if not all, of the bases in the region, and shifting to "underway replenishment," i.e., ship-to-ship refueling. This change might invite other wealthy or rising powers to contribute forces of their own; it might also reduce the U.S. costs of underwriting the world's shipping and resource markets. In the Pacific Rim, Air-Sea Battle implies a heavy investment in strike capabilities at the expense of ground forces. Proponents of Landpower, however, argue that Landpower possesses unique attributes that make it in many cases a superior option to naval and air power, and thus American engagement in these regions ought to include significant development and augmentation of allies' land-based forces.

It is difficult to think clearly about the various ways forward in both Asia and the Middle East, though, without a firm understanding of what exactly the United States intends to do in the coming years. The demands of offshore balancing are quite different than those of hegemonic stabilization; working alongside China during its rise is quite different than undertaking containment in the South China Sea. Without clear thinking about national strategy, trying to think clearly about Landpower is premature. On the other hand, a number of lesser questions may prove relevant to the larger question of U.S. strategy in these regions. What are the intentions of Iran and China — both in terms of their "near-abroads" and in terms of investing in global security? How should military signals — investments in new weapons systems, for instance — be understood to reflect intentions? What is the relative effectiveness of land forces compared to other types of national power? How does Landpower factor differently in the regions of vital interest to the United States? What is the impact of emerging Army capabilities—missile defense, cyber, and space in particular—on the Asian and Middle Eastern security environments?

Prevent, Shape, Win in Context: Lessons Learned in Africa and South America.

The strategies that leaders of U.S. Landpower are currently developing with a view to regions of vital interest are in many cases the very same strategies that have been pioneered in regions of peripheral interest. In Latin America, it has been more than 20 years since a significant number of U.S. ground forces were deployed into combat and more than a decade since a significant number were stationed abroad.[36] In Africa, much the same is true.[37] A DoD official has recently claimed that the U.S. military's Africa Command will have succeeded if "it keeps American troops out of Africa for the next 50 years."[38] The U.S. Southern Command would likely agree. In both cases, prevention has long been recognized as a winning strategy.

But to say that the U.S. military has been truly "out of" Africa and Latin America would be to neglect the role that shaping strategies have played in this "win." A small number of troops, many of them Special Forces, have, in fact, been used—sparingly but efficiently, as their impact has far surpassed what their numbers alone would lead one to believe. In Columbia, for instance, engagement with local leaders, military training, and strategic deployment of nonmilitary aspects of U.S. power (witness the U.S.-Columbia Trade Promotion Agreement of 2006) have all contributed to an important strategic advance against the drug trade and toward greater regional stability. Central America proved a model for Central Africa. In 2011, President Obama deployed 100 U.S. troops to assist local forces in their pursuit of Lord's Resistance Army leader Joseph Kony. Although as of this writing Kony remains at large, this operation has so far been considered a success—and the skills acquired, intelligence gathered, and relationships formed have the potential, at least, to enable future U.S. influence over a deeply unstable region. Ounces of shaping have proven more efficient and more effective than pounds of cure.

This can sometimes seem to be the case, however, up to the point that prevention and shaping metastasize into something more problematic. What prevents these early interventions from escalating into more prolonged engagements? Are certain prevent-shape strategies more likely to avoid escalation than others? Apart from concerns over escalation, what strategies have proven most successful in these regions, and which of these can be effectively transferred to other regions? What force structures have proven most effective? Are tiny Special Forces teams sufficient, or are there ways to bring more numerous Landpower units productively to bear?[39]

CONCLUSION

Since the time of its founding, U.S. insularity was considered an achievement to be won. "If we are wise enough to preserve the Union," Hamilton wrote in 1787, "we may for ages enjoy an advantage similar to that of an insulated situation."[40] From New York City, Hamilton could turn already from the Atlantic and peer over the horizon to the point where the continent descended back into the sea. He knew that Great Britain's shores had kept her (mostly) innocent of standing armies, and, in so doing, had preserved her liberty — the very same liberty he and his heirs would enjoy, if only they kept in view what has come to be called the "stopping power of water." Hamilton considered it a sort of special providence — the benevolence of nature and, perhaps, of nature's God.

But water starts as much as it stops. It is true, as Corbett knew, that humans live on land, but, for most of their history (and still today), humans have travelled more rapidly through elements foreign to them — the sea and now the air. Hamilton knew this, too. He envisioned a great trading nation — the world's emporium, ideally positioned between the two ends of the globe's great land mass, destined to be more pivotal to global communication and commerce than even her British parent had been. Here, too, Hamilton has proven prescient.

What Hamilton did not know — or at least, chose not to dwell on in the writings that have come down to us — is how water's starting power could work at counterpurposes from its stopping power. He had before him a cautionary tale to this effect: an island playing the part of a Landpower and failing. The United States has achieved the insularity Hamilton foresaw; it has met the commercial destiny Hamilton prophesied; it now remains for it to enter into regions Hamilton left uncharted. How should an island nation, no longer as insular as islands ought to be, conceive of Landpower?

ENDNOTES - CHAPTER 1

1. Julian Corbett, *Some Principles of Maritime Strategy*, Annapolis, MD: U.S. Naval Institute Press, 1988 [1911], p. 16.

2. Funding for Special Operations has not recently faced the same scrutiny as funding for the Army and Marines; however, debates about the core identity of Special Operations—between those who favor "direct" tactics like targeted raids and those who favor "indirect" tactics like building partner nations' militaries—are more intense now than perhaps ever before. On this and related debates, see in particular Linda Robinson, *The Future of U.S. Special Forces*, Council Special Report No. 66, New York: Council on Foreign Relations, April 2013. For considerations of how the Army and Marines might coordinate with Special Operations, see Fernando Luján, *Light Footprints: The Future of American Military Intervention*, Washington, DC: Center for a New American Security, March 2013; and John Nagl, *Institutionalizing Adaptation: It's Time for a Permanent Army Advisor Corps*, Washington, DC: Center for a New American Security, June 2007.

3. On the varied worldviews and priorities of U.S. military branches, see in particular Carl Builder, *Masks of War: American Military Styles in Strategy and Analysis*, Baltimore, MD: Johns Hopkins University Press, 1989.

4. For this formulation, see John Lewis Gaddis, "What is Grand Strategy?" Lecture delivered at Duke University, February 26, 2009, available from *tiss.sanford.duke.edu/DebatingGrandStrategyDetails.php*.

5. For lamentations of the absence of U.S. grand strategy, see the Gaddis lecture cited previously and the sources collected by Daniel Drezner's article on the theme. See Drezner, "Does Obama Have a Grand Strategy? Why We Need Doctrines in Uncertain Times," *Foreign Affairs*, Vol. 90, No. 4, July-August, 2011, pp. 57-68, especially p. 57.

6. John Mearsheimer, "Imperial By Design," *The National Interest*, Vol. 111, January-February, 2011, pp. 16-34.

7. For the Obama administrations two grand strategies, see Drezner, "Does Obama Have a Grand Strategy?" p. 58. For the United States' four grand strategies, see Walter Russell Mead, *Special Providence: American Foreign Policy and How It Changed the World*, New York: Routledge, 2002.

8. John Quincy Adams, "Speech to the U.S. House of Representatives on Foreign Policy," July 4, 1821, available from *millercenter.org/president/speeches/detail/3484*. One might compare Adams' notion of the exemplary power of American liberty to more recent iterations of the theme. Immediately following the passage quoted, Adams argues that the United States can "recommend the general cause, by the countenance of her voice, and the benignant sympathy of her example." The 2010 *National Security Strategy* claims that the United States promotes "universal values abroad by living them at home, and will not seek to impose these values through force," pp. 5, 10, 36.

9. For a study of military and strategic reforms in the wake of Vietnam, see for instance Andrew Krepinevich *et al.*, *Strategy in Austerity*, Washington, DC: Center for Strategic and Budgetary Assessments, 2012.

10. In *The Soldier and the State*, Cambridge, MA: Belknap, 1957, Samuel Huntington describes this period of reform in some detail. "The withdrawal of the military from civilian society at the end of the 19th century," he argues, "produced the high standards of professional excellence essential to national success in the struggles of the 29th century," p. 229.

11. For versions of this dual identity in the study of American political thought, consider the difference between Louis Hartz's *The Liberal Tradition in America*, Orlando, FL: Harcourt, 1991 [1957]; Rogers Smith, "Beyond Tocqueville, Myrdal, and Hartz: The Multiple Traditions in America," *The American Political Science Review*, Vol. 87, No. 3, September 1993, pp. 549-566; and *Civic Ideals: Conflicting Visions of Citizenship in U.S. History*, New Haven, CT: Yale University Press, 1997. One might also consider the distinction Mead draws between the Jacksonian and alternative strategic traditions in *Special Providence*, and Huntington's evolution from *American Politics: The Promise of Disharmony*, Cambridge, MA: Belknap, 1983; and *Who Are We? The Challenges to America's National Identity*, New York: Simon and Schuster, 2004.

12. The 2010 *National Security Strategy* lists "the security of the United States, its citizens, and U.S. allies and partners" as the first of America's enduring interests, p. 7.

13. The second, third, and fourth of 2010 *National Security Strategy*'s enduring interests have to do with the economy, universal values, and the international order, p. 7.

14. On the "pivot" to Asia, see in particular Hillary Clinton, "America's Pacific Century," *Foreign Policy*, November 2011; and "Sustaining U.S. Global Leadership: Priorities for 21st Century Defense," Washington, DC: DoD, 2012.

15. On Air-Sea Battle, see Andrew Krepinevich, *Why AirSea Battle?* Washington, DC: Center for Strategic and Budgetary Assessments, 2010; and Jan van Tol, *AirSea Battle: A Point-of-Departure Operational Concept*, Washington, DC: Center for Strategic and Budgetary Assessments, 2010.

16. As the military entered its last major period of budget stringency in the 1990s, for example, *International Security*, the leading academic journal in security studies, published a wealth of work in a single edition recommending new policies, but few works that attempted to evaluate a period of stringency after the fact. See, for example, Gordon Adams and Stephen Alexis Cain, "Defense Dilemmas in the 1990s," *International Security*, Vol. 13, No. 4, Spring 1989; Robert F. Ellsworth, "Maintaining U.S. Security in an Era of Fiscal Pressure," *International Security*, Vol. 13, No. 4, Spring 1989, pp. 16-24; Cindy Williams, "Strategic Spending Choices," *International Security*, Vol. 13, No. 4, Spring 1989, pp. 24-35.

17. Quality historical works do examine specific periods of stringency, but even in these works, stringency itself is not the key "study variable," and works, such as Williamson Murray and Allan Millett, *Military Innovation in the Interwar Period*, Cambridge, MA: Cambridge University Press, 1996, rarely focus exclusively on the Army as an organization.

18. Michael Meese, "Defense Decision Making Under Budget Stringency: Explaining Downsizing in the United States Army,"

Ph.D. Dissertation, Princeton, NJ: Princeton University, 2000. Meese examines three periods of budget stringency: the interwar period between the World Wars, the post-Korean War period, and the post-Vietnam period. He measures the effectiveness produced by Army policy during this period across a range of areas, including personnel, force structure, leadership, readiness, modernization, sustainability, and doctrine.

19. Note that these inclinations fit well with Carl Builder's characterization of Army culture in *The Masks of War: American Military Styles in Strategy and Analysis,* Baltimore, MD: Johns Hopkins University Press, 1989.

20. Meese, "Defense Decision Making Under Budget Stringency." Until 1940, the Army had little training at the large unit (Corps) level at all, while small scale training sometimes required uniting multiple companies under a single commander to provide a large enough force to maneuver. Compare Ronald Spector, "The Military Effectiveness of the US Armed Forces, 1919-1939," Allan R. Millett and Williamson Murray, eds., *Military Effectiveness, Volume 2: The Interwar Period,* New York: Cambridge University Press, 2010, p. 92.

21. The Pentomic Army was a success in breaking the traditional mold of Army culture. Chief of Staff Maxwell Taylor created a significantly smaller force structure, but one fully manned and functional without augmentation. More importantly, the Army dramatically shifted focus from personnel to technology. If this change was successful, however, due to the Army's need to remain relevant in the nuclear era and the force of personality of war hero Taylor, it was a failure in terms of effectiveness, sacrificing personnel and leadership for technology. The Army quickly abandoned the Pentomic concept after Taylor's departure as Chief. See Andrew J. Bacevich, *The Pentomic Era: The U.S. Army Between Korea and Vietnam,* Washington, DC, National Defense University Press, 1986; Meese, "Defense Decision Making Under Budget Stringency," pp. 113-184.

22. For this argument, see Suzanne C. Nielsen, "Preparing for War: The Dynamics of Military Reform," Ph.D. Dissertation, Cambridge, MA: Harvard University, 2003.

23. Importantly, Meese, Nielsen, and Stephen Rosen all find that the most important agent for (or obstacle to) change is senior Army leadership. On the role of the executive decision maker, consider James Q. Wilson, *Bureaucracy: What Government Agencies Do and Why They Do it*, New York: Basic Books, 1989, Chaps. 10-12. Contrast Barry Posen's classic *The Sources of Military Doctrine*, in which Posen argues that militaries are largely incapable of innovation or significant change in peacetime. Posen finds that Allison's organizational process model best explains militaries in peacetime and require intervention by political leaders in wartime to force change. Barry R. Posen, *The Sources of Military Doctrine: France, Britain, and Germany Between the World Wars*, Ithaca, NY: Cornell University Press, 1984.

24. On the role of generational experience in military leadership, see Edward Cox, Kent Park, Rachel Sondheimer, and Isaiah Wilson III, "Growing Military Professionalism Across Generations," *Military Review*, Special Edition, September 2011.

25. Even containment during the Cold War, often considered U.S. grand strategy par excellence, was marked by tremendously costly, unexpected deviations such as Korea and Vietnam, which perhaps distracted policymakers from the goal of containing the Soviet Union.

26. For a compelling treatment of these and related questions, see Isaiah Wilson III, "Educating Holistic Warriors," Chap. 10, *Thinking Beyond War: Civil-Military Relations and Why America Fails to Win the Peace*, New York: Palgrave Macmillan, 2007. See also Gaddis, "What is Grand Strategy?"

27. For a strong version of this claim, see Huntington, "The Military Mind: Conservative Realism of the Professional Military Ethic," Chap. 3 in *The Soldier and the State*.

28. Sun-tzu, *The Art of War*, John Minford, trans., New York: Penguin Books, 2002, p. 14.

29. Following the publication of the SDSR in 2010, the British Ministry of Defence, Foreign and Commonwealth Office, and Department for International Development jointly published the *Building Stability Overseas Strategy* (BSOS) in 2011. This strategy emphasizes preventing war by addressing the socio-political, eco-

nomic, and natural drivers of conflict. It envisions three means to this end: early warning, rapid crisis prevention and response, and investment in upstream operations, such as resilient institutions within fragile societies. While the BSOS is in every sense of the word a "government-wide" strategic planning framework, all three pillars, especially the second and third, rely heavily upon a flexible, adaptive, and responsive Landpower component.

30. The **reaction force** will be comprised of a division headquarters, three mechanized infantry brigades, and an air assault brigade. Seen as the British government's main source of landpower deterrence, the reaction force will be trained and equipped for "very high readiness" missions. The **adaptable force** will be comprised of division headquarters and up to seven UK regionally-based infantry brigades. In addition to the tasks mentioned in the text, the adaptable force will meet enduring security commitments in Cyprus, Brunei, the Falklands, and ongoing UN missions. The **force troops**, like the adaptable force, will be composed of regulars and reserves, and will include multiple brigades.

31. A recent publication explains the logic informing the UK Army 2020 concept. See The British Army, *Transforming the British Army, July 2012: Modernising to Face an Unpredictable Future*, London, UK: Ministry of Defence, July 2012, p. 13:

> *Army 2020* is an imaginative and practical response to an extreme challenge: that of confronting an era of strategic uncertainty, exacerbated by economic austerity, with smaller land forces. It will provide a range of capabilities that can be adapted to the nation's security needs at home and overseas, resetting the Army to meet the unexpected and deal with future contingencies.

32. Chief of the Australian Army Staff Lieutenant General D. L. Morrison has addressed the relation between whole-of-government approaches and the security threats Australia faces: "The Defence White Paper 2009 allocates tasks to the ADF according to a scale of priorities," he says.

> All of these tasks make heavy demands on the Army. The thread binding all these tasks together is the direction that the ADF implement a maritime strategy in the Defence of

Australia. In order to execute this strategy the ADF requires a comprehensive understanding of, and an ability to conduct decisive operations within, the Primary Operating Environment, the archipelagic approaches to Australia. This necessarily requires a focus on joint, inter-agency and whole of government operations, concepts.

33. *Army's Future Land Operating Concept*, Canberra, Australia: Australian Army Headquarters, 2012, p. iv.

34. The name "Beersheeba" refers to a World War I battle in which Australian troops were victorious over Ottoman forces in Palestine, owing in no small part to changes in technology, tactics, and doctrine in the months leading up to the battle.

35. On the use of military-to-military engagement in Asia as a strategic tool, see in particular Isaiah Wilson III, "Countering the Terrorism Threat, Preemptively, through Peacetime Military Engagement," Bryan Lee Cummings, ed., *Beyond the Campaign*, New York: Council for Emerging National Security Affairs, 2004. Wilson argues that foreign arms sales and transfers have helped to maintain U.S. reputation, influence, and access in strategic Asia, and might in the future be used to U.S. advantage in this and other theaters.

36. With respect to Latin America, the last significant use of ground forces in combat was the invasion of Panama in 1989. After control of the Panama Canal passed from the United States to the Panama Canal Authority in 1999, the American troops stationed at Soto Cano Air Base in Honduras have represented the largest deployment in the region; these troops number in the hundreds. These data are available from *www.vetfriends.com/US-deployments-overseas/*.

37. In Africa, the last significant use of ground forces in combat was the peacekeeping mission to Somalia in 1993.

38. Comments by then-Principal Deputy Under Secretary of Defense Ryan Henry at a Meeting of USAID's Advisory Committee on Voluntary Foreign Aid, ACVFA, May 23, 2007, cited in Lauren Ploch, "Africa Command: U.S. Strategic Interests and the Role of the U.S. Military in Africa," Washington, DC: Congressional Research Service, July 22, 2011, p. 6.

39. On the question of how to involve U.S. Army forces in missions traditionally reserved for Special Forces, see the sources cited in Endnote 2. On the potential uses of heavy arms in "light footprint" operations, see Irvin Oliver, "Cavalry in the Future Fight: An Environment for Cavalry Forces," *Armor*, Vol. 122, No. 1, January-March 2013, pp. 19-22.

40. "Publius" [Hamilton], "Federalist Paper No. 8," available from *thomas.loc.gov/home/histdox/fed_08.html*.

PART I:

AMERICAN GRAND STRATEGY

CHAPTER 2

THE RISE OF CHINA AND THE DECLINE OF THE U.S. ARMY

John Mearsheimer[1]

What is the future of U.S. Landpower? This is another way of asking: What is the future of the U.S. Army? The Army has been the most important of the three major military services over the past decade, mainly because of the prominence of the Afghanistan and Iraq wars. The Air Force and especially the Navy have played secondary roles in those conflicts. I have spoken with more than a few officers from those two services over the past decades who have complained about how all the attention focused on Afghanistan and Iraq has been detrimental to the interests of the Air Force and the Navy.

This situation is likely to change significantly in the next 2 decades, and the Army is likely to be treated as the least important of the three services, which means it will be allocated less of the Pentagon's resources than either the Air Force or the Navy. Indeed, the Army will probably have to work extremely hard to secure large numbers of defense dollars.

THE CHANGING THREAT ENVIRONMENT

We are at what I would call a plastic moment in the history of America's relations with the wider world. Fundamental changes are taking place in our strategic environment that are likely to have a profound effect on U.S. grand strategy, and on the Army in particular. To be more specific, three changes are occurring in

37

America's strategic calculus that will have a marked effect on the Army's fortunes. Those changes will interact in ways that make the Army a less important instrument to policymakers in Washington than it has been in recent memory.

First, the United States is pivoting to Asia to deal with a rising China. The threat environment in the Asia-Pacific region, however, does not require large numbers of American ground forces. If anything, it is a region in which the geography appears to favor the Air Force and Navy over the Army. Second, the Iraq war is over, and hopefully America's combat role in Afghanistan will end soon. All of the Army's combat units are scheduled to be out of Afghanistan by the end of 2014. Both of these wars are widely—and correctly—regarded as disasters and the United States is not likely to fight another war like them anytime soon. Occupation, counterinsurgency, and nation-building are likely to remain dirty words for years to come. Indeed, American presidents and their lieutenants are sure to go to great lengths to avoid fighting another protracted land war in the developing world. That means the mission that has been the Army's main force driver over the past decade will probably be of secondary, if not tertiary, importance in the foreseeable future.

Third, given the troubles afflicting the American economy, especially its huge budget deficits, the military's budget is likely to be exposed to the knife in the decade ahead, forcing the Pentagon to make lots of hard choices about the kinds of military forces it should buy. To justify large expenditures, each service will need a compelling story that explains why it is essential for protecting the national interest. The Army is going to have a particularly hard job doing that, because counterinsurgency and nation-building will be a hard sell, and because the Army is of limited utility for dealing with a rising China.

There is one additional factor that is unrelated to the strategic environment that will make life difficult for the Army in the years ahead. That factor is the Marine Corps. As you all well know, the United States has two separate land armies — the Marine Corps and the Army — and the Marines are going to want to play a key role in Asia. The Marines are brilliant in public relations, which means they will be very effective at securing scarce defense dollars. Furthermore, the Marines are joined at the hip with the Navy, which will have a big role to play in the Asia-Pacific region, and will be inclined to privilege the Marines over the Army more often than not. All of this is to say that the Army will have to work overtime to be an important player as the United States becomes increasingly focused on checking a rising China.

THE ARMY AND U.S. GRAND STRATEGY

Before laying out my thinking on these matters in detail, I want to emphasize that I am not hostile to the Army in any way. Indeed, I have a special place in my heart for that institution. Besides being a former enlisted man in the Army as well as a West Point graduate, I have long argued that Landpower is the principal ingredient of military power, and that most wars are ultimately won or lost on the ground. These are central themes in my book, *The Tragedy of Great Power Politics*, where I also emphasize the limits of independent airpower and independent sea power for winning wars. Furthermore, when the Vietnam war finally came to an end in the mid-1970s and the United

States refocused its attention on Europe, I argued that the Army was of central importance for deterring a Warsaw Pact attack, and that extra defense dollars should be spent on buying additional armored and mechanized divisions and the tactical aircraft needed to support them, **not** on procuring more aircraft carriers or more nuclear weapons. But the Asia-Pacific region is not Europe, and when you look at the possible conflicts that might involve the United States in that region, it is hard to see circumstances in which we will need a large and powerful Army.

Let me explain my thinking about the future of the Army in more detail. How a country thinks about building its military forces should be largely a function of its grand strategy. Because people define grand strategy in different ways, it is important to spell out exactly what I mean by that concept. For me, fashioning a grand strategy involves answering three questions. First, what areas of the world are strategically important? In other words, what areas of the world are worth expending substantial American blood and iron? Second, what are the main threats in those regions that might require a military response? Third, what kinds of military forces are necessary to counter those threats? To be more specific, what are the optimum mix of forces for deterring adversaries and defeating them if deterrence fails and war breaks out?

It seems to me that when today's Army leaders talk about why we need a large and powerful Army, they rarely make the case by framing it in terms of U.S. grand strategy. Instead, they talk in broad generalities about the fact that we live in a large and complicated world where change happens rapidly and where it is therefore hard to anticipate where trouble might come from in the future. They maintain that we have to be prepared for a wide variety of threats, none of which are defined with much specificity. One has the sense from listening to the Army leadership that there is no mission too difficult for the Army to do expeditiously. It is an all-purpose Army. This is not a smart way to strategize, and is not going to help the Army make its case in a world in which the defense budget is shrinking. Army leaders need to say where their service is likely to fight, whom it is likely to fight against, and why the Army is especially well-suited for dealing with that adversary or those adversaries.

Let me spell out my views on American grand strategy and explain how the Army fits into the big picture. I believe we are in the early stages of a fundamental shift in America's grand strategy. There are three areas of the world outside of the Western Hemisphere that have been of great strategic importance to the United States since the early part of the 20th century. They are 1) Europe, 2) Northeast Asia, and 3) the Persian Gulf. The first two are vital interests because the world's other great powers are located there, and we care greatly about those countries as they are potential rivals that could cause us lots of trouble. The third area—the Persian Gulf—matters because oil is located there, and it is an enormously important natural resource for countries around the world.

For all of America's history, Europe has been by far the most important of those three areas. Remember that the United States had a "Europe first" policy before it entered World War II; and even though Japan, not Germany, attacked us at Pearl Harbor, we maintained a "Europe first" policy throughout the war. During the Cold War, Europe was strategically more important to the United States than Asia, which is why—when we ran war games involving a major conflict between the superpowers—we would "swing" American forces out of Asia to Europe. Some of my Asian friends maintained that we swung forces out of Asia to Europe because most Americans had European roots and were more concerned about the fate of their fellow Westerners. But this was not true. We privileged Europe over Asia during the Cold War because the heart of the Soviet threat was sitting in the center of Europe, not in Asia.

This pecking order is now beginning to change. Mainly because of China's rise, Asia is becoming the most important area of the world for the United States, and Europe is likely to become not the second, but the third most important region. We talk today about pivoting to Asia, which obviously involves shifting American forces to Asia from other locations. This pivot, which is rather low key at the moment, is likely to accelerate if China grows increasingly more powerful. But if a country pivots to a particular area, that must mean it is pivoting away from some other region. That other region in this case is almost certain to be Europe, not the Persian Gulf, which is likely to be the second most important region for the United States.

There are two reasons the Gulf will remain especially important to the United States. First, it is long-standing American policy to make sure that no single power in that region establishes hegemony and gains control over the energy resources there. Second, China and India will both increasingly depend more on oil and gas from the Gulf in the years ahead, which means both of those Asian countries will pay serious attention to that region. In a very important way, Asia and the Gulf will be tied together. In other words, I believe that the security competition, which is likely to develop in Asia between the United States and China, will extend into the Persian Gulf. However, that security competition will not extend into Europe. Simply put, Asia and Europe will remain worlds apart militarily. Indeed, it is not clear Europe will help the United States in any meaningful way to contain China. Instead, it is likely to sit on the sidelines.

There is another reason Europe will not be a source of major worry for the United States in the next few decades. There is no threat on the horizon in Europe that is likely to command our attention. Both Germany and Russia — our two principal competitors in the 20th century — are depopulating. Moreover, there is not going to be a united Europe that might challenge the United States in some meaningful way. If anything, Europe looks to be fragmenting, not integrating — largely because of the Euro crisis, which is like acid eating away at the foundation of the European Union. Simply put, Europe is not likely to matter that much in the decades ahead. Asia and the Gulf are likely to be the focus of our attention. Again, this represents a historic shift in America's strategic priorities.

This shift in how we think about the key regions of the world will have profound ramifications for the Army. Europe is a region where Landpower has always mattered greatly. Large armies have settled all the major wars in European history. Thus, when the United States entered World War I, it built a huge Army — the American Expeditionary Force — to fight against Imperial Germany. It did the same in World War II with Nazi Germany, although that conflict was largely settled by the massive land battles that took place on the Eastern Front between the Red Army and the Wehrmacht. During the Cold War, we maintained a large Army on the Central Front to deter the Warsaw

Pact ground forces on the other side of the inter-German border. Thus, when the Vietnam War ended in 1975 and the United States began to focus laser-like on Europe, it was easy to make the case for maintaining a formidable American Army.

The geography of Asia, however, looks markedly different from Europe. Most importantly, there is no equivalent of the Central Front in the Asia-Pacific region. When you look at the possible conflict scenarios involving the United States and China, it is hard to see where a large American Army would be needed. This is not to say that no U.S. ground forces will be needed in the region, just that it is hard to imagine a major conventional war on land between America and China.

POTENTIAL CONFLICT SCENARIOS

Probably the most Army-friendly contingency in Asia is a possible war on the Korean Peninsula. Remember that more than 200,000 U.S. Army troops fought the Chinese Army between 1950 and 1953. While it is certainly possible to imagine a future war between South and North Korea, this time the Republic of Korea (South Korea or ROK) military will be able to handle the North Korean Army. In fact, the ROK forces are likely to clobber the North's Army. None of this is to deny that the United States could get dragged into a future Korean conflict. After all, we have about 19,000 troops stationed in South Korea, and it is imperative that they remain there for purposes of trying to convince South Koreans that our nuclear umbrella is firmly in place over their heads. Regardless, any American involvement in another Korean war would most likely involve relatively small numbers of U.S. ground forces. It is difficult to imagine a repeat of the conflict that took place in Korea during the early-1950s.

The other potential conflict scenarios in the Asia-Pacific region that might involve American military forces include 1) Taiwan, 2) the Senkaku/Diaoyu Islands, and 3) the South China Sea. None of them, however, are likely to involve large-scale American ground forces. Indeed, it is not even clear that U.S. troops would be involved in any of those fights. If they were needed, it might very well be the Marines — not the Army — that do the fighting.

The United States and a powerful China will not only compete in the Asia-Pacific region; they are also sure to do so in the Indian Ocean and the Arabian Sea as well, because those large bodies of water link China with the Persian Gulf. China will want to control those waters because large amounts of gas and oil destined for China move across them. However, the U.S. Navy and countries like India will bear the burden of countering Chinese efforts to control those critically important sea lines of communication. The Army will play a minor role at best.

The Persian Gulf itself is the one area where the Army is likely to have an important role in the decades ahead. The United States, as noted, has a deep-seated interest in making sure that no country dominates that strategically important region. The main threat to become a regional hegemon is Iran, which is why the Ronald Reagan administration supported Saddam Hussein in the Iran-Iraq War that ran from 1980 to 1988.

American policymakers can deal with threats in the Gulf in basically two ways: 1) they can rely on other countries in the region to check an aggressor, as happened in the Iran-Iraq War; or 2) they can build and deploy U.S. military units to handle the job. Those American forces can either be stationed outside of the region—"over the horizon" as they say—or on the territory of an ally in the region. Regardless, those forces would be comprised of a substantial number of Army units, whether they were stationed in the region or outside of it. Some of you, I am sure, remember the Rapid Deployment Joint Task Force (RDJTF), which the Jimmy Carter and Reagan administrations established in the last decade of the Cold War to intervene in the Gulf if there was a serious threat to upset the balance of power. It was comprised of four Army divisions (9th Infantry Division, 24th Infantry Division, 82nd Airborne Division, 101st Airborne Division) and a cavalry brigade (6th Cavalry Brigade). It also contained a substantial number of Marines.

Given America's dismal experience in its recent wars in Afghanistan and Iraq, future U.S. leaders are likely to rely on countries in the Gulf to check dangerous aggressors rather than sending American troops to do the job. Nevertheless, there will always be the possibility that the local powers cannot handle the task, in which case the United States—and here we are talking mainly about the Army—will have to move in and remedy the problem. This is essentially what happened in the 1991 Gulf War. The United States and its allies intervened and threw the Iraqi Army out of Kuwait, because no local power had both the will and the capability to reverse Saddam's aggression. All of this is to say that the Army is likely to play a key role in protecting America's interests in the Persian Gulf.

Let me conclude this discussion of grand strategy with a few words about Europe. As noted, it will remain an area of strategic importance to the United

States, but it will not command the attention from Washington that it has in the past. My sense is that how much attention future American policymakers pay to Europe will depend on how powerful China becomes in the years ahead. If China's rapid rise continues, the United States will have its hands full containing China and will sharply reduce its presence in Europe, maybe even remove all of its troops so it can focus its attention on Asia and the Persian Gulf. If that happens, it would have serious consequences for the Army, because the "American pacifier" in Europe is built around U.S. ground forces. The more likely scenario, however, is that the United States will gradually and inexorably decrease its presence in Europe, which will leave the Army with a diminishing role in that region.

My bottom line regarding grand strategy is that Asia is rapidly becoming the most important area of the world for the United States, and the Army will have a small role to play there. The region where the Army is most likely to play an important role is the Persian Gulf, where a substantial body of U.S. land forces will still be needed to prevent a regional hegemon and counter Chinese influence. Europe, which has always been an Army-friendly theater, is not likely to be a major concern for the United States in the years ahead.

THE DEVELOPING WORLD

Let me now switch gears and talk about conquest and occupation in the developing world. As part of the so-called Global War on Terror, the United States has fought two major wars of conquest since 2001, one in Afghanistan and the other in Iraq. The American military went to war in Afghanistan in mid-October 2001, and by early December, it had toppled the Taliban from power and appeared to have won a quick and decisive victory. That led many people in the American national security community, and especially in the George H. W. Bush administration, to think the United States had found the magic formula for conquering countries in the developing world, affecting rapid regime change, and then getting almost all American combat forces out of that country quickly so as to avoid a costly and difficult occupation.

This belief that the Afghan model was a harbinger of more easy victories to come is what underpinned the decision to invade Iraq in 2003 and the Bush Doctrine more generally. President Bush and his key advisors were convinced that the U.S. military could win a quick and easy victory in Iraq, avoid occupation, and then put its gun sights on the next rogue state in the region. The choice was obviously between Iran and Syria. In fact, it might not even have been necessary to attack either of those countries, because they might have been so fearful of being defeated by the mighty American military that they would have surrendered without a fight. As we now know, the victory in Afghanistan in the fall of 2001 was a mirage; the United States had not found the magic formula for winning quick and decisive victories in the developing world. Instead, it ended up in protracted and costly occupations in Afghanistan as well as Iraq, engaged in both cases in counterinsurgency operations and nation-building.

The Army, of course, has been the key service in these two conflicts, which explains in good part why the Army has grown significantly over the past decade. The central problem, however, is that there is almost no way the Army can win a meaningful victory in these type of wars; the mission is simply too difficult. Even in those rare cases where the United States might succeed, it would take many years and a huge amount of resources. In addition, the Army would pay a significant price in the process, and the war would have a corrosive effect on our politics at home, as well as our foreign policy.

Not surprisingly, there is remarkably little enthusiasm in the American national security community for invading another country and trying to do social engineering at the end of a rifle barrel. Just look at how the United States has dealt with Libya, Iran, and Syria. In the Libyan case, the Americans put no regular Army troops on the ground and instead relied largely on airpower to help topple Colonel Muammar Kaddafi. Furthermore, one White House advisor emphasized that the United States was "leading from behind" in Libya. Regarding Iran, there is no serious threat of sending American ground forces into that country. If the United States takes military action against Iran's nuclear facilities, it will be done with airstrikes and cruise missiles. But even so, it is evident that there is hardly any appetite for a war with Iran in the United States. The same is true regarding Syria, where the Barack Obama administration has gone out of its way to avoid intervening in that civil war, even with just airpower.

Perhaps former Secretary of Defense Robert Gates best summed up what will surely be the conventional thinking about future wars of conquest when he told a West Point, New York, audience in February 2011 that: "In my opinion, any future defense secretary who advises the president to again send a big American land Army into Asia or into the Middle East or

Africa should 'have his head examined,' as General MacArthur so delicately put it."[2]

The present situation reminds me of the post-Vietnam period. After that devastating defeat, American policymakers went to enormous lengths not to get involved in another costly occupation in which we had to fight a major counterinsurgency while simultaneously doing nation-building, a task of enormous difficulty. I am confident that it will be a long time before the United States tries to conquer another country in the developing world and transform its political system.

None of this is to say that we are going to get out of the business of fighting terrorists targeting the United States. But we will rely on special operations forces, allies, and especially drones, to get the job done. The lead article in *The New York Times* on April 8 nicely captures where the war on terror is headed. It reads: "Targeted Killing Comes to Define War on Terror."[3] If I am right, this means that one of the chief reasons for maintaining a large and powerful Army will be effectively taken off the table. When this happened after the Vietnam War—the last time we ran away from doing counterinsurgency—we turned to Europe with a vengeance, and, of course, Europe during the Cold War was Army-friendly in the extreme. But this time, we are turning to the Asia-Pacific region where the Army will only have a minor role to play. It is hardly surprising that today we talk about Air-Sea Battle, whereas in the Cold War we spoke about Air-Land Battle.

THE SHRINKING DEFENSE BUDGET

Finally, there is the shrinking defense budget. The Pentagon is already reeling from sequestration, which mandates that the Pentagon cut its budget by $41 billion in 2013 and about $500 billion over the next decade. That comes on top of another $487 billion in cuts that are already being implemented. There is no reason to think these troubles are going away anytime soon, given America's huge budget deficits, coupled with the difficulty of curtailing spending on entitlements. Indeed, the situation is likely to get worse. Secretary of Defense Chuck Hagel said on April 3, 2013, in a speech at the National Defense University that the military must make fundamental changes in how it operates to deal with new fiscal realities. He made it clear he was not talking about "tweaking or chipping away at existing structures and practices but, where necessary, fashioning entirely new ones that are better suited to 21st century realities and challenges." Hagel went on to say, "Much more hard work, difficult decisions and strategic prioritizing remains to be done."[4]

In a world where there is an abundance of defense dollars—like the decade after September 11, 2001—there is usually not much pressure to prioritize, and it is relatively easy for each service to get a large chunk of the pie. However, when the pie is shrinking and there are serious threats on the horizon, which will surely be the case if China continues its impressive rise, policymakers are forced to pay more attention and be more ruthless about their spending decisions. This situation can only be bad news for the Army, because its importance relative to the other services will be less than it was during the Cold War, when containing the Soviet Union was the Pentagon's overarching mission, or as it has been over the past decade, when the Pentagon was consumed by the wars in Afghanistan and Iraq.

CONCLUSION

I want to be clear. I am not saying the Army will have no role to play in defending the country's interests in the years ahead. Nor I am hinting that the Army should be drastically downsized. But I am saying that when you look at America's likely grand strategy in the next few decades, the Army is probably going to be the least important of the three services. Its role will certainly be limited in the Asia-Pacific region, which is likely to be the most important strategic area because China is located there. The Army's situation could be especially grim if the Pentagon's budget is severely constrained and China's economy continues growing at a rapid clip, necessitating an accelerated pivot to Asia.

Of course, the Army can help its case by fashioning a clear and concise story that describes the threats to critical American interests that the Army is best suited to counter. But even then, there are significant limits to what can be done, because the future security environment is unlikely to involve the United States in major land wars. That is surely good news for the country as a whole, but not for the Army's budget.

ENDNOTES - CHAPTER 2

1. Dr. John Mearsheimer was invited as the keynote speaker to the U.S. Army War College annual Strategy Conference on April 25, 2013. This speech is reprinted with slight revisions here.

2. Robert Gates, "Speech at the United States Military Academy, West Point, NY," February 25, 2011, available from *www.defense.gov/speeches/speech.aspx?speechid=1539*.

3. Scott Shane, "Targeted Killing Comes to Define War on Terror," *The New York Times*, April 8, 2013.

4. Chuck Hagel, "Remarks by Secretary Hagel at the National Defense University, Ft. McNair, Washington, D.C," April 3, 2013, available from *www.defense.gov/transcripts/transcript.aspx?transcriptid=5213*.

CHAPTER 3

AMERICAN GRAND STRATEGY AND THE FUTURE OF LANDPOWER IN HISTORIC CONTEXT

Scott A. Silverstone

One of the maxims in the field of international relations is that the future is inherently uncertain. Most observers, however, refuse to accept this proposition at face value. For those responsible for making decisions in the present, those who must develop budget priorities, make force structure choices, train our military professionals, and determine where in the world they should deploy, the inherent uncertainty of the future is a tremendous challenge they cannot avoid. Decisions made in the near term about the future of Landpower will have deep structural effects lasting years, so the task begs for some method or framework for making the right choices. To deal with this problem, we typically develop theories that help us generalize about causes of war and peace and hope that their predictive power will allow us to prepare for the future. We follow trends in economic performance, in technology, in political and social phenomena, and in environmental variables that might reveal future trajectories in the threat environment. We develop forecasting models and track "prediction markets" that seek to open a window on world events to come. Unfortunately, despite the great energy poured into the endeavor, systematic research has shown that with time, expert predictions prove to be grossly disappointing.[1]

But the question at the heart of this book—what is the future of Landpower?—still stands. Where do we look for guidance to make informed present day decisions? Rather than base my approach to the question on shaky predictions for the rest of the 21st century, I prefer to start from a different perspective. A truly strategic analysis of the question must begin with a clear understanding of the strategic-political objectives that the United States seeks to secure and advance through its foreign policy. Only by starting with an assessment of our strategic goals can we then move on to an informed debate about the wide range of political, economic, and military instruments best suited to achieve them and the threats that might put these strategic goals at risk. In other words, what are we trying to achieve, and what contributions might Landpower make in the effort?

Arguably, the present-day dilemma over what role Landpower can play as an instrument of U.S. policy resembles the dilemma faced by President Harry Truman in 1949 over whether to authorize the development of thermonuclear weapons. One group of advisors was arguing passionately that the United States must develop and deploy the H-bomb before the Soviets did, while a rival group was arguing just as vigorously that it would be a grave escalatory mistake to pursue this new atomic capability. In frustration, Truman observed that until someone could tell him what America's overall strategic objectives were in the post-World War II world, there was no way he could determine what role this particular instrument of national power might play, if any. What would an H-bomb be used for? What political ends would it help achieve in American foreign policy? How would it stack up against alternative tools for pursuing those strategic ends? Out of this debate came National

Security Council Memorandum No. 68 (NSC 68), that iconic piece of analysis that guided American Cold War strategy for the next 40 years.[2]

This chapter seeks inspiration from this earlier moment of uncertainty to frame the dialogue on the future of Landpower. It does so by laying out what seem to be the key strategic objectives from recent American history, objectives that have in no way been left behind by history, but capture enduring goals that are directly relevant to what the United States will pursue in the years to come. I cannot predict the specific threats to these goals that will emerge over time. I have no crystal ball to tell me what surprises world events have in store for U.S. foreign policymakers and military professionals. Nor can I offer specific recommendations on what the future of Landpower ought to be. But I do assert that, to start thinking about this problem, we should first study enduring American strategic goals. From this vantage point, we will be in a much better position to make decisions about the alternative means, including Landpower, best suited to pursue them.

The enduring strategic goals pursued by the United States that incorporated Landpower as an essential element can be distilled into four basic categories: 1) grand area access, 2) hemispheric policing, 3) contain and neutralize remote projectable threats, and 4) contain and mitigate politically-driven humanitarian crises. While each has distinctive historic roots and historic conditions have changed over time, the objectives remain as relevant today as they were in the past.

Strategic Objective #1: Grand Area Access.

The single most important strategic objective that Americans have been willing to accept heavy burdens and pay severe costs to secure over the past 100 years is what can be called "grand area" access. In its simplest terms, the objective has been to maintain open access to, and a balanced political order within, Europe, East Asia, and the Middle East. It is a simple strategic concept that links the costliest commitments of American power in our history: two million Soldiers mobilized and deployed to Europe with the American Expeditionary Force by the end of World War I; a total of 16 million Americans in uniform to support the fight across the European and Pacific theaters in World War II, over 8 million of them in the U.S. Army[3]; millions more who helped shoulder the burden of the U.S. commitment to the defense of Western Europe during the Cold War and who fought in Korea and Vietnam; and over 600,000 service personnel for the fight against Iraq during the 1991 Gulf War. While the world has changed in profound ways since 1917, nothing has altered the importance of this core objective for the United States in the years between World War I and the early-21st century.

There is a two-pronged explanation for such heavy commitments of American blood and treasure over such a long period of time. One explanation emphasizes a harm to avoid — preventing a hostile state from establishing hegemonic control in one of these key regions; the other explanation emphasizes the great gains to be made for American domestic values — access to these regions is seen as an indispensible buttress to liberty and prosperity. Neither explanation alone can adequately account for how Americans have conceived of the critical importance of these geographic regions to American interests since the early-20th century, so both must be explored as components of U.S. strategy for the future.

Realist Counter-Hegemonic Balancing.

It is useful to start with the kind of argument advanced by John Mearsheimer in Chapter 1, which is essentially the negative argument: great power threats to America's physical security can originate from these regions. Mearsheimer is certainly correct when he points out that, for the past 100 years, American leaders were willing to make massive commitments of military power to prevent a hostile state from achieving dominance in Europe, East Asia, and the Middle East. Why? According to realist theory, the inherent uncertainties and dangers of an anarchic world compel great states to seek security through material power.[4] For Mearsheimer, all great powers have two basic objectives: 1) to achieve hegemonic dominance within their own geographic region, and 2) to prevent other states from achieving hegemony in their own parts of the world. The fear, according to his Offensive Realist theory, is that once another state achieves regional hegemony, it is free to roam into other regions, projecting power abroad in a way that might fundamentally threaten others' survival or core interests.[5] The strategic objective then, is a negative objective: the prevention, containment, and defeat of power maximization by other major states.

Consider the strategic value of this objective for the United States. The United States is the only great power in modern history to have achieved and sustained regional hegemony successfully. As a result, for generations the United States has been liberated from the need to focus on threatening powers within the Western Hemisphere, and it has therefore been free to project massive military power on a global basis with virtually no fear that it left itself vulnerable closer to home. When we consider the advantages this offers in contrast to the regional threat environment faced by the other great powers in history — France, Great Britain, Germany, Russia/the Union of Soviet Socialist Republics (USSR), Hapsburg Austria, Japan, China — which were never free from immediate geographic threats — it is hard to deny that sustaining regional hegemony will remain a core American strategic interest.

From the offensive realist perspective, the most serious commitments of U.S. power abroad, particularly Landpower, have been motivated by the imperative to defeat the violent quest for regional hegemony by Germany and Japan in the world wars, and by the Soviet Union or its proxies in Europe, Korea, and Vietnam during the Cold War. A stark example of this fear from World War II is found in the work of the great geopolitical thinker Nicholas Spykman. His detailed analysis of the power potential of a hegemonic Germany and Japan, when in control of the resources of the European and Asian rimland, led him to conclude that, if these hostile states joined forces, there was little the United States could do to resist their efforts to bottle up the United States physically within the North American continent. Breaking their hegemonic drive, therefore, was imperative.[6]

Liberal International Order-Building.

While this realist perspective clearly is a valuable theoretical explanation for America's strategic choices over the past century, as well as its future strategic outlook, it provides only a partial explanation. American leaders certainly worried about the potential for other regional hegemons, using the secure footing, the resources, and the industrial base of Europe or

Asia to make trouble for the United States **within the Western Hemisphere**.

Yet there is another element to American grand strategy motivating the huge commitments of land and other forms of power in these cases, a more positive strategic objective to be pursued in the political and economic space created **within these other regions** in the absence of a hostile hegemon. This positive strategic objective is best captured by a phrase developed in the late-1930s as Europe descended into war: "grand area" access. Simply put, securing America's core political values, its prosperity, vitality, and strength depended on open access to the markets and resources of Europe and East Asia, as well as the Middle East. In other words, the primary motive is not simply to keep other great powers out of our neighborhood, **but to guarantee that the United States can maintain access to theirs**.

A series of memoranda produced in the early-1940s by the War and Peace Studies group of the Council on Foreign Relations, which had been commissioned by an understaffed State Department, demonstrated that, for a robust American economy to survive, it had to maintain access to European markets and critical resources from Southeast Asia. Co-existence with a Nazi-dominated continent with its closed economic system in one critical part of the world, and Imperial Japan's Greater East Asia Co-Prosperity Sphere in the other, would force the United States to fall back on hemispheric self-sufficiency. But as the War and Peace Studies group concluded, self-sufficiency was impossible.[7] Spykman came to the same conclusion.[8] An American economy that provided growth and opportunity for its citizens in industry, labor, and finance demanded an open international economic order.

NSC 68.

We find this exact strategic outlook underpinning America's assessment of the Soviet threat and the containment response, just a few years after victory over Germany and Japan rescued grand area access from the violent expansion of these aspiring hegemons. Specifically, grand area access is the core strategic objective articulated in NSC 68, the seminal document of the early Cold War that made the case for containment as the long-term American approach to the postwar threat environment. While NSC 68 had its origins in a different historic context, the document still has great value for our contemporary study of Landpower, past and present, because it presents a simply articulated characterization of the United States of America and the grand strategic political ends that its foreign policy must ultimately support. Just as important, NSC 68 presents a claim about the global conditions necessary to achieve those political ends that has enduring relevance as a grand strategic perspective connecting at least 100 years of history to the present and the future.

According to NSC 68, the "**fundamental purpose** of the United States . . . is to assure the integrity and vitality of our free society." One of the "realities" it claims to "emerge as a consequence of this purpose" is "our determination to **create conditions under which** our free and democratic system can **live and prosper**."[9] In other words, the vitality of a free society and the prosperity of its citizens depend on "maintaining [a] **material environment in which they flourish**. Logically and in fact, therefore, the Kremlin's challenge to the United States is directed not only to our values but to our physical capacity to protect their environment."[10]

In yet another section of NSC 68, its authors go so far as to acknowledge that containment of Soviet power — despite the heavy commitment of resources to this negative goal — is not the essence of American grand strategy. Containment serves a deeper strategic purpose:

> *Our overall policy at the present time* may be described as one designed to foster a world environment in which the American system can survive and flourish. . . . This broad intention embraces two subsidiary policies. One is a policy which we *would probably pursue even if there were no Soviet threat.* It is a policy of attempting to develop a healthy international community. The other is the policy of "containing" the Soviet system. . . . The policy of striving to develop a healthy international community *is the long-term constructive effort which we are engaged in. . . . It, as much as containment,* underlay our efforts to rehabilitate Western Europe. Most of our international economic activities can likewise be explained in terms of this policy.[11]

This deeper strategic purpose is largely forgotten in how we typically remember postwar U.S. foreign policy, which tends to fixate on military competition with the USSR as though this were the only objective being served by U.S. grand strategy. The deeper strategic goal was to sustain access to key geographic regions, more specifically, politically stable regions populated by states stitched together through institutions that open markets, allow for maximum participation, facilitate dense networks of social and economic interaction, enhance the predictability of behavior, and reduce the role of coercion and dangerous threats within them.[12] As NSC 68 declared, "the role of military power is to serve the national purpose by deterring an attack upon us **while we seek by other means to**

63

create an environment in which our free society can flourish."[13] This is realist power politics in the service of liberal institutional order that ultimately sustains American domestic political values.

Defeating German and Japanese aggressive expansion before 1945 and deterring the geographic expansion of Soviet power afterwards served the same underlying goals; the massive commitment of American power was a prerequisite for "the long-term constructive effort" to break open, defend, and sustain grand area access, institutionalize progressively wider sections of the planet, and ultimately secure the material environment that will help maintain vitality and liberty at home. Nothing changed in the U.S. underlying grand strategic framework when the Cold War ended and the Soviet Union collapsed. This profound historical event simply broadened the geographic scope — most immediately in Eastern Europe and former Soviet republics — that Americans could consider as ripe for integration,[14] while stoking debate on what other parts of the globe should be included in the material environment that is truly vital for American interests and worth the commitment of blood and treasure to safeguard and stabilize.

Realist Balancing, Liberal Order, and Landpower Today.

The specific identity, character, and intensity of threats to this open, stable, institutionalized order certainly have changed since the end of the Cold War (the so-called rogue state problem — Iraq, North Korea, and Iran, for example[15]), but the objective of preventing, containing, or defeating these threats to guarantee unfettered access to the grand areas has not. In the 1990s, force structure decisions hinged on the "Two

Major Regional Contingencies" concept. In one sense, this is a threat-based planning assumption: as a worst-case scenario, the United States might find itself at war concurrently in Northeast Asia and Southwest Asia, based on aggression from North Korea in one region and Iraq or Iran in the other. But these scenarios are considered threatening in the first place and serious enough to justify a massive Landpower response, because they put grand area security at risk. Our contemporary fears of a nuclear armed Iran do not really spring from scenarios in which Iran uses this capability to project offensive power against the United States itself. The fear is that nuclear weapons will allow Iran to deny the United States and its allies the freedom of action they now enjoy in a geographic region that is critical to the global economy.

It is within this same grand strategic framework that we can assess the implications of China's rising economic, political, and military power and the American response. More specifically, America's grand strategic tradition helps explain why China's "Anti-Access/Area Denial" (A2/AD) strategy creates such anxiety in Washington. It cuts directly against the very core objectives American strategic thinkers settled on in the late-1930s and have worked so hard to sustain over the ensuing 70 years. Anti-Access, Area-Denial; it is hard to think of a policy label that would be more provocative for American strategic thinkers.

Within official Chinese sources, A2/AD is certainly cast as an inherently defensive concept.[16] Chinese ballistic missiles that threaten American airbases in the western Pacific, anti-ship missiles designed to sink aircraft carriers, interceptor aircraft meant to blunt American and allied airpower, and submarines on patrol from the East China Sea to the Straits of Malacca are all characterized as military capabilities necessary for defending China's legitimate security interests along its Pacific coastline and for breaking maritime blockades that could strangle China's export-dependent economy and importation of oil. According to realist international relations theory, China's military investments are perfectly understandable. From this perspective, no major state should tolerate such a gross imbalance in relative power, which makes China vulnerable to American power projection right on China's doorstep.[17]

Many Americans tend to dismiss the notion that China's military modernization is driven by legitimate fear for its security. Secretary of Defense Donald Rumsfeld once declared, "since no nation threatens China, one must wonder: Why this growing investment? Why these continuing large and expanding arms purchases?" But as Professor Charles Glaser rightly notes:

> The answer should have been obvious. If China were able to operate carrier battle groups near the U.S. coast and attack the U.S. homeland with long-range bombers, Washington would naturally want the ability to blunt such capabilities.[18]

Yet the same capabilities that China develops to defend its territory and contiguous waters can also be used offensively to coerce neighboring states into conceding their claims to contested territory, or to seize this territory outright (such as in the Senkaku/Diaoyu islands or the South China Sea). Perhaps, as realist theory suggests, a more powerful China will be a more confident, ambitious, and risk-acceptant China,[19] willing to enforce the sovereignty it claims over the entire South China Sea. China might make a play to forcibly reunite Taiwan with the mainland, or intimidate American allies or partner states (such as Japan, South Korea, the Philippines, Thailand, and Singapore) to abandon their close political and economic ties with the United States, to include compelling the withdrawal of American military forces from their territory.

These are the scenarios that American political leaders and security professionals worry about. It is not that a strengthened China will actually send carrier battle groups to patrol the waters of the Western Hemisphere or seek partner nations in the Americas willing to provide bases for their strategic bombers or their marines. The fear is that China will turn a putatively defensive A2/AD capability into a robust force that will shield aggression and intimidation that ultimately dissolve U.S. deep political, economic, and military connections that have extended across the entire western Pacific and East Asia for generations. The fear is that the United States will lose grand area access.

If there is a role for American Landpower in Asia, it should contribute to the neutralization of aggressive forms of A2/AD. How might the Army be used to convince China that aggressive or coercive uses of its growing military capabilities are likely to fail, thus reducing their temptation to even try aggressive or coercive tactics? Alternatively, how can American Landpower help sustain the political desire, the political will, and the ability of regional states to remain active members of the broader system of unhampered interaction that the United States seeks to secure? This is the challenge for the most creative strategic thinkers, particularly those responsible for adapting the American Army to changing regional dynamics.

Of course, the Army will continue to play a critical role in deterrence and defense on the Korean peninsula. North Korea remains what we might call a "legacy threat," born in a radically different global context that no longer exists, yet it lingers as a legitimate threat to our South Korean ally. This threat matters only because South Korea is a critical member of the Asian grand area that the United States is determined to protect. But beyond this particular hotspot, Landpower planners should be focused on how this particular type of military force might support U.S. efforts to maintain access and partnerships across the wider region.

Strategic Objective #2: Hemispheric Policing.

Each state has a special interest in its own geographic region, its security environment, the political character of its neighbors, and the region's distinctive economic opportunities and disruptions. States have a special interest in their region's migration patterns, the movement of goods, disease, and criminals, and a keen interest in the rules that shape regional behavior and the rights that neighboring states claim. Simple geographic proximity suggests that potential dangers and opportunities have greater impact when they appear in the immediate neighborhood rather than halfway around the world.

The United States exemplifies the special attention that states tend to pay to regional affairs. In fact, the United States has more forcefully articulated its special interest, and its special obligation and right, to shape its own region than any other major state. President James Monroe's "doctrine" of 1823 was an expression of exceptionalism and separation of the

Americas from the violent and corrupting European balance of power system, a demand that the great states of the period refrain from intervention in the affairs of "our" hemisphere. Of course, the United States of the early-19th century did not have the power to actually enforce this demand, nor was Monroe's doctrine a declaration of U.S. intentions to take a leadership role in hemispheric affairs. By the turn of the 20th century, however, with the United States emerging as the most productive economy in the world and the Western Hemisphere free of any great power except the United States, America was in a position to pursue, in President Teddy Roosevelt's words, "the exercise of an international police power" to "see the neighboring countries stable, orderly, and prosperous."[20]

It is true that the Roosevelt "Corollary" to the Monroe Doctrine was the product of a particular historic context, when American leaders still worried about European great powers intervening in Latin America and the Caribbean. The notion of hemispheric policing might seem like an irrelevant anachronism, a throwback to the days when 5,000 American Soldiers under General John Pershing chased Pancho Villa across the northern Mexican desert for 9 months or when the U.S. Marines governed Haiti for nearly 2 decades. Teddy Roosevelt's declaration of the U.S. right to regional intervention was actually renounced in 1928; Presidents Calvin Coolidge, Herbert Hoover, and Franklin Roosevelt took pains to convince their regional neighbors that the United States was not going to mimic the rough hewn imperialism that other great powers pursued around the world. Cold War regional policing with Landpower—from preparations for a massive assault on Cuba in 1962 through the invasions of the Dominican Republic in 1965 and

Grenada in 1983—certainly follows the strategic logic of the Monroe Doctrine, yet these cases seem less relevant to an era that is not dominated by great power rivalry that could spill over into the U.S. backyard.

While the historic details have changed dramatically since the early-20th century and the Cold War era, those responsible for the future of U.S. Landpower should not be so quick to write off hemispheric policing as a mission left behind by history. The U.S. interventions in Panama in 1989 and Haiti in 1994 illustrate the kinds of scenarios that might indeed be replayed in the future, and which might certainly lead future political leaders to demand a similar response from the U.S. Army. In December 1989, approximately 26,000 U.S. military personnel launched Operation JUST CAUSE to overthrow Panamanian strongman General Manuel Noriega. The list of American grievances was long: Noriega was under indictment for drug trafficking by a U.S. federal court; his Panamanian defense forces had racked up over 300 incidents of harassment against American service personnel and family members serving in the canal zone; Noriega undermined a democratic turn in Panamanian politics by invalidating the results of presidential elections in the spring of 1989 that his candidate lost; and Noriega's regime was declared an unacceptable threat to the security of the Panama Canal. The U.S. Army deployed thousands of Soldiers from a wide range of units for the high-intensity assault.[21]

The U.S. occupation of Haiti in September 1994 also fits this hemispheric policing category. The motivation for the operation was twofold. First, as the operation's name—UPHOLD DEMOCRACY—bluntly points out, the most public motive was democratization and humanitarian stabilization. In 1991, democratically elected president of Haiti Jean-Bertrand Aristide was ousted in a military coup by Lieutenant General Raul Cedras. Diplomatic pressure and economic sanctions eventually led Cedras to sign an accord in July 1993 conceding power. But a year later, with Cedras still in Port-au-Prince, the United Nations (UN) Security Council passed a resolution authorizing the use of military force to restore democracy, the first time in the organization's history the UN has approved forcible democratization of a member state.[22]

A second motivation for the invasion was just as important, perhaps more so: to stop the relentless flow of thousands and thousands of Haitian "boat people" trying to reach the United States in flimsy crafts between 1991 and 1994. To keep the refugees from reaching the beaches of Florida, the George H. W. Bush administration set up an interdiction operation that would gather refugees at sea and bring them to camps at Guantanamo Bay, Cuba. During this period, approximately 30,000 Haitians passed through the camps, the maximum population reached nearly 13,000 refugees at one point.[23] When the Bush administration realized that this process was actually enticing more Haitians to flee into U.S. custody, they controversially changed policy and began to return all refugees to Haiti. President Bill Clinton had campaigned against this "cruel" policy, but during his first year and a half in office, the United States continued to interdict and return. By September 1994, President Clinton was ready to pull the trigger on military intervention in Haiti to resolve the problem at its source. With the 82nd Airborne in the air en route for an assault, and the 3rd Special Forces Group and the 10th Mountain Division staging out of Guantanamo Bay for the invasion, a last ditch diplomatic effort by former President Jimmy Carter,

Senator Sam Nunn, and retired General Colin Powell managed to convince Raul Cedras to leave. The planned invasion was converted into a peacekeeping and nation-building operation, but it was a close run thing.

Strategic Objective #3: Contain and Neutralize Remote Projectable Threats.

Since 2001, U.S. Landpower has been consumed with this strategic objective. The case of Afghanistan is a perfect illustration of the problem and the goals sought by American leaders. Under Taliban rule, Afghanistan harbored al-Qaeda, which used this secure territorial base to plan, organize, train, and direct its jihadists in attacks against U.S. targets in Africa, Yemen, and in the homeland. In the words of Ambassador Michael Sheehan, former Assistant Secretary of Defense for Special Operations and Low-Intensity Conflict, Afghanistan became a "sanctuary of impunity," an immensely valuable remote and unmolested zone within which U.S. enemies could develop and execute operations.[24]

Since the invasion of Afghanistan, which had as its strategic goals the destruction not only of al-Qaeda but the elimination of this particular unmolested base of operations, al-Qaeda and affiliate organizations have migrated, seeking new "sanctuaries of impunity" in Pakistan, Yemen, Somalia, and across North Africa. While this threat has morphed since 2001, the United States still has a keen strategic interest in preventing the emergence of true sanctuaries in remote regions of the world that violent extremists will use to build, plan, and deploy. Few dispute this objective. Yet the continuing challenge is to determine the best ways to deny these sanctuaries.

The United States pursued the regime change model in Afghanistan, followed by long-term counter-insurgency operations, nation-building, and continuing strike operations to neutralize al-Qaeda and its Taliban allies. But when former Secretary of Defense Robert Gates bluntly asserted that any future defense leader who advised the President "to again send a big American land army into Asia or into the Middle East or Africa should have his head examined," he was admitting deep skepticism about the regime change and nation-building option.[25] But skepticism over this Landpower-intensive and immensely complicated, ambitious approach does not mean that the United States can turn its back on the "sanctuaries of impunity" problem. The debate will go on regarding the right mix of other ways to seek our objective—from drone strikes, special forces, and law enforcement operations to training indigenous security forces and fostering economic development. Along the way, however, it is important to clearly define the ultimate strategic goal in those parts of the world that the U.S. targets: denying sanctuary to violent extremists who seek to strike targets of high value to the United States, and not to transform these remote parts of the world into Western-leaning progressive democracies.

Invasion and regime change in Iraq in 2003 is a more complicated case. Despite the mixed messages coming from the Bush administration, the President acknowledged that there was no evidence linking Saddam Hussein's regime with the September 11, 2001, attack, nor was there a prior concern that Iraq was serving as a sanctuary of impunity for al-Qaeda operatives, like Afghanistan had. The affiliated group "al-Qaeda in Iraq" that the American military battled was a product of the political upheaval following the downfall of the Ba'athist regime, the emergent insurgency and sectarian violence, and mere opportunism. Once the jihadist threat emerged, however, the fear that a post-Saddam Iraq might actually become a sanctuary of impunity became a key motive for continuing U.S. counterinsurgency and nation-building operations. As part of the broader U.S. counterterrorist strategy in these years, the hope was that if Iraq could be developed into a tolerant, prosperous, representative democracy, it would be a model for the rest of the Islamic world to adopt and thus "drain the swamp" that supported violent ideologies and terrorist action.

While the specter of terrorists in Iraq was part of the larger strategic narrative in this war, the claim that Iraq had active weapons of mass destruction (WMD) programs took a central role in how the remote threat was defined, and the heavy Landpower option was justified. Along with terrorism, WMD proliferation has been defined as the most serious remote threat faced by the United States and its allies since the early-1990s. Given that Iraq had no actual WMD programs, this war will never serve as a positive case of successful counterproliferation that will inspire future invasions of other suspected proliferators. Moreover, the high costs and frustrations it produced will continue to generate Gates-like reluctance to use heavy armies in this way again. It is virtually inconceivable that U.S. leaders will purposefully replicate the Iraq model as a way to neutralize the Iranian nuclear program. However, it is conceivable that airstrikes against Iran's nuclear infrastructure will set us climbing up an escalation ladder that eventually leads to consideration of some form of Landpower commitment to establish escalation dominance and end this conflict on U.S. terms. Army planners would be wise to consider

Landpower options in Iran should a preventive strike unintentionally produce escalating conflict.

Strategic Objective #4: Contain and Mitigate Politically-Driven Humanitarian Crises.

During the 1990s, U.S. leaders directed ground forces to intervene in civil conflicts that were producing or threatened to produce significant humanitarian tragedy on several occasions. The list is familiar: Operation PROVIDE COMFORT in Kurdish northern Iraq (1991); Somalia (1992); Bosnia (1995); and Kosovo (1999); these are a small sample of the much longer list of political-humanitarian crises that generated international angst and intervention by non-U.S. forces over the past 2 decades.[26] Many defense analysts, political leaders, and military professionals went so far as to declare in the 1990s that intervention in civil conflicts was the primary new mission for U.S. Landpower, a mission that should drive force structure, training, and doctrine. The ability to deter and defeat conventional threats on the Korean peninsula and in Southwest Asia remained, but civil conflict seemed to be the new game that the U.S. Army had to address.

During the first decade of the 21st century, U.S. interventionist energies were fully absorbed by Afghanistan and Iraq. But as the years move us further away from these wars, it is inevitable that the new humanitarian tragedies that appear will produce pressures for intervention, and U.S. political leaders will occasionally be tempted to respond (or at least ask the military for an analysis of the options). Perhaps the greatest variable shaping this particular strategic objective is the political will in the United States to actually commit land forces to contain and mitigate the humanitarian consequences of civil conflicts. Just as the "Somalia Syndrome" stifled American will to intervene in Rwanda in 1994, a similar "Afghanistan/Iraq Syndrome" will seriously dampen enthusiasm to turn to the muddy boots option in places like central Africa. Intervention in Libya in 2011 was restricted largely to air power, while there was virtually no willingness to apply direct American military power to stanch the killing of the Syrian civil war — and intervention with ground forces was openly rejected.

If the 1990s provide any clue to the conditions that could increase the likelihood of robust U.S. intervention in civil conflicts, something to watch is whether U.S. political leaders talk about (or perceive) the ongoing crisis as a direct test of American prestige on the international stage. More specifically, the United States is more likely to intervene if failure to do so would represent a severe blow to America's reputation for power and leadership.

It was this concern, not the horrible images of starving babies, that compelled President George H. W. Bush to volunteer an American interventionist force for Somalia. The international outcry for American action in the fall of 1992 took a particular form: the President was hearing from leaders around the world that his failure to deploy a military relief mission would fundamentally undermine the incredible prestige that the United States had generated during the Gulf War of 1991. In turn, it would erode the President's efforts to use the image of this superpower acting to help right the world's wrongs as the foundation of continuing American leadership in the post-Cold War era. For Bush, it was better to accept the risks of intervention than to damage American credibility this way, and thus undermine a great source of American power.

CONCLUSION

This chapter has not ventured specific predictions about developments in world affairs that the United States must confront in the years ahead. Instead, it has been a retrospective on how U.S. leaders have defined core strategic objectives over the past 100 years. Each of these strategic objectives has been met with a mixture of national resources, tools of potential power, and a mixture of concepts for how to achieve them. This includes the use of American Landpower. While the chapter began by warning against the prospects of prediction as the key to answering our core question—what is the future of Landpower?—it will end with a prediction of sorts. The four strategic objectives discussed previously—grand area access, hemispheric policing, containing and neutralizing remote projectable threats, and containing and mitigating politically-driven humanitarian crises—will endure in U.S. foreign policy. As a starting point, Landpower planners should take a hard look at how this particular form of power might contribute to these enduring goals and interests.

ENDNOTES - CHAPTER 3

1. Philip E. Tetlock, *Expert Political Judgment: How Good is it? How Can We Know?* Princeton, NJ: Princeton University Press, 2006.

2. "Terms of Reference," National Security Council (NSC) 68: *United States Objectives and Programs for National Security*, Washington, DC: NSC, April 14, 1950.

3. Kent Roberts, Robert Palmer, and Bell Wiley Greenfield, *The United States Army in World War II: The Army Ground Forces, the Organization of Ground Combat Troops*, Washington, DC: U.S. Department of the Army, Historical Division, 1947.

4. The most important work to make this argument is Kenneth N. Waltz, *Theory of International Politics*, New York: McGraw-Hill, 1979.

5. John Mearsheimer, *The Tragedy of Great Power Politics*, New York: W. W. Norton, 2001.

6. Nicholas J. Spykman, *America's Strategy in World Politics: the United States and the Balance of Power*, New York: Harcourt, Brace and Co., 1942; Nicholas J. Spykman, *The Geography of the Peace*, New York: Harcourt, Brace, and Co., 1944.

7. The most detailed archival study of the War and Peace Studies memoranda has been conducted by Carlo Maria Santoro, *Diffidence and Ambition: The Intellectual Sources of U.S. Foreign Policy*, Boulder, CO: Westview Press, 1992, pp. 75-82.

8. Spykman, *America's Strategy in World Politics*, pp. 198, 266, 272-275.

9. NSC 68, section II. Emphasis added.

10. *Ibid.*, section IV b. Emphasis added.

11. *Ibid.*, section VI a. Emphasis added.

12. G. John Ikenberry, *Liberal Leviathan*, Princeton: Princeton University Press, 2011.

13. NSC 68, section IV c.

14. For example, see President Clinton's national security strategy, "A National Strategy of Engagement and Enlargment," Washington, DC: The White House, 1995.

15. K. P. O'Reilly, "Perceiving Rogue States: The Use of the 'Rogue State' Concept by U.S. Foreign Policy Elites," *Foreign Policy Analysis*, 2007, pp. 295-315.

16. Peter J. Brown, "The PLA Raises its Voice," *Asia Times*, March 9, 2010.

17. Andrew Nathan and Andrew Scobell, "How China Sees America," *Foreign Affairs*, September-October, 2012.

18. Charles Glaser, "Will China's Rise Lead to War? Why Realism Does Not Mean Pessimism," *Foreign Affairs*, March-April, 2011.

19. See Fareed Zakaria, *From Wealth to Power*, Princeton, NJ: Princeton University Press, 1998.

20. President Theodore Roosevelt, Address to Congress, December 6, 1904.

21. R. Cody Phillips, *Operation Just Cause: the Incursion into Panama*, CMH Pub No. 70-85-1, Ft. McNair, DC: U.S. Army Center of Military History.

22. Office of the Historian, "Intervention in Haitia, 1994-1995," Washington, DC: U.S. Department of State, available from *history.state.gov/milestones/1993-2000/haiti*.

23. Harold Koh, "Captured by Guantanamo," *Open Democracy*, September 2005, available from *www.opendemocracy.net/globalization-institutions_government/guantanamo_haiti_2867.jsp*; Barbara Crossette, "U.S. to Close Refugee Camp at Guantanamo to Haitians," *The New York Times*, May 29, 1992.

24. Spencer Ackerman, "Mike Sheehan on Counterterrorism," *The Washington Independent*, October 10, 2008.

25. Thom Shanker, "Warning Against Wars Like Iraq and Afghanistan," *The New York Times*, February 25, 2011.

26. The U.S. intervention in Haiti is discussed in the section on hemispheric policing. The direct impact of the Haitian crisis on American territorial interests puts it in a different category from humanitarian interventions in other parts of the world.

CHAPTER 4

RECONSIDERING AMERICAN POWER

ISAIAH WILSON III

The author would like to acknowledge and thank members of the Department of Social Sciences' faculty at the U.S. Military Academy at West Point, New York, who participated in development of the guiding theme paper for the 62nd Student Conference on U.S. Affairs (SCUSA), and in particular the conference's executive secretary, Major Irvin Oliver, for their collective insights and research in the early development of this author's "power vs. force" thesis put forward in more mature form in this chapter. Parts of this chapter have appeared previously in "The True Tragedy of American Power," *Parameters*, Vol. 43, No. 4, Winter 2013-14, pp. 15-26, and *Thinking Beyond War: Civil-Military Relations and Why America Fails to Win the Peace*, Revised Edition, New York: Palgrave Macmillan, 2013.

What individuals do is related to what they think. . . .
Since wars begin in the minds of men, it is in the minds
of men that the defences of peace must be constructed.

Francis Beer[1]

If the past 12 years of long wars in Afghanistan and Iraq were not sufficient lessons, the current and developing complex and muddied situation in ("greater") Syria only amplify the clear inconvenient truth: a blunt reconsideration of American power, its purpose, its promise, and the perils that come if and when its limits are not respected, is long overdue. It is time to reconsider the American story, our national narrative, and from our beginnings as a nation and always at the heart and soul of our constitutional self, rethink the limits of American **power**.

In this chapter, I will distinguish between force and power. On the basis of that distinction, I will assess the limitations of Air-Sea Battle and the promise of "Prevent-Shape-Win." I will then conclude by considering how American power, properly understood, might contribute to a renewed national grand strategy.

POWER AND FORCE

As every graduate of Physics 101 knows, Sir Isaac Newton defined power with the following equation: Power = Force x Displacement/Time.

Newton could not account for power without force, but he did not consider the two to be identical. In addition to force, one had to account for both time and displacement, the imaginary straight path from the initial and final positions of a point, the length and direction of which one expresses in the displacement vector. All of these variables stand in harmonious symmetry in nature as reflected in Newton's equation.

When one applies Newton's elegant equation to the world of power politics, however, each variable suddenly springs to life and asserts its primacy. Force proves the most assertive of all, at least if the American case and the traditional "American Way of War" are any indication. For some time now, the United States has possessed a preponderance of force, especially the force generated by industry and the military, and this preponderance has led American strategists to equate the capacity to generate force with the capacity to generate and sustain power. Like nations laboring under a "resource" curse, a bounty of windfall riches too bountiful for their own good, so the United States suffers from a "force" curse. All problems seem to have military or economic solutions; even right seems vulnerable to might. Elements of power other than force thus can far too easily fade from the strategists' view.

Newton's force was couched always and everywhere in these complicating variables; naked force alone was a monstrosity, incapable of manifesting as power. For long stretches of its history, the United States shared something like Newton's sensibility. The basis of the constitutional discussions during our founding centered on how to maximize liberty and prosperity, and how to shape and order force with a view to these ends. Force was viewed as an instrument because the Founders understood themselves to be establishing "a nation of laws, not of men" (as John Adams put it), a regime in which force was prevented from endangering popular rule—in short, a republic. The goal was sufficient centralization of force to ensure citizen's rights and no more than the minimum necessary to protect and ensure liberty. By using principle to restrain force, the ends of government to limit and define its means, the Founders understood, the nation could generate true power.

Where does American power stand today? U.S. force is unsurpassed; American power, however, is limited by appearing only in the guise of force. American military force has had a mixed record of success, particularly over the past decade in Afghanistan and Iraq. These and other irregular wars and military-humanitarian operations (MHOs) the United States has engaged in have demonstrated the inability of mere military force to generate the conditions necessary to resolve conflicts: political agreement among internal factions, improved capacity in host nation civil governance, and increased economic development. Force of arms can bring down regimes with far greater ease than it can build them up. Partly as a result of the prominence of force in the American disposition toward the world, the persuasive and alluring aspects of America's "soft power" — its ability to attract other states through its ideals, ideas, and culture — is also in question. And with good reason, as the U.S. focus on force led it in many cases to compromise its own core ideals with greater effectiveness than any enemy could have done.

This is the heart of the paradox we face: a system of government that generates power by restraining force has produced a nation commanding unsurpassed force, and with it the tendency to place force rather than power at the core of its international relations. As the Founders knew, military force is an essential element of American power. But this power rests equally on its capacity to effect or prevent change by means of its prestige and legitimacy, which have as much to do with the opinion of those subject to American power as with the opinions of Americans themselves. True power is legitimate, purposeful, and strategic in securing national interests; it includes and exceeds mere force.

AIR, SEA, AND LAND "POWER"

Our challenge is to think beyond force — beyond war, as it has come to be understood — and to think instead about power. American power is not, at bottom, a military matter. Rather, it is an instrumentally effective, legal, and ethically legitimate, and, above all, strategic appropriation and deployment of our nation's bounty of force — all for the grand purpose of achieving better solutions to the compound security challenges our nation faces. Nonetheless, our conception of power and force does have profound consequences for how we understand and structure our military. In debates over the future structure of the U.S. military, our nation's tragic obsession with force assumes the form of an equally tragic focus on technology.

Many are already advocating a national strategy, Air-Sea Battle (ASB) that focuses on high technology threats to the global commons or a peer competitor (such as China) with a corresponding commitment never again to fight a low technology, protracted, counterinsurgency war. Such a strategy seductively appeals to those concerned by the growing cost of land forces in the midst of austerity. It also appeals to those who would minimize "fog and friction" in war by using high technology intelligence, surveillance, and reconnaissance (ISR), which leverages traditional strengths of the American military industrial complex. It appeals so strongly, in fact, that it has risen in a re-markably short period of time to become the de facto national strategy. A critic of Air-Sea Battle, Brigadier General (Retired) Huba Wass de Czege compares this development to other attempts to derive strategy from technological superiority:

> An idea that began life as a concept for overcoming the new and envisioned anti-access tactics of a great and modern power like China gained legitimacy in the new American way of high-end war, laden with the faulty logic of its predecessor of a decade ago, Rapid Deci-sive Operations (RDO). RDO informed the logic and design of the 2001 and 2003 invasions of Afghanistan and Iraq to depose the Hussein and Taliban regimes; both invasions depended on overwhelming precision air and naval firepower and a light presence of U.S. ground forces to change intolerable situations on the

ground. The approach endorsed by Secretary Gates would rely entirely on overwhelming precision air and naval firepower. This approach applies the logic of economic sanctions to bring a foreign government to terms by indirect pressure on the public it governs.[2]

The Air-Sea Battle concept is an operational approach that prioritizes assured access to the global commons of the sea, air, space, and cyberspace domains while relying heavily on continued American air and naval superiority. It also envisions a greater reliance on regional alliances and an increased acceptance of risk in other areas. The leading advocate of Air-Sea Battle, Dr. Andrew Krepinevich argues that it amounts to "a strategy of assured access [and] reflects a sense of what the U.S. military can realistically achieve."[3] The realism of Air-Sea Battle arises from both its suitability to a nation unwilling to pay the high costs of maintaining a standing army and its suitability to the high technology U.S. economy. It is a strategy that speaks simultaneously to American fiscal anxiety and to American economic and military pride.

But is Air-Sea Battle in fact a strategy? Even its advocates seem uncertain about the appropriate scope of Air-Sea Battle. Seen as a "new paradigm" for national military strategy, however, Air-Sea Battle raises a host of difficult questions. Foremost among them is the place of Landpower. What size and type of force structure would be necessary to complement air and naval assets? Air-Sea Battle also rests on a questionable notion of deterrence. Air-Sea Battle represents a capability that can be used against our enemies but lacks a strong signaling mechanism to show resolve. Carriers and aircraft come and go quickly into a region; they are excellent signals of capability but poor signals of commitment. Without demonstrating resolve, it is difficult to reassure friends and fence-sitters in regions of interest that the United States is "there," not only virtually or "from-a-distance" but in a substantial and sustainable way. Without considerable land forces, it is also more difficult to dissuade actual or potential adversaries from testing U.S. will and resolve. So while Air-Sea Battle, as an operational concept, represents an effective military doctrine and method for gaining access in areas where our enemies have adopted Anti-Access/Area Denial (A2/AD) tactics and weapons systems, it does not adequately address the strategic issue of how to avoid conflict in the first place, nor does it speak to what happens after you gain access. It addresses the how but not the why. For that reason, it is better understood as an operational idea rather than a strategy. Ironically, it is Sir Julian Corbett, Britain's greatest maritime strategist, who best expressed this point. The central theme of his work, he said, was "the powerlessness of a navy without an army equally well organized to act where the power of the fleet ends."[4]

The current vogue for Air-Sea Battle has been useful, however, insofar as it has forced military and civilian leaders to reconsider the very nature of Landpower. Again, we can turn to Sir Julian Corbett for an expression of the Army's essential *raison d'etre*: He wrote:

> Since men live upon the land and not upon the sea, great issues between nations at war have always been decided—except in the rarest cases—either by what your army can do against your enemy's territory and national life, or else by the fear of what the fleet makes it possible for your army to do.[5]

Since war is ultimately a human endeavor, "fog and friction" are inherent in all warfare. And since human beings live on land, not in the sea or air, human engagement by soldiers and marines in shaping, combat, and post-combat operations must always figure prominently in the larger and diverse ensemble of forces available to a nation.

To turn to our technological preeminence for solutions to vexing human problems is to confuse the fruit of our success with the cause of it. We do not enjoy power because of our advanced technology; we enjoy advanced technology because of our power. It is not in the air and on the sea, nor on cyber or outer space that wars are won. In the final analysis, they are won where the humans who wage them live, and this is on land. If the centrality of Landpower in national strategy raises difficult challenges, these are much better confronted with humility than ignored with **hubris**.

PREVENT, SHAPE, WIN

How, then, can our legions succeed militarily in a manner consistent with the principles of the American regime? In answering this question, the first step is to recognize that, for the past 60 years, tactical military excellence alone has not translated to strategic success. This is the heart of the paradox that haunts the American way of war and peace, or rather how America intervenes with force: the United States frequently proves better at winning battles than wars. In light of this fact, our future thinking and preparation must do two things. First, we must maintain the capacity to fight and win on the battlefield; for while victories in battle do not necessarily lead to victories in war, strategic success cannot be built upon battlefield failure. Second, we must think beyond the battlefield, and consider what is required of the land force so as to realize national strategic goals. Fundamental to this second line of thought is the strategic value of the land force itself. While tactical and operational success rests on controlling the air, sea, land, cyber, and space domains, strategic success lies in "controlling and influencing" the human "domain." Since, as Corbett recognized, humans dwell on land rather than in other domains, Landpower will — or should — continue to play a central role in national strategy.

The U.S. Army has put forward the "Prevent-Shape-Win" strategic solution to envision how Landpower might contribute to national strategy. I discuss the significance of each of these terms — prevent, shape, and win — elsewhere in this volume.[6] Here, I address two specific challenges associated with this strategic solution: regional alignment and the difficulty of recognizing "wins."

First, let us consider regional alignment, the current Army initiative to align brigade combat teams to specific regions of the world. Making U.S. forces regionally aligned is an important first step, but it is insufficient unless these forces are led by regionally acculturated talent, i.e., commissioned and noncommissioned officers familiar with not only the military forces in a given region, but the region's languages and cultures as well. The effective power of our forces aligned with the Middle East will be multiplied exponentially if they are led by modern-day T. E. Lawrences. But to attract and develop this sort of talent requires a system of professional development and promotion quite different than the one the Army currently uses. For an institution to produce Lawrences, it must have the investment strategy of a Warren Buffet; it must embrace the long-term view, for the most valuable human capital is not accumulated overnight. "Shaping" strategies, like the Individual Retirement Account, penalize early withdrawals while rewarding expectation management and, above all, strategic patience.

Patient prevention and shaping are awarded with "wins." But the wins they lead to are not always the ones the Army, and our U.S. Armed Forces more generally, are prepared to acknowledge, for the ultimate goal of these kinds of strategies is victory without battle. To gain a clearer sense of what this entails, consider the case of Turkey. After World War II, the Turkish military was a poorly-trained manpower-heavy force on the North Atlantic Treaty Organization's (NATO) flank. Through the deployment of military advisers, military equipment transfers, and whole-of-government support over the span of decades, Turkey developed into the second largest power in NATO and a lynchpin of American Middle East security. With the fall of Communism, Turkey emerged as a regional pivot state, connecting Europe and the Middle East, and providing vital support during the First Gulf War and Operations PROVIDE COMFORT and NORTHERN WATCH. Because Turkey acted in its own sovereign interests in the lead-up to the Second Gulf War, a number of observers have questioned Turkey's value as an ally; however, they fail to acknowledge that Turkey has continued to provide support to U.S. efforts in Iraq throughout the most recent war, and today supports U.S. efforts in the Syrian conflict. None of this was fated. It is the long-term return on an investment seeded nearly half a century ago, one which has continued in ways small and large over that entire span. The Turkey case represents a clear win—not on the battlefield, but through prevention and shaping strategies. As we look to possibilities for an extended diplomatic-military intervention in Syria, the 90-year investment in the U.S.-Turkey relationship may be coming to maturity, bringing large dividends to the United States, with the possibility of Turkey taking on some form of lead role in a future regional coalition aimed at protecting humanitarian safe zones, or in the longer term, containing and stabilizing conditions at and within the boundaries of a widening Syria civil war.

These questions will be at the core of our political debates in the years to come. While it is beyond my intent (and ability) to address each of them here, there are a few principles that can help us to consider how the military might maximize its contribution to national strategy in the face of budget stringency:

- A diverse spectrum of talented personnel provides an important hedge against uncertainty. Investments here, and now, will bear countable positive returns in the long run.
- Risk can be accepted by focusing service, command, and functional capability and by reducing redundancy and interservice competition.
- Limited focused research and development can develop technologies that hedge against uncertainty.
- Personnel quantity is costly; personnel quality is priceless.
- Reductions should facilitate and, indeed, require "draconian" cuts to preserve only what is truly value-added.
- Engagements with foreign military personnel to shape the strategic environment have long-term strategic benefits.
- We need a holistic campaign-quality solution.
  - Modules of unique and specialized functions and roles — packages of multi-composition

forces that are capable of semi-independent action—can be "plugged-in-for-play" with other modules or into a "mother ship" headquartering node depending on the breadth and nature of the intervention itself. This paradigm could conceivably be broadened as an organization and operational (O&O) model for integrating not only differing kinds of national military power (joint integration), or for that matter national power in general (interagency and intergovernmental integration), but also multinational power.

— This "Joint, Interagency, Intergovernmental, and Multinational (JIIM)-based" construct would provide a national and beyond constabulary-quality and campaign-quality force for international intervention. Postmodern crises and conflicts have already proven themselves to be complex, compound, and protracted affairs—long wars.

• Strategic prioritization, adherence to guiding principles, and powerful leadership are essential to achieving the most effective military at the conclusion of a period of budget stringency.

Observing these principles will make it more likely that this period of fiscal austerity leads not to "American decline" but to a fundamental re-examination and renewal of American grand strategy.

CONCLUSION: RENEWING AMERICAN GRAND STRATEGY

A renewed American grand strategy would acknowledge the nation's tragic flaw: its pride in its force and technology. It would also acknowledge the proximity of this flaw to the nation's virtue: the set of principles and institutions for restraining force that have proven uniquely adept at producing abundant prosperity, power, and with them—unsurpassed force. It would, finally, **exorcise**—or at least contain—the ghost that has haunted American intervention by casting war as a matter of mere force rather than an element of American power.

The great challenges and opportunities that lie before U.S. statesmen and statesmanship lie in questions of **American Power**. Power is about **choices**—choices over how to generate force, in different quantities and of different qualities; whether we choose to generate force on our own, or in genuine partnership with others. But as Newton taught us centuries ago, the bigger determinant over the strength and direction of power is found in how we **displace** force over time. Displacement of force, or rather how we as a nation choose to use our force, and the manner of behavior behind our uses of that force, independently and in collective actions with others, is a strong determinant of power . . . just and rightful power . . . legitimate power.

Austerity in terms of dwindling dollars and cents does nothing to deny citizens or elected leaders from making these power choices. Only a self-imposed austerity of sense and sensibility can deny a great nation like the United States of all the opportunity that "rides on the dangerous winds" of future times ahead that are, undeniably, ambiguous, and ripe with crisis.

ENDNOTES - CHAPTER 4

1. Francis Beer, *Meanings of War and Peace*, College Station, TX: Texas A&M University Press, 2001, p. 6.

2. Huba Wass de Czege, "The Hard Truth About ''Easy Fighting' Theories: The Army is Needed Most When Specific Outcomes Matter," Landpower Essay No. 13-2, April 2013, p. 1, available from *www.ausa.org/publications/ilw/DigitalPublications/Documents/lpe13-2/files/0.html*.

3. Andrew F. Krepinevich, Jr., "Strategy in a Time of Austerity: Why the Pentagon Should Focus on Assuring Access," *Foreign Affairs*, Vol. 91, No. 6, November-December, 2012, pp. 58-69, especially 67.

4. Sir Julian Corbett, *Some Principles of Maritime Strategy*, Annapolis, MD: U.S. Naval Institute Press, 1988, p. 16.

5. *Ibid.*, p. 336.

6. See Wilson's Chapter 19, this volume.

CHAPTER 5

THE MILITARY POWER TO DETER, DEFEND, ENFORCE, AND PACIFY

Huba Wass de Czege

Any discussion of grand strategy must begin with a common understanding of the eternal logic for keeping and employing arms. Western political elites responsible for recent defense policy have been sadly innocent of this field of knowledge, believing that new weapons and modern concepts have overturned ancient wisdoms. Both in antiquity and today, application of military force is justifiable only if it has a high probability of causing humans to react as intended. Only then does applied **force** become **power**.

As consequential as military power is, it is surprising that the language with which concepts of military power are formulated and expressed is so crude. Thinking in terms of air power, sea power, Landpower, space power, and cyber power may be useful to the proponents of these categories of "power" in budget battles at home, but it impedes clear and imaginative thought about defense policy and military strategies toward the world at large. These powers promise the control of certain conceptual "domains," but the sort of control envisioned is difficult to achieve in water, air, and space, while being nearly impossible on land—where most human activity takes place. The very term "Landpower" therefore confuses more than it clarifies.

Instead of classifying powers according to their domains, strategists would do better to divide power according to its functions. Military power can **deter** attack, **defend** against attack when deterrence fails, attack in order to impose and **enforce** a new and better peace where an intolerable one exists, and **pacify** an intolerably violent situation. Strategists through the ages have brought military force to bear for these broad categories of purpose, and so will strategists today. Strategists have not always been successful, however. Even when subject to overwhelming military force, humans do not always react as intended. This is so because force is not power, and because force potential is transformed by a logic specific to each of these broad categories of strategic purpose. Those making the very consequential decisions of national and military strategy must be aware of these logical distinctions, or their strategies will fail.

WHAT IS MILITARY POWER?

Before turning to the specific functions of military power — to deter attack, defend against attack, attack to enforce a better peace, and pacify a violent and armed population — it will be useful to address a more general question: What is military power? Wise strategists think of power, to whatever purpose it is put, in relative rather than absolute terms. All the sides in a conflict try to cause the humans on the other side to react as they intend. The outcome of the conflict is determined by a relative superiority of power specific to the case at the essential points of confrontation. Thus relative military power is not determined by mere comparisons of the military potential inherent in the capabilities each side has at hand. Although the amount and quality of military capabilities and resources available to each adversary are important, relative power is determined in the main by how these capabilities and resources affect the humans on each side of the conflict when they are brought to bear.

From Potential to Power: Intangibles and Pyrrhic Victories.

The conversion of potential to power is largely a function of intangible and nonquantifiable factors. Superior knowledge of war and sound decisionmaking, better training, higher motivation, greater firmness of purpose, and, above all, the ability to learn and adapt more rapidly while operating, have caused armed forces and their leaders to succeed, even against numerical odds. The great captains of history—Alexander, Hannibal, Caesar, Gustavus Adolphus, Fredrick, Napoleon, Mao, Ho Chi Minh, and others—had the ability to upset simple force ratios.

Wise strategists also understand the difference between the power to win battles and the power to win wars. Winning battles is important, but the battles have to count toward winning wars. Understanding which battles do and which do not is purely an intellectual matter. Vietnam is the classic example. Although the U.S. Army demonstrated superior combat power in battle after battle and the Vietnamese suffered far greater casualties than the Americans, the United States did not succeed in causing Ho Chi Minh's government to withdraw its forces from South Vietnam and settle for a divided nation. The North Vietnamese regime's ability to absorb far more losses than the American side thought possible ended up tipping the power balance and caused American combat forces to withdraw instead. Ho Chi Minh's final victory over the South Vietnamese regime in 1975 resulted from his ability to win key battles against the American-armed and -supplied Army of the Republic of Vietnam, and then to consolidate power in all the human habitations (cities, towns, and villages) of South Vietnam.

The power to decide battle is also relative and a matter of transforming given combat forces into the power to influence the decisions and options of adversaries. It does not matter what service or combination of services comprise combat forces, nor whether battles are fought at sea, in the air, in space, or on land. The logic is everywhere the same.

From Potential to Power: Maneuver, Firepower, Protection, and Leadership.

Prior to battle there exists only capability. Leaders and the forces of their environment, to include the actions of the enemy, transform this capability into the power to contest the outcome. Superior leaders and units can generate enough power on the battlefield to prevail against forces vastly superior by any objective criteria. Combat potential transforms into superior power at the decisive point and time to win the battle, by means of the appropriate combination of four factors: maneuver, firepower, protection, and skilled leadership.

Maneuver is the dynamic element of combat. It is achieved by concentrating forces in critical areas to gain and to use the advantages of surprise, psychological shock, position, and momentum to leverage available combat capabilities and thereby create a decisive relative advantage vis-à-vis an opponent on the battlefield. It may be the movement of forces to achieve a position on the battlefield from which to destroy or threaten destruction of the enemy. Its effect can be to throw the enemy off balance by uncovering or taking advantage of a weakness in dispositions, by unhinging his coordination, by invalidating his planned or current actions, by capitalizing on his unreadiness to counter our actions, or any combination of these.

It is the effects thus created which contribute to combat power. Mobility or movements in and of themselves do not create this effect although relative mobility or relative movements are enabling capabilities. These other factors, and the capabilities which contribute to them, are also important to create maneuver effects: knowledge of the enemy and terrain generated by study of the enemy, reconnaissance, and other intelligence activities; effective command and control of subordinate forces; flexible operational practices; sound organization; and reliable logistical support.

Firepower provides the enabling, violent, destructive force essential to realizing the effects of maneuver. It is the means of suppressing the enemy's fires, neutralizing his tactical forces, and destroying his ability to fight. This is done by killing, wounding, or paralyzing the enemy's soldiers and by damaging the materiel and installations necessary for his continued combat effectiveness. In combat, personal arms, crew-served direct fire weapons, mortars, artillery cannons and missiles, air defense guns and missiles, attack helicopters, Air Force and Navy aircraft, and Naval gunfire bombardment all deliver firepower.

Again, it is the effect of firepower, which contributes to combat power, and not its unapplied or misapplied potential. Counting available weapons and munitions is an insufficient predictor of the effects they can achieve. It is the accuracy and volume of fires, the lethality of munitions, and the flexible employment of weapons systems, which combine to create this effect. Therefore, efficient and effective target-acquisition systems, viable and effective command and control, a steady supply of the right munitions, and the tactical and operational mobility necessary to place weapons within range of critical targets are necessary ingredients of this element of combat power.

There has been a tendency to focus exceedingly on kinetic killing potential in defense planning — in essence, on weapons and their precise and lethal munitions. But for weapons and munitions to produce valid firepower effects, they depend highly on relevant knowledge; strategic mobility; flexible sustainment; and robust, integrated command and control. In the recent military interventions and in the wargames the Services use to explore future force requirements, weapons and munitions were abundantly available at every stage. But shortages in the key **enablers** of firepower make it difficult to bring this impressive potential to bear. The tendency, ahead of operations, is to consider these enablers burdensome overhead, and to underestimate the **value** of investments in having more of them. Analytical wargames replicate lethal effects easily, but the enablers not as well. This biases outcomes toward the contribution of weapons and munitions based on their numbers rather than on the lethal effects they can realistically produce. For instance, it will be very difficult to gather the volumes of information needed to perform the high tempo large-scale firepower-based operations some strategists imagine for the future. In reality, the capacity to produce relevant knowledge will limit the tempo of any such operations. When that capacity does not materialize in actual situations, the tempo and effectiveness of firepower-based operations will slow.

Protection is the shielding of the fighting potential of the force so that it can be applied at the decisive time and place. Protection has two components. The first includes all actions to counter the enemy's firepower and maneuver by making soldiers, systems, and units difficult to locate, to strike, or to destroy. Among these actions are security, dispersion, cover, camouflage, deception, suppression, and mobility. These actions routinely include the reinforcement and concealment of fighting positions, command posts, and support facilities. They also include the need to protect force elements from attack by irregular forces wherever they are—from fort to foxhole. The second component includes actions to keep soldiers healthy, to maintain their fighting morale, and to diminish the impact of severe weather. It also means keeping equipment in repair and supplies from becoming lost. As in the other elements of combat power, the effects of protection contribute to combat power. These effects are measured by the fighting potential actually available at the moment of decisive combat.

Leadership is the component upon which all others depend. It provides purpose, direction, and motivation in combat. Leaders function through personal interaction with their soldiers and through command and control systems and facilities. The primary function of leadership in battle is to inspire and to motivate soldiers to do difficult things in trying circumstances. While leadership requirements differ by echelon, leaders must be men and women of character; they must know and understand soldiers and the physical tools of battle; and they must act with courage and conviction. Leaders must understand how to control and to integrate fire, maneuver, and protection effects. In short, it is the overall effect the leader creates on the battlefield vis-à-vis the enemy through proper application of his potential maneuver, firepower, and protection capabilities which generates relative combat power.

Prior to battle, leaders set the pre-conditions which make winning possible. Superior combat power has its roots in proper preparation. Preparation includes many matters of long-term concern at the highest levels — force design, equipment design, procurement resources, doctrinal development, and the training and education of soldiers and their leaders, to name only a few. The tactical commander on the battlefield has a more immediate perspective. To him, preparation involves logistic readiness and motivation. It means continuous **planning** and training to the moment of, and even during, active combat. It means training throughout campaigns because every endeavor causes the unit to learn either good or bad habits and to gain valuable insight about an ever-evolving situation. Winning commanders and leaders in all Services and at all echelons must demand excellence under all conditions and must strive to make it habitual.

The outcome of battle can therefore be thought of as the complex interaction of the antagonists in a two (or more)-sided equation in which the sides attempt to maximize the effects of their leadership, maneuver, firepower, and protection, while simultaneously taking actions to degrade the ability of the other side to do the same. The leader who strives to win must operate on both sides of this equation before and during battle.

Transforming force potential into power is not a matter of brawn but brain. This way of thinking about military power applies to any purpose, but master strategists must take one further conceptual step because the logic of power is specific to the end it serves. As long as other states or groups exist and are capable of advancing hostile agendas by violent means, they will keep arms and the ability to use violence to serve them in four essential ways: to **deter** others from using arms against them; to **defend** themselves when others attack; to **attack** others to enforce their will on them; and to **pacify** armed internal subgroups. These basic purposes apply to nation-states and alliances of states, as well as tribes, clans, and families in the absence of states.. These basic purposes also apply to stateless political and criminal movements, as well as to state-based insurgent movements. Success in them requires mastering the logic unique to each.

THE LOGIC OF DETERRING MILITARY POWER

Military capability-in-being deters others from using force to advance their own hostile ends. The mere existence (without the need to act) of sufficient capabilities can guarantee a status quo and free the state from coercion by the violent threats of others. The art of deterring is based on understanding only two fundamentals.

Two Fundamentals of Deterrence: Image and Risk.

First, deterrence, like beauty, is in the eye of the beholder. As difficult as it might be to project the fully deterring image, under the right circumstances such images of a military force-in-being exert the power to influence events as usefully as any other. In fact, a properly constructed deterrent is the most economical use of military capability: a less costly way to preserve the status quo than to be forced to defend it. In many cases, the same military force standing in "uncommitted" readiness can project a deterring image to more than one potential adversary when an active diplomacy prevents collusion among them. In a strategic sense, such forces are hardly uncommitted.

Deterrence is wholly psychological. What matters is the image, not the reality. For example, if Country A can convince its neighbors that it has a terrible weapon which it would unleash if attacked, then it need not actually have it—maintaining the illusion of having it is enough. The deterring threat must be credible to the object. (Was this the game of bluff Saddam Hussein was playing with his Iranian neighbor prior to March 2003?) During the Cold War, both sides were concerned about the credibility of the mutually deterring nuclear threat each posed to the other. Europeans worried whether the United States would retaliate if they were attacked, thus inviting retaliation against American cities. The North Atlantic Treaty Organization (NATO) alliance is based on the promise each member makes to all others to come to the aid of any member who is attacked. Establishing an integrated and standing defensive command structure, and the commitment of national forces to it, underwrote the credibility of this promise. American forces stationed in Europe, and the annual reinforcement of these troops to exercise with their NATO partners, further bolstered the credibility of this deterrent. The United States has made such promises to individual nations on the Pacific Rim such as Taiwan, Korea, Japan, and The Philippines. Will the United States risk going to war by intervening in an attempted aggression against these Allies? Or can the potential aggressor produce a rapid *fait accompli*, thus preempting intervention? These are vital questions for strategists today.

The second fundamental of deterrence is that the deterring image's value must exceed the threshold of acceptable cost in light of anticipated gain. In other words, it must make the enemy ask, Is the risk of losses worth the prize? Humans generally value life and limb, especially their own or those of people they know and care about. Historically, however, political leaders have bargained the lives and limbs of their citizens for ends they value more. Policemen, firemen, airmen, sailors, marines, and soldiers risk life and limb daily to do their duty. Historically, aggressors have been notoriously over optimistic beforehand about the losses they would endure, and the time it would take to seize their prize. When Hitler launched Operation BARBAROSSA, he thought the Soviet Union would fall as rapidly as Poland and France.

It is equally important to appreciate that some people, in some circumstances, simply cannot be deterred. In fact, in some societies, individuals willingly sacrifice life and limb because the reward for the sacrificial act itself is greater than the goal for which it is offered. Such attitudes confound the usual logic of deterrence, as with today's Islamic fundamentalist suicide bomber.

In every case, a deterrent has to be tailored specifically to those people who are most likely to decide whether or not to act. The projection of deterring images plays an important complementary role in all other uses of military force at all levels, from the grand strategies of nation-states to the single combat of armed individuals. For instance, a force could more easily pursue any number of intentions merely by positioning a detachment of it just large enough to check several options of its opponent. The art, of course, is to know how to project the right image so that it is appropriately recognized and therefore sufficient.

Deterrence and Modern Technology.

Sometimes advances in technology pose dilemmas for deterrence because new problems need to be solved. In the years between World Wars I and II, the French built a defensive marvel of modern technology across most of the German World War I invasion avenues. Of course, they encountered political problems when they considered walling off the avenues through Belgium, and they considered the Ardennes impenetrable. The Germans solved the problem with new technology of their own—a rapidly mobile army supported by close support aircraft in lieu of lumbering artillery. And they saw the Ardennes differently than the French.

New technologies pose dilemmas for strategists because they pose new threats to the tactics formerly used by responding allies to deter an aggressor's attack. Any aggression is preceded by preparatory maneuvers and repositioning. Deterring maneuver and pre-positioning is possible within a narrow window of time—from when an aggressive pattern is recognized and acted on to the moment the aggressor commits to attack. On the one hand, modern military capabilities can enable the aggressor to narrow this window. On the other hand, some modern defenses, now called anti-access/area denial (A2/AD) systems by U.S. planners, can extend from a country's sovereign soil far over the land, waters, and airspace a reinforcing power needs for deterring maneuver and repositioning.

If countries fearing aggression could acquire and deploy these kinds of defenses themselves, they would increase the deterrent value of their defenses. But when they do not take full advantage of these capabilities themselves, and rely instead on the old tactics of protection by allied response, a new set of problems results. Coming to the aid of an ally already under attack is made more difficult because these extended defenses (A2/AD) need to be suppressed, and this requires engaging immediately in acts of war deep in the aggressor homeland, without diplomatic or political preliminaries. This is one thing when the responding ally already has its own troops under attack in the allied country. But this is increasingly not the case. Is, then, an ally's promise to respond to a sudden attack a credible deterrent? If the ally's intervention is meant to deter by means of maneuver and repositioning, knowing that there is a very narrow span of time during which these acts of deterrence must occur raise dilemmas of timing that tempt preemption. It may be difficult to know whether the aggressor is merely posturing for political effect or is actually attacking. Acting before unequivocal evidence of aggression can be found risks triggering hostilities, but waiting until the evidence is clear risks acting too late.[1]

When the aggressor is shrewd, the act of aggression occurs in a very brief "blitzkrieg" — a period so short that the potential counteraggression force arrives to a consolidated outcome. This would put the responding ally in the position of having to choose one of several poor options. One is to abandon an ally entirely, an obviously bad choice. Another is to commence a counteroffensive to recover the sovereign soil of an ally at the cost of a ground invasion force of impossibly large proportions (per lessons of Iraq), which risk triggering a nuclear and cyber escalation about the time the aggressor's regime senses an existential threat. A variant of this option would be to begin a negotiation while building a larger and more powerful coalition to recover the ally's seized terrain.

Finally, one could respond with the tactics of sea and air action advocated by the authors of "Air-Sea Battle: A Point of Departure Operational Concept."[2] We will suspend critiquing these last two options until we address the logic of military power that applies to defense and offense. But clearly, extensive deployments of A2/AD systems, though defensive, affect the workings and stability of deterrence postures. Strategies must be found to stabilize these postures. Such strategies will stem from examination of how modern technology can affect the logic and power of defense and offense, the task to which we now turn.

THE LOGIC OF DEFENSIVE MILITARY POWER

When deterrence is not enough to check the several options of each of several equally potent dispersed enemy forces, the first fallback is to defend and thus buy time for other options. Military capability employed defensively is the status quo guarantor of last resort. When deterrence, combined with diplomacy and all other peaceful means, fails to preserve the status quo, people will fight others to preserve it. These others who chose to use force rather than peaceful means to change the status quo may be external powers, internal insurgents, or a combination of both, as in the Vietnam War.

The Fundamentals of Defense: Bringing Real Potential to Bear against an Attack.

Like deterrence, defense has its own peculiar logic. While deterrence depends on the adversary's interpretation of an image of potential, what matters in the art of defense is the real potential and how best to bring it to bear in order to defeat the attack. In general, it is less costly for the defender to retain the status quo than it is for the aggressor to change it. All other things being equal, the defender merely has to cause the attack to fail to achieve its aim. Well-prepared defenses tend to improve the reach, accuracy, and protection of weapons and the morale of their operators. Those who defend their home turf usually know the ground better, can find concealed positions, and are more likely to surprise their opponents.

During the 20th century, military professionals widely believed—and often proved—that tactical military forces defending a position could deny success to a force three times as large if they were equal in quality, which of course, is not always true. Small, determined, poorly armed but well-led defenders have held off capable forces exponentially larger than themselves. A relatively poor and small nation without aggressive designs but strong determination can create a strong defense against invasion by combining its geography and its infrastructure of cities, towns, canals, roads, railroads, and other man-made obstacles to make military invasion difficult. In addition, its regular forces can specialize in one thing—defense of their homeland. Finally, the defender can create an inexpensive paramilitary "home guard" that complements the regular force by avoiding and hiding from the attacker's strength only to emerge after being bypassed to attack supporting forces and functions, the intent being to avoid losing as long as possible in the hope of a negotiated peace or some other kind of relief.

The challenge and major preoccupation of the defense is to seize the initiative from the attacker and to cause the attack to culminate before it succeeds. Successful defense depends on leveraging inherent advantages: better knowledge of the country; increasing vulnerability of the attacker's logistics and other supporting structures as these extend into the defender's country; the support of the population for regular, paramilitary, and irregular defenders; and the greater motivation of fighting for home and family. (Just because a regime is unpopular does not mean it cannot claim the "home court advantage" against foreigners.) These advantages, when aimed systematically at eroding the attacker's momentum and constraining his freedom of action, cause the attack to culminate. The problem, then, is to restore lost towns and territory through counteroffensive action, perhaps with the aid of allies, who by this time have managed to respond. When this is not possible, counteroffensive action can begin "underground" by initiating a resistance movement. Early initiation of guerrilla action and subversion in occupied areas can cause the attack to culminate short of victory and then provide leverage to the conventional counteroffensive. Causing the attack to culminate via guerilla action can also establish the basis for a viable insurgency.

   This struggle is also a contest of will. Success by either side in the physical clash hardens will. Early losses dishearten the attacker disproportionately because they suggest misjudgments about the defender's potential and cast doubt on other judgments yet to be tested. The defender must capitalize on these. In the contest of will, evidence of success or failure indicates a trend and foretells the future. Evidence of a coming culmination of the attack short of success emboldens defenders and depresses attackers. In the contest of will, time is on the side of the defender: The attacker needs to complete his business before the people at home tire of the effort. The defender merely needs to outlast the attacker and deny him his goal.

Ultimately, it is the defender and not the attacker who decides when to end the fighting, and he does so when either of two conditions occur: He has given up hope of success, or the attacker has eliminated all means of resistance. All of these factors combine to support Carl von Clausewitz's assertion that defense is the stronger form of war.[3]

Defense and Modern Technology.

The discussion of defensive logic up to this point is based on historical experience, and it remains a sound basis for defense in the future. Modern technology has the potential to strengthen the defense more than the offense. The wide deployment of counteraccess and area denial weapons and networks has already been mentioned. We only need to flip our understanding of these around to realize how technology has strengthened the power of defenses.

In the late-1980s, the Soviets saw "strike complexes" as the next major military development. They meant the synergistic combination of sensors connected to processors; connected to decisionmakers; connected to various lethal, destructive, and suppressive weapons served by robust networks, and **tuned to a specific purpose**. Those tuned to defensive purposes were labeled "surveillance strike complexes." These can be set to react automatically to the initiative or intrusion of an adversary. Such surveillance strike systems have been under development for some time. Well-planned defenses for most of the last century included such rudimentary defensive strike networks. Their sensors were forward observers or manned radars linked by radio or telephone to fire direction centers. These were further linked to aircraft or to cannons on the ground or afloat. The replacement of analog with digital technology greatly speeds the "kill chain," and renders it far more efficient. Elaborately integrated air defenses of industrialized armed forces are surveillance strike complexes that can evolve to be much more potent and far-reaching.

Though highly effective, the logic of surveillance or defensive strike networks is relatively simple, consistent, and **predictable**. Any penetration of the area of surveillance of a defensive strike network is immediately identified "friend or foe," an engagement decision is made, the best available response is selected, targeting data is sent to the responding weapon system, the target is engaged, damage is assessed, and the cycle may repeat again if required. This entire kill chain can be automated, or it could contain human nodes as sensors or decisionmakers. Some elements could be very low tech. The power of integrated strike networks derives from the combination of the very short time from initial sensing to striking (making it more likely dynamic targets are engaged) and from the precision and potency of the strike.

The possibilities for various kinds of integrated strike networks will explode. The science of automatic target recognition is advancing at great speed. Civilian wireless networks are rapidly expanding around the world, and both wireless technology and computer processors are being integrated in more commonly available devices daily. The very technologies most likely to proliferate soonest will prompt rational opponents fearing attack to defend from "urban web" defenses covered by integrated defensive strike networks. Savvy irregulars, for instance, will use rapidly proliferating technologies to deny access to large cities (or specific urban neighborhoods), jungle and mountain redoubts, and their base areas.

The United States and its allies could establish systems to respond instantly to every **recognizable** hostile attack phenomenon. This application of technology has the potential to strengthen defenses to a remarkable degree. This would be especially true against a high tech blitzkrieg attack on one of our allies, in which target discrimination is not a great technical problem. We should devote as much energy and innovation to improving the defenses of our allies, as we now do to schemes for going to war without an army. When our allies become blitzkrieg proof, the most dangerous dilemmas of deterrence are solved.

THE LOGIC OF OFFENSIVE MILITARY POWER

Military forces also fight to change the status quo when persuasion, compensation, bribery, and intimidation fail, and others choose to defend the status quo by force. This is the purpose of offensive wars, campaigns, battles, and even offensive engagements within defensive wars. In other words, this logic applies to counteroffensives to restore sovereign territory lost to an aggressor.

Offense has its own peculiar logic as well. To change the existing status quo is the most ambitious of all intended uses of military forces, requiring the most preparation, effort, expertise, and good luck.

The Fundamentals of Attack: Bringing Real Potential to Bear Against Defense.

What matters in the art of attack is also real potential and how best to bring it to bear to defeat the defense. Once launched into his enterprise, the attacker will test his own potential against the image that failed to deter. To counter the defense's strengths, the attacker has the advantage of deciding when and where initial engagements will be fought. The defender is obliged to react and either shift and expose reinforcing forces or meet local attacks with inferior forces in prepared positions.

All offensive endeavors—any effort to change the status quo—require a two-armed strategy. One arm **communicates** threats or inducements aimed at the intellect, or will, of the opposing chief decisionmakers. Such communications, whether through actions, words, or images, are intended to shape decisions and elicit desired responses. For best results, the intended recipient must perceive the communication, understanding and interpreting it in such a way that the message compels him to act in the way intended by the sender.

Because of the extraordinary difficulty of achieving the desired change in the status quo through this arm alone, the other arm must act to **force** the desired change in the status quo, regardless of the decisions or actions of the opponent. This arm creates new and very relevant facts, sometimes in plain sight, sometimes hidden, until the new reality is fact.

The real enemy of the attacker is culmination before ends are achieved. Sound intelligence is vital to the attack: Having misjudged the situation is the most frequent cause of premature culmination. While understanding physical systems such as transportation, industrial, financial, and communications infrastructures is challenging for modern intelligence, it is relatively easy compared with learning how a complex society will react to attack. The logic of a society's response can be learned only through a combination of very intrusive intelligence sources prior to action and purposeful interaction during offensive operations. Even then, the attacker's understanding of his opponent's response will be imperfect.

The single advantage of the offense over the defense is having the initiative to optimize all available potential, but knowing what potential is available and relevant and how to optimize it depends on a sound theory of the situation. Such theories then become the provisional "truth" upon which optimum plans are made and actions taken. The trick is to understand the provisional nature of such truths and revise them as the situation changes and learning takes place; plans and actions must adapt *in media res*.

All of this takes time, however, and time is the enemy of the impatient attacker. The traditional answer to such complexity has been shock and overwhelming force, which simplify complexity by treating much of it as irrelevant. Such methods require the willingness to accept heavy collateral damage and the potential loss of internal allies as the acceptable price for the desired change in status quo. The alternative is to be patient. Although modern democratic states lack patience when wars are costly and they have difficulty accepting the heavy collateral damage associated with traditional ways to simplify complexity, when sufficiently aroused, modern democracies will send their troops to war for a change in the status quo, even though they do not fully comprehend the complexities they will encounter. When that happens, it pays to understand the logic of the offense and its dilemmas.

The offensive schemes of sophisticated modern authoritarian states will be governed largely by similar logic and its dilemmas. They, too, will respond to internal pressures to change a status quo that is broadly believed to be intolerable, especially when leaders see responding to such pressures will enhance remaining in power, the deterrent of opponents is not credible, and the risks are acceptable. They, too, will misread the logic of those they attack.

Attack and Modern Technology.

If the argument so far is based on historical evidence, how will modern military technology affect it? There have been at least three stages in the recent application of technology to attack. Let us consider each in turn before turning to the weaknesses they share.

1. The 1980s: Reconnaissance Strike Complexes. In the 1980s, the Soviets developed the idea of reconnaissance strike complexes. Offensively oriented networks with high tech reconnaissance elements initiating the kill chain could be a prominent feature of all future offensive actions, at every scale. These networks could be reliably keyed to finding and destroying specific key components of the enemy's man-made systems of defense. Such proactive systems could also carry out deliberate ambush-like engagements with devastating effects on the enemy. The greatly expanded ability to acquire, track, and process more targets at greater ranges would make it possible for proactive offensive systems to strike many discrete targets that comprise the essential elements of an opposing military formation or functional grouping, **all at once**. This would affect forces mounted in land, sea, or air vehicles far more than dispersed light infantry.

There are great advantages to employing precision weapons in large numbers and within compressed time frames. The concept of "time-on-target" artillery strikes is not new. The advantage of precision fires is greatest against unwarned enemy mechanized air, sea, and ground formations or against fixed sites. Their effectiveness against such forces when mobile begins to degrade rapidly once the enemy is warned and begins to evade. Such evasion greatly increases the difficulty of subsequent targeting. The greatest challenge for such tactics is dispersed conventional or paramilitary infantry, or irregulars in sophisticated urban web defenses.

Equally important will be a planning mindset that sees target sets in terms of their systemic significance. This mind-set merely requires the adaptation of the principles of "target value analysis" developed by the Army artillery school in the early-1980s. This approach to "deep battle" targeting was used to identify the highest payoff targets in a large force array based on our knowledge of enemy doctrine, the context of the engagement, and the mission of the friendly force.

The role of reconnaissance strike complexes will grow as a prominent feature of modern offensives because of their efficiency in finding and dismantling man-made systems of the defense and vital physical infrastructures, even when hidden and well guarded.

2. The late-1980s and early-2000s: Warden's Concentric Rings. Prior to the First Gulf War, thinkers such as Colonel John Warden of the U.S. Air Force thought along similar lines.[4] Warden's important innovation was to introduce a new way to think about how to achieve desired results, or effects, using rapidly evolving aerospace technologies. He argued against the current serial approach to bombing campaigns and advocated attacking many targets in parallel, using the new capabilities of the Air Force. Older technology required many aircraft carrying many bombs

to concentrate on a few strategically valuable targets at one time. Bombing campaigns proceeded in series from target to target. This lengthy and predictable process exposed many aircrews to achieve a particular outcome. New technology permits many such targets to be attacked in parallel by fewer aircraft, and each aircraft can attack more than one target because the bombs they carry are far more precise and more potent. Warden reasoned that enhanced technical intelligence permits a greater knowledge of how man-made enemy defensive systems combine, and where to strike for maximum effect.

In theory, attacking large numbers of targets in parallel within a very compressed time frame should yield greatly magnified shock effect at greatly reduced aircrew exposure. The demonstration of Warden's methods and new airpower capabilities have been truly awesome in recent conflicts such as the Kosovo air war and the opening campaigns to depose the Taliban regime of Mullah Omar in Afghanistan and the Baathist regime of Saddam Hussein in Iraq.

But Warden went further. He also argued that the modern industrial state is very vulnerable to precision weapons delivered by American Airmen in stealth aircraft, especially if they attack large numbers of targets in parallel within a very compressed time frame. The key to this sort of an attack was Warden's concentric rings theory. He saw the modern state in terms of five concentric rings of targets with the power grid in the center and military communications next, followed by fuel supplies, normal communications, and the transportation system. Destroying these would paralyze an enemy without destroying his people. Field forces would be of little consequence because the enemy leadership would capitulate before the campaign of precision bombardment completed the final ring of targets. This strategy of striking vital infrastructure rapidly and surgically, Warden believed, would guarantee rapid success with limited risk and without the great loss of life of earlier bombing methods. This implied that the old two-armed logic of offensive strategy no longer applied — the arm necessary to enforce the desired change in the status quo regardless of the decisions or actions of the opponent would not be needed.

Source: *en.wikipedia.org/wiki/File:Warden%27s_Five_Rings.svg.*

Figure 5-1. Warden's Five Rings.

3. Today: Air-Sea Battle. In 2010, other innovators proposed a variant of Warden's theory. The second or enforcing arm of offensive campaigns would be un-

necessary in a war with rising powers, they suggested. These authors revised Warden's concentric rings theory to "distant blockading" the flow of goods and resources from and to an adversary power's economy for as long as it takes for its leadership to come to terms. And they argued that, applied long enough and competently, distant blockade — their form of "shock and awe" — would prove decisive. In its fundamental assumptions, "Air-Sea Battle" is revised Warden. Like Warden's theory, Air-Sea Battle has already proven to be widely popular, but like Warden's theory, it neglects the decisive element of military power: the capacity to force a change in the status quo regardless of the opponent's decisions.

4. The Weakness of One-Armed Attack. Proponents of concentric ring theory and Air-Sea Battle share a common flaw: they use only the arm of strategy that attempts to **communicate** with the intellect or will of opposing decisionmakers, and not the arm of strategy that attempts to **force** a change in the status quo regardless of the opponent's decisions. Some will argue that only one arm of offensive strategy is required because, according to Warden's concentric rings theory, air forces can essentially deprive the opponent of the capacity to decide since modern states (and modern warmaking) depend on networks vulnerable to air strikes. But will such operation enforce our will on the enemy? While leaders cannot communicate as before and the country may not be able to fight as before, the fighting will not be over after this first major shock and awe battle and a desirable peace will not be in sight. If all outcomes, beyond such a point, are acceptable, then one arm will do.

Once chosen, one-armed offensive strategies are roads to unpredictable and unfavorable outcomes; they are not reliable ways to change intolerable status quos. This is so because, within these strategies, cause and effect are weakly linked; between bombing campaigns and capitulation, there lie the very human brains of war-stressed leaders, most of whom are only partly known to the attacker.

Regardless of what happens to networks and infrastructures, when countries like China or Iran are attacked based on this theory, enemy leaders and the people of the country would decide to continue resistance. Events will have solidified the people more than cowed them. This appears to have happened after the "London Blitz" according to the study of Canadian psychologist J. T. McCurdy.[5] During the summer of 1940, British military and civilian leaders prepared for hundreds of thousands to be dead, more than a million wounded, and mass panic in the streets. One military estimate predicted the Army unable to defend the British Islands because it would be preoccupied with controlling a traumatized public. They believed that an air campaign against London could cause the British to lose the war with Germany. During the fall of 1940, the Germans commenced 57 consecutive nights of devastating bombardment at the beginning of an 8-month-long concerted effort to cause the British government and its people to give up fighting and accept the will of their enemy. Tens of thousands of high-explosive bombs and a million incendiary devices fell, damaging a million buildings. Entire neighborhoods were laid waste, and the casualties were indeed high, if not as high as expected. The British leadership had assumed that a traumatic effect, like being bombed, would have the same effect on everybody, and that the difference between near misses and remote misses would be the degree of trauma they suffered. This was not the finding of McCurdy's study. It found that those who survived near misses were indeed traumatized, but those who survived remote misses were affected in an unexpected way. They became hardened by the experience of surviving the severe bombardments, and ever more determined to persevere. And, as we know, Winston Churchill's government became all the more determined not to give in, but to pursue unconditional surrender instead. They will fall back on low-tech communications. National security and political organs now in existence in such countries stretch to the grass roots. The final fall back for populations in such disastrous straits are traditional social frameworks. Soon varied suppressed contending forces (ethnic, religious, political, or other) will spring into action with various change agendas. If matters are left to the remaining forces and frameworks to resolve, some new order will evolve. But the outcome is as likely to be as intolerable as the situation that warranted offensive operations in the first place. It would be as unwise to have caused it deliberately as it would be to try to predict the outcome.

We have already mentioned how well Wardian theory performed in the first battles of the Afghan and Iraqi wars. But such thinking also fueled over-optimism about the course and outcome of those wars. It also caused high-level leaders to believe in an ill-designed and puny second strategic arm—one that was not able to impose an acceptable status quo within politically acceptable costs and time.

Distant blockading compounds this weakness by setting in motion causal chains affecting globalized

122

economic interdependencies in unpredictable, fratricidal, and even suicidal ways. For instance, China is now America's third largest export customer after Canada and Mexico. How broad would be the economic ramifications of a distant blockade of China? Are we confident they would harm China more than the United States? How certain can we be in regarding the response of Chinese leadership? So not only might unpredictable causal chains transform China into something more intolerable than it was when war started, but unpredictable causal chains will surely shrink the global economy intolerably as well.

It is one thing to modify or disrupt man-made systems; it is quite another thing to modify or disrupt the intentions of actual men. Because we can only ever guess what strangers are thinking and what factors matter to them, we cannot know with certainty whether air and naval attacks on high value targets will cause submission, or how long it will take before decisions to submit are taken, or what form these decisions will take. Democracies may respond one way to damaged infrastructure, while tyrants, who are as likely as not to have let infrastructure crumble while constructing palaces, may respond differently. All decisionmakers are dealing with varied pressures, some unknown to us, and these pressures arise from various directions and constantly change in direction and amplitude. We can predict with some confidence, however, that once we attack a determined enemy, that enemy's definition of winning will promptly become not losing, or delaying defeat (indefinitely, if possible) until the coalition tires of pursuing its original strategic ends. Rather than trust in our predictive powers, we should recall how powerless we were against Ho Chi Minh's unification of Vietnam, and allow this memory to inspire strategic modesty and prudence. Above all, we should assume an inscrutable and implacable enemy.

Naval and air forces play the leading role in the first arm of offensive strategy, and they figure prominently in the second. Naval, air, and space forces can gain information about objects and activities on the ground, and they can influence adversaries' activities and strike objects. Nevertheless, only truly integrated operations containing a sufficiency of ground forces can control the activities of adversaries and enforce desired outcomes. When implacable foes have to be defeated and the desired outcome is a specified new condition or behavior, only unified action including a significantly large land force can secure it. We should also be reminded beforehand how difficult such undertakings remain.

THE LOGIC OF MILITARY POWER FOR PACIFICATION

The fourth basic purpose of military forces is pacification. Pacification is necessary because groups of people within a state have gone to war, and normal policing agencies can no longer enforce the peaceful and lawful behavior of potentially hostile forces, warring factions, or violent criminals.

The Fundamentals of Pacification: Overwhelming Force and Its Alternatives.

In the past, great powers treated insurrections with overwhelming force, often exterminating offending cities, towns, villages, ethnic groups, tribes, or clans to eliminate the source of resistance swiftly — at least for a generation — and to "advertise" a deterring example.

Pacifying the old-fashioned way does not work for modern democratic states that hope to remain influential and popular in this transparent, globalized world.

The undesirability of extermination as a mode of pacification requires modern democratic states to compensate in two ways, both difficult. First, the armed security forces of the state can seize the initiative from the national level down to the local, and apply focused and discriminating force. Knowing the enemy very well, having very good intelligence, and being more creative and strategically savvy than the enemy is essential. In addition, the state has to separate the enemy from the support of the people; it must know the people and retain their trust. Put another way, successful pacification in the modern era requires a very surgical two-edged strategy that combines the fundamental logic of offense (because one aspect of the situation requires change) and defense (because another important aspect of the situation must be defended).

The status quo changing (offensive) arm of a pacification strategy must also embody two arms (like any strategy to enforce a change in the status quo must) — one arm unifies physical and psychological pressure to affect the choices of insurgent leaders, followers and supporters; and the other arm takes away their best options one by one, and relentlessly. This pressuring arm must include a relentless pursuit into sanctuaries, giving the insurgent no respite from evasion. The defensive arm must provide real around-the-clock security from the armed propaganda and reprisals of insurgent fighters. A fearful and exposed population is lost to the government.

The worst possible conditions for making war on irregulars occur in the wake of changing regimes, when the fundamental choice of legitimate government is between a foreign occupier and a homegrown competitor. The key to regime change is not the knocking down of the regime and its forces, but the successful immediate pacification of the population despite the power vacuum that follows regime change. And this has to be achieved before the legitimacy, in the eyes of the population, of a liberator becomes the illegitimacy of an occupier.

Pacifying unruly ungoverned space is very difficult to do; there are no shortcuts. It takes keeping people safe and getting them on the side of peace. It is also very expensive in terms of trained and armed manpower. Some studies, based on rare historical successes, have judged the price to be no less than 20 security personnel per 1,000 citizens.[6] This approach also requires legitimate and efficient courts and prisons. It takes patience, time, evenhandedness, and consistency of word and deed. The benefit, however, is that the state decides when normal is attained, and warring factions as well as insurgents are eventually integrated into a peaceful society.[7]

Second, the state can simultaneously war and police in the same area of operations. This is the far more complex practice, and the one actually more common today. Success at warring and policing requires keeping straight who it is you are fighting and with whom you are enforcing the law of the land — confusing this point incurs great penalties. The principle of policing violence is to suppress it (and resulting property damage) to tolerable levels by creating and reinforcing the perception that perpetrators will face a high probability of being caught and prosecuted, and that there is no honor in this. Policing successfully requires retaining the moral high ground, and strong and legitimate institutions of justice — courts, laws, and police.

For policing to succeed, more and more of the population must see the insurgents' violent acts as crime. Going to war with an insurgent is admitting defeat in that regard.

Warring successfully requires being able to defend favorably a desired status quo on the one hand (by causing the insurgents' attacks upon it to fail), and on the other, to cause a movement of committed warriors of a sacred cause to submit to the rule of the sovereign state's authority. Some argue that the one facilitates the other, but to work well in tandem, they must both be perceived to succeed by the population and by the insurgents. In practice, they sap strength from, and undermine, one another when one or the other is seen to fail. It is possible to switch from warring to policing once a moral high ground and stronger legal institutions are established, but switching back to the warring approach is an admission of weakness and failure.

Weak states with weak institutions condemn themselves to perpetual pacification by warring until they win legitimacy with the people and the armed struggle with their armed opposition. Aid by outsiders must be provided without delegitimizing the government in the eyes of the people. This is very difficult to do.

Pacification and Modern Technology.

Volumes could be written about technique and experience, all worthy of attention, but this is the simple, yet difficult to follow, logic of pacification — enforcing peace in communities of people at war with each other and their governments. Unlike deterrence, defense, and attack, pacification is not altered significantly by modern technology. The challenge for the pacifying power has less to do with new weapons than with the fact that each case of pacification is unique.

The most recent U.S. experience with pacification illustrates the point. American and other NATO soldiers and marines found themselves in the worst possible situation by 2006 when the most recent American counterinsurgency manual, Field Manual (FM) 3-24, was written. They were strangers in lands where the government was ineffective and where their primary task was to cause people to trust their own governments and institutions for physical and economic security. In addition to this, as stated earlier, pacification is a very people-intensive business. There were too few U.S. and allied soldiers at first—at the time there should have been many more, and when they were still seen by many as liberators. There should have been far fewer soldiers when the surge of more forces came because, by this time, they were seen as occupation forces.

With a view to future strategy and force planning, the question is under what conditions will U.S. Soldiers and Marines be employed for this broad purpose? It is hard to imagine the need for rapid response formations of specially trained pacification Soldiers to be rushed to faraway and strange lands at short notice and at the invitation of foreign governments. It is more likely that pacification missions will follow an internal breakdown in governance or a deliberate regime change. In either case, the pacification effort would be anticipated and would begin immediately in the wake of active or potential combat operations to seize and secure inhabited localities. It is also likely that governments that face internal turmoil will at some point request support by training cadres of experts that trickle, rather than flood, into the country. U.S. strategists need not prepare for a land war in Asia, yet they cannot neglect pacification scenarios like the ones described here. Pacification, like attack, can succeed only on the basis of integrated operations containing robust ground forces.

CONCLUSION: BEYOND AIR-SEA BATTLE

We should never again put ourselves into situations in which we are unprepared and powerless to do what we intend with the forces we are willing to commit. We should have no delusions about the difficulty of using war to bring about desired change in human situations. In both Afghanistan and Iraq, the faultiness of over-simplified Wardian thinking was vividly displayed. In both cases, an opening shock and awe battle-winning strategy was not followed with a well-thought-through war-winning strategy. As a result, we failed to enforce the peace on our terms. What is worse, we have failed to learn **why** we failed.

The reason, in brief, is that we do not yet understand what military power is. Military power is not raw destructive force. Military power, at bottom, is the ability to influence human decisions and behavior; it entails the focused and constructive use of force alongside other instruments of power. Indeed, it is a matter of brain as much as brawn. Strategists must understand both military power in general—how maneuver, firepower, protection, and leadership translate combat potential into real effects—and military power in its specific functions—**deter** attack, **defend** against attack when deterrence fails, attack in order to impose and **enforce** a new and better peace where an intolerable one exists, and **pacify** an intolerably

129

violent situation—before they can properly assess the role of military power alongside other instruments of national power in an overarching grand strategy.

The makeup of the Armed Forces should reflect what each service contributes to causing human adversaries to react as we intend when these very different strategic purposes must be achieved. While capable forces in being are essential, our ideas about how to use them are far more so. Our past actions suggest that we confuse potential lethal force with power. As of this writing, the emerging consensus regarding the role of military power in U.S. grand strategy is badly flawed. We think much more about winning the first tactical battles of the next war rather than the construction of robust and stable deterrents, and powerful defenses. We have far too little respect for the difficulty of enforcing the peace we desire when we attack.

The fundamental goal of U.S. military in Asia should be not to prepare for war with China in such a way which risks increasing the likelihood of war, but to craft a deterrent of sufficient strength to prevent war. Developments in technology, interacting with the eternal logic of defense and attack, facilitate **this** goal as much as they enable rising powers to deploy A2/AD capabilities at U.S. expense. Defensive strike networks enable the United States to make its allies blitzkrieg proof, and, in the event that defenses falter, commitment of U.S. troops to allied countries can act as an insurance policy, signaling U.S. resolve. Prudently stationed and regionally aligned ground forces at home can support those stationed abroad while checking several options of our opponents simultaneously. Additionally, the same overconfidence in our own air and sea power to force decisions on opponents leads strategists to overestimate the significance of the enemy's air and sea power. Just as we cannot control intractable and inscrutable enemies via bombing and blockade, so enemies cannot control us or our allies. Our allies can deploy the same A2/AD capabilities that we foresee China developing, and, given their proximity to China and their cumulative economic strength and interest in global trade, they have every incentive to do so. In short, creation of an effective deterrent that exploits advances in technology, utilizes the defense capabilities of our allies, and properly estimates the role of air, sea, and Landpower in the two arms of strategy (that which strongly communicates our will to leaders, followers, and supporters, and that which decisively enforces our terms) is more likely to advance U.S. interests than the alternatives offered by proponents of Air-Sea Battle.

Military power is but one component of such a strategy, and Landpower is but one component of military power. Indeed, to christen a strategy Air-Sea (or for that matter, Air-Land) is to obscure the jointness inherent in all forms of modern combat, and to weaken national strategy by diminishing one of its parts. What is the proper name for the incorporation of Air, Sea, and Land in a balanced national strategy? Perhaps it is simply "military power." It is the nature of this power and its essential purposes that I hope to have illuminated here.

ENDNOTES - CHAPTER 5

1. Brigadier General Huba Wass de Czege, "The Costs and Risks of AirSea Battle," *Army*, November 2011.

2. Jan van Tol, *AirSea Battle: A Point-of-Departure Operational Concept*, Washington, DC: Center for Strategic and Budgetary Assessments, 2010.

3. Carl von Clausewitz, Michael Howard and Peter Paret, eds. and trans., *On War*, Princeton, NJ: Princeton University Press, 1976, p. 358.

4. John Warden, *Air Theory for the Twenty-First Century*, available from *www.airpower.maxwell.af.mil/airchronicles/battle/chp4. html*. Also see John Andreas Olsen, *John Warden and the Renaissance of American Air Power*, Washington, DC: Potomac Books, 2007.

5. J. T. McCurdy, *The Structure of Morale*, Cambridge, United Kingdom: Cambridge University Press, 1943.

6. See James T. Quinlivin, "Force Requirements in Stability Operations," *Parameters*, Winter 1995-96.

7. This is the approach the British government chose to pacify the Irish Republican Army (IRA) and to transform the IRA into a political movement that has forsworn the use of violence. This successful example of policing as a strategic alternative to warring is also a good illustration of the elegantly simple logic of the policing approach. While the IRA side certainly employed a warring logic during the conflict, Great Britain did not dignify the conflict as war. Instead, they insisted that the fundamental right of sovereign states is to monopolize the use of force. Internal and transnational stateless groups did not posses that right. They treated IRA violence, although politically motivated, as criminal behavior in all respects and very consistently. In fact, they treated all warring social factions neutrally. While they treated all acts of violence as crimes, they invited any and all disaffected groups to participate in the political mainstream. A great many arrests were made, and the system of justice sorted out the criminal from the innocent. There were missteps along the way, and the justice system occupied a large portion of the British Army for a very long time. When the level of violence subsided enough, the government offered terms including political inclusion and legitimacy in exchange for disarmament. Violations will inevitably occur, but they will be addressed through the police and the established legal system. For a more detailed discussion of this approach, see Huba Wass de Czege, "On Policing the Wild Frontiers of Freedom," *Army*, July 2006.

PART II:

FORCE PLANNING AND THE U.S. ARMY

CHAPTER 6

STRATEGY AND FORCE PLANNING IN A TIME OF AUSTERITY

Michael J. Meese

An earlier version of this article was published as an Institute for National Security Studies Strategic Forum paper. The views expressed in this article are the author's own and do not necessarily reflect the views of the American Armed Forces Mutual Aid Association or any government agency.

On February 13, 1989, General Colin Powell, who was in transition between his job as National Security Advisor and Commander of the U.S. Forces Command, gave a speech at Princeton University, Princeton, NJ. In answer to a question about grand strategy as the Cold War was ending, Powell replied, "All of the sophisticated talk about grand strategy is helpful, but show me your budgets, and I will tell you what your strategy is."[1] This chapter reinforces Powell's observation and focuses on the **means** part of the ends, ways, and means of grand strategy to explain how austerity affects strategy and force planning. By first examining theory about budget reductions, we can then describe the current, austere U.S. budgetary environment. We conclude with the current strategic options that will likely characterize the contemporary discussion of strategy and force planning.

DECREMENTAL SPENDING[2]

The defense budget system is most accustomed to and works better when budgets are growing, not shrinking. In fact, in the 63 years of Department of Defense (DoD) budgets, the budget grew in 49 of those years, with only 14 years in which the defense budget was reduced.[3] From a functional perspective, most U.S. federal government processes are designed for "incremental" spending, where much of last year's budget provides the base for the following year and budget debates concentrate on where best to allocate any incremental increases. With "decremental" spending, there is rarely an obvious reduction of strategic ends to guide the reduction in means. As budget expert Allen Schick explains, "Decrementalism diverges from incrementalism in at least three significant ways. Decremental budgeting is redistributive rather than distributive; it is less stable than incremental decisions; and it generates more conflict."[4]

As a practical matter, budgeting in austere times is different because of the strategic context in which decision are made. With an increasing budget, advocates of particular programs argue for increases to those programs from the overall increase to the budget. If successful, in the following year, they can ask for more funding; alternatively, programs that were not favored previously may receive additional funding in the following year's increment to compensate for smaller earlier increases. In contrast, with a decreasing budget, a reduction that is taken in one year may not insulate a particular service or program from continued or increased reductions in the future. Quite the contrary, if a program "survived" with a 10 percent cut last year, the reduced level is the new starting point for next year's budget negotiation. This places a premium on defense leaders understanding the long-term budgetary conditions so that they can make well-informed strategic decisions.

Even if the budget system could be used to make relevant cuts, political, institutional, bureaucratic, and other factors can lead to continuing obsolete weapons, forces, bases, and concepts even though they are likely not the most effective way to accomplish the ends of grand strategy with the means available. As Carl Lieberman states:

> Decrementalism tends to apply cuts broadly, but often fails to establish clear-cut priorities for reducing expenditures. Moreover, in a period of decremental spending, powerful political forces are likely to seek exemptions from proposed reductions for their preferred agencies or programs.[5]

In the extreme, austerity may cause political leaders to scramble to preserve constituent interests, military officers to fight to protect pet projects, decision-makers to placate the demands of competing groups, and no one to focus on the security needs of the nation. Consequently, during a period of austerity, when it is most important to maximize the effectiveness of each defense dollar, billions can be diverted to goals that may not provide the most effective contribution to national security. Strategy and force planning under austerity is different from normal budgeting and requires full understanding of the current U.S. budgetary and fiscal realities.

TODAY'S AUSTERITY

The austerity in national security spending is a function of a drawdown from the wars in Iraq and Afghanistan, the need to reduce all parts of the budget to address the federal fiscal crisis, and a concomitant re-prioritization within national power to support a new, albeit incompletely defined strategy. The federal fiscal crisis largely stems from the often polarizing and challenging national debate concerning the appropriate size of the federal government. As Figure 6-1 shows, the gap between the top line (spending) and the bottom line (tax revenue) represents the federal deficit, which has averaged about 2 percent of the gross domestic product (GDP) during nonrecession years.[6] The deficit expands during recessions (with spending up to maintain government programs and revenues down as fewer workers are paying taxes) and shrinks as the economy grows, even achieving surpluses, as it did from 1998-2001. On average, prior to the 2008-09 Great Recession, the United States was taxed at about 18 to 19 percent and had nonrecession federal spending averaging about 20 to 21 percent. While not ideal, this 2 percent fiscal gap was manageable.

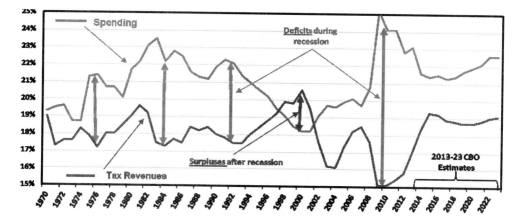

Figure 6-1. U.S. Federal Spending and Revenue
as a Percent of GDP.

With the Great Recession of 2008, leaders of both political parties took significant, unprecedented action with the American Recovery and Revitalization Act in February 2009. This "Stimulus Bill" authorized $787 billion (5.67 percent of GDP) in infrastructure spending, need-based aid, and tax expenditures, increasing government spending to 25 percent of GDP and reducing taxes to 15 percent of GDP. This exacerbated the national debt, which has now grown to over 100 percent of GDP for the first time since World War II.[7]

The fundamental question of means that confronts the Nation is on the right side of Figure 6-1. The 2013-23 lines reflect the Congressional Budget Office (CBO) projection for the federal budget, optimistically assuming there is no recession in the future. The gap between 19 percent of GDP in revenue and 22-23 percent of GDP in spending cannot be sustained indefinitely. Consequently, there is substantial need to reduce all forms of spending, including defense spending. To make matters worse, increasing numbers of the baby boom generation are over 65, living longer, and receiving Social Security and growing Medicare benefits.

Over the past 50 years, the main role of the federal government has evolved with the gradual expansion of mandatory entitlement spending and a commensurate reduction in the role of defense. In 1960, for example, 52 percent of the federal budget was spent on national defense, and 21 percent was spent on entitlement programs. Today, the roles have more than reversed with defense comprising just 18 percent of the federal budget and entitlement spending totaling 60 percent of the 2013 budget. Consequently, as reflected in Figure 6-2, as federal spending on defense is reduced, the growth in individual payments or government health care spending will likely—and very rapidly—absorb any reductions in defense spending.

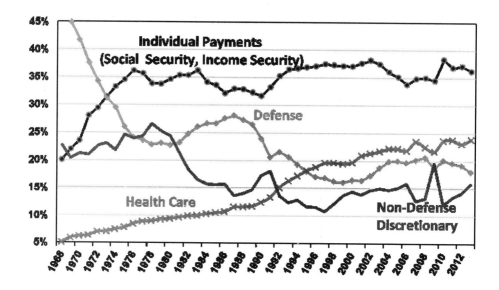

Figure 6-2. Components of U.S. Federal Spending.

The United States has actually had this problem before — in 1983 — when the nation was in a significant recession, Social Security was rapidly becoming bankrupt, and the national deficit and debt were approaching historically high peacetime levels. The difference was that political leaders, primarily Republican President Ronald Reagan and Democrat Speaker of the House Tip O'Neill, found a way to solve the fiscal crisis through a compromise facilitated by a commission headed by Alan Greenspan and bipartisan compromise between Senators Pat Moynihan and Bob Dole, which significantly reformed Social Security and extended its solvency by over 50 years. Reagan and O'Neill had to accept higher taxes, lower benefits, and other reforms, but they compromised and solved the problem.[8]

Sadly, the political environment today is characterized by extreme polarization, which significantly limits the chances for coherent strategic choices to enhance national security. Instead of compromise, national leaders narrowly averted a debt ceiling crisis with the Budget Control Act of 2011, which prescribed sequestration. Sequestration was viewed as so draconian and anti-strategic that it would force political leaders to compromise, but it failed to do so. As a result, the nation faced a "fiscal cliff" in January 2013, delayed sequestration until March 1, and then allowed budget formulas instead of coherent policy to dictate federal spending. The government shutdown and difficulty extending the debt ceiling in October 2013 reflects the continuing political paralysis in Washington. The Murray-Ryan Bipartisan Budget Conference Agreement in December 2013 forestalls an immediate crisis in 2014, but does not provide substantial movement toward a comprehensive solution in the future.

Without a national consensus on the systemic budgetary challenges described earlier, cuts in defense programs will have little impact on the national fiscal crisis. If cutting an Army or Marine division might save $5 billion per year, such savings would merely represent $5 billion in entitlement reform that would not be done, tax revenues that would not be raised, or domestic programs that would not be cut.

So, under these economic and political circumstances, what should be done with regard to force planning in an era of austerity? First, defense leaders need to engage in a credible dialogue about austerity as part of grand strategy so that as defense is cut those savings are actually used for deficit reduction — that is, to improve the nation's fiscal position and not for other political priorities. Second, defense leaders should not just notice, but focus on, other parts of government because of their effect on national security. Arguably, one of the greatest threats to U.S. national security is the unchecked expansion of entitlements without commensurate revenues which leads to increased federal debt, retarded national growth, and further austerity that undermines U.S. national security. While some might argue the military should not comment on domestic programs or entitlement spending, it is not only appropriate, but it is essential that leaders provide their best military judgment about the impact of those programs on economic security and national defense. Finally, with this as context, defense leaders still need to make strategic choices with regard to national security priorities, which is the focus of the final section of this chapter.

CURRENT DEFENSE SPENDING CHALLENGES

Strategy in an age of austerity must carefully consider current defense spending and the levels from which proposed reductions begin. First, the historical approach to DoD spending has been for the Army to receive roughly 25 percent of the defense budget, nearly consistently, for the past 60 years. The exceptions have occurred when Army spending—as a percent of the overall DoD budget—increases in support of combat operations during wartime. The fiscal year (FY) 2014 budget reflects that return to the 25 percent level, as noted in Figure 6-3.[9] As sequestration was imposed, it affected all DoD budget accounts, except military pay and a few other programs, with a proportional reduction of spending.[10] It was certainly not a strategic decision on how best to take the cuts. It was the easiest, albeit least thoughtful, method of impos-

ing austerity — across-the-board "salami slice" reductions of all parts of the defense budget.

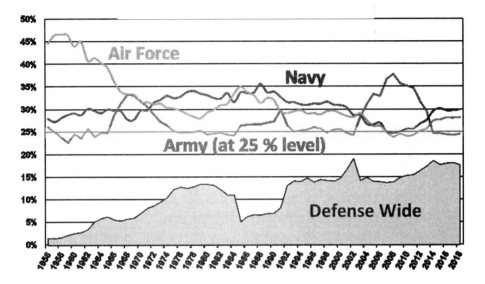

Figure 6-3. Service Budget Shares.

Understandably, defense leaders thought that im-
position of cuts through sequestration was the absence
of a strategy, and Secretary of Defense Chuck Hagel
directed DoD leaders to conduct a Strategic Choices
and Management Review (SCMR):

> to help ensure the Department of Defense is prepared
> in the face of unprecedented budget uncertainty . . .
> [and] to understand the impact of further budget re-
> ductions on the Department and develop options to
> deal with these additional cuts.[11]

In addition to identifying specific management reforms, overhead reductions, and proposed reductions
to military compensation, the SCMR identified, but

did not decide between, two broad options going forward, each of which would represent a distinct strategic direction. Hagel outlined these two broad options in this way:

Approach 1 concentrates on technology and acquisition and trades away size for high-end capability:
- Army would be reduced from the 490,000 that is planned for now to between 380,000 and 450,000 active duty Soldiers for the future force.
- Navy would be reduced from 11 carriers to 8 or 9 carriers.
- Marines would be reduced from 182,000 currently to between 150,000 and 175,000 active Marines.
- Continued modernization, especially against anti-access and area-denial threats with long-range strike, submarine cruise missiles, joint strike fighters, and special operations.

Approach 2 concentrates on force structure and trades away high-end capability for size:
- Army, Navy, and Marines would generally retain projected sizes to sustain capability for regional power projection and presence.
- Modernization programs would be cancelled or curtailed, with slower growth to cyber and other programs.
- Defense would, in effect, take a "decade-long" modernization holiday.

While Hagel made no decision among these approaches, these kinds of strategic options effectively illustrate substantial tradeoffs among defense priorities. Either approach would be substantially different from the current across-the-board cuts and would represent a fundamental strategic choice. Mark Gunzinger, from the Center for Strategic and Budgetary Assessments, argues that 1993 *Bottom Up Review* was "the last time the Pentagon created a new vision for how the U.S. military should prepare to meet the nation's security challenges."[12] If adopted, either of the SCMR's fundamental approaches would have a similar strategic impact on national defense to that of the 1993 *Bottom Up Review*, which provided the general vision for DoD force planning over the past 20 years. For those looking for a strategic choice, the recently published 2014 *Quadrennial Defense Review* (QDR) was disappointing. Instead of articulating a clear choice, it made the force smaller overall and emphasized the calamitous impact of continuing sequestration levels of cuts.

In an uncharacteristically blunt section of the QDR entitled "Implications of Sequestration-Level Cuts on the Defense Strategy and Force Planning," the report concludes:

> The return of sequestration-level cuts in FY2016 [the current law] would significantly reduce the Department's ability to fully implement our strategy . . . risks associated with conducting military operations would rise substantially. Our military would be unbalanced and eventually too small and insufficiently modern to meet the needs of our strategy, leading to greater risk of longer wars with higher casualties. . . . Ultimately, continued sequestration-level cuts would likely embolden our adversaries and undermine the confidence of our allies.[13]

In the QDR, DoD has forestalled making fundamental strategic choices and instead has declared to

Congress and the public that, if we follow the current law, we will have longer wars, more casualties, emboldened adversaries, and undermined confidence in our nation's security. This is an alarming statement about the current political-military environment in which defense decisions are made.

When the Nation eventually does make a strategic choice, it is worth noting from a budgetary standpoint that Approach 2 described by Hagel is more consistent with most of the defense decisions that have been made by the United States in previous postwar periods. The need for military engagement in the world as either a global superpower or the leader of the West during the Cold War has meant that procurement budgets either rose or fell much more rapidly than the overall defense budget (see Figure 6-4) as services relied less on always replacing the latest equipment. Instead, they continued research and development and then procured equipment if and when funding became available.[14] The contrast is clear as the dashed line reflecting procurement has much greater annual fluctuations (both up and down) than either the defense budget as a whole (thick line) or military personnel spending (thin line). Since it is unlikely that the U.S. Armed Forces will confront a technologically-superior military competitor in the next decade, deferring fleetwide procurement of new technology may be the best way to allocate scarce funding in the near future.

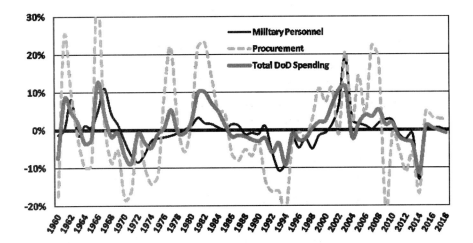

Figure 6-4. Annual Changes in Spending
Components.

The best example of deferring modernization was
the Army during the 1970s, which maintained its
16-division, 770,000 Soldier force structure, but had
very little money for modernization. General Creighton Abrams, the Chief of Staff of the Army at the time,
put the Army's limited research and development
funding into the "Big Five" weapons: the Abrams
Tank, the Bradley Fighting Vehicle, the Blackhawk
and Apache helicopters, and the Patriot missile. He
also streamlined Army organizations, improved acquisition practices, and revitalized training. Then,
when funding was available in the 1980s, procurement
could be increased to provide the basic systems that
remain the mainstay of the Army today. Some investment in research and development as a hedge against
technological surprises is appropriate, but, during this
period of strategic uncertainty and fiscal austerity,
large-scale procurement should not be funded at the

expense of forces that can shape the current international environment.

CONCLUSION

Strategy and force planning concepts are fundamentally different in a time of austerity because the defense budgeting process that may work with spending increases has significant problems executing budget reductions. To make strategic choices effectively, leaders must understand the context of their decisions, which includes the current U.S. fiscal and political circumstances that make strategic planning extremely difficult. As a result, the absence of strategy was implemented through the sequestration cuts imposed by the Budget Control Act of 2011, which reduced spending across-the-board. There is a chance for coherent strategic choices, and DoD has identified fundamental choices in the *Strategic Choices and Management Review*, but it avoided making those choices in the 2014 QDR, preferring to wait until there was greater potential relief from sequestration-imposed austerity. If a strategic choice is made, it may help resolve the connection between ends, ways, and means and be an important step forward in developing an effective U.S. grand strategy.

ENDNOTES - CHAPTER 6

1. Colin Powell, "The Changing Foreign Policy Environment," Lecture to Woodrow Wilson School, Princeton University, Princeton, NJ, February 13, 1989.

2. For further insights on decremental spending, see Michael Meese, "Defense Decision Making Under Budget Stringency: Explaining Downsizing in the United States Army," Ph.D. Diss, Princeton, NJ: Princeton University, 2000.

3. Of the 49 years of growth, over half (32 years) included real (inflation-adjusted) growth and 17 included nominal growth. Calculations based on DoD Comptroller, *National Defense Budget Estimates for FY 2014 (Green Book)*, Washington DC: Department of Defense Comptroller, May 2013, Table 6-1, recording changes in Total Obligational Authority from FY 1948 to FY 2013.

4. Allen Schick, "Incremental Budgeting in A Decremental Age," *Policy Sciences*, Vol. 16, September 1983, pp. 1-25.

5. Carl Lieberman, *Making Economic Policy*, Englewood Cliffs, NJ: Prentice-Hall, 1991, p. 19.

6. Calculations based on data from Council of Economic Advisors, *Economic Report of the President*, Washington, DC: Government Printing Office, 2013, Tables B-80 and B-1 for fiscal years 1970-2013 (hereafter EROP); and Congressional Budget Office, *Budget Projections – February 2013 Baseline Projections*, Washington, DC: Congressional Budget Office, February 5, 2013, Table 1.

7. Calculations based on EROP, 2013, table B-79. The 2013 National Debt is projected to be $16.7 trillion, which is 107.7 percent of GDP. Of this total, $11.9 trillion (77.5 percent of GDP) is debt held by the public, and the balance is the portion of debt which is held by government agencies (such as trust funds).

8. See Robert G. Penner, "The Greenspan Commission and the Social Security Reforms of 1983," *Triumphs and Tragedies of the Modern Presidency*, Washington, DC: Center for the Study of the Presidency, available from *www.thepresidency.org/storage/ documents/Greenspan_Commission_and_Social_Security_ Reforms.pdf*.

9. Calculations based on DoD Comptroller, Table 6-13.

10. Sequestration could have also affected military pay, but President Barack Obama chose to exempt military personnel from the automatic reductions for both fiscal year 2013 and 2014. See Andrew Tilghman, "Military Pay to Be Exempt from Sequestration in 2014," *Army Times*, August 9, 2013.

11. Chuck Hagel, as quoted in "Statement on Strategic Choices and Management Review," July 31, 2013, available from *www.defense.gov/Speeches/Speech.aspx?SpeechID=1798.*

12. Mark Gunzinger, "Shaping America's Future Military: Toward a New force Planning Construct," Washington, DC: Center for Strategic and Budgetary Assessments, 2013, p. ii.

13. *Quadrennial Defense Review 2014*, Washington, DC: Department of Defense, March 4, 2014, p. 53.

14. Calculations based on DoD Comptroller, Table 6-8.

CHAPTER 7

STRATEGIC MEANS: BUILDING AN ARMY FOR AN ERA OF STRATEGIC UNCERTAINTY

Douglas Macgregor

Today, Americans are disinclined to support military interventions in conflicts where the United States itself is not attacked, and American economic prosperity is not at risk.[1] In 1975, it was "No more Vietnams"; today, it is "No more Iraqs!"[2] This attitude is reinforced by both the current absence of an existential military threat to the United States and the American public's demand for jobs and economic growth instead of military spending.[3]

Yet, it would be wrong to conclude that the public's attitude emanates from complacency about the nation's security or from some naïve view of international politics.[4] On the contrary, American public support for a robust defense establishment remains strong. The American experience in Iraq simply imparted the lesson that open-ended missions involving masses of U.S. ground troops designed to occupy backward, hostile societies are unaffordable and strategically self-defeating.[5] For the first time in decades, the pressure on American political and military leaders to formulate strategic aims worth fighting and dying for before American blood and treasure are sacrificed is enormous and growing.

Regrettably, the growing demand for a new and less belligerent foreign policy has yet to be matched by coherent strategic guidance to the armed forces from the President and the Secretary of Defense. The resulting mismatch between forces and capabilities on the one hand, and missions and political-military objectives on the other, is staggering.[6] The Army, along with the rest of the U.S. Armed Forces, is adrift, floating on a sea of strategic uncertainty. A new U.S. *National Military Strategy* will eventually emerge, but until it does, the U.S. Army's leadership confronts austere, interwar levels of defense spending and constrained budgets that require an effective and efficient organization of Army fighting power for conflicts in 5, 10, or 15 years.[7]

In fact, future conflicts are more likely to resemble the Balkan Wars of the early-20th century; brutal conflicts involving Bulgaria, Greece, Romania, and Turkey in fights to secure ports, cities, and territory abandoned by the retreating Turkish armies. Today and in the future, similar fights for regional power and influence will overlap with interstate competition for energy, water, food, mineral resources, and the wealth they create. These conflicts promise to be far more lethal and dangerous than any the United States has experienced since 1991.[8] More important, without a robust and capable integrated Army warfighting component, salvos of precision guided weapons from the nation's aerospace and naval forces will become the 21st century equivalent of siege warfare. They will decide little of strategic importance on land. In this new environment, shrinking the 1990s Army to a lower number of divisions and brigades while maintaining the three- and four-star headquarters to expand the old Cold War Army if needed is not the formula for success.

Instead, the U.S. Army should be organized for the unexpected, strategic surprise; a "Korea-like Emergency" in 1950 or a "Sarajevo-like" event in 1914; punitive expeditionary operations to destroy imminent threats or deployments of ground forces to support allies already engaged in conflict will take center stage. The changes in technology, society, and the international system already underway make the case for a new 21st century Army that can do the following:

- Organize scalable, self-contained, lego-like Army formations for joint, "all arms" operations in a nonlinear, nodal, and dispersed, mobile warfare environment—a future battle space potentially more lethal than anything seen since World War II.

- Develop ground forces packaged for joint warfighting operations; formations that integrate functional capabilities—Maneuver, Strike, Intelligence, Surveillance, Reconnaissance (ISR), and Sustainment—across Service lines inside an integrated framework for joint, operational command and control (C2).

- Train and equip Army formations that punch above their weight, mobilizing fighting power disproportionate to their size (high lethality, low density); formations with the capability to close with the enemy, take hits, sustain losses, keep fighting, and attack decisively (mobile, armored firepower).

- Prepare formations to surge from a joint rotational readiness base, not from a tiered readiness, Cold War mobilization posture.

- Demand that all Soldiers from squad leader to four stars demonstrate performance against an objective standard in training and readiness; character, competence, and intelligence (C2I) must trump all other considerations in the context of promotions in order to nourish a new, core group of military leaders prepared to cope with the unexpected when it arises.

Now is not the time for the Army's senior leadership to cling to the past. Poorly thought out solutions rooted only in tradition will cause the future Army to relive the past, not master the future. For the present, the Army's senior leadership does not have the luxury of knowing precisely which power or alliance of powers the United States may eventually confront in war. Thus, the Army's task is to build a mix of capability-based expeditionary fighting formations that will be strategically decisive wherever and whenever they come ashore to fight. A new Army organization for combat is indispensable to this process.

PAST AS PROLOGUE

With the end of the 30 Years' War in 1648, interstate warfare transformed into a minimally destructive contest for the acquisition of land, resources, and productive populations (human capital). The French Revolution, 150 years later, and its martial offspring, Napoleon Bonaparte, reversed this evolutionary process by making warfare an unlimited struggle of peoples. This sort of warfare faded during the 19th century (in Europe, at least) when Europe's great powers deliberately sought to contain the forces of internal revolution and the wars of German and Italian unification between 1848 and 1871, but in the two World Wars of the 20th century, the "nation in arms" returned with a renewed capacity for the wholesale destruction of human life and property.[9] The U.S. Army trained and equipped millions of American citizens, the human foundation for victory in wars that had already consumed tens of millions of lives long before the U.S. Armed Forces arrived to fight.

Clearly, things have changed since the end of World War II. Post-industrial warfare will not require the conversion of enterprises from private to public management or the mobilization of millions of men in Army uniform. The lion's share of U.S. defense dollars fund specific technology and capability-based equipment and forces. Single-Service warfare—together with the industrial age air, land, and sea based forces it supports—is being supplanted with highly mobile, joint, integrated, aerospace, and sensor-dominated force structures, all with more devastating firepower and effect than anything seen in World War II.

ISR capabilities, long-range strike (air, land, sea, and space-based stand-off attack) forces (kinetic and nonkinetic) now decisively influence not only tactical maneuver, but the operational and strategic conduct of operations. These conditions give rise to the requirement for mobility and dispersion in land warfare—a development that elevates tactical dispersion on land to the operational level of war.

To survive and flourish in this post-industrial age, the U.S. Army must recognize that masses of superficially trained citizen Soldiers with rifles designed to "hold ground" no longer equal military power.[10] Holding ground made sense when the purpose was to systematically cleanse millions of square miles of enemy forces in Europe and Asia. Holding ground along the 38th Parallel in Korea made sense when the American people refused to support an offensive to reunite the Korean Nation in 1952.

But holding ground in the face of today's massive commercial and military surveillance increasingly linked to an array of precision guided weapons is suicidal. U.S. ground forces that immobilize themselves in defensive works on the World War II model or, worse, inside large, forward operating bases, will not succeed. Smaller, highly mobile, and lethal formations will dominate warfare. Commanders at the lowest tactical level will have to operate autonomously on the basis of the operational commander's intent.

This recognition demands a shift in Army thinking away from holding ground and toward enemy-oriented maneuver and strike operations. "Ground" or topography must be viewed from the vantage point of mobility or moving, not holding. The goal in American warfighting operations should be to achieve area dominance through the skilled employment of persistent ISR and strike assets, combined with the rapid maneuver of ground combat forces to close with and destroy the enemy. The goals should not be to flood the battle space with vulnerable light forces.

There will always be times when control of critical points on land is vital, but control must be achieved without concentrating vulnerable light forces in static defensive positions that invite destruction by future enemies' strike assets. Put another way, M-16 versus AK-47 warfare is an unrewarding exchange, something Americans want to avoid, not pursue.

Like modern, post-industrial economies, the Army must become leaner, faster, flatter in command and control, and much more capable of dispersed, decentralized operations to both survive and dominate land warfare. Maneuver in this sense diverges sharply from the linear concepts of the past with phase lines, excessive control measures, and terrain-oriented goose eggs. These control measures were designed by commanders during World War I when senior officers feared that without tight control from above millions of citizen Soldiers would be impossible to manage or control in combat. Today, Army ground forces must be designed for dispersed, mobile warfare, a type of warfare that requires greater independence at lower levels than in the past. In this new strategic setting Army ground forces must be capable of conducting deep operational maneuver to key strategic objectives, bypassing or selectively attacking enemy elements immobilized by air, space and missile power. To attain this capability, the Army must become formation-based.

NEW FORMATIONS FOR JOINT, "ALL ARMS" OPERATIONS

Benjamin Graham, the intellectual father of value investing, described the marketplace in terms that should resonate with professional Soldiers who study and understand war:

> In the short run, the market is like a voting machine, tallying up which firms are popular and unpopular. But in the long run, the market is like a **weighing machine, assessing the substance [intrinsic value] of a company**.[11] (emphasis added).

War is much like the market. War assesses the substantive strength and capability of the participants. War rewards superior firepower, survivability, and agility. War punishes vulnerabilities, fragility, and immobility.[12] When Soviet and Imperial Japanese Army (IJA) forces collided on the plains of Nomonhan in 1939,[13] superior Japanese aircraft outranged and outfought the opposing Soviet air force to a draw,[14] but Japanese airpower could not compensate for the IJA's weakness in mobility, armor, and firepower. The IJA's infantry-centric ground force was decisively defeated. Japan sued for peace.

The hard lesson that mass and athleticism do not equate to fighting power were not lost on postwar Japan's Self Defense Force (JSDF). Despite its constitutional restrictions, today's JSDF fields armored forces larger and more capable than the combined armored strength of the French and British armies. Emperor Hirohito's observation that "Our military leaders put too much emphasis on (fighting) spirit and forgot the significance of science,"[15] still resonates in Japan.

The Japanese experience is one contemporary Army ground forces must not repeat with Army forces too light to survive and fight effectively in a battle space where mines, rocket-propelled grenades, machineguns, mortars, chemical agents, barbed wire, tanks, air defense systems, and unmanned combat aerial vehicles are plentiful. To say that Army Forces should be leaner and more agile is not to say that they must be lighter and, hence, more vulnerable to destruction. In land warfare, the keys to success are better sensors, more robust information system designs, and accurate, devastating firepower from a variety of armored platforms, integrated with better — more effectively organized, trained, and commanded — Soldiers.

The aforementioned trends point to a 21st century Army that consists of self-contained formations, mission-focused force packages organized around maneuver, strike, ISR, and sustainment capabilities for employment under **Joint C2**. These formations are self-contained, survivable mobile combat formations rich with firepower of 5,000-6,000 troops under brigadier generals with robust staff structures (see Figure 7-1). They are designed to deploy and fight as unreinforced, stand-alone formations and operate inside a joint military command structure that tightly integrates ground maneuver forces within the Joint ISR-Strike complex that in many ways Air-Sea Battle (ASB) tries to create.[16]

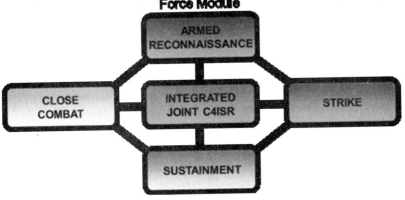

Figure 7-1. Combat Maneuver Group:
A Permanently Organized Capability-Based
Force Module.

Early in any conflict on the Eurasian landmass, Army combat groups would provide critical warfighting capabilities to halt or preempt enemy action. Early arriving formations would team with naval and air forces to rapidly secure ports and air fields, and fix enemy forces for destruction by joint strike assets. Given the embedded Joint command, control, communications, computers, and intelligence surveillance and reconnaissance (C4ISR) and robust staff organization, combat groups provide the nucleus for coalition and allied land forces that will eventually mount counteroffensive operations. Joint theater missile defense in particular is vital to the provision of Army cruise and ballistic missile defense that otherwise threatens U.S. and coalition operations.

In today's environment of "no-notice" crisis and conflict, Army combat forces must be capable of moving rapidly from widely dispersed staging areas in the continental United States deploying into a crisis or regional conflict and initiating an attack, all without pausing. The only way for the Army to achieve this capability and provide a pool of ready, deployable combat troops is to link the unit replacement policy to a training and readiness structure that deploys Army units in a peak state of readiness to fight.

A rotational readiness system that moves Army forces through four 24- to 36-month readiness phases or windows—training, deployment, reconstitution, modernization/education/leave—ensures the Army can always provide 35,000 to 50,000 ready, deployable troops inside combat groups at all times. This approach also ensures the National Command Authorities (NCA) always know what Army forces/capabilities can deploy and manages operations and maintenance funds more efficiently. In addition, Army combat groups or mission-focused capability packages are precisely aligned with the strategic air and sea lift required to move them. The advantages of the combat group organization within this system are numerous:

1. Combat groups offer more capability with less overhead at lower cost.

2. The mission-focused character of combat groups expands the nation's range of strategic options by offering the modular continuum of response the joint force needs;

3. Combat groups enable the Army to shed unneeded equipment, rationalizing modernization within a joint rotational readiness system. The system also preserves depth in the fighting force that is at risk of further cuts;[17]

4. Within the proposed joint readiness system, combat groups are also faster to deploy and cheaper to maintain and modernize than the current division-centric structure;

5. Combat groups are "high lethality, low density" formations, organized and equipped to mobilize fighting power disproportionate to their size. In short, they punch above their weight and are scalable.

Today, the Army's leadership is once again trying to re-equip the old, shrinking ground force by building and inserting updated versions of old equipment—the ground combat vehicle—into old organizations. This was the French army's approach to modernization between 1920 and 1940. It is the road to ruin, not future victory. High risk development programs like the Future Combat Systems (FCS) are unaffordable and unlikely to result in funding. Rapid prototyping *using a proven platform* is far more promising because it mitigates risk and speeds up delivery. Today's Army cannot risk binding Army modernization efforts through massive programs intended to stamp out ideal designs over 20-year production runs (FCS).

Rapid prototyping's principle disadvantage lies in smaller production runs and retooling costs, but this disadvantage is offset by the closer interaction with the user community. However, when tied to a **new force design**, rapid prototyping is a better, more cost-effective way to explore and develop new capabilities quickly with smaller inventories of new equipment in

Soldiers' hands before larger investments are made. Once we know which technologies and platforms are promising, it is easier to assess which ones will provide mission essential force attributes. High resolution modeling can be employed to refine desired attributes, but field trials with real Soldiers are still critical.

Since technologies are really designs for instrumental action to achieve a desired effect, only the use by Soldiers and technicians of new technology — **in rigorous field trials or against a capable opponent** — can reveal vulnerabilities and advantages. The light reconnaissance strike group (LRSG) is the right test bed for new platforms. The LRSG is a "dispersed mobile warfare" design explicitly organized and equipped for rapid decisive operations inside a joint force. It employs manned and unmanned aircraft and sensors forward with ground maneuver elements to provide the coverage needed to exploit the formation's potentially devastating, precise firepower. Along with strategic and tactical mobility, the LRSG has the striking power, superior mobility, and survivability to conduct armed reconnaissance and drive any enemy force on the ground into kill zones for joint precision strikes or to destroy a dispersed enemy in detail.[18] (See Figure 7-2.)

All of these points suggest the Army senior leadership link modernization to the development of new formations or combat groups of roughly 5,000-7,000 troops commanded by brigadier generals. These formations should be designed to be capability-based force packages for dispersed, mobile warfare within a new joint C2 structure designed to integrate Army capabilities into larger joint forces.

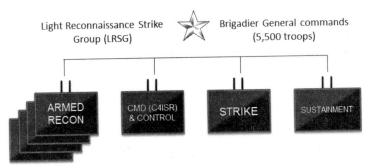

Light Reconnaissance Strike Group (LRSG)

Brigadier General commands (5,500 troops)

ARMED RECON

CMD (C4ISR) & CONTROL

STRIKE

SUSTAINMENT

New equipment must be tied to *a new force design with a Joint purpose*!

✓ Provides a credible land component with the mobility, firepower, protection and organic sustainment to operate autonomously under Joint C2; integrates all arms/all effects;

✓ Magnifies the striking power of aerospace and naval forces and signals escalation dominance to the enemy;

✓ Bypasses or punches through enemy resistance for operational maneuver to encircle and destroy nation-state forces or sub-national groups;

✓ Shifts rapidly as needed between close combat and peace enforcement;

Figure 7-2. New Equipment Tied to a New Force Design with a Joint Purpose.

As a result, they should be organized with manned and unmanned aviation, reconnaissance, standoff attack and artillery systems, Service support, and close combat troops. Formations must include logistical support groups, missile defense, and new forms of strike groups, organized in peacetime for the way they would deploy and fight in a crisis or conflict.

In an Army of roughly 400,000 to 450,000 troops, a 250,000-man field Army that consists of combat groups (see Figure 7-3) rotates through a joint readiness system of 6 to 9-month phases. Depending on the national command authorities, 30,000 to 50,000 troops inside combat groups can be maintained in a state of readiness to deploy and fight on a moment's notice. Since they are pre-determined force packages, the required transportation—rail, air, and sea lift—can be aligned with them. This approach also puts an end to the customary last minute, hasty assembly of units and equipment for deployment in crisis or conflict.

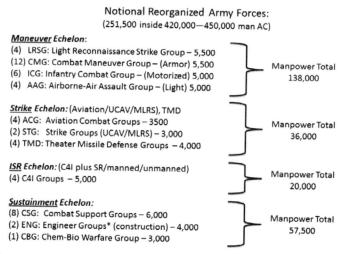

Figure 7-3. Notional Reorganized Army Forces.

Inspector generals with the rank of major general and supporting inspection teams can be constituted from existing Army resources to test and evaluate combat groups at the outset of the readiness phase to ensure standards for readiness and deployment are met. XVIII and III Corps headquarters could be tasked with the responsibility to provide these teams. Such a system would create the basis for an orientation that focuses attention on the demands of operational readiness, not the needs of garrison life in an Army composed of first, second, and third class units, depending on when the unit is placed in the Army's old Cold War mobilization system.

In the event a major war breaks out, either part or, all of the 250,000-man field Army could be deployed in a matter of 3-5 months while additional reserve units mobilize at home. Formations can be assembled in whatever mix is needed in a particular theater. It is worth remembering that at the height of the Korean Conflict, the Army maintained force of 201,000 troops on the Korean Peninsula. The deploying force described here is larger. It would arrive faster and in a much higher state of readiness. Its lethality and mobility, thanks to its equipment and integration within the ISR-Strike framework of the Joint Force, would be many times greater.

The rotational readiness and formation replacement scheme will go a long way toward achieving the goal of creating a new culture that supports joint expeditionary warfare by thoroughly grounding young officers in their profession and engendering trust and confidence in the Soldiers that their officers are competent and caring leaders. By making training cycles and deployment cycles predictable, the struggle for time and resources at the lowest levels should become less stressful.

For the Soldiers living in this system, enlistments of 36 months or longer would guarantee assignment for the duration of their service to a combat group stationed on a permanent basis at a designated home garrison in the United States. If Soldiers elected to stay in the Service, they would have the option of continuing to serve with the same combat group for years. All of these factors seem to create the stability Soldiers and their families need.

In summary, integrated "all arms" warfare is an operational concept that integrates capabilities across Service lines to maximize synergy and economize losses. However, all arms warfare also requires a force design with fewer echelons of C2 and a faster decision cycle that employs joint/integrated sensors with maneuver elements to provide the coverage needed to exploit the joint potential in the U.S. Air Force/U.S. Navy ISR-strike-maneuver-sustainment complex, as well as advanced aviation and ground combat platforms. Ideally, everything above the brigadier general commanded formations should be stripped away and replaced with a single layer of headquarters that has the Joint C4ISR capabilities, the expertise and command authority necessary to integrate ground forces into a joint/combined theater campaign plan.

THE ARMY AND JOINT C2

Unity of Effort across Service lines demands that regional unified command structures direct warfighting operations from a unified, "all arms" perspective.[19] The Goldwater-Nichols Act, like the Articles of Confederation, was a profound improvement over the ad hoc arrangements of the past, but like the Articles of Confederation, the legislation failed to endow the new unified order it created with the authority required to unify its parts.[20]

Today, the multitude of single-Service operational, two, three, and four star headquarters that proliferate inside the regional unified commands militate against unity of effort in ways that also overlap with the destructive inter-Service fight for shrinking defense dollars. They too will eventually be transformed and consolidated into single-integrated command structures capable of commanding and employing whatever modular capability-based forces — ISR, strike, maneuver, or sustainment — the Services send to them. If the strategic vision fails to produce this outcome, fiscal reality eventually will. The anticipated reduction in the number of unified commands will simply accelerate this process.

Building the integrated, joint C2 inside the regional unified commands will take time, but the coming interwar period is the right time to experiment, test, and evaluate the potential alternatives. The Army is ideally positioned to lead this process. As a first step, the Army can stand up two "Joint Force Land Component Commands" (JFLCC), one oriented to the East or the Pacific and, the other oriented to the West or North Africa and the Middle East. (See Figure 7-4.)

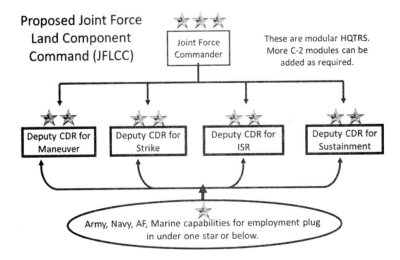

Figure 7-4. Proposed Joint Force Land Component.

With the expansion of strike and ISR assets, the JFLCC Commander must have deputies from the Navy and the Air Force, together with staffs committed to employ the full complement of air, ground, electronic, and information operations capabilities. Sensor systems that detect, locate, track, and target vehicles and groups of people moving within a large area of the earth's surface provide unprecedented capabilities. A deputy for maneuver, an Army major general, is included in the JFLCC, making the deployment of division headquarters unnecessary.

This is not to suggest that in the future U.S. Forces will always know everything all the time. On the contrary, perfect situational awareness is an illusion. But it does suggest that the integration of maneuver and strike capabilities through the integration of Army, Air Force, and Navy capabilities is the path to decisively exploit what U.S. Forces will know. Thus, "all arms" warfare requires a force design with fewer echelons of C2 and a faster decision cycle that employs joint/integrated sensors that reside primarily in the aerospace and naval forces with maneuver elements land.[21]

The contemporary Army leadership should take note of conclusions reached decades ago by a generation of senior officers who fought the world's last Great War. In November 1944, General Courtney Hodges, Commander of First Army, was asked to testify before the Joint Chiefs of Staffs Special Committee for the Reorganization of National Defense. Hodges's testimony emphasized the following points:

> That there was no necessity for separating the ground and air forces, but that it was imperative in future years especially at the War College and at Leavenworth, the officer be thoroughly trained in both ground and air operations so that logically by this system an air force officer could command a corps or an army.[22]

Hodges's comments highlight a critical issue for today's Army: **The deficit the Army's senior leadership should worry most about is intellectual, not**

fiscal. Joint operational concepts in the sense of integrating maneuver and strike on the operational and tactical levels must be developed in ways that utilize basic, learned principles, but are still flexible enough to permit the maximum number of approaches to unforeseen operational challenges. Contingency war is warfare with unexpected parameters, waged with insufficient time to prepare, and fought in a place where the political and military leadership did not anticipate fighting. If the Army is to posit future conflict scenarios successfully, and then to infer from them the need for capabilities that may not yet exist inside a force with an adaptive force design, a small body of talented, professional officers is needed to study the range of operational and strategic problems and recommend solutions.

Eliminating the unneeded echelon of brigade command will offer the opportunity to promote younger officers faster to flag rank. While this change would constitute an improvement, by itself, it would not be enough. For a new human capital strategy to have any meaning, it must institutionalize a selection system that values talent more than longevity of Service (C2I = Character, Competence, Intelligence). The officers selected to perform these tasks must be chosen on the basis of demonstrated performance against objective standards: examinations for entry to the Staff College, testing and evaluation at the training centers, and assessments during deployments. Simply selecting those who have cultivated influence at the four-star level by serving as aide-de-camps or marrying the general's daughter is not the answer. Developing officers with the courage and imagination to explore new ways of doing things is too important to ignore. Observations about the character and talents of a serving officer must come from more than one source — his or her immediate superior.

Serving Army officers continue to express dissatisfaction with an Army that lacks objective measures to discriminate between levels of performance, thus undermining leadership development. Graduates of Army schools are criticized for the inability to quickly develop creative solutions to complex problems in a time-constrained environment.[23] Clearly, a better means for talent management is desperately needed in the Army.

To get the right leaders into the right positions of authority and responsibility, leaders at every level (squad leaders through four stars) must demonstrate performance against an objective standard. Standards for technical competence are rigorously enforced at sea in the U.S. Navy. Pilots who fail to master the required skills are washed out of flight school. Similar standards must be established and enforced across the Army. Without concrete standards of performance and tests for competence, an environment conducive to initiative and independent action within a commonly understood operational framework from lowest to highest levels will simply not emerge. For example, once a captain has completed command, his or her file should be stamped "validated" and then set aside. At this point, the skills and knowledge required for further advancement will be fundamentally different and not simply an extension of the first 5 or 8 years of service.

A written examination required for admission to the General Staff College is essential. By publishing the list of required reading and study material, "validated" captains would know precisely what areas would be tested and what skills they would need to perform well. The top 25 percent of the officers tested would be admitted once the test results were compiled. Every captain would be given three opportunities over 3 years to take the examination and qualify for admission to the residence course.

CONCLUSIONS

Americans tend to forget that, long before we were an independent Nation-State, we were, first and foremost, an Army. It was the professional core of that American Army, the Continental Army, that endured the years of hardship and despair, cooperated closely with the army and navy of France, and finally defeated the British army at Yorktown. In the end, the combination of character, competence, and intelligence gave Americans victory at Yorktown and, with that victory, independence.

In fundamental terms, the Continental Army was an early vindication of Helmuth von Moltke's ageless principle, "The most outstanding institution in every nation is the Army, for it alone makes possible the existence of all other institutions."[24] In this sense, the U.S. Army's central role in American society as the guarantor of American liberty and the rule of law that supports it has changed little since Washington commanded America's first Regular Army on the battlefield at Yorktown. The time for the reemergence of America's "regulars" is upon us. Now is the time to deploy intellectually and professionally, both to restore the foundations of economic prosperity inside the United States and to create the basis for future unassailable American military power.

Soldiers know what is required: ready, deployable Army forces-in-being, highly trained forces capable of decisive action on land within a joint warfighting framework. Bold new initiatives to create the Army forces described in this chapter can succeed, but incremental changes on the margins of the Cold War status quo court failure and will produce few real savings with no qualitative increase in the Army's warfighting capability.

Unfortunately, the Army, grounded as it is in the past, is seldom adept at dealing with the future. During the last interwar period, end-strength fell, and dollars dried up. New ideas and new organizations for combat were treated as disruptive. Officers who did not conform to the party line vanished. General of the Army George C. Marshall spent 6 years (1939-45) replacing the Army's generals and recovering Army Forces from 20 years of professional neglect.

In 1996, Andrew Grove, former chairman of the board of Intel Corporation, described a strategic inflection point as a point in time when the balance of forces shifts from the old structure, from the old ways of doing business and the old ways of competing, to the new, leading large organizational structures to adapt and thrive or simply decline and die.[25] The Army has reached an historic strategic inflection point. How the Army's senior leadership organizes, trains, and equips its forces to deal with strategic uncertainty now will determine whether the Army thrives to fulfill this mission, or is marginalized and defunded.

ENDNOTES - CHAPTER 7

1. Paul Richter, "Americans Turning toward Isolationism," *The Los Angeles Times,* October 25, 2012, p. 1.

2. Daniel Tencer, "GOP Congressmen: Everyone Agrees Iraq War a 'Horrible Mistake'," *The Raw Story,* March 19, 2010.

3. Walter Pincus, "Pentagon Officials: Spending Is Bloated. Senate Panel Is Told about Need to Reduce Costs," *The Washington Post*, September 29, 2010, p. 1.

4. Eric Nordlinger, *Isolationism Reconfigured*, Princeton, NJ: Princeton University Press, 1995, p. 50.

5. Amitai Etzioni, "'Bottom-up Nation Building' Afghanistan, Pakistan, and Iraq," *Policy Review*, No. 158, Hoover Institution, Stanford University, December 2009/January 2010.

6. James Kitfield, "A Decade of War: What the U.S. Military Learned," *NationalJournal.com*, March 22, 2013.

7. "Only Two US Army Brigades Now Combat Ready, Chief Says," *Defense News*, October 21, 2013, available from *www.defensenews.com/article/20131021/DEFREG02/310210035/Only-Two-US-Army-Brigades-Now-Combat-Ready-Chief-Says*.

8. Colin Freeman, "Saudi Arabia Targeting Iran and Israel with Ballistic Missiles," *The Telegraph*, July 10, 2013. Also see *"Ballistic and Cruise Missile Threat,"* NASICR-1031-0985-13 July 2013, Report prepared by the National Air and Space Intelligence Center with participation of the Defense Intelligence Agency Missile and Space Intelligence Center and the Office of Naval Intelligence, Washington, DC, July 2013.

9. Will and Ariel Durant, *The Lessons of History*, New York: Simon and Schuster, Inc., 1968, p. 82.

10. Russell F. Weigley, *The American Way of War: A History of the United States Military Strategy and Policy*, Bloomington, IN: Indiana University Press, 1973, p. 359.

11. Benjamin Graham, *The Intelligent Investor*, New York: Harper Business Essentials, 1973, p. 121.

12. Wendell Minnick, "Heavy Armor Still Has Role in China," *Defense News*, April 19, 2010. "Heavier vehicles are for real wars," said, Dean Cheng, a research fellow at the Heritage Foundation looking at Chinese military development. "China's periphery is not like Europe, with well-paved super-highways."

13. Alvin Coox, *Nomonhan: Japan Against Russia, 1939*, Stanford, CA: Stanford University Press: 1985, p. 84. Also known as the Battle of Khalkha River, the battle took place between the cities of Nuren Obo and Nomonhan. The total area spanned no more than 100 kilometers wide and at a depth of a little less than 30 kilometers at the widest. In this small area would be the largest and most costly defeat for the Kwantung Army by the Soviets until August 1945. Japan was simply outmatched with about half the troops, almost a fifth of the aircraft, and a tenth of the tanks that the Soviets had.

14. Dimitar Nedialkov, *In the Skies of Nomonhan: Japan versus Russia May-September 1939*, Manchester, United Kingdom (UK): Crecy Publishing Limited, 2011, pp. 140-141.

15. Stephen Large, *Emperor Hirohito and Showa Japan: A Political Biography*, New York: Routledge, 1992, p. 132.

16. General Norton A. Schwartz, USAF, and Admiral Jonathan W. Greenert, USN, "Air-Sea Battle—Promoting Stability in an Era of Uncertainty," *The-American-Interest.com*, February 20, 2012.

17. According to retired Army Major General Robert Scales, "Affordable readiness can best be achieved by adopting some form of rotational deployment scheme for the entire U.S. Army both at home and overseas." Robert H. Scales, Jr., USA, *Yellow Smoke: The Future of Land Warfare for America's Military*, Lanham, MD: Rowman & Littlefield Publishers, 2003.

18. John Matsumura *et al.*, *Lightning over Water, Sharpening America's Light Forces for Rapid Reaction Missions*, Santa Monica, CA: RAND National Defense Research Institute, 2000, p. 103.

19. "Cross-domain synergy: The complementary vice merely additive employment of capabilities in different domains such that each enhances the effectiveness and compensates for the vulnerabilities of the others . . ." *Joint Operational Access Concept* (JOAC), Version 1.0, January 17, 2012.

20. General (Ret.) Pete Chiarelli, "Beyond Goldwater-Nichols," *Joint Forces Quarterly*, Autumn 1993, p. 71.

21. Lieutenant General David A. Deptula, USAF, and Major R. Greg Brown, USAF, "A House Divided: The Indivisibility of Intelligence, Surveillance, and Reconnaissance," *Air Power Journal*, Air University, December 2008, p. 21.

22. Major William C. Sylan and Captain Francis G. Smith, Jr., *Normandy to Victory: The War Diary of General Courtney H. Hodges and the First US Army*, John T. Greenwood, ed., Lexington, KY: University of Kentucky Press, 2008, pp. 166-167.

23. See the "2011 Center for Army Leadership Annual Survey of Army Leadership," Technical Report 2012-1, Ft. Leavenworth, KS: U.S. Army Combined Arms Center, May 2012.

24. Helmuth von Moltke, *Kriege und Siege (Wars and Victories)*, Berlin, Germany: Vier Falken Verlag, 1938, p. 645.

25. Andrew Grove, *Only the Paranoid Survive: How to Exploit the Crisis Points that Challenge Every Company*, New York: Currency-Doubleday, 1999, pp. 30-33.

CHAPTER 8

REBALANCING LAND FORCES IN THE UNITED KINGDOM AND AUSTRALIA

Matthew Cavanaugh

On July 4, 1918, four infantry companies from the American 33rd Division fought alongside the 4th Australian Division at the Battle of Hamel.[1] American Corporal Thomas A. Pope earned the Medal of Honor while serving under the higher command of Australian Corps Commander Lieutenant-General Sir John Monash, who in turn was commanded in the British sector by General Sir Douglas Haig.[2] As this episode suggests, American, British, and Australian soldiers have a deep tradition of shared sacrifice.

Nearly a century later, "austerity" accurately describes the zeitgeist in Washington, DC, London, United Kingdom (UK), and Canberra, Australia. The British Army is reducing from an active force of 102,000 to 82,000.[3] An Australian foreign policy think tank director recently wrote, "Australia's military spending has slipped to 1.6 percent of gross domestic product . . . this is the lowest it has been since before World War II."[4] In the United States, a recent *Reuters* story highlighted the reduction of 10 brigade combat teams and cuts which total 80,000 soldiers over the next 4 years.[5] Moreover, as U.S. Army Chief of Staff General Raymond Odierno recently acknowledged in *Foreign Affairs*, the organization is adjusting to "major changes" like "declining budgets, due to the country's worsened fiscal situation."[6] All three governments face resource constraints.

Austerity, however, is not a strategy. Scholars have defined strategy as the art of balancing ends, ways, and means.[7] The American, British, and Australian ground forces each face a meaningful reduction in "means" and broadly consistent "ends," which can shift due to the nature of elective politics. It is therefore important that the "ways" ought to be adjusted to keep each country's strategy in balance. It is in this context that this chapter addresses the following questions: Are there viable options for collaborative rebalancing strategies? Which partnered policies — e.g., coproduction, joint-venture[8] — might be most mutually beneficial for the United States and its closest allies? When the American, British, and Australian armies collaborate, **can** they be greater than the sum of their parts? If so, **how**?

SEA POWER SOLUTION?

First, are there recent examples of viable options for collaborative rebalancing? Interestingly, it appears that one comes from the sea. The U.S. Navy faces a similarly resource-constrained environment: observers note the steep decline in fleet size (from roughly 600 to less than 300) since the end of the Cold War.[9] Others counter by looking at "relative" numbers like the "displacement of the U.S. battle fleet" which is larger than "at least the next 13 navies combined, of which 11 are our allies or partners."[10] While the United States has fewer ships (or "means"), the opportunity clearly exists to look for new international collaboration ("ways") to achieve similar "ends." As Admiral Michael Mullen once commented, he was "after that proverbial 1,000 ship Navy — a fleet-in-being, if you will, comprised of all freedom-loving nations."[11]

Mullen's realization: international collaboration can extend limited resources.

In October 2007, the U.S. Navy, U.S. Marine Corps, and U.S. Coast Guard collaboratively published *A Cooperative Strategy for 21st Century Sea Power*, a "historical first" document intended to "create a unified maritime strategy."[12] The strategy highlights efficiencies gained by pooling resources, as well as reaching out to other nations and organizations to "form partnerships of common interest to counter . . . emerging threats."[13] This initiative resulted in the 26-nation Combined Maritime Forces, an organization formed to enhance maritime security, counterterror, and counterpiracy cooperation.[14] Though sea power approaches are clearly different than the land domain, here one can find contemporary evidence for a feasible, multinational solution to a resource-constrained military environment. But **how** should these three forces collaborate?

CO-PRODUCTION AND JOINT-VENTURE

Both co-production and joint-venture among the American, British, and Australian armies appears impracticable. The massive gap in overall defense spending among the three — America approached U.S.$700 billion in 2010, while Britain went below $60 billion, and Australia came in around $25 billion in the same year — these figures demonstrate the significant imbalance in resources.[15] There is one noteworthy exception from World War II that is helpful in explaining why this imbalance matters. In 1942, an American test pilot flying a "problematic" American test plane ("Pursuit Fighter 51" or P-51) at a British airfield — successfully recommended that a British-designed engine (Rolls-Royce Merlin 61) be put in the P-51 to improve performance.[16] This co-production enterprise made the plane's performance "outstanding," and a meaningful asset in the Allied effort.[17] At first glance, one might conclude that this is a mark in favor of co-production. However, crucially, the context in which this success occurred is radically different to the contemporary environment. Compared with World War II, today's relative poverty of military investment and the lack of impending external threat makes it doubtful that each public would accept anything less than full national control and accountability of national defense expenditure (particularly the United States).

Joint-venture does not appear workable either. The 2010 Franco-British Defense and Security Treaty was lauded as a model of joint-venture, but ahead of the 2012 North Atlantic Treaty Organization (NATO) Summit in Chicago, some assessed that "a number of political and military challenges remain" in the relationship between the two equipment-sharers.[18] Though co-production and joint-venture enterprises have practical challenges, there is an even greater reason to be skeptical. Elective politics can subtly shift the "ends" which a country seeks in a particular conflict. One can see verification of this in the wrangling over potential intervention in Syria.

SYRIA AND SHIFTING POLITICAL WINDS

At the time of this writing, the civil war in Syria is roughly 2 years old, has killed over 100,000 and sentenced two million Syrians to flee the country.[19] Nearly 1 year after President Barack Obama remarked that the Syrian government's use or transfer of chemical weapons would be a "red line," it appeared that the line had been crossed. The U.S. intelligence agencies assessed with "high confidence" that the Syrian government used a nerve agent in the Damascus suburbs.[20]

Despite British Prime Minister David Cameron's support for military involvement, his parliament voted 285-272 against any type of military intervention.[21] Columnist Roger Cohen opined that this "marks a watershed moment that leaves the 'special relationship' in search of meaning."[22] Cohen found Ed Milliband, the opposition Labour Party leader, counseling that the "lesson for Britain" is it must sometimes strike out on its own, even if that means separately from America.[23] Oxford University historian Hew Strachan has recently recorded similar thoughts.[24]

There appears to be a divergence afoot in Australia as well. Michael Fullilove rightly notes that, "Australia is the only country to have fought beside the United States in all of its major conflicts over the past century, including Vietnam and Iraq."[25] Past may not be prologue, however: a poll from the "Lowy Institute found that only 38 percent of Australians" would support "American military action in Asia . . . in a conflict between China and Japan."[26] So, Australian attitudes might be changing about the use of force in ways that are not favorable to the United States.

Australia is serving a 2-year term on the United Nations Security Council, making it a part of the response to the Syrian conflict.[27] Also, the 2013 Australian parliamentary election shifted power from the Labor Party and (outgoing) Prime Minister Kevin Rudd to a Liberal-National coalition led by (incoming) Prime Minister Tony Abbott.[28] Immediately after the election, the press speculated about a policy shift, with some noting that Abbott "has been far less vocal than Mr. Rudd in his support for an American-led strike against the Syrian government."[29]

In sum, both with respect to the British and Australian armies, one should assume that co-production and joint-venture endeavors would be subject to the vagaries of shifting political winds, thereby rendering such collaboration difficult at best.

ENABLE THE HUMAN NETWORK[30]

Bearing this in mind, what partnered policy might fit this ever-changing reality? General Stanley McChrystal once wrote about the importance of understanding the enemy network.[31] U.S. policymakers would also do well to understand the "friendly" network. The human network is there when needed, but can be unplugged when politically necessary. Armies often simplify their common tasks to a three-word slogan: "Shoot—Move—Communicate." All three are underpinned by morale and trust.[32] Though each country may use different weapons to "shoot" and separate vehicles to "move," the ability to "communicate" in a common language can make each force compatible without commitment. This is a desirable collaborative "way" in an environment marked by reduced "means" and brimming with questions about policy "ends."

There are a number of policies that would promote this sort of communication:

1. International Staff Integration: Americans, British, and Australian officers have served together intimately for the past decade in war. To maintain these relationships, international assignment service should continue in peacetime. Australian Major General Richard Burr currently serves as the Deputy Commanding General for Operations at U.S. Army Pacific, for instance.[33] This sort of staff integration can be expanded.

2. International Doctrine: One study from the 1990s found that less than half of all doctrinal publications carried multinational sections.[34] The default should be to include sections devoted to international partner operations — that is how America typically fights wars.[35]

3. Communications Architecture: Colonel John Angevine has argued that "The number one tactical-level interoperability issue" among the Americans, British, and Australians "is the lack of an integrated tactical-level COP [Common Operating Picture]."[36] He further reports that, "the absence of a tactical-level COP has proved deadly in the past" and "significantly inhibit[s] coalition" operations.[37] Higher headquarters and staffs often work well together, but interaction on the tactical and operational levels (i.e., brigade and below) should be fused more effectively.

4. Defense Diplomacy: Too often policymakers react to reduced budgets by cutting travel spending. The relationships gained in the crucible of war must be maintained through to the next conflagration. Cost-effective, online networking initiatives like the Australian "Ikahan" program, as well as private efforts like Rally Point, ought to be explored.[38] The focus, however, should be shared experience in order to develop the trust that enables communication. The commander of U.S. Army Pacific recently stated his commitment to defense diplomacy despite austerity, "We've been able to fence our engagements throughout our theater of operations. . . . In this business . . . relationship building is building trust, and that's the part I want to make sure we hold onto."[39] This is a helpful sign, precisely what it means to "enable the human network," but there is more that could, and should, be done.

CONCLUSION

The challenge, as Steven Jermy of the British Royal Navy has written, is that "Strategy making is problem solving of the most complex order, because it deals with three of life's great imponderables: people, war, and the future."[40] Supporting the human network is simply better policy than co-production and joint-venture because it is there when needed, yet can be rapidly disconnected when politically expedient. In an environment of significantly reduced "means" and loaded with questions about policy "ends," this is a feasible, collaborative "way" that empowers the American, British, and Australian ground forces to be greater than the sum of their parts.

ENDNOTES - CHAPTER 8

1. Gary Sheffield, *The Chief: Douglas Haig and the British Army*, London, UK: Aurum Press, 2011, p. 293.

2. *Ibid.*, p. 294. See also "Pope, Thomas A.," Washington, DC: Center of Military History, available from *www.history.army.mil/html/moh/worldwari.html#POPE*.

3. Andrew Chuter, "Reductions Will Limit Armed Forces' Capabilities, UK Military Chief Warns," *Defense News*, August 22, 2013, available from *www.defensenews.com/article/20130822/DEFREG01/308220013/Reductions-Will-Limit-Armed-Forces-Capabilities-UK-Military-Chief-Warns*.

4. Michael Fullilove, "Caught Between the U.S. and China," *The New York Times*, September 5, 2013.

5. David Alexander, "Army To Eliminate 10 Brigades at U.S. Bases in Drawdown: Odierno," *Reuters*, June 25, 2013, available from *www.reuters.com/article/2013/06/25/us-usa-army-idUSBRE95O1IR20130625*.

6. Raymond T. Odierno, "The U.S. Army in a Time of Transition: Building a Flexible Force," *Foreign Affairs,* May-June, 2012, p. 11.

7. See Arthur F. Lykke, "Toward an Understanding of Military Strategy," *The U.S. Army War College Guide to Strategy,* Carlisle, PA: Strategic Studies Institute, U.S. Army War College, 2001, pp. 179-185.

8. Note: Both "co-production" and "joint-venture" should generally be considered multinational shared investment in, and the development of, new military technologies for those participating nations.

9. See Robert D. Kaplan, "America's Elegant Decline," *The Atlantic Monthly,* November 2007.

10. Robert Gates, quoted in *Ibid.*

11. *Ibid.*

12. James T. Conway, Gary Roughead, and Thad W. Allen, *A Cooperative Strategy for 21st Century Sea power,* Washington, DC: Department of the Navy, United States Marine Corps, and United States Coast Guard, October 2007, p. 1.

13. *Ibid.,* p. 5.

14. See "Combined Maritime Forces," *Wikipedia,* available from *en.wikipedia.org/wiki/Combined_Maritime_Forces#Combined_Maritime_Forces.*

15. *The Economist: Pocket World in Figures,* 2013 Ed., London, UK: Profile Books, 2013, p. 102.

16. Paul Kennedy, *Engineers of Victory: The Problem Solvers Who Turned the Tide in the Second World War,* New York: Random House, 2013, p. 121.

17. *Ibid.,* p. 122.

18. Benoit Gomis and Andrea Barbara Baumann, "U.K.-France Defense Cooperation in Spotlight Ahead of NATO Summit," *World Politics Review*, March 21, 2012.

19. United Nations Human Rights Committee, "Number of Syrian refugees tops 2 million mark with more on the way," September 3, 2013, available from *www.unhcr.org/522495669.html*.

20. Office of the Press Secretary, "Government Assessment of the Syrian Government's Use of Chemical Weapons on August 21, 2013, Washington, DC: The White House, August 30, 2013, available from *www.whitehouse.gov/the-press-office/2013/08/30/government-assessment-syrian-government-s-use-chemical-weapons-august-21*.

21. Roger Cohen "A Much Less Special Relationship," *The New York Times*, August 30, 2013.

22. *Ibid.*

23. *Ibid.*

24. Hew Strachan, "British National Strategy: Who Does It?" *Parameters*, Vol. 43, No. 2, Summer 2013, p. 51.

25. Fullilove.

26. *Ibid.* See also "The Lowy Institute Poll 2013," Sydney, Australia: Lowy Institute, June 24, 2013, available from *www.lowyinstitute.org/publications/lowy-institute-poll-2013*.

27. "United Nations Security Council," United Nations Website, available from *www.un.org/en/sc/members/*.

28. Matt Siegel, "Australian Labor Party Is Dealt Sharp Blow in Vote, Ending 6 Years in Power," *The New York Times*, September 8, 2013.

29. *Ibid.*

30. Note: "Human network" refers to person-to-person linkages in any meaningful professional form (i.e., voice, electron-

ic). In this case, the objective is to cut across organizations and national boundaries.

31. Stanley McChrystal, "It Takes a Network," *Foreign Policy*, March-April 2011, available from *www.foreignpolicy.com/ articles/2011/02/22/it_takes_a_network*.

32. Colin S. Gray, *The Strategy Bridge: Theory for Practice*, Oxford, UK: Oxford University Press, 2010, pp. 214-215.

33. Amber Robinson, "USARPAC Honors Deputy Commanding General for Operations," *Army: News Website*, January 17, 2013, available from *www.army.mil/article/94570/*.

34. See Jay M. Vittori, "Making the Case for Multinational Military Doctrine," *Joint Forces Quarterly*, Spring 1998, pp. 109-115.

35. Note: The only exception ought to be those that just do not make sense, i.e., funeral arrangements.

36. John Angevine, "Dangerous Luxuries: How the Quest for High-End Capabilities Leaves the ADF Vulnerable to Mission Failure and More Dependent on the United States," Sydney, Australia: Lowy Institute for International Policy, June 2011, pp. a2-vi, a2-vii.

37. *Ibid.*

38. See "Ikahan Alumni Pertahanan Indonesia-Australia," available from *Ikahan.com*. See also "Rally Point," available from *RallyPoint.com*.

39. Kevin Baron, "U.S. Army 'Fences Off' Military Diplomacy from Sequester," *Foreign Policy.com*, May 14, 2013, available from *ering.foreignpolicy.com/posts/2013/05/14/us_army_fences_off_ military_diplomacy_from_sequester*.

40. Steven Jermy, *Strategy for Action: Using Force Wisely in the 21st Century*, London, UK: Knightsone, 2011, p. 6.

CHAPTER 9

MAINTAINING AND MODERNIZING
THE FORCE
IN PERIODS OF REDUCED RESOURCES

Conrad Crane

The U.S. Army once again faces the challenge of maintaining and modernizing the force. American resources devoted to defense decline after every major conflict. During these recoils from wars, threats are usually poorly or narrowly defined, domestic economic concerns and a desire to "return to normalcy" overshadow foreign policy, and the Army struggles to define its missions as policymakers decide to rely more on other services. Army Chiefs of Staff generally find themselves with much flexibility and little direction in determining cuts and priorities, while facing a widening gulf between strategic commitments and resources. Far-sighted leaders have met this enduring challenge by maintaining trained and educated Soldiers who could rise to their responsibilities when danger again threatened, by concentrating on a few key and relatively inexpensive weapons systems when money was scarce, and by laying the groundwork for more extensive acquisitions when policies changed and conflicts erupted.

HISTORICAL CONTEXT

The service has responded to this challenge in many different ways. By and large, the Army has not had the opportunity to undertake major modernization programs. Instead, it has moved incrementally

189

while preparing to take advantage of rare opportunities for more abundant funding: a long war with a buildup, or a national security policy reemphasizing land forces.

The United States did not concern itself with building and sustaining the military forces of a world power until the 20th century. Before then, the peacetime Regular Army was always very small, with the expectation that militia and volunteers could be called up for emergencies. While the Navy worried about keeping up with the latest technology, the Army did not. This all changed after World War I. The primary security threat to the United States was perceived as a rising Japan, with a resulting focus on the Pacific and the Navy (the first American strategic "pivot" to that region), but the solution to such danger was thought to lie mainly in naval arms limitations treaties. Meanwhile, the National Defense Act of 1920 did establish a base active force of 280,000 Soldiers to defend the homeland and perform expeditionary duties. The legislation was heavily influenced by the Guard lobby in Congress, and depended on the Guard and an Organized Reserve to help mobilize almost 2 million draftees in 60 days for a war. The Army also made some effort to incorporate promising new technologies from World War I such as the tank and airplane, but internal opposition to those weapons systems, the absence of imminent threats, and the reluctance of the executive and legislative branches to provide much funding limited the options of the "Roaring Twenties." Indeed, in some circles, the solution to the threat of war was just to sign a treaty outlawing it.[1]

The Great Depression of 1929 made matters worse. As budgets got even tighter and the depression deepened, the Army Air Corps nevertheless proved adept at procuring money to purchase new aircraft. The rest of the force was less successful at such modernization. Though the Army knew that it needed tanks, trucks, and general mechanization, when budget priorities were set, Chiefs of Staff almost always favored trained Soldiers over new weapons. There was an assumption that the next generation of technology would be better, and that educated leaders would be able to build and adapt the Army when necessary. Consequently, the service school system thrived in the 1920s and 1930s, and the best officers were assigned as students and faculty. In the meantime, the service successfully developed and fielded less expensive but still important weapons like the MI Garand rifle and a new 105-mm howitzer.[2]

The big explosion of modernization, however, occurred during the buildup and execution of World War II, when the planning and priorities of those interwar Chiefs of Staff were generally vindicated. Much of this success was due to a board system where each branch developed requirements which the Chief of Staff then prioritized. When the budget floodgates opened to prepare for war, there were plenty of well-developed concepts on the table for programming. The Air Corps and Quartermaster Corps also proved especially adept at working with manufacturers to advance their technology in aircraft and motor vehicles. Probably the greatest failure was in tank development, which was due in major part to the lack of a distinct armor branch.[3]

The end of that war produced a similar drawdown and neglect of the Army. International Communism was the new threat, and the Navy and a newly independent Air Force squabbled over who should have the primary responsibility for deterrence. By 1948, when the Army had been reduced to 1/16th of its peak World War II strength, General Omar Bradley declared that it was in a "shockingly deplorable state," with "almost no combat effectiveness."[4] Armored forces were so depleted that some tanks had to be removed from museum display pedestals for deployment to the Korean War.[5] That conflict surprised everyone, but the Dwight Eisenhower administration's assumption that nuclear threats had finally forced the Communists into the armistice in 1953 only reinforced the focus on such weapons. Ike's "New Look" de-emphasized conventional forces, and the Army developed the short-lived Pentomic Division concept for relevance on the nuclear battlefield.[6] Strategic Air Command thrived, but the Army and Marine Corps lost manpower and modernization programs as the administration held fast to budget limitations. Korea did spark more reliance on civilian scientific advisors and the development of a new Army Combat Developments System, which did produce the designs for the M60 main battle tank, M113 APC, and M14 rifle by the early-1960s.[7] But there was not yet money to field them. A robust Reserve Component (RC) program again would meet any major conventional war contingency, and in the Reserve Forces Act of 1955 Congress set the ceiling for such forces at 2.9 million men. By 1960, there were almost a million drill-pay reservists on the rolls. Again relying on the RC was seen as the hedge against a major ground war; yet again, when that war came, draftees would be used instead for most manpower needs.[8]

John F. Kennedy's shift to a national security policy of "Flexible Response" provided major impetus to reinvigorate conventional forces, including the purchase of new armored vehicles and support for the Army's investment in air mobility. Secretary of Defense Robert McNamara's emphasis on systems analysis helped motivate the Army to set up a new Combat Developments Command in 1962, which brought into use the AR-15 rifle along with the new helicopters.[9] These would soon be tested in Southeast Asia. The Korean War had globalized the national security strategy of containment beyond Europe, and now Communism had to be stopped in Vietnam. But counterinsurgency against light and guerrilla forces does not provide much justification for force modernization. In the aftermath of war in Southeast Asia, the Army again suffered severely, ending up with the "Hollow Force" of the late-1970s. Army leaders realized that the force needed to modernize, especially after the 1973 Arab-Israeli War, but defense budgets were again shrinking. One of the main reasons for the shift of combat support and combat service support assets to the RC by Creighton Abrams was to free up funding for long-delayed modernization of active combat units. However, by 1979, six of 10 continental U.S.-based divisions were rated "not combat ready," as was one of four in Europe. The U.S. Army in Europe commander complained that his force had become "obsolescent." Even for a substantially smaller force, budgets were inadequate to achieve production rates to replace aging equipment with new models which were ready to field, such as the Abrams tank and Apache helicopter. The Congressional Budget Office's explanation for that state echoes eerily today:

> Yet the underlying problem may have been an imbalance between defense resources and national security commitments that made it impossible for DoD [the

Department of Defense] to buy both readiness and modernization.[10]

In the 1970s, the Army had neither.

The Army's last great opportunity for modernization occurred with the Ronald Reagan defense buildup in the early- and mid-1980s. After an unsatisfactory period where doctrine writers were given primary responsibility to determine Army needs, the 1973 war jolted the Army into a new approach. The newly created Training and Doctrine Command reinvigorated combat developments. Again, farsighted leaders during tough times laid the groundwork to exploit service opportunities, and the "Big Five" systems developed and fielded between 1971 and 1990—Abrams tank, Bradley fighting vehicle, Apache and Blackhawk helicopters, and Patriot missile system—still provide the backbone of the force today. All the services thrived during this period, but a national security strategy reemphasizing strong conventional forces to further deter the Soviet Union aided the Army greatly. Reagan's defense policies really envisioned a fusion of the New Look with Flexible Response.[11]

Operation DESERT STORM in 1991 revealed the impressive results of Army modernization. It also began another period of ground force drawdown and neglect. Chief of Staff Gordon Sullivan realized the risks the service faced in trying to maintain its preeminence. He set four goals to guide change—Reshape the Force, Resource the Force, Integrate and Strengthen the Force, and Maintain the Edge—and gave specific guidance to all his key subordinates about managing that risk.[12] He warned his new Deputy Chief of Staff for Operations:

My sense is that tight resources will drive many to try and eliminate the complementary capabilities that give joint forces such powerful synergy; that there will be, in some quarters, an undue willingness to rely on technological solutions; and that wishful thinking will lead some to sacrifice readiness to other motives.[13]

His concerns are very recognizable today.

Sullivan set up the Louisiana Maneuvers and battle labs to define requirements further, and his successors continued to refine the system under increasing budget pressures. There have been numerous congressional debates about returning hollowness since Operation DESERT STORM. The fate of the Comanche helicopter, Crusader artillery system, and Future Combat Systems demonstrates the vulnerability of major Army modernization programs in periods of vague threats and tight budgets. Generally, the Army has not fared well in maintaining its share of modernization since the era of Joint Requirements began in 1986. DoD studies at the opening of the new millennium faulted the Army for its branch procurement focus that was perceived as inefficient, and Congress ordered more centralization. Secretary of Defense Donald Rumsfeld and Vice Chairman of the Joint Chiefs of Staff General Peter Pace then drove the establishment of a Joint Requirements Oversight Council to further streamline the acquisition process with a purely top down approach.[14] While these changes did make the system more efficient, it can be questioned whether it has been as effective as the more decentralized branch approach in developing and meeting Army needs for modernization.

RECOMMENDATIONS FOR THE FUTURE

By the time of the 2001 *Quadrennial Defense Review,* declining budgets had again put considerable strain on the Army to balance readiness, modernization, and manpower. As during the 1920s and 1930s, Chiefs of Staffs in this stressful period tended to emphasize keeping trained and ready personnel over weapons procurement. The aftermath of September 11, 2001, solved that budget dilemma for the moment. However, like earlier counterinsurgency in Vietnam, the long war against terrorism and insurgency in Afghanistan and Iraq, in which the Army has been so deeply engaged, again has not nurtured congressional support for ground force modernization. Past experience highlights three key insights that senior Army leaders should keep in mind during yet another period of constrained resources.

1. Keep professional military education and training programs robust. The future remains unknown and unpredictable, and the ability of Soldiers to learn and adapt under fire has always been an important Army strength. Many studies have shown that having trained and ready Soldiers led by adaptable leaders are more important than having the most modern equipment.

2. Even when budgets are tight, the Service can still pursue the development and fielding of one or two relatively inexpensive "game-changers." These could range from a new infantry weapon to revolutionary cyber capabilities. Innovation does not stop just because money is scarce. Thinking might be hard, but it is cheap.

3. That also means that more extensive modernization programs should still be developed. The service

must be prepared to quickly take advantage of more abundant resources when they become available.

The difficulties balancing modernization and readiness for future crises will be exacerbated by the demise of the draft. Instead of bringing draftees into an expansible active component for a crisis, now Guard and Reserve forces must be deployed instead, requiring a new emphasis on their modernization as well. Even more problematic for the Army and the Armed Forces is the current economic and budgetary situation, with the additional impact of sequestration from the Budget Control Act of 2011.

But the Army has faced and overcome such problems previously, even when the Great Depression worsened funding from a nation little inclined to spend money on the military in the first place. As this review of the Army's history of responding to periods of reduced resources has shown, far-sighted leaders have met this enduring challenge by maintaining trained and educated Soldiers who could rise to their responsibilities when danger again threatened, by concentrating on a few key and relatively inexpensive weapons systems when money was scarce, and by laying the groundwork for more extensive acquisitions when policies changed and conflicts erupted.

ENDNOTES - CHAPTER 9

1. Allan R. Millett and Peter Maslowski, *For the Common Defense: A Military History of the United States of America*, New York: The Free Press, Revised and Expanded Ed., 1994, pp. 380-400.

2. *Ibid.*, pp. 396-404. On the schools, see Peter J. Schifferle, *America's School for War: Fort Leavenworth, Officer Education, and Victory in World War II*, Lawrence, KS: University Press of Kansas,

2010; and Harry P. Ball, *Of Responsible Command: A History of the U.S. Army War College*, Carlisle, PA: Alumni Association of the U.S. Army War College, 1983.

3. Edgar F. Raines, Jr., *The Army Requirements System, 1775-2009*, Washington, DC: U.S. Army Center of Military History, 2009, pp. 34-61.

4. Garry L. Thompson, *Army Downsizing Following World War I, World War II, Vietnam, and a Comparison to Recent Army Downsizing*, Fort Leavenworth, KS: Command and General Staff College, 2002, pp. 34-35.

5. Arthur W. Connor, Jr., "The Armor Debacle in Korea, 1950: Implications for Today," *Parameters*, Spring 1992, pp. 66-76.

6. A. J. Bacevich, *The Pentomic Era: The U.S. Army between Korea and Vietnam*, Washington, DC: National Defense University Press, 1986.

7. Raines, pp. 77-82.

8. Millett and Maslowski, pp. 534-552.

9. Raines, pp. 82-92.

10. Andrew Feickert and Stephen Daggett, *A Historical Perspective on "Hollow Forces,"* Washington, DC: Congressional Research Service, 2012, pp. 5-8; James T. Currie and Richard B. Crossland, *Twice the Citizen: A History of the United States Army Reserve, 1908-1995*, Washington, DC: Office of the Chief, Army Reserve, 1997, pp. 212-215.

11. Raines, pp. 99-105; Millett and Maslowski, pp. 614-618.

12. For example, see Letter, General Gordon Sullivan to Lieutenant General Leon Salomon, undated, Letters to Commanders Binder, Papers of Gordon Sullivan, Carlisle, PA, U.S. Army Heritage and Education Center.

13. Letter, General Gordon Sullivan to General John Tilelli, July 21, 1994, Letters to Commanders Binder, Papers of Gordon Sullivan, Carlisle, PA: U.S. Army Heritage and Education Center.

14. Raines, pp. 114-123; Feickert and Daggett, pp. 10-19.

CHAPTER 10

THE ARMY IN TIMES OF AUSTERITY

Michael J. Meese

Winston Churchill famously said, "Gentlemen, we have run out of money. Now we have to think."[1] Although neither the Department of Defense (DoD) nor the Army have run out of money, in the current period of austerity, coherent strategic thinking will be essential. The Army has a compelling strategy that can resonate with the American public and decisionmakers, but Army leaders must both understand and effectively articulate the Army's role in the context of American grand strategy to effectively make the case for Landpower.

To explain the role of the Army in times of austerity, this chapter will review the Army's history confronting budget stringency over the past century. In doing so, it will identify the four fundamental tendencies that have dominated the Army's approach during past periods of stringency and explain how they are affecting the Army today. Finally, with this perspective, the chapter provides a specific proposal that could help the Army emphasize its appropriate role in U.S. grand strategy and improve its ability to contribute to national security.

THE ARMY'S HISTORY DURING STRINGENCY

The Army has undergone several periods of austerity throughout the past century; indeed, they have occurred regularly every 20 years—during the interwar 1930s, the post-Korea 1950s, the post-Vietnam 1970s, and the post-Cold War 1990s. A comprehensive examination of each of those periods of downsizing reflects significant continuities, even though the international situation, domestic politics, and budgetary stringency were different in each case.[2] This is not surprising, both because of the relatively stable institutional culture within the Army and the fact that, in almost all cases, the generals who were making decisions for the Army during one period of stringency were field grade officers during the previous stringency (20 years earlier) and were commissioned during or soon after the stringency prior to that (40 years earlier).[3] The Army itself is a prisoner of its own experiences, and it is important to understand those experiences if Army leaders are to make effective policy.

In examining previous periods of austerity, it appears that the Army has a deeply ingrained approach to peacetime decisionmaking, which I call the peacetime "Army Concept." The peacetime Army Concept consists of four tenets, which have a subtle, but profound, impact on the Army and the Army's effectiveness.[4] The first is the Army's consistent emphasis on **people**, with the tendency to trade all other factors — equipment, readiness, sustainability, and others — to preserve the emphasis on Soldiers and officers already in the Army. The second is the Army's emphasis on **expansibility**, so that Army leaders will generally maintain large organizational structures that can be filled quickly in the event of rapid expansion rather than cut down those structures. The third is the emphasis on **equitable allocation of resources** among all major commands and branches, with less of a tendency to redistribute power or radically reorganize the Army to meet new conditions. The fourth tenet is that the Army will **adopt inappropriate strategy** for its doctrine, using a tailored form of the national strategy rather than concentrate on the Army's role in that strategy. These tenets, which are consistent over time, are not in and of themselves wrong, but strategists should consider and understand them as they plan for Army downsizing. Each will be described with their historical antecedents and contemporary recommendations.

Emphasis on People.

Concentrating on people is understandable because war is a human endeavor and soldiers are fundamental to accomplishing the Army's mission. The Army has always been the most manpower-intensive service and the relationship between the society and the military often focuses on the Army more than other services. During the 1930s interwar years, the Army went to great lengths to emphasize citizen-soldiers, while maintaining and expanding the number of officers and Soldiers. During the 1970s, the Army emphasized making the All Volunteer Force work as the draft ended on July 1, 1973. After the Cold War, even as the size of the Army reduced by one-third (from 780,000 to 495,000), Army leaders made exceptional efforts not to separate any officers involuntarily.[5] This emphasis on people is not wrong, but it needs to be properly understood within the context of the decisions concerning Army force structure.

Today, the nation has the benefit of having the most experienced Army that it has ever had as it enters a period of downsizing; once again there is an emphasis on people. There is an understandable desire to retain all of those leaders, and decisions about separation policies are particularly difficult when one considers the human faces behind the budget numbers. However, it is important to recognize that, while personnel **quality** is priceless, personnel **quantity** can be very expensive. Because the Army is the most personnel-intensive force, the increasing military compensation over the past decade has most significantly affected the Army. Military pay has become a huge, mandatory expenditure within the Army budget that significantly constrains flexibility, as noted in Figure 10-1. Civilian pay is a large part of Operations and Maintenance spending and is also difficult to control. In other words, once the end strength of the Army is set, personnel numbers will drive the budget spending.

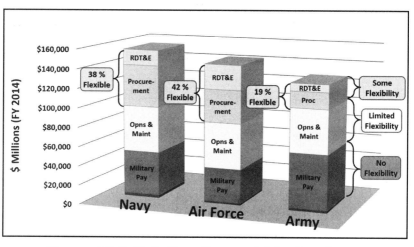

Figure 10-1. Relative Costs within Services.

Obviously, it would not be wise, or even possible, for the Army to stop emphasizing people, but the Army can leverage austerity to improve the long-term effectiveness of its people. There are several steps, however, that the Army can take now: First, the Army can continue to emphasize personnel quality, even as end strength is reduced. In each of the previous periods of stringency, the Army invested in leader development programs, whether it was at the U.S. Military Academy, the U.S. Army War College, the Noncommissioned Officer Academy, or other programs. Those relatively modest expenditures retained the leaders who were interested in expanding their education, and in each future conflict those investments in leader development paid huge dividends.[6]

Second, as the most personnel-intensive service, the Army should champion effective compensation reform to reduce overall personnel costs. For example, the recently published "10-15-55" plan offers an alternative retirement system that would result in significant savings (a projected $3.84 billion per year) and could actually enhance the quality of personnel in the Army.[7] Programs such as this should not just be "reluctantly forced upon the Army," but should be championed by the Army as a way to reduce costs and enhance personnel quality.

Third, in previous periods of stringency, the Army had great difficulty whenever there was significant uncertainty regarding future personnel cuts. Until and unless Army leaders can establish the long range end strength of the Army, the annual budget cycle can become paralyzed by just fighting for a personnel number. However, the Army has solved this problem in the past. Most famously, Chief of Staff of the Army Creighton Abrams had an explicit agreement with Secretary of Defense James Schlesinger—which became known as the "golden handshake"—that fixed the Army's declining personnel strength and permitted the Army to restructure within that new, lower fixed number (of 785,000 Soldiers).[8] While difficult to achieve, gaining a definitive decision on the quantity of Soldiers after the drawdown would permit the Army to focus on the quality of those that remain.

Expansible Units.

In previous periods of austerity, the Army frequently emphasized the need to maintain relatively larger units, even if they lacked Soldiers to fill those units. Historically, larger units provided the superstructure into which newly recruited Soldiers could be mobilized—as they were during World War II. Organizationally, larger units provided greater senior leadership responsibility and more headquarters for operations, planning, and training of leaders and staffs. After Vietnam, Abrams had a choice between 11 robust divisions or 16 expansible divisions. He deliberately chose to retain more units that were explicitly designed to be "hollow," supported by "round out" units mobilized from the National Guard to bring them to full strength.[9] In the late-1990s, when the Army had to reduce its forces from 495,000 to 480,000, a relatively small reduction, it took Soldiers from existing units without reducing the overall structure of the Army. This led to a degradation of readiness within many of the Army's units, which was criticized by many observers at the time as a step back toward a hollow Army.[10] Finally, there is a great propensity to maintain larger structures with more headquarters in more locations, because divisions, brigades, and other elements of force structure are extremely difficult to justify and recreate after it is cut.

Today, the Army may have broken with this precedent, at least within Active Duty forces. It appears to be choosing relatively fewer, but more robustly manned units. For example, the Army recently decided to reduce the number of brigade combat teams (BCTs) from 43 to 32. Concurrently, the Army will take some of the personnel authorizations that were saved from those units that are eliminated to add one maneuver battalion into each remaining armored and infantry brigades.[11] This approach of fewer, but more robust brigades, would be a break from past reductions and would recognize that there is less need or justification for large expansible units today, given the need for more robust units that have a higher degree of readiness.

Equitable Resource Allocation.

The Army has always had a tendency toward equitable resource allocation for several reasons. Functionally, land warfare requires combinations of teams, and it is difficult during a particular period of stringency to know with certainty that a particular force or capability will not be important in a future war. Organizationally, many of the different parts of the Army have strong constituencies and substantial bureaucratic effort can be expended with limited results if Army leaders try to reduce any particular group. Finally, from a practical standpoint, across-the-board cuts, which treat all organizations similarly, are the fastest and easiest way to implement reductions. The sequester imposed by the Budget Control Act of 2011 reinforced this tenet of the Army Concept with a "salami slice" to all aspects of the budget. With greater time and strategic study, however, it may be possible to establish priorities and preserve specific parts of the Army while cutting others.

DOCTRINE — ADOPTING NATIONAL STRATEGY AS ARMY STRATEGY

During peacetime austerity, the Army frequently confuses its service doctrine with national strategy. In each of the four major cases of downsizing in the last century, the Army adopted a scaled-down version of the existing national strategy as doctrine. In the 1930s, as national strategy emphasized pacifism, disarmament, and a defensive military, the Army followed suit and did not develop a doctrine of offensive, combined arms warfare until the outset of World War II. In the 1950s, as national strategy emphasized massive retaliation with nuclear weapons, the Army developed the "Pentomic Army" without any doctrine for fighting on a non-nuclear battlefield, thus requiring rapid changes in Vietnam. In the 1970s, as national strategy emphasized détente, the Army followed with a defensive doctrine, called "Active Defense." Active Defense primarily emphasized only deterrence instead of the offensive steps that would be taken when deterrence fails, and the Army had to respond rapidly in 1983 with "AirLand Battle." In the 1990s, as the nation became fascinated with the post-Operation DESERT STORM "Revolution in Military Affairs," the Army invested in "Force 21" high technology, and then had to scramble to fight protracted counterinsurgencies against low-technology enemies in Iraq and Afghanistan. Army doctrine needs to be **consistent** with national strategy, but that does not imply that it must be **the same as** national strategy. When the Army has followed national strategy too closely, it has led to significant, rapid changes at the outset of the next war.

Today, many people support a national strategy that focuses on either high-technology threats to the global commons or a peer competitor (such as China); there is a corresponding commitment never again to fight a low-technology counterinsurgency war. This kind of approach is articulated as part of the Air-Sea Battle Concept, which supports the emphasis on countering anti-access, area-denial systems that will likely be employed against U.S. Forces.[12] Such a strategy seductively appeals to those who argue for minimizing "fog and friction" in war by using high technology intelligence, surveillance, and reconnaissance (ISR), which leverages traditional strengths of the American military-industrial complex. While the destruction of targets with precision strike weapons is necessary, it is not a sufficient condition for the United States to achieve all of its objectives when the nation goes to war. Just as "shock and awe" failed to win the war in Iraq rapidly in 2003, advocates of a strategy that maximizes standoff and minimizes risk will likely not be able to achieve the desired effects necessary to support U.S. national security.

Grand strategists should recognize that "fog and friction" are inherent in all warfare, and that war is ultimately a human endeavor. While technology is helpful and indeed necessary, the human engagement by Soldiers and Marines in pre-combat, combat, and post-combat operations must always be the focus of land forces. Does that mean that the Army has a role in a potential long-term conflict with China? Yes. However, that role is not likely to involve confronting China or Chinese forces on their mainland. The Army's part of the "pivot to Asia" is to engage in pre-combat shaping operations throughout the world, just as Chinese forces and industry expand the Chinese sphere of influence in Central Asia, Africa, and South America. Through security assistance, exchanges, partnership exercises, peacekeeping missions, building host nation forces, and other military engagements, the Army can shape the international environment to enhance all aspects of U.S. security. The proper doctrine is not for the Army to stake out a position in Air-Sea Battle, but to determine how Landpower most effectively contributes to the overall grand strategy.

A PRACTICAL PROPOSAL: REGIONAL ALLOCATION

A good example of the kind of engagement that would support U.S. policy throughout the world is to build on the Army's development of regionally aligned brigades.[13] For the past decade, all Army units have practiced this kind of regional focus in their preparations for combat deployments to Iraq or Afghanistan. The Army should expand on regional alignment to actually allocate units in support of combatant commanders, just as the Navy allocates "steaming days" for carrier battle groups.[14]

For example, if the Army had 32 active BCTs, during steady-state operations with the Army Force Generation (ARFORGEN) 3-year cycle, one-third of those BCTs would be available for deployment or engagements in any given year. Assuming that 11 active BCTs would be available for 12 months each, the Army could provide a total of 132 BCT-months in each year, in addition to BCTs from the National Guard. The BCT-months could be allocated to combatant commanders in a manner roughly analogous to the forward presence of Navy carriers. If ongoing operations in Afghanistan required three brigades, that would be 36 BCT-months for Central Command (CENTCOM) and that command may be allocated 10 additional months for exercises and partnerships, for a total of 46 months. Additional allocations might be something like the following:

Central Command (CENTCOM)	46 BCT-months
Pacific Command (PACOM)	24 BCT-months
European Command (EUCOM)	18 BCT-months
African Command (AFRICOM)	20 BCT-months
Southern Command (SOUTHCOM)	12 BCT-months
Northern Command (NORTHCOM)	12 BCT-months
Total	132 BCT-months

The details of this plan would certainly need to be worked out, to include recognizing that BCTs that were training for one mission could always be reoriented to another more urgent crisis as circumstances warrant.

The general approach, however, would allow regionally allocated BCTs to deploy to those commands as part of exercises, work with host-nation units, participate in partnership exercises, or deploy as part of ongoing operations. Within the ARFORGEN 3-year cycle, units would be preparing for these requirements during their training year—possibly participating in Leadership Training Program visits the year before they are in the window for operational missions. This would provide continuity and planning for the combatant commander. The result would likely be that combatant commanders would have additional requirements beyond the limited number of months available and would be advocates for sustaining—or potentially increasing—Army units to better support their theater plans.

This proposal would take into consideration all four of the tenets discussed earlier and would help reinforce the most important aspects of the Army as it adjusts to current and future conditions. First, it recognizes the valuable contribution of people and provides a specific region for leaders to become experts in as they prepare for their regional deployment. An even more radical proposal would leverage the concept of Talent Management and actually assign people with expertise in specific areas to units prior to deployment.[15] Using Talent Management would both enhance the capability of the units and the career satisfaction of those assigned to the units.

Second, the regional allocation of units would counter the tendency for the Army to hollow units as it has during past periods of austerity. Since those units are committed to support combatant commanders, the Army has an incentive to ensure that they are at or near full strength as a commitment to those who depend on them.

Third, this proposal would counter the tendency for equity in resource allocation, because units that are preparing for deployment would naturally get the priority. As resources are cut, they would not be implemented "across-the-board," but would fall on those units recently returning from their regional commitments; these units would have more time to recover from any resourcing shortfall before the next deployment cycle.

Finally, this proposal would ensure that the allocation of Army units was a vital part of the national security discussion among combatant commanders, the Joint Chiefs of Staff, and other senior defense leaders. Combatant commanders would likely make robust use of the BCTs allocated to them to enhance their theater security plan in support of the overall National Security Strategy. Ideally, combatant commanders would become advocates for ensuring that there were enough Army units to create the BCT-months necessary to support their overall strategy.

CONCLUSION

The Army has significant experience reacting to budget austerity as it has regularly faced budget reductions every 20 years since 1930. In each of those cases—the 1930s, 1950s, 1970s, and 1990s—the decisions that Army leaders made had a significant influence on the effectiveness of Army forces that fought in major conflicts during the decade following each period of stringency. With the stringency of the 2010s, what should the Army do to prepare for the "unforeseeable" conflict of the 2020s? Army leaders should recognize the four tendencies that the Army will follow in its downsizing: focusing on people, expansible units, equitable resource allocation, and conflating national strategy with Army strategy. By understanding those tendencies, Army leaders can make better decisions, one of which could be to expand the current work to align Army brigades with specific regions of the world. Careful decision making by national leaders can enhance the ongoing contribution of Army forces to national security both today and in the future.

ENDNOTES - CHAPTER 10

1. Churchill's quote, which is also associated with New Zealand physicist, Ernest Rutherford, is cited in numerous places, including Lawrence P. Farrell, "Gentlemen, We Have Run Out Of Money; Now We Have to Think," *National Defense*, November 2011.

2. For a comprehensive examination of the Army during periods of austerity, see Michael Meese, "Defense Decision Making Under Budget Stringency: Explaining Downsizing in the United States Army," Ph. D. Diss: Princeton, NJ: Princeton University, 2000.

3. For example, the Army leaders who are executing the decisions today were commissioned in the midst of the post-Vietnam austerity and remember what then Chief of Staff of the Army Edward "Shy" Meyer described to Congress as "a hollow Army" in 1979. When those same leaders were majors, they were all offered (and declined) a "voluntary separation incentive" as the Army was paying people to leave in the 1990s. These common experiences undoubtedly influence their reactions to the current period of stringency.

4. The "Army Concept" is a phrase borrowed from Andrew Krepinevich, *The Army and Vietnam*, Baltimore, MD: Johns Hopkins University Press, 1986, pp. 6-7. He brilliantly used it to describe the wartime Army Concept, which focused on a large, conventional land war which relied heavily on firepower and failed to prepare it adequately for the counterinsurgency warfare of Vietnam.

5. The only forced separations in the post-Cold War drawdown were 277 officers who were commissioned in 1979 and were separated as a reduction-in-force board in 1992. See David H. McCormick, *The Downsized Warrior: America's Army in Transition*, New York: New York University Press, 1998, p. 114.

6. The description of leader development during each period of downsizing is described in Meese. For specific details, see also Mark C. Bender, *Watershed at Leavenworth: Dwight D. Eisenhower and the Command and General Staff School*, Fort Leavenworth, KS: Command and General Staff College, 1990; William W. Whitson, "The Role of the United States Army War College in the Preparation of Officers for National Security Policy Formulation," Ph.D. Diss., Medford, MA: Tufts University, Fletcher School of Law and Diplomacy, May 1, 1958; and *Leadership for the 1970s*, Carlisle, PA: U.S. Army War College, October 20, 1971.

7. See Roy A. Wallace, David S. Lyle, and John Z. Smith, *A Framework for Restructuring the Military Retirement System*, Carlisle, PA: Strategic Studies Institute, U.S. Army War College, July 2013.

8. Lewis Sorely, *Thunderbolt: General Creighton Abrams and the Army of His Times*, New York: Simon and Schuster, 1992, p. 363.

9. Specifically, nine of the 16 divisions relied heavily on the RC. Four divisions had their third "roundout" brigade in the National Guard, and five other divisions required dozens of reserve battalions to complete their structure. See Secretary of Defense, *Annual Report of the Secretary of Defense on Reserve Forces, Fiscal Year 1975*, Washington, DC: DoD, 1976.

10. See Mark E. Gebicke, Testimony, *Military Readiness: Observations on Personnel Readiness in Later Deploying Army Divisions*, GAO/T-NSIAD-98-126, Washington, DC: General Accounting Office, March 20, 1998.

11. Michelle Tan, "Army Announces 10 Brigade Combat Teams to be Cut," *Army Times*, June 25, 2013.

12. General Norton A. Schwartz, U.S. Air Force, and Admiral Jonathan W. Greenert, U.S. Navy, "Air-Sea Battle: Promoting Stability in an Era of Uncertainty," *The American Interest*, February 20, 2012.

13. General Raymond Odierno, "Regionally Aligned Forces: A New Model for Building Partnerships," *Army Live: The Official Blog of the United States Army*, March 22, 2012, available from *armylive.dodlive.mil/index.php/2012/03/aligned-forces/*. See also Steve Griffin, "Regionally-Aligned Brigades: There's More to This Plan than Meets the Eye," *Small Wars Journal*, September 19, 2012.

14. Navy carrier battle groups have a certain number of "steaming days" in which they in operate each year. Combatant commanders are supported by carriers as part of routine operations—recognizing that a crisis can always adjust the priorities among ships at sea. Secretary of the Navy Ray Mabus's discussion of steaming days is discussed in "FY 2013: The Year the Navy

Sprinted in Circles," *Maritime Security,* September 18, 2013, available from *maritimesecurity.asia/free-2/maritime-security-asia/fy2013-the-year-the-navy-sprinted-in-circles/.*

15. See Casey Wardynski, David S. Lyle, and Michael J. Colarusso, *Toward a U.S. Army Officer Corps Strategy for Success: A Proposed Human Capital Model Focused upon Talent,* Carlisle, PA: Strategic Studies Institute, U.S. Army War College, April 2009.

CHAPTER 11

TRANSLATING STRATEGIC ENDS INTO MEANS

Kerry J. Schindler

How large should be the Army or any of the Services? Given the potential costs of Army forces in the future, this is literally the trillion dollar question. In the past, this question was answered with another question, "to do what?" It is in attempting to answer this second question that national strategy is formed. So what do you do when the answer to that question, your strategy, exceeds what you can afford? Some would argue that either your strategy must be adjusted or your budget must increase, but neither option is always possible. A third option exists: optimize your force structure to be more versatile, and thus try to do more with what you have, while articulating the risk to the decisionmakers. News headlines tend to focus on the important issue of end strength, but the mix of capabilities occupying the ranks of the Service end strength is an equally important issue. The Army is a tool of national policy; end strength determines the size of the tool while shaping the force determines what kind of tool the Army will be. Decisions regarding the Army's capabilities have far reaching effects because if what the world or problem planners anticipate proves an illusion, then future decisionmakers are left to rely on the flexibility of chosen capabilities. Can the nation's tools adapt to the problem, not try to force the problem to adapt to them? As an Army Force Manager, focusing on determining the best mix of Army capabilities to meet the strategy is how we spend our days.

THE DEPARTMENT OF DEFENSE VISION

Every several years, the Secretary of Defense issues *Defense Planning Guidance* (DPG) to provide specific instruction to each of the Services regarding their strategic requirements, objectives, and constraints. In 2012, the DPG raised two questions with respect to the Army's force development: How large should the force be ("Sizing")? What should the force be able to do ("Shaping")? Though these two questions seem symbiotic and critical to meeting past *Quadrennial Defense Review* (QDR) guidance, they become divergent and antagonistic when bound by the DPG guidelines and pre-sequestration fiscal constraints. Additionally, sequestration has caused the Defense community to reevaluate the DPG and QDR guidance to determine, within the new fiscal reality, what strategy can we afford. This emerging strategy will likely still lean on the DPG constructs to provide analytic rigor to this new question, as development of new scenarios and modeling would take several years.

In answering the first question (regarding "Sizing"), the DPG requires Services to consider one of three possible futures referred to as Integrated Security Constructs (ISCs).[1] Of the three developed (ISC-A, ISC-B, and ISC-C), the DPG allows only the first two to be used as "Sizing" constructs to determine the required size of each Service. These ISCs are a compilation of two large operations (usually one defeat and one deter),[2] homeland defense activities, and multiple small scale engagements ranging from partner building to peace enforcement to kinetic force on force over a 13-year timeline spanning the near to mid term (within the next 20 years). In answering the second question (regarding "Shaping"), the Army must ensure its force is capable of performing 11 primary mission scenarios[3] given the likely adversaries across the full Range of Military Operations (ROMO). The ROMO includes offensive, defensive, foreign stability and defense support to (Domestic) Civil Authority (DSCA) Operations. The DPG further specifies Services must use Office of the Secretary of Defense (OSD) approved scenarios or Combatant Command War Plans to develop "Shaping" constructs.[4] The Army tries to vary the climate, geography, and weather to ensure demand pictures for each capability span the full ROMO and encompass Army equities in the 11 DPG primary mission areas.

The conflict within the DPG is that of the three ISCs, it allows the Services to use only one of two ISCs (ISC-A and -B, and only ISC-B has significant ground forces) to determine the "Size" of the Service when each ISC contains coverage of only a few of the 11 required DPG primary mission areas. The use of only one ISC also fails to address the full range of environmental considerations as it contains only two specific fights which neglect other possible situations involving those adversaries as well as other possible adversaries all together. Even using the one ground force-centric ISC to "Size" the Army would lead to an end-strength well below what is required to accomplish the 11 DPG primary mission areas and ensure America's security.

TOTAL ARMY ANALYSIS

Because the Secretary of Defense, through the QDR process, and Congress, through appropriations, specify the "Size" of the Army, the Army focuses on the "Shape" of that given end-strength. The mechanism by which the Army determines its "Shape" is the

Total Army Analysis (TAA). Like the defense budget process, TAA is conducted annually, but it takes much more than a year to complete. Army planners spend up to 18 months to model and analyze, a year to build a budget, 8 months to compile, and 9 months for testimony and debate on Capitol Hill. As a result, several TAAs are ongoing simultaneously. Each determines the appropriate "Shape" of the Army and provides Army budget builders with a "Budget Force" (Program Objective Memorandum Force or POM Force) to build the Army Budget submission, which covers 5 years at a time.

TAA consists of two phases: Capability Demand Analysis (CDA) and Resourcing (see Figure 11-1). The CDA process usually takes just over 12 months and numerous inputs to produce a thoroughly analyzed modeling output. This becomes the "Science" of the demand for each capability. The Army puts the "Human-in-the-Loop" to temper the "Science" of the demand with the "Art" of military experience to decide what to resource and where to assume risk. For example, TAA uses average dwell time (how long a unit spends at home between deployments for the modeled ISC) to determine which units have higher capacity and those requiring additional resources to meet modeled demands. If the dwell time was only slightly higher for a Combat Aviation Brigade (CAB) than for a Composite Truck Company and the Army was required to divest several hundred spaces, the "Science" would say get rid of the CAB. The "Art" would likely select the Truck Company for inactivation as it can take up to four years to build and train a CAB, while it requires considerably less time to build a Composite Truck Company, contract for a truck company, nationalize the Teamsters or train an unutilized Firing Battery to move cargo.

Figure 11-1: Total Army Analysis:
"End-to-End" Shaping Process.

The Resourcing phase is not as much about where to apply resources as about determining where to assume risk and identifying what risk is acceptable. Furthermore, just because a POM Force fits within the directed end-strength does not mean the Army will have the funds for readiness or modernization. Risk will need to be assessed as to whether to maintain the capability or the capacity; fewer modern, ready forces vs. more, less modernized, less ready forces.

The length of time it takes to complete a TAA process presents challenges to Army leadership. Senior leaders provide strategic guidance for "Shaping" at the beginning of the TAA process, which will come to fruition a full 4 years later. Since the average length of term in office for the Secretary of the Army (SA) and Chief of Staff, U.S. Army (CSA) is 4 years, senior leaders generally execute the budget from the previous office holder.

This does not mean, however, that the SA and CSA are totally constrained. To the contrary, if the SA or CSA decided tomorrow to move the 82nd Airborne Division to Fort Campbell, Kentucky, from Fort Bragg, North Carolina, they could. It may result in Soldiers marching to Kentucky without their families, living in shelter halves, and eating surplus meals ready-to-eat from the first Gulf War, but it could be done. When the plan does not make it into the Army Annual Budget submission, senior leader plans are constrained by the discretionary funds available for reprogramming[5] in the year of execution. If this hypothetical move of the 82nd Airborne Division were to make it into the budget submission, those Soldiers would have barracks, moving expenses, training facilities, and other Soldier and family services available when they arrived at Fort Campbell. Generally, decisions resulting in a requirement for Military Construction (MILCON) could mean the final decisions may actually have been from previous administrations to ensure the facilities are available for the Soldiers, as the MILCON process can take up to 5 years from decision to building occupation.

Because TAA requires about 38 percent of the time between senior leader initial budget guidance and year of execution (18 months of the 4 years), TAA is often called unresponsive. In reality, if the strategy does not change, TAA can use previous modeling and analysis and go right into a Resourcing Phase, reducing the budgeting process to less than 3 years (TAA is about 4 out of 32 months; 12.5 percent). While this still takes a considerable amount of time and likely still leaves execution to the predecessors of the senior leaders making the decision, the process is still faster. To the contrary, if a change in strategy creates the need for a new scenario or vignette, the 4-year timeline would likely expand an additional 12 to 24 months to allow the Secretary of Defense and the Joint community time to develop an agreed upon construct and the Army time to develop the appropriate concepts of support, model the scenarios, and analyze the results.

THE ARMY'S CHARTED PATH

In July 2013, the CSA and SA announced they would reorganize the Army brigade combat teams (BCTs) no later than the end of fiscal year (FY) 2017 in conjunction with end-strength reductions in the Active Component (AC) to 490,000 (from a wartime high of 570,000), Army National Guard (ARNG) to 350,200 from 358,200 (a reduction of 8,000) and the U.S. Army Reserve (USAR) suspension of a 2007 Grow the Army decision to increase from 205,000 to 206,000 (1,000 spaces) in 2012. The Army has since decided to accelerate those end-strength and organizational changes to complete them prior to the end of FY 2015.

The AC will accomplish both the end-strength reduction and BCT reorganization by inactivating a Corps Headquarters and 13 BCT headquarters while maintaining significant combat power through redesigning the remaining BCTs and aligning combat power (a third maneuver battalion) to them from the inactivating BCTs. The Army will transition from 45 AC BCTs with a total of 98 maneuver battalions to approximately 32 BCTs with about 92 maneuver battalions. The BCT reorganization allows the senior leaders the ability to build a highly versatile mix of tailored and networked organizations to provide a sustained flow of trained and ready forces for current commitments and to hedge against unexpected contingencies.

Additionally, by maintaining the maneuver battalions, the Army maintains the strategic base to expand the number of BCTs to meet future surge requirements. The Reserve Component (RC) will accomplish its reductions by removing unencumbered spaces from RC jobs currently unoccupied by RC Soldiers. The BCT reorganization also eases the burden on multiple installations and their communities. Instead of reducing eight or nine AC BCTs at approximately 3,500 spaces each from a like number of installations, the BCT reorganization spread the reductions across every installation with BCTs.

Finally, we must never underestimate the political pressure associated with end-strength reduction. With personnel costs accounting for over 50 percent of the Defense budget, personnel cuts become inevitable. Most elected officials generally agree we must reduce Defense spending, but many generally agree personnel cuts should come in someone else's district, making any unit reduction difficult politically. The Army considers this during the Resourcing Phase of TAA.

THE ARMY'S FUTURE STRATEGY?

The Army and the other Services are poised at a crucial budget crossroads that will shape the nature of each Service. How ready will the Army be? How much modernization will occur over the next decade? What core competencies will the Army maintain and from which must it walk away? Ongoing budget negotiations and legislated reductions in Total Obligation Authority (TOA)—how much money the Army was appropriated by Congress—will force the Army to an end-strength below 490,000 in the AC, 350,000 in the ARNG, and 205,000 in the USAR. The "Shaping" question for TAA will no longer only be where to assume risk, but what can the Army still do; essentially, what strategy can we afford?

The Army has always struggled with the proper balance between end-strength, readiness, and modernization. Over the past 12 years, this balance was easy to achieve with the additional appropriations of Overseas Contingency Operations (OCO) funding to the TOA. But with the elimination of OCO and the TOA reductions, the Army is entering into uncharted challenges. As shown in Figure 11-2, the TOA line is fixed (and declining). If you over-invest in personnel, readiness and/or modernization will suffer. The Army would have untrained personnel lacking adequate equipment to meet the challenges of an ever-changing enemy. If you continue with modernization and/or readiness, you may not have the number of forces required.

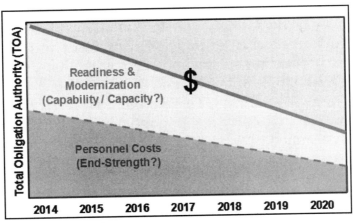

Figure 11-2. Declining Budgets, Readiness/Modernization, and Personnel Costs.

At the legislated spending levels, choosing where to set the spending line for personnel will not only change the strategy for how the United States is able to interact with the world, but the Army strategy on how it will be manned, trained, and equipped. The Army has several options to explore:

Manning.

The Army could choose to build more units than it has people (over-structure) to maintain the leadership opportunities and depth in capabilities, which could be expanded to meet a surge. Since senior non-commissioned, warrant and commissioned officers can take decades to develop, the Army may need to relook unit designs and the nature of the generating force to keep higher grades to accommodate future growth. This would be like a factory having a once a year increase in production needing 100 employees (80 of which are highly skilled jobs) and 80 employees (70 highly skilled) during the slow production season. By laying off the 20 lower skilled, entry-level jobs (which are more easily and quickly trained) during the slow production season and keeping the more costly highly skilled employees, the company is able to meet its surge requirement. This would mean fewer people (lower skilled, entry level) in the Army and units not fully manned.

Moreover, the Army may need to evaluate compensation and pay levels to find a more affordable solution (the less you spend per Soldier, the more Soldiers you can afford). Assess the length of time spent in a grade and potentially expand the pay scale to make it possible to retire as say, a captain. Speaking of retirement, changing the service requirements for retirement from 20 years to 25, 30, or even 40 would also save funds.

Training.

The Army could choose to change the length of schools (officer, warrant, noncommissioned, even basic and advanced individual training) by either removing instruction and/or by requiring the Soldiers' new units to provide the deleted instruction to the Soldier or the individual Soldier to make up the missed curriculum through correspondence. Reduce the number of seats at certain schools and require some Soldiers to complete via correspondents courses. Additionally, the Army may need to reduce the number of units funded to train beyond the squad or platoon level.

Equipping.

The Army could rely more on pre-positioned equipment sets (forward deployed equipment the units would use to fight) and reduce the equipment in units to the minimum level required to train; forgo modernization or cancel procurement programs; and divest specialized equipment in favor of more general purpose equipment. These are all ways for the Army to minimize equipping costs.

At present, Congress is still debating the 2014 budget and the OSD has begun QDR 2014 to address what the defense strategy will become. The Army continues to explore all options for building a force capable of fighting and winning the nation's wars. TAA will find the best mix of forces within the given end-strength and strategy while minimizing the impact to our Soldier, their families, and all those communities that have provided our Army with such great support. We Army Force Managers are truly living in interesting times.

ENDNOTES - CHAPTER 11

1. ISCs were built to represent multiple military operations or "demand signals" of various size, complexity, and duration integrated into a time-phased response over a 7-to-13-year time period. See *2010 QDR Report*, Washington, DC: U.S. Department of Defense, pp. 42-43.

(ISC-A): A major stabilization operation, deterring and defeating a highly capable regional aggressor, and extending support to civil authorities in response to a catastrophic event in the United States. This scenario combination particularly stressed the force's ability to defeat a sophisticated adversary and support domestic response.

(ISC-B): Deterring and defeating two regional aggressors while maintaining a heightened alert posture for U.S. forces in and around the United States. This scenario combination particularly stressed the force's combined arms capacity.

(ISC-C): A major stabilization operation, a long-duration deterrence operation in a separate theater, a medium-sized counterinsurgency mission, and extended support to U.S. civil authorities. This scenario combination particularly stressed elements of the force most heavily tasked for counterinsurgency, stability, and counterterrorism operations.

2. "Defeat and Deter." See *Defense Planning Guidance*, Washington, DC: Department of Defense, April 11, 2012. U.S. forces will remain capable of deterring and defeating aggression by any potential adversary. As a nation with important interests in multiple regions, our forces must be capable of deterring and defeating aggression in one region even when our forces are committed to a large-scale operation elsewhere. Deterrence is described in (*Joint Publication 3.0, Joint Operations*, Washington, DC: Department of Defense, March 22, 2010.) The prevention of action by the existence of a credible threat of unacceptable counteraction and/ or belief that the cost of action outweighs the perceived benefits.

3. The 11 DPG Primary Mission Areas are Counter Terrorism (CT) and Irregular Warfare (IW); Deter and Defeat Aggression; Project Power Despite Anti-Access/Area Denial Challenges; Counter Weapons of Mass Destruction; Operate Effectively in

Space; Operate Effectively in Cyberspace; Maintain a Safe, Secure and Effective Nuclear Deterrent; Defend the Homeland and Provide Defense Support to Civil Authorities (DSCA); Provide a Stabilizing Presence; Conduct Stability and Counterinsurgency Operations; and Conduct Humanitarian, Disaster Relief and Other Operations.

4. Not all of the OSD scenarios reside in the three ISCs. OSD continues to update and build its library scenarios by changing locations, adversaries, events, duration, timing, coalitions, Joint integration, U.S. interests, etc. Any scenario from this library can be used for "Shaping." Additionally, combatant commanders are constantly building and updating war plans for potential contingencies in their area of operations to prepare a better detailed, well-thought-out response, which can be quickly applied. War plans are an important "Shaping" tool.

5. The Army may not spend or obligate more than the Congress has appropriated and can use funds only for purposes specified in law. The Antideficiency Act prohibits them from spending or obligating the Government to spend in advance of an appropriation, unless specific authority to do so has been provided in law. *H. R. 4310 – 643, SEC. 4301. Line 010,* specified the Army had $1,223,087,000 for operations and maintenance for maneuver units in 2013. The Army had an internal plan going into 2013 on how it will use those funds (it was the basis for the amount requested). The Army leaders can change the plan for using those funds in the year of execution as long as it has not already been obligated (spent).

CHAPTER 12

NEW CHALLENGES FOR THE U.S. ARMY

David W. Barno
Nora Bensahel

The U.S. Army, like the nation as a whole, is facing difficult new strategic challenges. Thirteen years of constant warfare will end in 2014, when the last U.S. combat troops leave Afghanistan — the longest war in U.S. history. At the same time, the battles in Washington continue about the future role and size of the Army. Substantial cuts to the defense budget will reduce Army end strength below 490,000 active-duty troops — down to 450,000, 420,000, or even as low as 380,000 under one severe scenario.[1]

Yet these challenges are not unprecedented. Cycles of drawdown and rebuilding have occurred repeatedly in the past — often with similar and even deeper funding cuts than the U.S. military faces today[2] — and the Army has adapted in response. In the 1930s, for example, the United States retrenched from the world after the carnage of World War I, and military budgets shrank substantially. With Army end strength slashed precipitously from wartime highs, the service responded by investing in education and leader development, rebuilding its intellectual capability for warfare when budgets were tight. That investment paid off in growing a generation of officers who went on to win World War II. In the 1950s, the Army faced serious questions about the continuing relevance of ground combat in the nuclear era, while seeing substantial defense resources shift to the rapid growth of U.S. strategic airpower and the beginnings of space

231

competition. Echoes from both of these gloomy periods can be heard today in arguments about roles and missions, budget share, and the future of land warfare.

Today, the Army once again faces similar problems of constrained resources and questions of relevance, especially given the rapid technological innovations that enable increasing standoff and unmanned capabilities. Yet the United States will continue to need ready and capable ground forces that can address unexpected threats, and fight and win wars that cannot be resolved simply through applying standoff weaponry, but require ground and populations to be controlled. In order to ensure that it can respond to the full range of challenges with capabilities that the nation may demand in this fast-changing, resource-constrained future, the Army will need to address six key challenges: 1) redefining land warfare; 2) leveraging technology for the close fight; 3) reshaping the roles of the active and reserve components; 4) making expansibility work; 5) attracting and retaining talent; and 6) addressing the paradox of coming home.

REDEFINING LAND WARFARE

Since at least the end of World War II, the U.S. military has embraced a deeply-held value of maintaining technological dominance over current or potential adversaries — an unwavering commitment to develop and employ advanced weaponry whenever possible instead of sacrificing the lives of men and women. This has been seen most clearly in the continuing U.S. commitment to air and space superiority, which has not been seriously challenged in the last 5 decades. Such a profound national commitment to military technological dominance in conflict can best be described as the American Way of War.[3] It continues today, yet remains a philosophy in which the Army fits only uncomfortably due to its close combat battlefield responsibilities.

Over the last 40 years, the Army's major conceptual contribution to warfare was known as Air-Land Battle. The development of this innovative concept and its diverse web of supporting doctrine, materiel, education, and organizations were prime examples of the Army's renaissance after Vietnam. Conceived in the 1980s as a means of defending Western Europe in the face of overwhelming Soviet conventional forces, Air-Land Battle provided a unifying concept of fighting that animated the Army's entire system of conventional warfare from the last stages of the Cold War through the beginning of this century.[4] Air-Land Battle was designed to attack the forces of the Warsaw Pact simultaneously in depth across all of its serial attacking echelons. It achieved this through unprecedented integration of air and ground strike capabilities ranging from the front lines of combat all the way to the enemy's deepest reserves.

Driven by this Air-Land Battle doctrine, the Army spent 40 years shaping its weaponry, force structure, training, leader development, and even its personnel system largely around the continental defense of Western Europe. The logic of this approach during the Cold War was unassailable given the massed armies of the Soviet Union and Warsaw Pact aimed like a dagger at the heart of Europe, presenting an existential threat to the West. But with the fall of the Soviet Union and shifts in global power toward the Pacific Rim, that era has ended—and no subsequent concept of land warfare has emerged in the 21st century to take the place of Air-Land Battle.

With the dominance of the maritime domain in the Asia-Pacific, U.S. warfighting constructs are increasingly being framed around this operating environment; the foremost construct is called Air-Sea Battle. This geostrategic rebalancing to the Pacific brings the maritime and expeditionary nature of the Pacific Rim to the forefront of military challenges, and reflects a set of demands much different from the continental nature of the European theater. Air-Sea Battle has become a central organizing construct around which the Navy and Air Force seek to confront the area denial and anti-access threats common not just in the Pacific, but arguably in many other regions of the world as well. The Army's role in this new construct is both unclear, and to date, seemingly limited. In effect, this shift away from a 20th century continental model to a 21st century maritime model has left the Army without a prime directive around which to organize its forces.

The Army needs to generate a compelling narrative about what land warfare will look like in the 21st century, and how it intends to organize and prepare itself for the challenges that it will face. Senior Army leaders have frequently argued against cutting Army end strength by noting that the United States has never accurately predicted the next war it will conduct. While true, this argument has failed to resonate because it does not articulate a positive vision for the future—what types of threats the Army will face, how it needs to reorganize and train to address those threats, and the end strength (balancing active and reserves) it will need to be successful. Crafting this strategic narrative should be among the Army's top priorities.

LEVERAGING TECHNOLOGY FOR THE CLOSE FIGHT

The Army, and land forces writ large, face the unique demands associated with closing with the enemy and killing or capturing him in face-to-face proximity. This "last 100 yards" has always been the most deadly domain of warfare, and remains today the portion of the battlefield least influenced by modern technology. Even in the first two major U.S. wars of the 21st century, the technology available to aid and protect Soldiers and Marines in close-in fighting was largely limited to improved body armor, robots for detecting and disarming roadside bombs, and mine-resistant vehicles.

The Army must aggressively push for better technological solutions to its squad-level problems of both protection and mobility. Infantry squads today on average carry far more weight on their backs than their counterparts from World War II; they have gained the least from the revolutions in information and material technologies that have transformed so many other warfighting functions. Robotics for load-carrying and more hazardous tasks associated with infantry combat offer promise, but the technology base has not faced demands to deliver truly innovative solutions. Ten years into our recent wars, both Army and Marine infantrymen were often maimed and killed by simple land mines that were discovered by stepping on the device. This threat has been present for more than 100 years on the infantry battlefield, yet Soldiers today have little to counter primitive explosive land mines beyond what their great-grandfathers employed on D-Day in 1944. This should be simply unacceptable.

The arena of ground mobility for infantry Soldiers also remains at a primitive standard. Despite immense advances in strategic and operational mobility enabled by massive military cargo jets and nimble assault helicopters, today's infantryman, upon arrival at the battlefield, often reverts to a human pack mule. Soldiers climb mountains carrying as much as 100 pounds of ammunition, batteries, communications gear, food, and water on their backs, unassisted by modern technology. Faster development of both robotics and exoskeletal augmentation could help provide substantial support to get cargo off Soldiers' backs and out of their rucksacks. Thirteen years into a ground war fought largely on foot, semi-autonomous, all-terrain robotic "mules" should be part of every foot-mobile infantry formation's kit. In the second decade of the 21st century, the lack of basic technology to unburden Soldiers in the close fight is scandalous.

RESHAPING THE ROLES OF THE ACTIVE AND RESERVE COMPONENTS

The success of the Army's reserve component—the Army National Guard and Army Reserve—over the last 13 years at war has been indisputable. The "shock absorber" capability provided by mobilizing large numbers of reserve formations permitted the Army to sustain an extraordinarily high set of operational demands as it simultaneously fought prolonged land campaigns in both Iraq and Afghanistan. Without the operational depth provided by these Guard and Reserve formations, the active Army simply would have been unable to meet these demands—and the all-volunteer force might well have been broken.

Not only did Guard and Reserve Soldiers and units repeatedly integrate into two combat theaters and fight with active formations for more than a decade, but they did so with a solid record of tactical success. They also brought a remarkably diverse set of civilian skills to environments where "nation-building" became a core mission of deployed Army forces. Moreover, the moral authority that the Reserve component of the Army now brings to the table in discussions of the future composition of the Army should not be underestimated. The permanent placement of a four-star National Guard officer on the Joint Chiefs of Staff reflects this dynamic. The Army Guard and Reserve will never go back to the days of much-derided "weekend warriors." They have paid a steep price in blood and commitment in the recent wars unmatched since at least the Korean war.

Moreover, recent studies have established some solid baselines for comparing Active and Reserve cost structures.[5] These figures demand a serious look at how the Army Guard and Reserve can be even better integrated with the Active force for a wide range of missions as budgets come down. There can be no return to the old model. Army forces that are not required to deploy and fight inside of perhaps a 6-month window now must be evaluated more seriously for placement in the Army Guard or Reserve, rather than kept in the Active component at high expense. These might include select tank and artillery formations not needed in the early days of expected conflicts; shifting those forces from Active to Reserve retains these key capabilities in the force at less cost (and readiness) during what could be a dramatic down-sizing of the active Army. Aggressive use of advanced training technologies (discussed later) could also help retain their combat readiness at higher levels than has been possible in the past. The Guard and Reserve also offer unique opportunities to leverage high end civilian talents of their members in fields where the military lags civilian industry such as cyber, media, mobile communications, and many other high technology fields.

MAKING EXPANSIBILITY WORK

Although it is not difficult to identify some key trends that will shape the future strategic environment—the increasing role of advanced technologies, for example—it is virtually impossible to predict exactly when and how U.S. military forces will be used in the future.[6] The Army must balance the need to maintain ready forces for the most likely (probably lower level) contingencies, while ensuring it preserves robust enough capabilities to deal with the most dangerous eventuality should it materialize. Military forces must always hedge against this uncertainty, but this is particularly critical for the U.S. Army as it absorbs the potentially large force structure cuts described previously. The cuts must be done in a way that prioritizes expansibility—the ability to regenerate capabilities and even force structure should unexpected scenarios demand them in the future.[7]

Expansibility requires ready Active and Reserve forces, since there is little hope that new force structure and end strength can be generated if existing forces cannot meet their missions. In 2012, the Department of Defense (DoD) explicitly stated that it would "resist the temptation to sacrifice readiness in order to retain force structure" when allocating future cuts,[8] and both Army Chief of Staff General Raymond Odierno and Secretary of the Army John McHugh have reaffirmed this principle.[9] Deep budget cuts driven by sequestration have already undercut that promise.[10] But even if readiness can be fully maintained, it is not enough. The Army will also need to retain more mid-grade and noncommissioned officers than it would otherwise, since these experienced leaders would become the core of any new units formed in any rapid expansion of the force. Regenerating junior personnel would not be easy, but given the right incentives for accession, it would be easier than regenerating the people who lead them.

Creating a more expansible Army—one that can be grown rapidly in the face of a major conflict—will require Army leaders to think innovatively about how to rapidly and efficiently bring Active and Reserve formations more quickly to high readiness. It will also require serious dedication to the planning and regular rehearsal of rapidly creating wholly new combat-ready units—something the Army has not done on a large scale since World War II. More Active Duty Soldiers need to be dedicated to both of these tasks, and to share this responsibility equally with the Army National Guard and Army Reserve. Ensuring that the Reserve component remains an operational reserve with resourced plans to upgrade quickly when activated for combat missions will require careful planning, commitment, and cooperation by both Active and Reserve leaders.

Returning to a version of the 1980s "round-out/round-up" model would be one way to better integrate Active and Reserve formations, increasing their readiness in peacetime and ensuring they have a wartime focus. Selected brigade combat teams (BCTs), for example, could be "blended" formations, and include both Active and National Guard battalions and companies. They could be designed so that they would be ready for combat within 4 to 6 months of activation. The Active Duty elements of these BCTs would have full-time responsibility not only for their own Active unit readiness, but also for shaping training for the National Guard elements to ensure that they work together seamlessly to achieve full unit readiness once the blended unit is activated.

A second set of units could be designed for growth from near-cadre status to full capability in 10 to 12 months. This would institutionalize the ability to regenerate parts of the Army that are shorn during the coming drawdown, should future circumstances demand more ground forces. The Army did this with some success during the last decade, when the end strength of the Army temporarily increased to 570,000, and it added numerous new BCTs to meet wartime rotational demands. The Army must now invest in the cadre units and individual structures to make expansibility a well-oiled Army capability for future conflicts. This "zero to full-up" ability to build new units should be exercised and evaluated by creating one new BCT per year (as another stands down) to test, adjust, and validate this vital new capability.

ATTRACTING AND RETAINING TALENT

As the Army faces the end strength cuts described earlier, it must ensure that the best of its talent remains in uniform. Regardless of the eventual size of the cuts, the Army cannot afford to simply shed its people at random to meet much lower authorizations. Strategic cuts are required.

The end of the Cold War in the early-1990s provides a cautionary tale for the next Army drawdown.

The Army was rapidly reduced in this era by nearly 40 percent, and multiple incentive structures encouraged officers and troops to exit quickly—often without regard to their future value to the force. West Point graduates, as one example, who are normally required to serve 5 years on Active Duty after graduation, were allowed to leave service after as little as 2 years in uniform.[11] Needless to say, such incentives robbed the force of some of its most expensive human capital investments without systematically assessing the future consequences.

The current military compensation and retirement systems are enormously expensive. They consume more than a third of the defense budget today, and they are projected to consume the entire defense budget by 2039.[12] These systems will likely be reformed in the coming years, especially since the congressionally-mandated Military Compensation and Retirement Modernization Commission is due to report its findings in early-2015. Any changes, however, will undoubtedly alter retention incentives in some unintended ways. For example, the Commission may recommend creating portable retirement benefits, similar to civilian 401(k)s. While this might make sense from a fiscal perspective, it would also make it much more difficult to retain talented personnel after 10 years of Active Duty service. Right now, most officers and senior sergeants who stay in for 10 years are likely to stay in until they become eligible for retirement benefits after 20 years of service. A portable benefits program would need to be accompanied by new incentives for the most talented personnel to remain in uniform.

Finally, the reality for Soldiers making career decisions in the coming years will be deeply influenced by the perverse reality that service in a peacetime Army may prove much less attractive to combat veterans than continued operational combat duty. Long hours performing mundane tasks in garrison, lack of training dollars, and perhaps even a less clear Army mission will all mitigate enthusiasm about a career in uniform for combat-experienced younger officers and sergeants alike. Moreover, this growing millennial generation of Soldiers may chafe against the peacetime leadership styles of a hierarchical institution after years of having broad autonomy and decentralized control in the combat theaters. Managing this transition and keeping the best in the force as pressure mounts for rapid cuts will be perhaps the most important leadership challenge for this generation of Army leaders in the current drawdown. Army leaders, from generals to company commanders, will need to take on this responsibility with fierce determination to fight for the best to remain in the force, and to relentlessly find and eliminate the bureaucratic and leadership frustrations that cause great leaders to leave.

THE PARADOX OF RETURNING HOME

The U.S. Army is returning home for the first time since before World War II. The United States forward-stationed numerous Army units around the world during the Cold War and beyond, especially in Europe and in Asia, and many other units rotated abroad for training exercises with allies and partners. During the past decade of war, operational tempo ran so high that many units and personnel deployed to Afghanistan or Iraq multiple times, often with a year or less at home for respite and retraining. Yet during this same time, the U.S. Force posture abroad changed significantly. The 2004 *Global Defense Posture Review* recommended forward-stationing fewer units and instead building forward operating sites and cooperative security locations that would leave very little permanent global military presence. As a result of that review and subsequent decisions, the number of U.S. Army units forward-stationed in Europe and in Northeast Asia has shrunk considerably.[13]

After the withdrawal of U.S. combat forces from Afghanistan, the vast majority of U.S. Army units will be based in the United States, with potentially only two of its BCTs permanently stationed outside the United States.[14] Furthermore, deep cuts in the defense budget will mean fewer dollars available for training and exercises, particularly those that require expensive deployments overseas. In the next couple of years, the U.S. Army will complete the transition from a forward-deployed wartime force into a garrison peacetime force, where far fewer troops will have the opportunity to train and serve abroad.

Yet at the same time that Army units and personnel return home, they will be just as isolated from the American people and the society they serve. Less than 1 percent of Americans choose to serve in the military. With many of those volunteers coming from military families, even fewer among the general population gain direct knowledge of or experience with the military. And even though the Soldiers in this "at home" Army will now have mailing addresses in the United States, many will remain nearly as physically removed from American society as they were when they were abroad. Many of them will even remain isolated from their local communities, since numerous food, shopping, and entertainment options exist entirely within base perimeters. Moreover, many Army bases are located in relatively remote areas, far distant from the diversity found on the coasts or in sprawling metropolitan areas where Americans increasingly reside. As a potentially (much) smaller Army is distributed across even fewer bases, the risk grows that the culture of the Army will become increasingly separate from—and less tolerant of—the diverse culture of most Americans, especially those living in growing urban centers. This would be profoundly unhealthy both for the Army and for the nation more broadly.

The Army (like the other services) will need to find ways to counter this trend. One option would be to increase outreach activities, such as speaking tours by young officers and veteran sergeants to urban areas and elites in the media, Hollywood, business, and academia. Another would be to significantly increase the opportunities for more members of these same key communities to visit Army bases and see troops and training. Finally, any future efforts to realign and close excess Army bases should carefully consider not only the potential budgetary savings, but the need to maintain an Army presence across as broad a swath of the U.S. population as possible—not just in rural low-cost areas, or on a small number of "Mega-bases." Americans deserve to better know the heart and soul of the military that their tax dollars support, and whose members are sworn to protect them. A drift into isolation between the two in coming years risks losing the support of the American people, as well as creating an Army that does not share the same values and outlook as the society that it defends.

CONCLUSION

The U.S. Army is at a key crossroads, coming out of two wars and entering into a period of strategic uncertainty. It will get smaller, perhaps substantially so. Its resources will decline, perhaps in greater share than those of the other Services. Its men and women, hardened by years of unrelenting combat, will be dealing with fiscal austerity and challenges in sustaining readiness not seen in over a decade and a half. It will be based largely at home, removed from both its recent combat theaters and the day-to-day view of the American people.

Drawdowns and tight resources after wars have been a normal part of the Army's 239-year history. Managed well, they present a unique opportunity to shape the force with the knowledge and experience gained from extensive recent combat experience, and to keep the best and most far-sighted veterans in the force for the future. Done badly, they can decimate morale and drive out much of the brightest talent. But at the end of the day, leadership will determine which path the Army follows. The requirements for hands-on, committed, and visionary leadership of this Army through the coming years are as vital at the company and battalion commander levels as they are for the Chief of Staff of the Army. They will build the next Army out of the reorganized remnants of today's force. They must strive to do it quickly, and well. And they need to be organized around a central vision for the Army's future.

Lieutenants and sergeants ultimately make decisions about staying in or leaving the Army because of belief in — or loss of confidence in — their immediate leadership. Battalion commanders and first sergeants, captains, and sergeant majors will have to shape this force into its next incarnation by working hard to lead though adversity with verve and confidence, informed by history. The Army's senior leadership needs to do all it can now to engage its mid-grade and junior leadership with the six challenges we outlined here. All the answers may not yet be evident, but the entire Army needs to be involved and committed to working the challenges. That is what the young men and women who comprise this peerless force deserve as they make decisions about service—the life decisions about continued service in the coming years. An Army that creates and sustains that conversation will be ready to fight and win once again when the next war erupts.

ENDNOTES - CHAPTER 12

1. When Secretary of Defense Chuck Hagel presented the results of the *Strategic Choices and Management Review*, he mentioned that one of the options for allocating sequestration-level cuts "would further shrink the active Army to between 380,000 to 450,000 troops." See Hagel, "Statement on Strategic Choices and Management Review," Washington, DC: DoD, July 31, 2013, available from *www.defense.gov/Speeches/Speech.aspx?SpeechID=1798*.

2. According to a report by the Center for Strategic and International Studies (CSIS), the defense budget decreased by 43 percent after the Korean war, by 33 percent after the Vietnam War, and 36 percent after the end of the Cold War. If the sequestration-level cuts take effect as mandated in law, the defense budget will decrease by 31 percent from the peak spending levels during the wars in Iraq and Afghanistan. See Clark A. Murdock, Kelley Sayler, and Ryan A. Crotty, "The Defense Budget's Double Whammy: Drawing Down While Hollowing Out from Within," Washington, DC: CSIS, October 18, 2012, available from *csis.org/files/publication/121018_Murdoch_DefenseBudget_Commentary.pdf*.

3. Russell F. Weigley, *The American Way of War: A History of United States Military Strategy and Policy*, Bloomington, IN: Indiana University Press, 1973.

4. Douglas W. Skinner, *Airland Battle Doctrine*, Alexandria, VA: Center for Naval Analyses, 1988.

5. In particular, the Reserve Forces Policy Board (RFPB) found that Reservists, when not activated, cost less than one-third the amount of their Active Duty counterparts. See Reserve Forces Policy Board, "Eliminating Major Gaps in DoD Data on the Fully-Burdened and Life-Cycle Cost of Military Personnel: Cost Elements Should be Mandated by Policy," RFPB Report FY13-02, Washington, DC: Reserve Forces Policy Board, January 7, 2013.

6. For more on the difficulties of national security prediction, see Richard Danzig, "Driving in the Dark: Ten Propositions about Prediction and National Security," Washington, DC: Center for a New American Security, October 2011, especially pp. 14-16.

7. The most recent *Defense Strategic Guidance* identified this principle as reversibility, described as an "ability to make a course change that could be driven by many factors, including shocks or evolutions in the strategic, operational, economic, and technological spheres." See *Sustaining U.S. Global Leadership: Priorities for 21st Century Defense*, Washington, DC: DoD, January 2012, pp. 6-7.

8. *Ibid.*, p. 7.

9. See the transcript of Odierno's comments at the Brookings Institution, Washington, DC, February 15, 2013; McHugh's statement to the U.S. Senate Committee on Armed Services, Washington, DC, March 8, 2012, available from *www.armed-services. senate.gov/hearings/2012/03/08/oversight-department-of-the-army;* and McHugh's statement to the U.S. Senate, Subcommittee of the Committee on Appropriations, Washington, DC, March 21, 2012, available from *www.gpo.gov/fdsys/pkg/CHRG-112shrg29104508/ html/CHRG-112shrg29104508.htm.*

10. Loren Thompson, "Why A Modest Cut to the Budget Will Cause Major Damage to the Military," *Forbes,* February 25, 2013, available from *www.forbes.com/sites/lorenthompson/2013/02/25/why-a-modest-cut-to-the-budget-will-cause-major-damage-to-the-military/.*

11. Other incentives included the Voluntary Separation Incentive and the Special Separation Benefit programs, which started in 1992, and the Temporary Early Retirement Authority, which started in 1993. See Bernard Rostker, "Right-Sizing the Force,"

Washington, DC: Center for a New American Security, June 2013, p. 22.

12. Todd Harrison, "Rebalancing Military Compensation: An Evidence-Based Approach," Washington, DC: Center for Strategic and Budgetary Assessments, 2012, p. 1.

13. Stacie L. Pettyjohn, "U.S. Global Defense Posture, 1783-2011," MG-1244-AF, Santa Monica, CA: RAND Corporation, 2011, pp. 86-90.

14. The Army currently bases two BCTs in Europe, and is currently assessing whether Army units should rotate through South Korea instead of being permanently stationed there. Michelle Tan and Lance M. Bacon, "Changing the Korean Tour," *Army Times*, July 22, 2013.

PART III:

FUTURE MISSIONS

CHAPTER 13

SHAPING STRATEGIES:
GEOPOLITICS AND THE U.S. ARMY

Richard Rosecrance

In the long term, the nations which control the most productive territories will have an edge in charting the future direction of the world. Globalization, economies of scale, and network primacy all have a territorial dimension. Together, they govern economic power which will ultimately determine political and military outcomes. This is why U.S. military bases in Europe are critical—they help to provide stability and political predictability in the most important economic areas of the world.

Economic power includes population, wealth, industrial skills, natural resources, and the capacity to use them effectively. These factors of economic power are clustered regionally in certain places. Insofar as the definitive capacity of Landpower is the control of territory, Landpower plays a vital role in the international distribution of economic—and with it, political—power. The presence of U.S. land bases in Europe and Asia help maintain the world's present prosperity and expanding Western power in the future. U.S. national interests are best served by using its Landpower prudently and proactively to shape power relations in Europe and Asia.

EUROPE, ASIA, AND EURASIA

Historically, the maintenance of power is partially the result of a competitive spirit and effective engagement with foreign countries. Interwoven with waterways and internal and external seas, Europe traditionally has provided the arena for an historical competition among its adjacent states. But mountain barriers and great rivers have made universal conquest a difficult option for any aspiring hegemon. Even small water-protected countries have usually been able to maintain their existence. Thus both defense and offense have been honed in the European context.

Over time, the economic development of European countries and their overseas offshoots has lent industrial primacy to these nations. Writing in 1904, Halford Mackinder claimed the "world island" (that is, Eurasia from the British Isles to the Kamchatka peninsula) would eventually come to control the world. It possessed huge resources, giant populations, and a dominant land mass. It was the locus in which the industrial spirit came to fruition. If Eurasia were controlled by a single power, even the possessors of America and Africa could not hope to contend effectively against it. As late as World War II and the ensuing Cold War, strategists believed that, if this Eurasian giant and productive region were to fall into a single pair of hands, it could write *finis* to opposition located elsewhere.

An America linked with Eurasia would be very strong; an America opposed by Eurasia, very weak. In many ways this is still true. Modern economies revolve around economies of scale industries, industries in which unit costs decrease with greater production. How many economies of scale industries are situated elsewhere? Where does the most sophisticated manufacturing occur? Where are the great agricultural and mineral resources but in Europe, Russia, and the United States?

It is the European Union (EU) which has begun this modern-day "enlargement" process in recruiting new members. It has enlisted one key country after another: Poland, Hungary, the Balkan countries, and the Baltic countries. Now the EU is encroaching upon the Caucasus: Moldova, Ukraine, Georgia, and later the "Stans" are lining up to join.[1] Robert Mundell, the Nobel laureate who coined the requirements for an optimum currency area, later forecast that, in time, 50 countries would join the Euro-zone. This may be an exaggeration, but five to 10 new countries are in the mix of applicants to join the existing 28 right now. As the EU proceeds into what was once Western Asia, the power of Europe will not only mount, but it will attract others as well. In geopolitical terms, the agglomerating Europe (joined with the United States in both North Atlantic Treaty Organization [NATO] and Transatlantic Trade and Investment Partnership [TTIP]) will represent the strongest geopolitical magnet seen in world politics as it integrates its members into a more coherent whole. The West, in other words, is not only resurging, it is growing stronger — developing Asian nations will have to sell there, and their technology will largely come from there.

NATO membership has brought in Albania, Iceland, Canada, and the United States as well as Norway. The EU has separately recruited Cyprus, Malta, Finland, and Sweden, as well as Ireland. Alternating offers have led one state after another to join one organization and then the other. The same will likely be true in the future as Ukraine and then Georgia are considered for membership in the West.

In recent years, and particularly after President Barack Obama's "pivot to Asia," many have come to believe that developments in the Pacific and Asian realm might outweigh the U.S. past emphasis upon Eurasia. According to this view, India, Japan, China, Indonesia, and perhaps South Korea (at some point joined with the North) could take primacy away from the northerly West. But that is unlikely to happen. East Asia's development has depended upon selling in North America and Europe. The value contributed by Asian exports typically is still less than 50 percent of the sale price of the product in question. Also, Asian countries are traditional rivals of each other. China, for instance, traditionally has opposed Japan, Vietnam, India, and Korea for regional influence. The East Asian area is unlikely consolidated into one vast bloc that can challenge Europe and the United States. Many East Asian countries are linked or contractually allied to the United States and Europe. Chinese coercive efforts result, not in bandwagoning, but with increasing regional resistance, bringing unlikely partners like Vietnam and India together.[2]

Thus the central truth is that a new balance of power will not be formed in Asia against the United States or Europe. The United States and Europe together constitute nearly one-half of world gross domestic product (GDP), an amount that is not likely to change. As Europe enlarges and the United States and Europe come more closely together economically, the lateral strength thus gained will more than compensate for China's economic growth, which, in any event, is slowing down.[3]

America's greatest strength in Asia and elsewhere is its democratic character. As democracy spreads in Asia, the United States and the West will benefit. Right now, in Southeast Asia, as one example, China has an advantage in local demographic terms. Overseas Chinese constitute key minorities in Indonesia (5 percent), Philippines (2 percent), Malaysia (25 percent), Thailand, and Burma (5 percent). As a proportion of GDP of the country concerned, overseas Chinese earn much more than their proportion of the population would suggest, ranging from 50 percent in Indonesia and 63 percent in Malaysia, to 60-70 percent in Burma and Thailand. The United States does not have any substantial American population in these countries; hence it will need economic (trade and investment) relationships that can serve broader social purposes. But as Bill Clinton told Jiang Zemin: "You are on the wrong side of history." As democracy proceeds in Burma, Singapore, and ultimately Vietnam and China, the United States will be strengthened.

As Joe Nye shows, to gain soft power, the United States needs high prestige results—in democratic decisionmaking, economics, culture, sports, art, movies and other activities—to demonstrate continuing Western and American clout.[4] Why emphasize these strengths? The answer is to achieve an overbalance of power.

OVERBALANCE OF POWER

Achieving a mere balance of power is not enough to guarantee favorable outcomes over the long term in broader world politics. The United States needs an overbalance of power to defuse opposition and avoid a hostile response.

This was the great mistake in 1914—the consolidation of the Triple Entente as a counterweight to the Triple Alliance represented a mere balance of power, not an overbalance. In the longer-term, winning over China will not come from the creation of a balance of power. The West will need an even stronger economic and political coalition to attract China. Beijing will need to be part of a Western economic powerhouse to achieve its long-term economic and political objectives.

The consolidation of such a grouping was also the key to the end of the Cold War. The United States had built an overpowering coalition which included more than 75 percent of world GDP. As a result, Russia was better off joining, than opposing the Western group. But Russia did not have the democratic credentials to become a full member of the West, and it still does not, despite "diplomatic" efforts in Syria.

How does this influence the strategy of the U.S. Army? It means that U.S. bases in Europe are absolutely critical politically. They assist the political and military stability that the EU needs to continue to project in attracting new countries to the East. Just imagine what repercussions—economic, political, and military—there would be if U.S. troops were to withdraw, especially as Russia is pressing Ukraine, Moldova, and Georgia to rejoin its economic space. The U.S. Army is not the sufficient cause of European success, but it is a likely necessary cause of continued Western unity and economic progress.

ON SHORE BALANCING

To assist democratic tendencies in Asia, trade will not be enough. The United States needs on-shore basing arrangements, which it has in Korea, Japan, and Australia. If choke points emerge in Malacca, facilities in Singapore may be helpful. But the key here is not naval bases, but politically relevant land bases on shore in Asia.

Land bases facilitate Asia's transition to democracy. It is no accident that the Communist Party School in Beijing is now examining a future in which the Communist Party of China (CPC) will either lose power or be diluted as a monopolistic political influence. Experts have studied the examples of Taiwan and Singapore as they coped with the prospect of opposition. Singapore is most attractive from the Chinese point of view because Lee Kuan Yew's People's Action Party has maintained its dominance since 1965. Chiang Ching-kuo ruled on behalf of the Kuomintang Paty (KMT) in Taiwan until the mid-1990s, but then recruited the Democratic Progressive Party as a loyal opposition, and it won the election in 1996. Gradually acknowledging the need for change, the CPC understands that until it achieves democratic openness both politically and economically, it will not be able to join key, high profile international groupings like the Trans-Pacific Partnership, the Organization for Economic Cooperation and Development, and the G-7. How can the United States sophisticatedly but not intrusively assist this process? As in Europe, the critical idea is provide a backstop to allies in the region so that they would not be victims of pressure or territorial expansion by the mainland.

THE ROLE OF THE U.S. ARMY: SHAPING RELATIONSHIPS

The U.S. Army has critical roles in two major U.S. objectives: (1) maintaining U.S. links to Eurasia and creating an overbalance of power; and, (2) securing the democratic transition in Eastern Europe and facilitating a similar transition in Eastern Asia. To perform these functions, the Army will ultimately need onshore facilities with access to Eastern Europe that are also close to East Asia. If the U.S. Army is to use shaping strategies, where better than in the critical states of the West which will ultimately determine the fate of the world?

Ultimately Europe will have to become even larger. This enlargement, however, will not be achieved through conquest. One trend often preceding the spread of the EU is the spread of military cooperation through NATO. Admission into NATO requires adherence to military standardization and compatible means of state governance. Potential NATO member states begin the process of changing domestic institutions. These domestic transitions frequently continue — states like Croatia, the newest addition to the EU, strive to meet the economic and political requirements of the EU. Land bases provide security. But, more importantly, these bases perpetuate a process of integration.

U.S. Army bases, however, except for the informal relationship with Poland based upon past requirements for missile defense, are not moving further east. *Aegis* cruisers will patrol the Mediterranean, but new military bases are unlikely to be set up. When expanding military influence, the United States must consider Russia — overt NATO expansion exacerbates tensions with Russia. The Army must take a gradual and measured approach to the expansion of military cooperation. Special Forces might test the political waters of military integration. In a passive form of maneuver warfare, relatively less problematic states can be "exploited" by regionally aligned brigades. U.S. Army units might collocate with host nation units, offsetting costs and furthering integration. Incirlik, Turkey; Ramstein, Germany; and other bases (to say nothing of those in Kuwait) allow the United States to assist imperiled allies. The careful introduction of military Landpower allows for the maintenance of an economic and political overbalance of power in the Euro-Mediterranean region.

Efforts such as TTIP create the overbalance of power necessary to maintain western power and international prosperity. But sustaining this overbalance requires the expansion of the EU into Eastern Europe. The U.S. Army has a unique opportunity to shape the East European security environment, allowing further economic, and eventually, political integration in the region. U.S. bases in East Asia help ensure the maintenance of the current military and economic status quo and thus facilitate the environment in which liberal democracy can emerge.

It is, of course, part of the conventional wisdom that air and sea systems are the wave of the future. They travel more swiftly over their continental spaces than land forces can do over ground terrain. But these forces, though present, are evanescent. They do not stay. They do not interact with populations and little with politics. The key to continental security are land forces which literally compel the United States to act in ways that air and sea contingents cannot do. Europe is secure today because it can concentrate on economics and culture instead of military dangers. Japan, Australia, and South Korea know the security which only comes from the presence of U.S. land forces. Perhaps the United States does not need new land bases in Asia, though in time Singapore and the Philippines may ask for them. But, it is certain that the EU cannot expand to the East without the guarantee that U.S. ground forces, stationed nearby, can offer. U.S. forces may not have to fight, but they provide a political and security reassurance that no other U.S. force can muster.

ENDNOTES - CHAPTER 13

1. These are aside from Albania, Bosnia-Herzegovina, Iceland, Kosovo, Montenegro, Serbia, and Turkey, currently in line to join the EU.

2. Though unlikely to be formed, any effective economic agreement among East Asian members would certainly involve the United States.

3. See e.g., Barry Eichengreen, Donghyun Park, and Kwanho Shin, "When Fast Growing Economies Slow Down," Working Paper 16919, Cambridge, MA: National Bureau of Economic Research, March 2011.

4. See Joseph Nye, Chap. 4, *The Future of Power*, New York: Public Affairs, 2011.

CHAPTER 14

OFFSHORE BALANCING OR OVERBALANCING? A PRELIMINARY EMPIRICAL ANALYSIS OF THE EFFECT OF U.S. TROOP PRESENCE ON THE POLITICAL BEHAVIOR OF REGIONAL PARTNERS

Jordan Becker

In this volume, John Mearsheimer and Richard Rosecrance address the role of U.S. Landpower in an era of U.S. strategic "rebalancing" toward the Asia Pacific region.[1] Their assessments differ significantly, but are not mutually exclusive. Mearsheimer emphasizes the importance of "dealing with" a rising China, the U.S. shift away from counterinsurgency in the wider Middle East, and the Army's lack of **operational** utility in a major conflict in Asia, as opposed to Europe. At the same time, he predicts that "the United States will gradually and inexorably decrease its presence in Europe, which will leave the Army with a diminishing role in that region." He envisions the United States maintaining an "over-the-horizon" capability in areas of concern, an approach which he and others have referred to as "offshore balancing."[2]

Rosecrance, on the other hand, focuses on the **strategic** utility of land forces. He emphasizes the geostrategic and economic importance of Europe, noting the importance of the Euro-Atlantic economic community, specifically highlighting ongoing Transatlantic Trade and Investment Partnership (TTIP) negotiations. He sees "the West" as an important strategic grouping, the continued cohesion of which is supported by U.S. land presence in Europe. Perhaps more critically, he argues that rather than offshore balancing, the United States should seek to "overbalance": to generate or maintain a cohesive Western strategic and economic sphere with which potential rivals (such as China) would be compelled to engage constructively, presumably in not only the economic sphere, but the realm of security as well.

Crucial to this argument is Rosecrance's claim that, in both Europe and in Asia, the presence of U.S. bases and troops is "absolutely critical politically." While Mearsheimer does not specifically address this claim, his over-the-horizon argument indicates an opposing strategic approach. Rosecrance makes his claim for three reasons: First, U.S. troop presence ensures continued "political and military stability" in Europe, a claim that resounds with Mearsheimer's earlier arguments regarding the role of the United States in **intra**-European peace,[3] and with more recent arguments that rely on Mearsheimer's theoretical framework.[4] Second, Rosecrance suggests that the presence of U.S. forces serves to enhance or cement broader political ties or "maintain links" with allies and partners—that, in essence, U.S. troops buy the United States influence among the states in which they are stationed. Finally, he argues that U.S. troop presence supports democracy and democratization in Eastern Europe and Asia.

This chapter attempts to deal systematically and empirically with the generally opposing, but occasionally complementary, claims made by Mearsheimer and Rosecrance. Based on the arguments sketched out by each in this volume and using panel data covering the years 1950-2011 for both Europe and East Asia, I develop and test a theory that a policy-relevant variable, the number of U.S. troops stationed in a particular country,[5] provides a useful (if only partial) explanation for the extent to which states align with the United States politically and strategically. I find that the more U.S. troops are stationed in a country, the more closely that country's foreign policy orientation aligns with that of the United States.

Because Mearsheimer's assessment of the role of the U.S. Army rests primarily on his appreciation of the **operational** utility of land forces in Asia, it offers less tractable material for empirical political analysis. Nonetheless Figure 14-1 captures the obvious historical fact that the United States has maintained (relatively) limited troop presence in Asia, punctuated with major inflows for the purposes of fighting wars. So, while the topography of Asia may not be "ideal" for the application of Landpower in combat, the United States has found it strategically necessary to use Landpower in Asia on two occasions in the last 60 years.[6] Figure 14-1 also speaks to Mearsheimer's prediction of a gradual and inexorable decrease in the U.S. presence in Europe. In fact, a dramatic exit from Europe began immediately following the Cold War, only stabilizing with the Balkan crises of the mid- and late-1990s. Decreases have continued incrementally in recent years, and after the removal of two brigade combat teams in 2012, the United States now has roughly the same number of troops in Asia that it does in Europe. In other words, the much touted "rebalancing" of the last 3 years has been taking place, at least in terms of troop presence, for 2 decades.

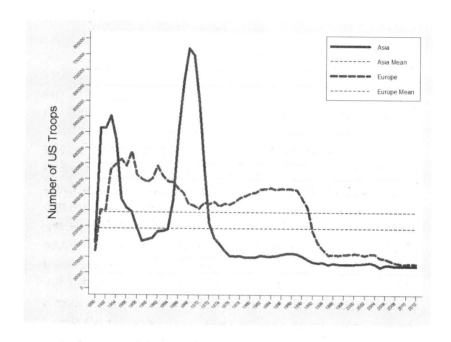

Figure 14-1. Number of U.S. Troops in Europe and Asia, Over Time.

Mearsheimer's broader concept of "over-the-horizon" use of U.S. power or "offshore balancing" can be contrasted to Rosecrance's conception of "overbalancing," which explicitly requires "onshore" capabilities. I make use of these contrasting theories of the strategic utility of U.S. Landpower to test the following hypotheses:

H1: The greater the U.S. troop presence in a state, the more that state's foreign policy orientation will align with that of the United States.

Secondarily, I test Rosecrance's claims about the role of U.S. troop presence in promoting democratization:

H2: The greater the U.S. troop presence in a state, the more pluralistic that state's domestic institutions will be.

RESEARCH DESIGN

Dependent Variable.

The dependent variable in this analysis is the alignment, or foreign policy orientation, of potential partners and allies of the United States, as measured by the proximity of a state's "ideal point" in the United Nations General Assembly (UNGA)[7] to that of the United States. **Ideal point proximity**, or the difference between state i's ideal point in UNGA votes in year t and that of the United States, is the best available indicator of attitudinal shifts and polarization in world politics—when global politics are more polarized, average ideal point proximity numbers increase (see Figure 14-2). Ideal point proximity is not only indicative of foreign policy orientation on issues of global importance; it also corresponds with more strategic and even operational measures of alignment. Among North Atlantic Treaty Organization (NATO) members, for example, ideal point is highly correlated with an "Atlanticist" (broadly pro-American)[8] strategic foreign policy orientation.[9] Among NATO members, an Atlanticist foreign policy orientation offers a powerful explanation for resource allocation toward military operations, a crucial indicator of not only strategic alignment, but willingness to share the burden of collective defense and security.[10] In short, ideal point proximity is a powerful measure for the influence the United States is able to exercise on other states across an array of strategically important areas, and therefore quite useful in testing the effect of U.S. troop presence on foreign policy alignment.

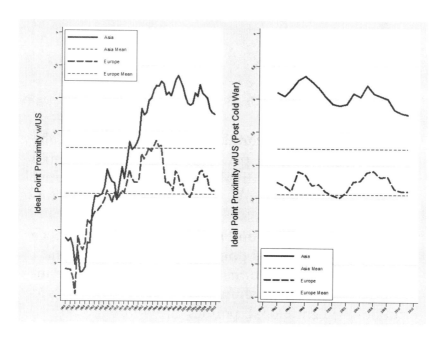

Figure 14-2. UNGA Alignment with the United States over Time, by Continent (Lower Score = More Aligned w/U.S.).

Independent Variable.

The independent variable in the analysis is the number of U.S. troops present in a particular country. I use the natural log of this number because, for most of the period studied, large troop presence is so highly concentrated in a few states (Japan and South Korea in Asia, Germany and Italy in Europe). In this way, the analysis can better capture the effect of relatively small changes in the number of troops present in a country, which is more relevant for policy questions about the use of, for example, Foreign Area Officers (FAO) in support of Special Forces or regionally aligned forces. Numerous studies have made use of this independent variable, measuring its effect on economic growth where troops are stationed,[11] U.S. Foreign Direct Investment in states in which troops are stationed,[12] and even the security behavior of the states in which U.S. troops are stationed as measured by their own troop levels, along with their propensity to initiate or become the target of interstate disputes.[13] However, no study has explicitly addressed the effect of troop presence on foreign policy orientation.

Control Variables.

To address the potential for omitted variable bias, I introduce a series of control variables to the analysis. First, I control for the **region** (or continent) in which U.S. troops are deployed. The United States has deployed troops at different times, in different numbers, and in varying patterns in Europe and Asia, as highlighted by Figure 14-1. The effect of those troops is likely to differ between the two — a difference in effect is, in fact, a core element of Mearsheimer's operationally-focused discussion of the irrelevance of ground forces in Asia.

Second, I control for the **gross domestic product (GDP) (natural log)** and **population (in millions)** of the state in which U.S. troops are deployed, based on the collective action logic that richer and more populous countries are more likely to assert more autonomous foreign policies, while poorer and less populous countries are more likely to align with larger powers.[14]

Third, I control for economic interdependence, in the form of **bilateral trade volume with the United States, in thousands of dollars per capita,**[15] based on Rosecrance's argument that economic interdependence has an effect on foreign policy behavior.[16]

Fourth, I control for **threat proximity**,[17] measured in thousands of kilometers from Moscow (for European states), and thousands of kilometers from Beijing (for Asian states), based on Stephen Walt's "balance of threat" logic.[18]

Fifth, I control for **veto points**[19] in order to account for the effect of domestic political constraints on a state's ability to adjust international positions.[20] This control is also consistent with Rosecrance's argument linking troop presence and domestic political institutions. The effects of veto points may, in fact, be mixed: While more veto players may slow a state's ability to adjust foreign policy positions quickly based on changes in U.S. troop presence, theories linking regime type and state alignment suggest that a state having a pluralistic institutional environment would simply make alignment with the United States more probable.[21]

Sixth, I control for the size of the force positioned in a particular country, or **troop contingent size**. This control stems from the intuition that states in which U.S. troops are stationed will respond differently to different sizes of troop contingent. Accordingly, I created four categories of contingents: First, contingents up to 200 personnel, which reflects the type of contingent that would be able to conduct ongoing military to military engagement and support a continued rotational presence, but do not represent even a company-sized element permanently stationed in a country; second, contingents between 200 and 2,000 personnel, which represent a forward deployed battalion-sized unit or smaller; and third, contingents between 2,000 and 25,000 personnel, which represent one or several forward deployed brigade-sized elements. The fourth category, 25,000 personnel or above, represents forward deployments of division or corps-sized organizations.

Table 14-1 provides the bivariate correlations of each dependent and independent variable, and Table 14-2 presents the descriptive statistics.

EMPIRICAL ANALYSIS

I begin with a bivariate analysis between U.S. troop presence and UNGA alignment, visually represented in Figure 14-3. Panel A provides the full sample of country years ranging from 1950 to 2011, whereas Panel B simply provides a snapshot of the relationship in 2011 with country labels. In both cases, we observe the hypothesized relationship that countries with more U.S. troops will align more closely with the United States, with ideal point proximity ranging from 1.5 in the United Kingdom (UK) to nearly 4 in Vietnam. Of some concern is the presence of a cluster of apparent outliers. However, those states are all in Asia, and when we parse the relationship by continent, as in Figure 14-4, we find that the relationship is much more consistent. This helps confirm the use of a region/continent dummy variable as a control.

Table 1: Bivariate Correlations of Variables Used in Core Analysis

	1	2	3	4	5	6	7	8	9	10	11	12	13	14
Bailey et al. FP Orientation Proximity (Lower Score = More Closely)														
1 Aligned with US in UNGA	1													
2 FP Orientation (Word Scores: Atlanticist=0; Europeanist=100)	0.1608*	1												
3 Biehl et al. FP Orientation (Atlanticist=1, Balanced=2, Europeanist=3)	-0.1252*	0.4345*	1											
4 US Troop Presence (ln)	-0.3959*	-0.3168*	-0.1239*	1										
5 GDP (ln)	0.0029	-0.1846*	0.1148*	0.4650*	1									
6 Population (millions)	0.2105*	-0.1848*	0.1063*	0.3546*	0.6016*	1								
7 Bilateral Trade Volume w/US ($000/cap)	0.1449*	-0.2738*	0.1055*	-0.0469*	0.0995*	-0.1084*	1							
8 Threat Proximity (000 km, Beijing or Moscow)	-0.0858*	0.0094	0.3708*	-0.0045	-0.0375	0.0349	0.0802*	1						
9 Veto Points	-0.5330*	0.0212	0.0369	0.1012*	0.1989*	-0.1630*	0.0860*	-0.1108*	1					
10 US Troop Presence (ln) x Checks	-0.4824*	-0.2273*	-0.1019	0.8248*	0.5498*	0.2125*	0.0049	-0.0592*	0.5658*	1				
11 US Troop Presence (ln) x Troops<200	0.2312*	0.1651*	0.2290*	-0.6193*	-0.0893*	-0.043	0.1360*	0.0621*	0.0002	-0.4982*	1			
12 US Troop Presence (ln) x Troops<2,000	-0.0138	0.2879*	0.297*	-0.2359*	-0.0502*	-0.1724*	0.1068*	0.2156*	0.0334	-0.1624*	0.2959*	1		
13 US Troop Presence (ln) x Troops<25,000	-0.2898*	-0.1503*	-0.0876	0.5459*	0.1253*	-0.0288	-0.0556*	0.0941*	0.0570*	0.4221*	-0.3761*	0.0799*	1	
14 US Troop Presence (ln) x Troops>0	-0.3959*	-0.3168*	-0.1239*	1.0000*	0.4650*	0.3546*	-0.0469*	-0.0045	0.1012*	0.8248*	-0.6193*	-0.2359*	0.5459*	1

* Significant at the .05 level

Table 14-1

Table 2: Summary Statistics of Variables Used in Core Analysis					
Variable	Obs	Mean	Std. Dev.	Min	Max
Dependent Variables					
Bailey et al. FP Orientation Proximity (Lower Score = More Closely Aligned with US in UNGA)	2053	1.73895	1.165609	-1.1622	4.91055
FP Orientation (Word Scores: Atlanticist=0; Europeanist=100)	191	15.2056	4.420492	0	26
Biehl et al. FP Orientation (Atlanticist=1, Balanced=2, Europeanist=3)	378	1.64021	0.677546	1	3
US Troop Presence (ln)	2053	5.09555	2.954165	0	12.3353
Control Variables					
GDP (ln)	1972	4.6567	1.641789	-0.0073	8.29615
Population (millions)	1972	25.6758	36.05011	0.14294	242.326
Bilateral Trade Volume w/US ($000/cap)	1877	0.58886	1.282483	-0.0023	11.7985
Threat Proximity (000 km, Beijing or Moscow)	2053	2.83939	2.021014	0.791	10.691
Veto Points	1298	3.55008	1.490459	1	8
Interaction Variables					
US Troop Presence (ln) x Checks	1298	17.9243	13.05429	0	67.9038
US Troop Presence: 1-200	2053	1.75551	1.673521	0	5.29331
US Troop Presence: 200-2,000	2053	2.72292	2.214794	0	7.5974
US Troop Presence: 200-25,000	2053	4.33712	2.779029	0	10.1022
US Troop Presence: >25,000	2053	5.09555	2.954165	0	12.3353

Table 14-2

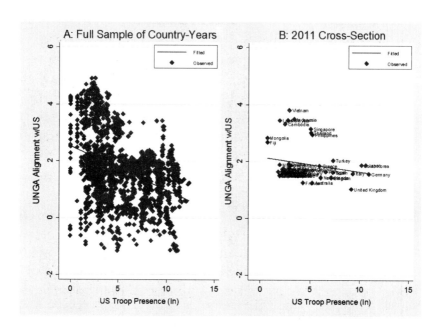

Figure 14-3. Bivariate Relationship between
U.S. Troop Presence and UNGA Alignment.

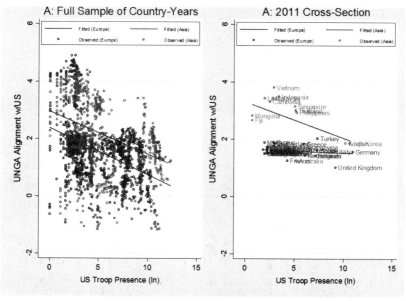

Figure 14-4. Bivariate Relationship between
U.S. Troop Presence and UNGA Alignment,
by Continent.

This bivariate analysis is almost certainly biased by omitted variables. In addition, states like Vietnam and the UK still appear to be slight outliers, appearing to be less (Vietnam) or more (UK) aligned with the United States than the number of troops stationed there would suggest, even in the continent-specific Figure 14-4. This concern about bias requires multivariate analysis that adequately addresses the particular strategies of various states.

Multiple Regression Specification.

To assess H1 more systematically, I estimate the following equation using Ordinary Least Squares (OLS) regression:
$$Y_{it} = \beta_0 + \beta_1 T_{it} + \delta X_{it} + \varepsilon$$

Y_{it} is the proximity of country i's foreign policy orientation in year t, as captured by Bailey $et\ al.$'s ideal point measure, to the United States, and T_{it} is the number of U.S. troops in country i in year t. X_{it} is the matrix of control variables, outlined earlier, employed to address omitted variable bias. Because the number of years in the analysis is relatively small compared to the number of observations, I employ panel corrected standard errors.[22]

The results are presented in Table 14-3. It is important to note that in Table 14-3, a negative correlation coefficient indicates **closer** proximity to U.S. foreign policy orientation. Note also that Vietnam and South Korea are dropped from the model during years in which the United States was engaged in armed conflict in those countries, as the objective of this analysis is to measure the effects of troop deployment in terms of **influencing allies and partners** in the way that Rosecrance indicates in this volume, and these massive combat deployments would bias that analysis.

Table 3: Correlates of Ideal Point Proximity (UNGA Alignment) with US Troop Presence

VARIABLES	(1) Baseline	(2) Region	(3) Collective Action	(4) Economic Interdependence	(5) Threat Proximity	(6) Veto Points	(7) Troop Contingent Size	(8) Country FE
US Troop Presence (ln)	-0.156***	-0.159***	-0.192***	-0.190***	-0.189***	-0.251***	-0.252***	-0.371***
	(0.009)	(0.010)	(0.011)	(0.010)	(0.011)	(0.022)	(0.033)	(0.053)
Europe Dummy		-0.649***	-0.518***	-0.421***	-0.918***	-0.950***	-1.130***	-1.805***
		(0.076)	(0.068)	(0.064)	(0.048)	(0.051)	(0.068)	(0.127)
GDP (ln)			0.041	0.007	0.024	-0.016	-0.003	-0.001
			(0.029)	(0.024)	(0.024)	(0.015)	(0.015)	(0.085)
Population (millions)			0.009***	0.011***	0.008***	0.003***	0.004***	0.022***
			(0.001)	(0.001)	(0.001)	(0.001)	(0.001)	(0.001)
Bilateral Trade Volume w/US ($000/cap)				0.126***	0.122***	0.033**	0.038***	0.134***
				(0.026)	(0.025)	(0.014)	(0.014)	(0.017)
Threat Proximity (000 km, Beijing or Moscow)					-0.168***	-0.125***	-0.159***	0.030
					(0.007)	(0.008)	(0.007)	(0.017)
Veto Points						-0.394***	-0.387***	-0.478***
						(0.042)	(0.044)	(0.063)
US Troop Presence (ln) x Veto Points						0.038***	0.039***	0.060***
						(0.005)	(0.005)	(0.008)
US Troop Presence: 200-1,999							0.014	0.008
							(0.037)	(0.038)
US Troop Presence: 200-1,999							-0.029	0.007
							(0.052)	(0.053)
US Troop Presence: 200-24,999							-0.324***	0.178*
							(0.114)	(0.098)
US Troop Presence (ln) x Troop Category (1-199)							0.119**	0.144**
							(0.049)	(0.061)
US Troop Presence (ln) x Troop Category (200-1,999)							-0.089*	0.298***
							(0.047)	(0.064)
US Troop Presence (ln) x Troop Category (2,000-24,999)							0.387***	-0.228**
							(0.143)	(0.094)
Constant	2.532***	3.009***	2.635***	2.592***	3.410***	5.016***	5.118***	3.394***
	(0.050)	(0.079)	(0.111)	(0.109)	(0.105)	(0.139)	(0.140)	(0.620)
Observations	2,053	2,053	1,972	1,877	1,877	1,207	1,207	1,207
R-squared	0.156	0.220	0.305	0.318	0.375	0.603	0.623	0.777
Panels	51	51	51	51	51	49	49	49
RMSE	1.071	1.030	0.940	0.945	0.905	0.593	0.580	0.454

OLS coefficients with Panel Corrected Standard Errors in parentheses; *** p<0.01, ** p<0.05, * p<0.1; ln: natural log

Table 14-3

Not displayed in the tables are the results of an analysis of H2, that greater U.S. troop presence will be associated with more pluralistic domestic institutional environments, represented in the model by veto points. While a model controlling for regional and collective action factors yields a correlation coefficient of .28 significant at the .05 level, the r-squared is very small, and the statistical significance of the correlation disappears when economic interdependence is added to the model, casting doubt on the hypothesis that U.S. troop presence affects the development or consolidation of democratic or pluralistic political systems.

The results in Table 14-3 progress through the 8 regression models sequentially, with Model 1 establishing the bivariate relationship visualized in Figure 14-3, followed by a testing of the strength of that relationship with the addition of control variables. Of course, these additions do not entirely rule out omitted variable bias, and even the fully specified model, which includes country fixed effects, accounts for only 62 percent of the variation in ideal point proximity.

In model 2, I add a dummy variable accounting for whether a state is in Europe or Asia. The logic for this variable is captured visually in Figure 14-4: European states are systematically more aligned with the United States than Asian states, represented by the .65 point downward shift of ideal point proximity in the baseline regression, equal to nearly 10 percent of the difference between the highest and lowest measures in the entire data set. In other words, European states are systematically 10 percent more closely aligned with the United States than are Asian states.

Model 3 adds national wealth and population in order to account for Mancur Olson and Richard Zeckhauser's collective action logic.[23] Model 4 adds a measure of economic interdependence with the United States, a variable that Rosecrance assigns great importance to elsewhere,[24] and that is also correlated with foreign policy alignment (see Table 14-1).

Model 5 adds a threat proximity variable (capital city distance from Moscow or Beijing) to capture Walt's balance of threat logic.[25] Model 6 adds veto points, under a variation of Witold Henisz and Edward Mansfield's logic that shifts in foreign policy are likely to be slower in states with more political constraints, quantified as veto points.[26] Veto points also help capture the extent to which a states' political regime is pluralistic.

Model 7 adds an interaction term between the independent variable and a categorical variable: the size of the U.S. troop contingent (rotational only, battalion-size or less, brigade up to division, and division or more, indicated by troop numbers). Figure 14-5 demonstrates the logic of the inclusion of this variable: the four troop contingent sizes demonstrate not only different intercepts, but different slopes in the scatter plotted bivariate relationship between foreign policy alignment and troop numbers. It is also worth noting that the relationships vary significantly during and after the Cold War, with the correlation being highest among small troop contingent countries during the Cold War, and highest among larger troop contingent countries in the years that followed.[27] The end of the Cold War affected both the independent and the dependent variable in this study: the end of the Cold War resulted in a less polarized world, and therefore lower ideal point proximity scores. It also resulted in the withdrawal of almost two thirds of the U.S. forces in Europe from 1990 to 1994, and a smaller, but perceptible reduction in Asia.

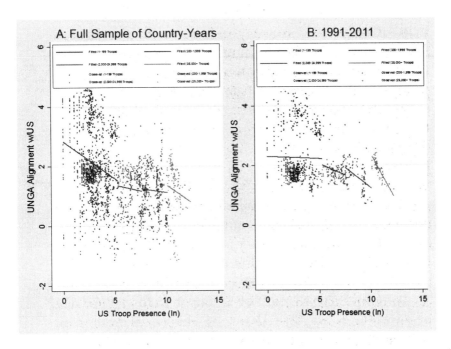

Figure 14-5. Bivariate Relationship between U.S. Troop Presence and UNGA Alignment, by U.S. Troop Contingent Size.

Model 8 makes use of the 60-year length of the period covered. If it is true that troop presence influences the foreign policy orientation of the state in which the troops are located in a way that causes them to align more closely with the United States, then as troop numbers increase in a state, that state should become more aligned with the United States. To test this hypothesis, I add **country-level fixed effects**, which eliminate country-level variation and measure the effect of shifts in U.S. troop numbers within individual countries. Model 8 is therefore particularly rigorous, helping ensure that results are not driven by unobservable factors particular to individual states, such as cultural or linguistic affinity or historical ties, which may affect both the number of U.S. troops present in a state and that state's foreign policy orientation. In Table 14-3, the coefficient remains negative and increases significantly. This suggests fairly robust results, and a strong relationship between U.S. troop presence and foreign policy alignment.

Results.

The key finding of Table 14-3 is that there is a strongly negative and significant effect—the more U.S. troops are in a country, the more closely aligned its foreign policy orientation is with that of the United States. The r-squared in the baseline model is .156, indicating that 15.6 percent of variation in foreign policy orientation is accounted for by the number of U.S. troops in a country. While not a huge number, this is still a fairly significant finding.

As each control is added into the model, the correlation coefficient remains stable as the r-squared increases. In the fully specified Model 7, which still allows cross-country variation, a one standard deviation (roughly 3 percentage point) movement in the number of troops in a country is associated with a .25 point shift in that country's foreign policy orientation. To put this figure in comparative perspective, .25 points was the difference between France and Bulgaria's respective proximities to the United States in 2011.

Moving through the other control variables in the fully specified model, we find that the Europe dummy is significant: European states are, all else equal, 1.13 points closer (over a quarter of the difference between the United States and the most distant state) to the U.S. foreign policy orientation than are Asian states.

Among the collective action variables, GDP is not significant, but population is positive and significant, indicating that more populous states are slightly less likely to align with the United States. This seems reasonable, given that the latent power associated with population might increase the likelihood of a state having a more autonomous foreign policy. The coefficient is very small, however.

The correlation between economic interdependence and foreign policy alignment is paradoxical: states that are more economically interdependent appear to be less closely aligned with the United States, although the coefficient is very small, particularly relative to the amount of trade. This could be related to trading states being less inclined to align politically with any large powers for fear of affecting the commerce on which they depend.

Threat proximity is associated with alignment with the United States, consistent with Walt's theorizing—the closer a state is to Beijing or Moscow, the more closely aligned it is with the United States. The analysis confirms Walt's claims.

Veto points behave interestingly—they correlate negatively with the dependent variable, indicating that states with more veto points are more likely to align with the United States. This is consistent with the basic outlines of theories of democratic peace,[28] but inconsistent with the notion that additional checks will limit a state's ability to respond quickly to international stimuli and incentives.[29] However, when interacted with troop numbers, more veto points shift states away from the United States, indicating a challenge for U.S. troops in pluralistic institutional environments—while states with more veto points are more closely aligned with the United States, the effect of troop presence in those states is limited. It is also important to note that the biggest shift in r-squared (from .375 to .603) takes place when adding veto points into the model, which suggests that regime type has a more significant effect on alignment than does troop location. Recall also that there is little evidence suggesting that troop presence has any effect on democratization.

The categorical troop variables also behave interestingly: shifts in numbers in very small and very large troop presence countries have the expected effect of moving those countries' orientations away from that of the United States; but in countries with brigade-sized contingents, the coefficient is small and negative. This result is also dependent on time period, with a significant shift taking place as the Cold War concluded. The bottom line finding — that troop presence is positively correlated with foreign policy alignment with the United States — remains unchanged.

In sum, the empirical analysis demonstrates a strong correlation between shifts in U.S. troop presence and foreign policy alignment among partners and allies. Countries hosting more U.S. troops appear inclined to align with the United States in the UNGA, and UNGA alignment also correlates, among NATO members, with Atlanticism and willingness to invest in military operations,[30] suggesting that this alignment has political and strategic significance beyond mere grandstanding in the General Assembly.

CONCLUSION

This chapter has introduced a theory explaining how U.S. troop presence might affect the foreign policy orientation of countries in which those troops are stationed. While other variables, in particular regime type, threat proximity and broader region-specific factors seem to exert a strong effect on foreign policy orientation, I observe that U.S. troop presence is a meaningful predictor of the extent to which a state's foreign policy orientation is likely to be aligned with that of the United States. More U.S. troops are associated with greater alignment states' foreign policy orientations with that of the United States.

This finding has theoretical implications in relation to the arguments presented by Mearsheimer and Rosecrance in this volume, as well as policy implications for the future of Landpower. I have used an extensive data set to empirically assess two hypotheses generated from Mearsheimer and Rosecrance's work: that the presence of U.S. troops increases U.S. influence with states in which they are stationed, and that the presence of U.S. troops fosters democracy in those states.

I find little evidence supporting the second hypothesis, but significant evidence supporting the first. This suggests that, if the United States is primarily concerned with troop placement as it affects the operational utility of those troops in combating potential adversaries, or even with the development of pluralistic and democratic political institutions around the world, an "over-the horizon" strategy such as that proposed by Mearsheimer may be good enough. But if the United States is interested in developing a strategically meaningful "Western" grouping, or even in influencing the foreign policy orientation of East Asian states in a way that aligns them more closely with the United States, a more robust military presence may be of use. While stationing troops is a costly endeavor, it is worth noting that troop presence is, in fact, a policy relevant variable that the United States can control directly, unlike the presence and proximity of threats, the wealth or population of partner states, or the nature of those states' regimes. Trade volume, which is, to an extent, amenable to policy decisions, appears less correlated with foreign policy alignment than does troop presence. In a period in which the United States and its partners are facing significant resource constraints and negotiating the Trans-Pacific Partnership as well as the TTIP, the United States would appear to have significant opportunities to achieve complementarity between the stationing of land forces and intensification of economic interdependence.

ENDNOTES - CHAPTER 14

1. See Mearsheimer, Chap. 2, and Rosecrance, Chap. 13, in this volume.

2. Christopher Layne, "From Preponderance to Offshore Balancing: America's Future Grand Strategy," *International Security*, Vol. 22, No. 1, 1997, pp. 86-124. John J. Mearsheimer, "The Future of the American Pacifier," *Foreign Affairs*, 2001, pp. 46-61. John J. Mearsheimer, *The Tragedy of Great Power Politics*, WW Norton & Company, 2001, p. 63.

3. John J. Mearsheimer, "Back to the Future: Instability in Europe after the Cold War," *International Security*, Vol. 15, No. 1, 1990, pp. 5-56.

4. Sten Rynning, "Germany is More than Europe Can Handle: Or, Why NATO Remains a Pacifier," NATO Defence College Research Paper No. 96, Rome, Italy: NATO Defence College, September 2013.

5. Tim Kane, "Global US troop deployment, 1950–2005," Report, Washington, DC: Center for Data Analysis, 2006, p. 2-6. *Active Duty Military Personnel Strengths — By Regional Area and by Country*, Washington, DC: Department of Defense, available from *www.defense.gov/faq/pis/mil_strength.html*.

6. The effectiveness of these engagements is, of course, well beyond the scope of this analysis, but their occurrence is worth noting.

7. Michael Bailey, Anton Strezhnev, and Erik Voeten, "Estimating Dynamic State Preferences from United Nations Voting Data," Social Science Research Network, 2013.

8. For the purposes of this analysis, I narrowly define Atlanticism as the perception that NATO, with active American leadership, is the central institutional component of European security, per Nina Græger and Kristin Haugevik, "The Revival of Atlanticism in NATO? Changing Security Identities in Britain, Norway, and Denmark,"Oslow, Norway: Norway Institute of International Affairs, 2010. Broader visions of the concept of Atlanticism are common; for a detailed discussion of the social, cultural political and economic aspects of Atlanticism see Kenneth Weisbrode, *The Atlantic Century: Four Generations of Extraordinary Diplomats who Forged America's Vital Alliance with Europe*, Cambridge, MA: Da Capo Press, 2009.

9. Bailey *et al.*'s ideal point has a bivariate correlation of .43 with the expert analysis of Biehl et al.'s Bundeswehr study of European strategic cultures, and of .16 with an automated content analysis of 95 strategic documents produced by NATO member states, significant at the .05 level. Heiko Biehl, Bastian Giegerich, and Alexandra Jonas, "Strategic Cultures in Europe," *Schriftenreihe des Zentrum für Militärgeschichte und Sozialwissenschaften*, Vol. 15, 2013.

10. Jordan M. Becker and Edmund J. Malesky, "Pillar or Pole? The Effect of Strategic Culture on Burden Sharing and NATO's Future," Social Science Research Network, 2013.

11. Garett Jones and Tim Kane, "US Troops and Foreign Economic Growth," *Defence and Peace Economics*, Vol. 23, No. 3, 2012, pp. 225-249.

12. Glen Biglaiser and Karl DeRouen, "Following the Flag: Troop Deployment and US Foreign Direct Investment," *International Studies Quarterly*, Vol. 51, No. 4, 2007, pp. 835-854.

13. Carla Martinez Machain and T. Clifton Morgan, "The Effect of US Troop Deployment on Host States' Foreign Policy," *Armed Forces & Society*, Vol. 39, No. 1, 2013, pp. 102-123.

14. Mancur Olson and Richard Zeckhauser, "An Economic Theory of Alliances," *The Review of Economics and Statistics*, Vol. 48, No. 3, 1966, pp. 266-279.

15. Katherine Barbieri and Omar Keshk, "Correlates of War Project Trade Data Set Codebook, 1009," Version 3.0, 2012, available from *correlatesofwar.org*; Katherine Barbieri, Omar M. G. Keshk, and Brian Pollins," Trading Data: Evaluating our Assumptions and Coding Rules," *Conflict Management and Peace Science*, Vol. 26, No. 5, 2012, pp. 471–491.

16. Richard N. Rosecrance, *The Rise of the Trading State: Commerce and Conquest in the Modern World*, Vol. 386, New York: Basic Books, 1986.

17. Christian Skrede Gleditsch, "Distance Between Capital Cities," *Data, Etc.*, available from *privatewww.essex.ac.uk/~ksg/data-5.html*.

18. Stephen M. Walt, *The Origins of Alliances*, Ithaca, NY: Cornell University Press, 1987.

19. Thorsten Beck, George Clarke, Alberto Groff, Philip Keefer, and Patrick Walsh, "New Tools in Comparative Political Economy: The Database of Political Institutions," *The World Bank Economic Review* Vol. 15, No. 1, 2001, pp. 165-176.

20. Witold J. Henisz and Edward D. Mansfield, "Votes and Vetoes: The Political Determinants of Commercial Openness," *International Studies Quarterly*, Vol. 50, No. 1, 2006, pp. 189-212.

21. Michael W. Doyle, "Liberalism and World Politics," *American Political Science Review*, Vol. 80, No. 4, 1986, pp. 1151-1169.

22. Nathaniel Beck and Jonathan N. Katz, "What To Do (and Not To Do) with Time-Series Cross-Section Data," *American Political Science Review*, 1995, pp. 634-647.

23. Olson and Zeckhauser, pp. 266-279.

24. Richard N. Rosecrance, *The Rise of the Trading State: Commerce and Conquest in the Modern World*, Vol. 386, New York: Basic Books, 1986.

25. Walt.

26. Henisz and Mansfield, pp. 189-212.

27. The results captured in Table 14-3 are also not robust to the introduction of year dummies into the fully specified model, suggesting further study of the effect of different time periods on the relationship between troops would be appropriate.

28. Bruce Russett, *Grasping the Democratic Peace: Principles for a Post-Cold War World*, Princeton, NJ: Princeton University Press, 1994.

29. Henisz and Mansfield, pp. 189-212.

30. Becker and Malesky.

CHAPTER 15

EUROPE, LANDPOWER, AND THEIR IMPORTANCE IN U.S. GRAND STRATEGY

Seth A. Johnston

What is Europe's place in U.S. grand strategy, and what are the implications for U.S. Landpower? The contemporary discourse on the U.S. "pivot" to the Asia-Pacific and the accompanying maritime-focused Air-Sea Battle doctrine discount the grand strategic significance of Landpower and of Europe. Yet, both remain deeply important and intertwined with one another. Landpower is central in European affairs, and Europe remains vitally important to the United States. As a result, U.S. grand strategy must avoid pivoting off balance by according too little consideration to the two. The most significant issues at stake concern the futures of the North Atlantic Treaty Organization (NATO) and U.S. military bases in Europe. Sound strategic and empirical reasons suggest that NATO will endure, and that force presence in Europe offers the United States significant advantages.

HOW IMPORTANT IS EUROPE TO THE UNITED STATES?

The rise of China and the U.S. pivot to the Asia-Pacific implies a relative decline in Europe's significance to the United States. Indeed, much of the controversy over the initial use of the term "pivot" stemmed from the concerns of America's European allies over the prospect of abandonment and of those elements of the U.S. foreign policy establishment that seek to maintain strong transatlantic links. These concerns seemed borne out by announcements of U.S. military force rebalancing that would see troops cut in Europe, while new basing arrangements sprung up in Australia and elsewhere in the Pacific.

But to see Asia's rise and the U.S. "pivot" (now referred to as "rebalance") as coming at Europe's expense is misleading in two ways: Such a view wrongly undervalues Europe's importance in the international system and to the United States, and it ignores the consistency of Europe's grand strategic objectives with those of the United States.

First, the relative emphasis on Asia's rise discounts Europe's significance, which is considerable, both in absolute terms and relative to other regions. Europe is a major pole of the world economy. The common market of the 28 member states of the European Union (EU) constitutes the largest economy in the world, its U.S.$17.6 trillion gross domestic product (GDP) now slightly larger than that of the United States. Its nearly 510 million citizens give it a population well greater than the United States and smaller than only India and China.[1]

Militarily, the 25 European members of NATO collectively spend U.S.$283 billion on defense, figures far exceeding China's $90 billion or Russia's $53 billion annual totals. The countries of NATO Europe maintain more than two million troops under arms, slightly fewer than China but more than double the next largest non-NATO countries, India and Russia.[2] Qualitatively, European forces are among the most technologically advanced, well equipped, and highly trained in the world. With many European countries also having participated in recent EU and NATO military operations—including the NATO-led International Security Assistance Force (ISAF) in Afghanistan since 2003—European forces are also experienced.

To be sure, there are reasons to worry that Europe's material power may decline. But fears about the collapse of the Euro currency following the 2008 financial crisis have largely abated. While Europe's population is aging and slowly shrinking, its labor force is among the healthiest, best educated, and most highly skilled in the world. By any material standard, Europe remains an enormously significant region.

The significance of Europe's material power is even greater when considered in view of its integration with the United States. The United States and Europe are each other's most important economic partners. The transatlantic economy accounts for as much as U.S.$5 trillion in total commercial activity per year and employs up to 15 million workers on both continents. The United States and Europe are each other's greatest source and destination for foreign direct investment (FDI), together accounting for approximately two-thirds of all global FDI. U.S. firms invested $37 billion in China between 2000 and 2010, relegating China to 12th place as a single-country destination for U.S. FDI, behind Belgium, France, Germany, Switzerland, Ireland, the United Kingdom (UK), and the Netherlands. U.S. investment in the Netherlands alone was nine times more than in China during the decade 2000-10. Despite the financial crisis, U.S. and EU financial markets continue to account for over two-thirds of global banking assets; three-quarters of global financial services; and more than half of global stock market capitalization. A remarkable 93 percent of global foreign exchange holdings were in dollars (62.1 percent), euros (26.5 percent), or sterling (4.2 percent) in mid-2010.[3] No other economic relationship in the world is as intertwined or influential as the transatlantic economy.

The same is also true of the military and security ties between Europe and America. NATO is in a class of its own among military alliances. Not only do NATO countries account for roughly two-thirds of total world defense spending while enjoying quantitative and qualitative strengths in military personnel and equipment, but NATO provides a highly institutionalized mechanism for security cooperation among its members. A political decisionmaking process in the North Atlantic Council approves the design and implementation of the Alliance's "strategic concept," while an integrated military command structure provides for a standing multinational chain of command, and various NATO agencies facilitate common standards for doctrine, organization, training, and operations. Given its capacity to organize strategic ends and the ways and means to achieve those ends, NATO might even be considered as a strategic actor in its own right. More than 60 years of longevity accords a certain expectation of durability to this status.

The integration of material capabilities between Europe and America points to the second major reason why it is misleading to see Asia's rise and the U.S. "pivot" coming at Europe's expense: Europe contains the strongest and most likely partners in U.S. grand strategy. Europe and the United States remain aligned in their grand strategic objectives and are willing and able to work together to a remarkable degree. Liberal democracies on both sides of the Atlantic continue to share common interests in individual freedom and human rights, economic prosperity and development, democratic governance, security, and the rule of law. Europe and the United States will not always agree on the particulars of every issue, of course. But the broad general consensus on objectives makes Europe a natural grand strategic partner of the United States in the future just as it has been in the past. Europe's substantial material capabilities provide considerable incentives to continued cooperation, while the highly integrated economic and politico-military relationships between Europe and the United States offer proven ways of organizing partnered action. Seen as a rebalancing of strategic means rather than ends, the U.S. pivot toward Asia demonstrates more continuity than change: on the enduring questions of desired grand strategic ends, the United States and Europe remain consistent and largely united.

HOW IMPORTANT IS LANDPOWER IN EUROPE?

Europe's place in U.S. grand strategy has powerful implications for U.S. Landpower. Landpower is a defining consideration in European politico-military affairs. Europe's continental strategic geography dates at least to Charlemagne, whose 800 AD foundation of the Carolingian Empire united European lands under a single ruler for the first time since the fall of the Western Roman Empire three centuries earlier. Its division in 843 AD established the broad outlines of the monarchies of France and the Holy Roman Empire, and ultimately the modern Landpower nations of France and Germany. For nearly 300 years, the House of Habsburg battled to establish continental dominance against the Ottoman Turks in the 16th century, against the Reformation in the 17th century, against commercial and philosophical liberalism in the 18th century, and against the unification of a rival German national state in the 19th century.[4] In the meantime, Napoleon came closer than anyone since Charlemagne in unifying Europe, not only through conquest but through the continental system that sought to employ Landpower in the service of economics between 1806 and his first abdication in 1814.[5]

Noncontinental powers have found Landpower decisive in their efforts to influence modern European affairs. Britain's historic policy of opposing any bid for continental hegemony depended on the deployment of Landpower, often in concert with allies, in the most crucial moments. While Napoleon met his demise at Waterloo against the combined forces of Wellington, Blücher, and others, the absence of British forces in Belgium a century later influenced Germany's strategic miscalculation in 1914.[6] The ensuing stalemate on the Western Front of World War I ultimately came to an end following the commitment of U.S. Landpower in Europe after 1917, and the war's consequences were measured in terms of their destruction of four monarchical land empires—German, Austro-Hungarian, Ottoman, and Russian. The withdrawal of U.S. and British land forces after the Great War reduced the risk to Hitler's remilitarization programs and left the Western powers fewer options to counter his expansion in the 1930s prior to the outbreak of general war. A reapplication of Landpower then decided the outcome to the European theater in World War II: Despite the punishing impact of strategic bombing and the vitality of maritime power in bringing U.S. resources to the continent, the land forces of the Soviet Union inflicted more than two-thirds of German losses, and the war ended only with the physical occupation of Germany by British, French, Soviet, and U.S. troops.[7]

The maintenance of strong Landpower commitments underpinned the tense but stable balance of power after the war. The Iron Curtain that descended across Europe after 1945 defined the battle lines of the Cold War and was a direct result of the Landpower situation at the end of World War II. Following the Cold War, the enlargement of NATO and the EU were among the most important instruments in creating a continental "Europe whole and free."[8] Even today, Landpower remains central to contemporary European political and economic life. However, noncontinental Britain remains outside two of the most significant features of the EU: the Euro common currency and the Schengen Agreement that allows passport-free travel across national borders.

The role of U.S. Landpower's consistent application as a contributor to peace and stability in Europe should not be taken for granted. Many of the same ingredients that historically have destabilized Europe persist today. Unresolved disputes and frozen conflicts in the region continue in Cyprus, Kosovo, Transnistria, Nagorno-Karabakh, Armenian-Turkish relations, and Greek complaints with (the former Yugoslav republic of) Macedonia. Ethno-linguistic differences lingering from Russification policies in the former Soviet Union loom in the Baltic states, Ukraine, the Caucasus, and others.

Europe's frontiers remain prone to more open conflict. In the past decade, war in the Middle East has twice bordered NATO territory in Turkey, leading the Alliance to deploy additional land forces there in the lead-up to the Iraq War in 2003 and during the Syrian Civil War following the shooting down of a Turkish jet and the shelling of Turkish territory by Syrian forces in 2012.[9] The revolutions of the "Arab Spring" beginning in 2010 have contributed to violence and instability across the Mediterranean in North Africa, where European and/or U.S. forces have since intervened in Libya, Mali, Niger, and the Central African Republic.[10]

Europe's risk of great power competition and conflict also remains real. The Cold War may be over, but that was not the end of history. Russia remains an enormously important country with vital interests in Europe. Russia is the largest country in the world by land area, possessed of territory stretching across nine time zones, the world's largest arsenal of nuclear weapons,[11] and an advanced conventional armaments industry. It is the second largest global producer of oil and of natural gas,[12] and is a major supplier to Europe.[13] Russia's leading political figure since the Cold War, Vladimir Putin, has sought to reestablish Russia's regional influence and has spearheaded such initiatives as the Collective Security Treaty Organization and Shanghai Cooperation Organization as multilateral alternatives to Western institutions like the Partnership for Peace and Organization for Security and Cooperation in Europe. More significant is Russia's demonstrated willingness to use force unilaterally. Russia invaded Georgia, its neighbor and a former Soviet republic, in 2008 following several years of Georgian overtures toward the EU and NATO. The United States transported Georgian troops home from their participation in the Iraq War coalition but otherwise avoided direct intervention in the conflict. Russian troops, deployed ostensibly to protect Russian minorities in the Georgian regions of Abkhazia and South Ossetia, still occupy these regions. Russia's relations with Ukraine appear to be following the model of Georgia. Following Ukraine's apparent turn toward Western-style democracy after the "Orange Revolution" in 2005, Russia twice disrupted natural gas flows to Ukraine, in 2006 and 2009, putting significant pressure on Ukraine and causing cascading shortages in the EU. Russia's 2014 invasion of Ukraine, home to Russia's Black Sea naval fleet at Sebastopol, also involved a justification of protecting ethnic Russian minorities in the Crimea. Ukraine is the largest country by land area wholly within Europe, and it borders four NATO members.[14]

ISSUES IN U.S. GRAND STRATEGY AND LAND-POWER IN EUROPE: NATO AND BASES

The most pressing issues, then, affecting Europe's place in American grand strategy with implications for Landpower are the futures of NATO and of U.S. military bases in Europe. There are strong reasons to believe that NATO's future is secure. Although U.S. forces in Europe are set to decline, there are strong arguments for maintaining bases there.

The Once and Future NATO (?):
Keeping Russia Out and Germany Down.

The future of NATO is promising because the underlying strategic aims of the Alliance remain sound. The memorable formulation of NATO's first Secretary General Lord Hastings Lionel Ismay on the Alliance's central purposes — to keep the Americans in, the Russians out, and the Germans down — still resonate for Europe today.[15] American involvement provides Europe with security at low cost, while America retains influence on the strategically important continent and proximity to other regions of interest. Russia's illiberalism, heavy-handedness with neighbors, as well as its support for undemocratic regimes in other regions (e.g., Syria) are of strategic concern to both Europe and the United States. The German question has been the central European Landpower issue since unification in 1871.[16] After 150 years and two world wars, the role of this large and powerful country at the heart of the continent remains an important concern for Germany itself, as well as its neighbors. America's security guarantee in NATO was instrumental in setting the conditions for Franco-German rapprochement and the leadership of those two states in European integration since the 1950s. As economic and monetary union and the financial crisis have increasingly pushed Germany to a position of greater leadership within the EU, a strong NATO militates against renewed concern in Europe about German power, while also increasing Germany's own confidence in assuming the leadership role appropriate for the continent's greatest Landpower by population and economy.

NATO In Afghanistan.

The continuing relevance of the Alliance's strategic rationale is the greatest reason to expect its continuing endurance, despite some post-Cold War predictions of its demise and more recent concerns that NATO's fate might be tied to the outcome of the war in Afghanistan. After all, its command of the ISAF in Afghanistan, starting in 2003 and set to end in 2014, has been the most ambitious military operation in NATO's history.[17] NATO's involvement in Afghanistan began as a direct consequence of Alliance politics following the terrorist attacks of September 11, 2001 (9/11). NATO promptly, and for the first time in its history, invoked its collective defense clause — Article V of the North

Atlantic Treaty—committing the Alliance to treat the 9/11 attack on the United States as an attack upon all. But the United States largely rebuffed NATO in its initial responses and invasion of Afghanistan, having concluded following the 1999 Kosovo air campaign that an ad hoc coalition would be more expedient than working through NATO.[18] The United States turned to NATO for assistance in Afghanistan 2 years later as it shifted its own resources to the invasion of Iraq. European allies that opposed the Iraq war but were already participating in the United Nations-mandated ISAF saw NATO's assumption of that mission in Afghanistan as a low-cost way to curry favor with the United States.

At the same time, NATO members lacked consensus on the purpose of the ISAF mission. Initially limited to peacekeeping in Kabul area in 2003, this mission expanded to cover the entire country and the full range of military operations by the end of the year 2006. Countries that had justified participation on peacekeeping or humanitarian grounds to their domestic audiences found these developments difficult to explain. This gave rise to a complex web of so-called national "caveats" on the use of force in Afghanistan: the NATO-led chain of command was nominally in charge, but many countries caveated their participation such that their forces were prohibited from certain kinds of operations. The result was often that countries conducted independent and largely uncoordinated campaigns in different parts of the country: for example, the British in Helmand province, Germans in Kunduz in the north, Italians in the east, Turks often in Kabul, and Americans in the east. Violence skyrocketed in Afghanistan following the NATO/ISAF assumption of responsibility throughout the country in 2006. Inefficiencies notwithstanding, the effort also suffered from a poverty of resources, as NATO force levels in much of the country were lower than what they had been during the preceding U.S.-led Operation ENDURING FREEDOM. Ultimately, the United States decided to increase dramatically its presence in Afghanistan after 2009, effectively Americanizing the NATO effort under the command of Generals Stanley McChrystal and David Petraeus.

Afghanistan revealed significant problems of burden sharing, national caveats on the use of forces, and other matters that make NATO less likely to undertake large-scale expeditionary military operations of the Afghanistan sort for the foreseeable future. The conflict in Afghanistan also helped reveal the factionalization of NATO's membership since its enlargement to 28 members since the end of the Cold War. Longstanding Western European NATO members have cut defense budgets amid economic concerns, while newer members in Eastern Europe remain concerned about territorial security risks, especially following the 2008 Russian invasion of Georgia. Meanwhile, the capabilities gap between Europe and the United States has widened to a point greater than at any time since the early Cold War era.[19]

But these problems of strategic ways and means do not undermine the potential for cooperation emanating from consensus over strategic ends. NATO is already moving beyond its experiment in Afghanistan. At its Lisbon Summit in 2010, NATO adopted a new Strategic Concept that declared its core tasks to be collective defense, crisis management, and "cooperative security" (i.e., political and military partnership). NATO confirmed its role as the institution of choice for organizing the limited military intervention in

Libya from February to October 2011. It has also pursued naval and counterpiracy operations off the Horn of Africa and the Gulf of Aden, a training mission in Iraq, and advisory assistance to the African Union, among others. At Chicago in 2012, NATO leaders recommitted to a winding down of the ISAF mission by 2014, while maintaining a longer-term political promise and also went on to address wide-ranging regional and global security concerns in a 65 point statement. NATO also embarked on a cost saving reduction of its integrated military command structure and promoted a "Smart Defence" initiative for states to cooperate and create efficiency in their force structure planning and equipment acquisitions.

NATO after Afghanistan.

NATO after Afghanistan therefore appears set to continue two seemingly contradictory trends: one regional and conservative, the other increasingly global and innovative. Both will be shaped not only by the last decade's experience in Afghanistan, but also by the widening gap in capabilities between the United States and its allies, as well as downward pressure on defense budgets across the Alliance.

First, NATO increasingly will emphasize its traditional purpose of territorial defense in Europe. This reflects a chastened appetite for large scale expeditionary operations like those in Afghanistan. It also reflects the maturing role of Eastern European NATO members, many of which joined the Alliance during the Afghanistan era but which value membership primarily as a guarantee against Russia.

Second, NATO will sustain an increasingly extra-regional or global outlook despite reduced likelihood of large-scale expeditionary operations. NATO's entry into niche areas such as cyber and missile defense contribute to this trend, as does the continued development of global partnerships with countries outside NATO's core Euro-Atlantic area. Even the concern of Eastern European NATO members regarding Russia requires some focus on the near-abroad. Budget concerns will keep the scale of these activities small, however.

NATO will continue to cultivate and leverage the global partnerships it built since the end of the Cold War and especially during the last decade. This reflects the willingness and capacity of non-NATO countries to partner with NATO or submit to its procedures, as Australia, South Korea, and more than 18 others have done in Afghanistan. It also represents a continuing ambition for NATO to assume modest, limited expeditionary operations such as its bombing campaign in Libya and counterpiracy efforts off the Horn of Africa. Future NATO initiatives are less likely to involve the unanimous participation of all members, and more likely to involve ad hoc coalitions within the Alliance and in concert with non-Alliance member countries. NATO's standards and procedures will continue to provide the common multinational framework into which members and partners alike interoperate in a "plug-and-play" fashion. Leading European states may turn to NATO both for this common framework and to access U.S. capabilities, as the UK and France did in Libya.

In reference to U.S. grand strategy, both trends in NATO—the regional and the expeditionary—serve American interests: a renewed emphasis on European security serves U.S. interests in that important region, while cultivation of NATO's expeditionary capabilities operationalizes European strategic means in ways that can serve mutually beneficial ends.

U.S. MILITARY BASES IN EUROPE

After the future of NATO, the status of permanent U.S. military bases in Europe is the next most important grand strategic issue with implications for Landpower. America's European bases have seen three major rounds of cuts during the last 25 years: The first was a result of the end of the Cold War and the success of arms control agreements such as the Conventional Forces in Europe treaty; the second was a result of the U.S. military's "transformation" efforts in the early-2000s, the wars in Iraq and Afghanistan, and transatlantic tensions during the George W. Bush administration; and the third is ongoing, as part of the post-Iraq drawdown and pivot toward the Asia-Pacific. Cold War U.S. force levels in Europe peaked at 425,000 just before the Berlin Crisis of 1958, declined during Vietnam and then leveled at just above 300,000 during the 1980s. The first post-Cold War reduction saw a two-thirds decrease to just above 100,000 troops. These levels declined by about one-quarter to 75,000 after 2003. Further force reductions announced in 2012 would reduce total U.S. forces by another one-quarter, and would reduce the size of the U.S. Army in Europe to approximately 30,000 troops.[20]

While many of these cuts were sensible, there are important reasons to consider maintaining permanent U.S. bases in Europe. On a continent where Landpower is so important, the presence of U.S. land forces demonstrates U.S. credibility and commitment to the transatlantic Alliance. They are, in other words, an important strategic means to support an important strategic end: peace and stability in Europe. One hundred years since World War I, the historical lesson of the U.S. failure to remain actively engaged in European security should not be forgotten. Sixty years since the end of World War II, the success of U.S. efforts to prevent another general European war is also noteworthy. Persistent American Landpower in Europe was an essential ingredient in winning the peace after 1945 and sustaining peace through the Cold War, the Balkan crises of the 1990s, and into the 21st century.

Furthermore, U.S. bases are important for facilitating combined training with European forces, building capacity, and maintaining capability for future combined operations. Habitual relations among European-based U.S. forces and their local counterparts allow forces to implement interoperable doctrine and develop standard operating procedures for efficient and effective interoperability. Combined training areas such as the U.S.-operated Joint Multinational Readiness Center in Germany allow tactical formations to conduct small and large unit training. U.S. presence at European headquarters such as Supreme Headquarters Allied Powers Europe in Mons, Belgium, and Southern European Task Force (Airborne, U.S. Army) in Vicenza, Italy, allows U.S. forces to plan military operations and to integrate more fully with other instruments of national power.

Europe's geographic proximity to other regions of interest to the United States — particularly the Middle East — further argues for the maintenance of U.S. bases in Europe. In the 1990-91 Gulf War, U.S. deployments to the Persian Gulf largely flowed through Europe and were built around the Cold War-era plans for the reinforcement of NATO forces along the inter-German border (the so-called REFORGER exercises).

In the Afghanistan and Iraq conflicts since 2001, U.S. bases in Europe have provided important logistical and training areas, as well as a vital medical waypoint for wounded service members evacuated from the combat theaters. The distance between Iraq and the U.S. Army's Landstuhl Regional Medical Center in Germany — the largest military medical center outside of the United States — is less than half the distance to the Walter Reed National Military Medical Center in Maryland or any other in North America.

A difficult-to-quantify but noteworthy implication of sustained U.S. bases in Europe is the potential for the cultivation of personal relationships, civil-military exchange, and cross-cultural understanding. Social liberals cite the popularity of transatlantic study abroad programs (in 2009-10, more than 188,000 students from the United States and EU studied abroad on the other side of the Atlantic[21]) and tourist volumes (more than 10 million EU tourists in the United States in 2010[22]) as evidence of close transatlantic ties. The millions of U.S. troops and their families based in Europe since World War II contributed to this impact, due not only to their numbers, but also to the fact that many of these Americans lived in Europe for several years. Forward basing of U.S. troops in Europe also has a practical military training value insofar as soldiers practice cross-cultural competences, an essential qualification for modern warfare, which frequently involves cooperation with multinational forces and local host nation populations.

EUROPE AND LANDPOWER: ENDURING FEATURES OF U.S. GRAND STRATEGY

Balance is an important consideration in grand strategy. U.S. grand strategy weighs global interests and objectives and employs a variety of military and nonmilitary instruments of national power as means. There is a sensible rationale for the rebalance of means to the Asia-Pacific and for the thoughtful uses of air and maritime power, as well as the sizeable U.S. economic, diplomatic, informational, and cultural capabilities. But there are also sound reasons to maintain a considerable focus on the importance of Europe, Landpower, and their combination with one another. Europe is one of the most important regions of the world in its own right, and its fortunes are integrated with those of the United States to a remarkable degree through economic, military, and institutional ties. Shared interests make Europe and the United States natural and mutually beneficial grand strategic partners. The history of European politico-military affairs is largely a history of Landpower, and there are important indicators that familiar historical patterns persist. These patterns should make U.S. leaders confident that their Landpower commitments have contributed to European peace and stability, but they should also make U.S. leaders cautious about overestimating that stability in the absence of U.S. commitment. In appreciation of the importance of Europe and Landpower there, U.S. grand strategy should accord continued attention to the maintenance of a strong NATO and permanent U.S. military bases in the region.

ENDNOTES - CHAPTER 15

1. See *europa.eu/about-eu/facts-figures/economy/index_en.htm*.

2. See *www.nato.int/nato_static/assets/pdf/pdf_2012_04/20120413 _PR_CP_2012_047_rev1.pdf*; International Institute for Strategic Studies, *The Military Balance*, 2012.

3. See *transatlantic.sais-jhu.edu/publications/books/Transatlantic _Economy_2011/te_2011.pdf*.

4. A. J. P. Taylor, *The Habsburg Monarchy, 1809-1918: A History of the Austrian Empire and Austria-Hungary*, Chicago: University of Chicago Press, 1948, p. 10.

5. See, for example, Norman Davies, *Europe: A History*, New York: Oxford University Press, 1996; Paul Kennedy, *The Rise and Fall of the Great Powers*, New York: Random House, 1987.

6. See, for example, Sidney Bradshaw Fay, *The Origins of the World War*, Vol. 1, New York: Macmillan, 1928, pp. 42, 204.

7. Casualty data varies widely, with some crediting the Eastern Front with up to three-quarters of German losses during the war. A recent statistical study places the figure closer to two-thirds: Rüdiger Overmans, *Deutsche militärische Verluste im Zweiten Weltkrieg (German Military Casualties in the Second World War)*, Munich, Germany: Oldenbourg Verlag, 2000.

8. George H. W. Bush, Remarks by the President of the United States to the Citizens in Mainz, Rheingoldhalle, Mainz, Federal Republic of Germany, May 31, 1989.

9. See *www.nato.int/cps/en/natolive/topics_92555.htm?*

10. See *www.eeas.europa.eu/csdp/missions-and-operations/*.

11. See *www.sipri.org/yearbook/2013/files/sipri-yearbook-2013-cha pter-6-overview*.

12. See *www.iea.org/publications/freepublications/publication/Key World2013.pdf*.

13. See *www.bbc.com/news/world-europe-26436291;* and *epp. eurostat.ec.europa.eu/statistics_explained/index.php/Energy_production_and_imports.*

14. Russia and Turkey are larger but have the bulk of their land areas in Asia.

15. Jaap de Hoop Scheffer, "A Transforming Alliance," Speech by the Secretary General of NATO, Cambridge Union Society, Cambridge, England, February 2, 2005.

16. See, for example, Wilhelm Röpke, *Die Deutsche Frage* (*The German Question*), Erlenbach-Zürich, Switzerland: E. Rentsch, 1945; David Calleo, *The German Problem Reconsidered: Germany and the World Order, 1870 to the Present*, New York: Cambridge University Press, 1978.

17. Afghanistan stretched NATO's institutional competencies in three important ways. First, operations in Afghanistan represented the first major land combat operation the Alliance had ever undertaken. Second, it was undertaken outside of NATO's traditional Euro-Atlantic geographic area. Third, NATO integrated many nonmember partner countries into the effort.

18. Ellen Hallams, *The United States and NATO since 9/11*, New York: Routledge, 2010, pp. 35-53.

19. See Robert M. Gates, "The Security and Defense Agenda, Future of NATO," Speech by the Secretary of Defense, Brussels, Belgium, June 10, 2011, available from *www.defense.gov/speeches/ speech.aspx?speechid=1581.*

20. *See www.eur.army.mil/news/2012/transformation/force-posture /02162011-dod-announces-plan-to-adjust-posture-of-landforces-in-europe.htm;* and Jordan Becker, "Offshore Balancing or Overbalancing? A Preliminary Empirical Analysis of the Effect of U.S. Troop-Presence on the Political Behavior of Regional Partners,"Chap. 14in this volume.

21. See *www.euintheus.org/what-we-do/eu-us-facts-figures/.*

22. *Ibid.*

CHAPTER 16

PREVENT, SHAPE, WIN IN CONTEXT: THE ASIA-PACIFIC

Albert S. Willner

The author is indebted to his Center for Naval Analyses (CNA) colleagues Dr. Tom Bickford, Dr. Alison Kaufman, Dr. Joel Wuthnow, Dr. David Finkelstein and Ms. Tamara Hemphill. Their U.S. Army in Asia research insights proved invaluable. Some of the concepts discussed in this paper are elaborated on in Joel Wuthnow et al, *The U.S. Army in Asia: Opportunities and Challenges – Report of a Workshop of Experts* (Alexandria: VA, CNA, August 2013) and forthcoming CNA reports on related topics.

The U.S. rebalance toward the Asia-Pacific region, officially announced by the Barack Obama administration in January 2012, has important implications for the role of Landpower and the U.S. Army.[1] Commonly known as the *Defense Strategic Guidance* (DSG), it lays out the rebalance strategy which includes shifting the U.S. focus in the post Iraq-Afghanistan campaign environment to a greater emphasis on seizing opportunities and meeting challenges in Asia. This shift is designed to occur even as the United States maintains its ability to meet commitments in the Middle East and other regions.

Former U.S. National Security Advisor Tom Donilon elaborated on the administration's vision and strategy:

> . . . the overarching objective of the United States in the [Asia-Pacific] region is to sustain a stable security environment and a regional order rooted in eco-

nomic openness, peaceful resolution of disputes, and respect for universal rights and freedoms. To pursue this vision, the United States is implementing a comprehensive, multidimensional strategy: strengthening alliances; deepening partnerships with emerging powers; building a stable, productive, and constructive relationship with China; empowering regional institutions; and helping to build a regional economic architecture that can sustain shared prosperity. These are the pillars of the U.S. strategy. . . .[2]

This chapter discusses how the Asia-Pacific landscape is changing, the potential implications, and how the United States Army can support the U.S. rebalance to the Asia-Pacific region.

THE SETTING: THE ASIA-PACIFIC REGION

In order to develop an understanding of how the Army can best support the U.S. rebalance while meeting obligations elsewhere, it is important to outline some issues for consideration:

- First, in terms of potential conflict, the North Korean challenge continues to be the dominant and most pressing one for the United States and its key allies and partners. The outbreak of hostilities on the Korean peninsula could potentially involve three nuclear powers and would have dramatic consequences throughout the region. U.S. alliance commitments to the Republic of Korea and Japan to deter and defend will continue to require critical U.S. military attention in order to keep peace and maintain stability on and around the Korean peninsula.
- Second, the rise of China has enormous consequences for the United States, the region, and the world. The United States is commit-

ted in part to building a cooperative bilateral military-to-military relationship in a way that is mutually beneficial and contributes to peace and stability in the region. New opportunities to advance the defense relationship will be important to develop and, if successful, are likely to have far reaching positive consequences.

- Third, due in part to the rise of China and changing power dynamics in the region, U.S. alliance partners—Japan, the Republic of Korea, Australia, Thailand, and the Philippines—and others are rebalancing as well to meet the changing economic and security environment. Understanding and taking into account their changing perspectives and efforts is critical to meeting the objectives of the U.S. rebalance.

- Fourth, the potential for large-scale interstate land wars in Asia appears to be receding. Although India-Pakistan and China-India land conflicts remain possibilities, only on the Korean peninsula is there the potential for a significant U.S. Army ground force engagement. As the likelihood of ground war in the Asia-Pacific region declines, states are likely to shift their strategic perspectives and defense requirements.

- Fifth, domestic and transnational challenges such as terrorism, insurgency, disasters, pandemics, piracy, narcotics, and human trafficking will require Asia-Pacific governments to devote greater attention and resources to internal defense and other ways of dealing with these security threats. This has important implications for how the United States will need to engage and understand the changing needs of the region.

- Sixth, in the past decade, for several Asia-Pacific states, economic and security issues in the maritime domain have led to a shift in attention and resources away from a traditional Landpower focus. This shift to the maritime has important implications for the U.S. military. In particular, U.S. Landpower leaders must consider how best to secure important land assets that are important to securing the maritime domain.
- Seventh, other powers of consequence are rising, most notably India and Indonesia, potentially opening up new opportunities for the United States. The U.S. military can play an important role in working with its counterparts to address common security interests in the region.
- Eighth, beyond the Republic of Korea and Okinawa in Japan, the willingness of states in the region to accept the basing of large numbers of U.S. ground forces on their soil appears unlikely in the near term. Maintaining a smaller footprint has implications for rotational and temporary deployments and perhaps a greater emphasis on engaging key states to preposition equipment offshore.
- Finally, regional institutions in Asia are playing a greater role in the development of international rules and norms, communication, and influence. Interactions with key allies and partners within these institutions are likely to become more important in meeting shared interests.

For the Army to properly support the rebalance to Asia, leaders must first endeavor to understand the interests and changing desires of other players in the region—most importantly those of key allies, partners, and potential adversaries. While the items listed previously are not a comprehensive list of areas of concern, these issues highlight the need to reengage with and appreciate the domestic pressures and strategic perspectives of key states, and the potential implications for the United States and its military in the region.

What the Army can likely sustain should, in part, influence how the Army rebalances to Asia. The global demand signal for Army capabilities and engagement remains high—clearly, the U.S. Army cannot be all things to all armies. It is no surprise, particularly in an era of dwindling resources and competing requirements, that intra- and inter-regional prioritization in a joint and combined context will be needed. Within the Asia-Pacific region, some are already asking whether the United States will be able to keep its rebalance commitment over the long term. As individual Asia-Pacific governments deal with a host of domestic and international challenges, their evolving perceptions of the U.S. commitment will likely influence significantly the strategic direction they decide to take.

SUPPORTING THE REBALANCE

U.S. national security obligations around the globe will test Asia-Pacific commitments. As the Army is pulled in multiple directions, it will be challenged to make meaningful and sustainable choices within the region. How, then, does the U.S. Army rebalance to Asia and what must leaders consider as it continues meeting national security obligations in other regions, particularly the Middle East? How does the Army effectively support key allies and partners? The rebalance to the Asia-Pacific region deserves a comprehensive Army plan in order to balance competing demands against regional security priorities. The following is offered as a starting point.

Maintain the Ability to Deter and Defeat Aggression.

While this seems fairly straightforward, the Army's ability to partner in both a joint and combined context is critical not only to meeting U.S. interests, but in reassuring allies and partners as well. U.S. Landpower forces, to include the Army, Marines, and Special Operations, often offer a visible and potent reminder of U.S. commitment and power. In places like the Republic of Korea, Japan, and the Philippines, for example, U.S. Landpower's contribution to deterrence and defense cannot be underestimated and deserves to be reiterated. Less visible perhaps is the Army's enduring contribution to setting the theater for others to deter and defeat potential adversaries. Missile defense, strategic communications, and logistics infrastructure capabilities are all examples of how the Army fulfills its enabling role. Even in a primarily air or maritime conflict, the U.S. military and others in the Asia-Pacific region are reliant on Army capabilities, particularly should operations take place over an extended duration.

Support Department of Defense (DoD) Efforts to Develop a Deeper U.S.-China Military Dialogue.

One of the pillars of the rebalance is to build a stable, productive, and constructive relationship with China. Bilateral exchanges between senior civilian and military leaders, a recently completed humanitarian assistance table top exercise, and multiple interactions in the Gulf of Aden between the United States, China, and others all have contributed to deepening the dialogue. The Army, through its mature institutional and functional area exchange program, is well positioned to further develop links to the Chinese military that are mutually beneficial and contribute to peace and stability in the region. China Foreign Area Officers (FAOs) are potentially a significant strategic multiplier for the United States, and selecting and retaining the right officers will be important to advancing dialogue with the Chinese military.

Redefine Forward Presence.

The Army's forward presence has historically been a key component in building and maintaining relationships with key allies and partners—in Asia, it has been doing so for over a century. As the United States rebalances to and within the Asia-Pacific region, however, its units and individuals will be interacting with countries and populations that have little appetite for a large U.S. presence on the ground. Making the Army's presence known and relevant will require revisiting traditional models of engagement. It may be necessary to 1) reprioritize rotational or temporary deployments and exercises in line with the DSG; 2) revisit where to focus institutional exchanges aimed at promoting alliance and emerging partners; 3) work with other U.S. services to limit unneeded and costly redundancies; and 4) rethink how Army attachés, security assistance, and liaison officers stationed in country can better meet DoD, U.S. Pacific Command (PACOM), and Army rebalance priorities.

Build and Retain Country and Regional Expertise.

Individual states in the Asia-Pacific region are undergoing significant changes that could affect U.S. interests dramatically. Understanding their domestic situations and their bilateral and multilateral relationships are of paramount importance. The Army may want to consider what adjustments need to be made to better develop and sustain broad language, cultural, and security expertise, all of which will be relevant for the long term. Repetitive regionally aligned assignments—to PACOM, to United States Army, Pacific (USARPAC), or DoD or joint positions in Washington and abroad, if managed well, can enhance the Army and joint community's understanding of the changing dynamics in the region. The Army FAO program should be reexamined. Is the current structure for developing and assigning highly skilled and peak performing FAOs aligned properly with rebalance and Asia-Pacific country priorities? Is the Army developing FAOs in a way that best supports combatant commanders in engaging key allies and partners? Is the Army retaining and promoting the right FAOs needed to support the rebalance and U.S. national policy objectives?

Determine Troops to Task Costs.

There are likely more tasks implied by the rebalance than there are troops to commit. Regionally aligned forces will only partially meet the demands of allies and partners in the region. Part of the Army's ability to successfully support the rebalance will probably depend on the ability to reach back to U.S. based units and individual soldiers — active, National Guard, and Reserve. One consideration may be focusing designated units for repetitive exchanges with key allies and partners to provide greater exposure and create opportunities to build more resilient relationships in country.

Reinforce and Highlight Combat Capability.

Army combat experience gained in Afghanistan and Iraq is likely to be of particular interest to key allies and partners. A focused effort that sends midgrade combat veterans, officers, and noncommissioned officers out to engage in a way that reinforces perceptions of U.S. capability and military-to-military cooperation may prove of value. The Army, along with the Marines, is especially well positioned to pass warfighting lessons learned on to those in the Asia-Pacific region facing their own counterterrorism or insurgent threats.

Revisit Partner Capacity Requirements in the Region.

The rebalance, coupled with declining resources, means that the Army's capacity will be stretched. Building partner capacity will be important to mitigating risk. Assessing key allies and partners changing needs and will and matching these against U.S. requirements will be an important first step in getting the right mix needed to advance common security interests. In some cases, even a small partner contribution may yield important benefits in advancing an important relationship.

Maximize Opportunities that an Army 4-Star Brings to the Region.

The 2013 elevation to the rank of general for the Commander, United States Army, Pacific, means that the United States and the Army will have a new leader well positioned to advance joint and combined engagement, exercise, command, control, and coordination initiatives of importance. In a region where the majority of countries' top uniformed military leaders are Army, this change has the potential to dramatically enhance PACOM and Army objectives among key leaders in key states.

CONCLUSION

The U.S. rebalance toward the Asia-Pacific region presents tremendous opportunities and challenges for the U.S. Army. Successfully implementing the rebalance in a diverse and complex strategic environment will not only require understanding U.S. intent and objectives, but those of key states in the region. As Donilon commented, "rebalancing means devoting the time, effort and resources necessary to get each [pillar of the strategy] right."[3] It is hoped that this chapter contributes to that endeavor.

ENDNOTES - CHAPTER 16

1. *Sustaining U.S. Global Leadership: Priorities for 21st Century Defense*, Washington, DC: U.S. Department of Defense, January 2012, available from *www.defense.gov/news/Defense_Strategic_Guidance.pdf.*

2. "Remarks by Tom Donilon, National Security Advisor to the President: 'The United States and the Asia-Pacific in 2013'," The Asia Society, New York, March 11, 2013, available from *www.whitehouse.gov/the-press-office/2013/03/11/remarks-tom-donilon-national-security-advisory-president-united-states-a.*

3. *Ibid.*

CHAPTER 17

PIVOTING WITHOUT STUMBLING IN ASIA

Joseph Da Silva
Douglas Ollivant

Air-Sea Battle (ASB) has been the topic of much discussion since the Barack Obama administration's announcements in 2010 of a strategic rebalance (popularly known as the "pivot") toward the Asia-Pacific region. The ASB concept envisions a combined Air Force and Navy team overcoming the anti-access (preventing an opponent from entering one's territory) and area denial (limiting an opponent's mobility once inside your territory) strategies (A2/AD) of potential adversaries. Since 2010, many policymakers have hailed ASB as the new paradigm of future warfare.[1] Andrew Krepinevich, one of the originators of the ASB concept, maintains that Air-Sea Battle is:

> focused less on repelling traditional cross-border invasions, effecting regime change, and conducting large-scale stability operations . . . and more on preserving access to key regions and the global commons, which are essential to U.S. security and prosperity.[2]

Air-Sea Battle is particularly important as the United States looks to the Pacific, say its supporters, since it can deter China from pursuing territorial expansion while reassuring U.S. allies of our commitment to their defense and, by extension, to regional stability. While many proponents of Air-Sea Battle (including the Navy and Air Force's Air-Sea Battle Office, created in 2011) claim that ASB is an operational concept rather than a strategy (perhaps in response to critiques of ASB as a strategy), it is clear that other proponents think of ASB in larger terms.[3]

A successful Pacific strategy against an emerging power, however, must accomplish two basic tasks. First, it must engage China in order to encourage its ongoing emergence within the international community as a responsible and prosperous stakeholder. Second, it must balance against Chinese territorial expansion through responsible and effective deterrence. To this end, Aaron Friedberg has suggested that:

> The engagement half of this strategy has been geared toward enmeshing China in global trade and international institutions, discouraging it from challenging the status quo, and giving it incentives to become what the George W. Bush administration termed a 'responsible stakeholder' in the existing international system. The other half of Washington's China strategy, the balancing half, has looked to maintain stability and deter aggression or attempts at coercion while engagement works its magic.[4]

We suggest that while ASB may serve as an effective operational concept in solving the A2/AD problem, it fails as a strategic concept for at least four reasons. Air-Sea Battle fails to effectively deter China, does not reassure U.S. allies in the region, exacerbates the security dilemma and thereby hinders engagement, and puts the United States on the wrong side of an economic cost equation.

HISTORY OF THE REBALANCE AND AIR- SEA BATTLE

The present prevalence of ASB cannot be understood apart from the decision to rebalance toward the Pacific; however, the genesis of ASB predates U.S.

strategic reorientation. The origins of the concept can be traced back to at least the mid-1990s and the Office of Net Assessment under Andrew Marshall. Marshall began his career as a nuclear strategist in the 1950s and in 1973 became the first (and so far, only) director of the Pentagon's Office of Net Assessment (ONA), a group tasked to search for potential threats to U.S. dominance.[5] Marshall's office ran a series of war game scenarios in the Asia-Pacific region that looked at potential challenges to U.S. dominance in the world. From ONA's viewpoint, the main challenger turned out to be a rising China which had invested large amounts of money in A2/AD capabilities to thwart U.S. offensive capabilities. In 2009, the Obama administration formed a China Integration team, based primarily around the Navy and Air Force, whose task was to look at how the United States could improve its capabilities in a potential conflict against China.[6] The results of their findings found their way into the 2010 U.S. Department of Defense *Quadrennial Defense Review*, which directed the Navy and Air Force to "develop a joint air-sea battle concept . . . for defeating adversaries across the range of military operations, including adversaries equipped with sophisticated anti-access and area denial capabilities."[7]

Air-Sea Battle rose to prominence as the United States began to draw down its wars in the Middle East and openly discussed its intention to reorient toward the Asia-Pacific region. Then-Secretary of State Hillary Clinton announced the new focus of U.S. strategy in January 2010: "One of the most important tasks of American statecraft over the next decade will be to lock in a substantially increased investment—diplomatic, economic, strategic, and otherwise—in the Asia-Pacific region."[8] This new strategy, which quickly became popularized as "the pivot," would proceed along six lines of action:

> strengthening bilateral security alliances, deepening our working relationships with emerging powers, including with China, engaging with regional multi-lateral institutions, expanding trade and investment, forging a broad-based military presence, and advancing democracy and human rights.[9]

While the new strategy intended to increase investments along diplomatic, economic, and military efforts, the diplomatic leg was to be the largest and leading element. However, as with many policies, the sequencing and timing of these lines of action has proven problematic, as has the intended emphasis on diplomacy. Soon after the pivot was announced, many think tanks and defense intellectuals began to write about and publicize ideas about the military portion of the rebalancing strategy, as did a number of the services most affected.

In April 2010, the Center for Strategic and Budgetary Assessments (CSBA) published a 123-page report: *AirSea Battle: A Point-of-Departure Operational Concept*.[10] While technically the product of a private think tank, this report has been seen in many quarters as a statement of the Pentagon's military intentions toward China. In August 2011, the Pentagon announced the formation of the Air-Sea Battle Office, and in January 2012, the Chairman of the Joint Chiefs published the Joint Operational Assured Access Concept (JOAC) and nested ASB underneath its overarching operational framework.[11] Finally, in May 2013, the ASB office published the official document detailing the ASB concept: "Air-Sea Battle: Service Collaboration to Address Anti-Access & Area Denial Challenges."[12]

As the timeline, discussed previously, details, the ASB concept spanned 2 decades of development and is only now beginning to be finalized. One could argue, however, that ASB comes in two versions. There is a modest version, promoted (at least officially) by the Air-Sea Battle office, that seeks merely to collaborate to address the A2/AD challenge. This version can be—and often is—justified as prudential military planning. However, there is a stronger version, as in the CSBA paper, that promotes ASB as the primary venue through which China should be approached. It is this second version that seems to have captured the imagination and to which most responses are directed.

The rise of China poses a challenge to the United States' accustomed freedom of action in the Pacific. While the economic growth of China directly benefits the United States, U.S. strategists are concerned that China will transform its economic wealth into military power. Indeed, it seems to have already started. China's military budget grew an average of 9.7 percent a year between 2003 and 2012, and currently stands at an estimated $114 billion, though still just a fraction of U.S. defense spending.[13] These expenditures are of concern to the United States because China continues to invest in A2/AD technologies designed to keep the United States out of key areas in the Pacific and increase the zone of Chinese influence. This is the crux of the military problem in the Pacific: As China's wealth increases and its military expenditure grows, the military balance will begin to shift against the United States and in favor of the Chinese, empowering the Chinese to exert more authority over its neighbors and ultimately (albeit indirectly) against U. S. interests in the region. In short, the Chinese will be able to use both geographical proximity and (relatively) cheap

A2/AD systems to deny freedom of action to the U.S. military, and the U.S. Navy particularly.

The greatest immediate concern for the ASB proponents appears to be that the People's Liberation Army (PLA) might use its military force in a dispute over Taiwan.[14] A PLA attack on Taiwan might involve a preemptive strike on Japanese and forward-deployed U.S. forces. According to proponents of ASB, "the overall PLA strategy may be to inflict substantial losses on U.S. forces, lengthen U.S. operational timelines and highlight the United States' inability to defend its allies."[15] Once the PLA achieved this goal, it could assume the defense and deny U.S. forces access to the theater until the United States determined it would be too costly to undo.[16] In order to accomplish these ends, the Chinese would have to gain surprise and achieve a quick, decisive victory, as a longer campaign would favor the United States and its global logistics network. Because of this issue, the PLA would conduct a multiphase attack so as not to draw out the conflict. First, in the opening minutes of a conflict, the PLA would seek to render U.S. and allied forces "deaf, dumb, and blind," by destroying or degrading U.S. and allied intelligence, surveillance, and reconnaissance (ISR) capabilities.[17] Second, the PLA would conduct ballistic attacks launched from various platforms supplemented by air strikes on key U.S. forward air bases. These attacks would be designed to deny the United States the ability to generate combat power for a counterattack.[18] Next, the PLA would launch land-based anti-ship ballistic missiles (ASBM) and anti-ship cruise missiles (ASCM) against all major U.S. Navy and allied warships in order to raise the cost of the U.S. operation to unacceptable levels. Finally, the PLA could interdict U.S. and allied sea lines of communication throughout Southeast Asia and the Western Pacific in order to divert resources.[19] In essence, the PLA would deny the U.S. sanctuary from its forward bases in the Pacific, raise the costs of recovering the lost area, and ultimately abandon its desire to influence these areas of the Pacific.

ASB attempts to prevent that scenario by "developing networked, integrated forces capable of attacking-in-depth to disrupt, destroy, and defeat adversary forces."[20] Forces would be integrated from all domains — air, sea, land, and cyber — prior to entering theater. In the event of a PLA attack, U.S. and allied forces would attack initially to disrupt the PLA command, control, communications, computers, and ISR networks. These attacks would come from allied stealth bombers, submarines, and cyber weapons. The next phase would focus on destroying the PLA A2/AD platforms and weapon systems providing freedom of action.[21] Finally, the United States would defeat PLA-employed weapons post-launch, thus defending friendly forces from attack and allowing for U.S. sustained operations.[22] ASB advocates believe that once the United States and its allies have defeated PLA A2/AD and follow-on weapon systems, they will cease their actions because the cost of further escalation will be too great.

CRITIQUE OF AIR-SEA BATTLE

While ASB claims to be only an operational concept, it continually makes strategic promises that it falls short of delivering. ASB fails to deter China, lends itself to uncontrollable vertical escalation, exacerbates the security dilemma, and places the United States on the wrong side of the cost equation.

Failure to Deter.

ASB's fundamental claim is its ability to deter China and other adversaries from exerting military influence in the region. Deterrence is a form of coercive violence that, when used appropriately, convinces an adversary not to take a certain action. In order to exercise effective deterrence a state must demonstrate both the capability to carry out the threat and the resolve or commitment to carry through on the threat if needed. ASB fails to deter China because both halves of this equation are not fully demonstrated.

Air-Sea Battle relies, by its very nature, on sea-based platforms. U.S. naval assets have enjoyed an asymmetric technological advantage over potential adversaries arguably since the end of World War II, and certainly since the end of the Cold War. However, the rise of regional powers such as China, equipped with their own high-technology industries and capable of producing cutting-edge electronic consumer goods, means that the United States' asymmetric advantage is likely to diminish. U.S. military assets may continue to have an advantage in terms of degree, but they will no longer have an advantage in terms of kind. Missile technologies produced by the Chinese, for instance, may be inferior to American versions, but they will be good enough that if employed in mass against an inherently vulnerable target, they will have a high probability of hit and kill.

In the cyber realm, while relative capacities are untested — at least at the unclassified level — it is far from clear that U.S. cyber defenses will stand up to an attack by Chinese military or closely aligned civilian "hackers" or "cyber militias."[23] Again, much of the hardware that forms the Internet backbone is produced in China, and there may be inherent vulnerabilities built into the core that would give the Chinese, and not the United States, the asymmetric advantage.[24] In at least two of the key aspects of ASB—naval and cyber power—it is not clear that, should push come to shove, they would survive an initial Chinese attack.

Air-Sea Battle also suffers from issues of demonstrated resolve. U.S. warships and airpower can serve as powerful signals of military capacity. However, because ships and planes can quickly move both in and out of a region, they do not signal **resolve**. This is a fact that is not lost on the Chinese or U.S. allies in the region. While ASB could help to demonstrate one limited form of capability, it works inversely against attempts to signal resolve or commitment because of the inherently transient nature of air and sea power. At the end of the day, if the situation in the South China Sea grows too fraught, air and naval assets can easily be pulled back to the second island chain.

Escalation.

While ASB has gained some popularity in the United States, it is perceived very differently among our Pacific allies. While the Pacific allies definitely seek assurances of both hard security guarantees and softer diplomatic attention, Australia, one of our strongest regional allies, has expressed concern over combined interoperability in the ASB concept. In Australia, the debate has begun over whether to purchase new submarines that can reach the distances that would be called upon in an ASB concept or continue with the current line of submarines merely focused on Australian coastal defense.[25] In order for ASB to be successful, it must be interoperable with both the Japanese and Australian forces. Debate in both countries is raising concern about the effectiveness of ASB and its potential to escalate conflict needlessly.[26] Escalation is of great concern to the neighboring states that must live with the long-term consequences.

U.S. foreign policy in the Pacific must include a clear deterrence framework in which ASB (as a capability, not a strategy) is part of an escalation ladder that is transparent to adversaries and allies alike.[27] ASB appears to lend itself to very rapid vertical escalation—one single and particular aspect of power moving very quickly to more extreme levels. In this case, the vertical escalation involves the need to execute "kill chains" against all the nodes of PLA A2/AD defenses—launchers, sensors, networks, and command and control—in order to prevent their use against inherently vulnerable sea-based platforms. This involves an immediate attack against the sovereign soil of a nuclear-armed power.

The ASB concept also fails to guarantee strategic results, failing to reassure allies who cannot help but notice this fatal flaw. Thomas Schelling famously argued that "military strategy can no longer be thought of, as it could for some countries in some eras, as the science of military victory. It is now equally, if not more, the art of coercion, of intimidation, and deterrence."[28] ASB is an operational concept that aims at achieving a military victory, and then makes the assumption that this military victory will lead to strategic victory. Ultimately, the United States wants to return the international system back to stability after hostilities have ended, but there is no guarantee that China will in fact change or moderate its behavior when faced with in-depth attacks on its industrial heartland. ASB is notably silent on how the international system returns to a state of equilibrium on "the morning after."

Security Dilemma.

Additionally, ASB might exacerbate the "security dilemma." The security dilemma is a classic international relations concept, which holds that one state's steps to increase its own security decrease the security of others;[29] as other states begin to take steps to also increase their security, a "back-and-forth" contest, and potentially instability, results. The situation might seem unavoidable, but Robert Jervis correctly suggests that states can increase their security and avoid the dilemma *if* states can distinguish between offensive and defensive measures — that is, if there exist some sources of security that do not threaten the security of another state.[30]

It is this scenario that exists in Asia currently. China's A2/AD capabilities are inherently defensive in nature. Admittedly, offensive actions could be taken within this defensive umbrella; any weapon can be seen as offensive within its range. But A2/AD capabilities are not weapons a state would purchase to pursue strategies of enlargement or adventurism. The United States in turn responded with a concept designed around offensive weapons, platforms, and doctrine — ASB. The authors of ASB maintain that the United States has benign intentions in the region and claim that the Chinese are trying to shift the balance of power in the Pacific; the Chinese, of course, consider their own intentions benign and claim the United States poses a threat to its interests. From the perspective of the Chinese, violations of state sovereignty by the United States in Serbia, Iraq, and Libya create a disturbing precedent. China's key vital interests are the security of its borders, which have been invaded repeatedly over the centuries, and the protection of its industrial base. The introduction of an offensive military concept that includes the destruction of vast cities deep in China's industrial heartland should be expected to receive a response. Last year in a debate sponsored by the Center for Strategic and International Studies, Gaoyue Fan, a senior research fellow at the PLA Military Science Academy said that, "If the U.S. military develops Air-Sea Battle to deal with the [People's Liberation Army], the PLA will be forced to develop anti Air-Sea Battle."[31]

The authors of ASB have used poor analogies to sell ASB as a viable strategy in the Pacific, comparing the U.S. standoff with a rising China to its Cold War competition with the Soviet Union. On the surface, this seems like a logical comparison. Since the United States emerged triumphant out of the Cold War, perhaps we should adopt similar strategies with respect to China. However, the analogy quickly breaks down. During the Cold War, the United States and the Soviets openly called each other enemies, threatened each other, and fought proxy wars; however, they could still keep diplomatic relations open along various levels of communication. This was possible because of the strategic architecture between the two states. This architecture prevented misunderstanding from turning into crisis due to the various levels of horizontal and vertical escalatory measures that could be metered at the highest levels. The introduction of ASB into the Pacific changes the psychological equilibrium between the two powers, leading (again) to near instant vertical escalation that can hardly be metered. How many Americans are willing to gamble that in a military exchange with China, after we have destroyed a large portion of China's industrial base, China will not react with its nuclear arsenal? Is this not how the United States would likely respond to an attack on its homeland by a near-peer competitor? How many of us want to make this gamble based upon a poor historical analogy?

Economics.

Finally, the ASB concept works against long-term U.S. interests in the region because it puts the United States on the losing end of the economic cost equation. In the previous security dilemma scenario, the introduction of ASB will result in a response by the Chinese or any adversary. Even if we are to assume that the Chinese will not respond offensively and instead will solely improve their defensive postures, ASB still does not improve U.S. security or influence in the region. A2/AD capabilities are comparatively cheaper than the means to defeat them, with the result that security competition with respect to A2/AD can become both iterative and exponential. The United States introduces ASB, China improves their A2/AD abilities to overcome it; the United States must then improve ASB, which will cost exponentially more than its first generation. In 2010, the *Economist* described this paradigm: "Missiles are good value. Compared with a fully equipped aircraft-carrier, which might cost $15 billion-20 billion, a missile costs about $1m."[32] The authors of ASB have repeatedly claimed that China wants to change the military balance in the Pacific without fighting, harking back to Sun Tzu's axiom, "To subdue the enemy without fighting is the acme of skill."[33] While supporters of ASB use this logic as an argument for the concept, it seems that if the Chinese wanted to swing the military balance without fighting, forcing an adversary to overspend their resources on offensive measures in the Pacific would be an intelligent strategy. It would seem that as China's rate of growth remains high, a better approach to keeping the balance in the Pacific would be to improve the A2/AD capabilities of our allies in the region and force the Chinese into the losing side of the cost equation.

CONCLUSION

The authors of ASB have done a tremendous job convincing both policymakers and defense officials of the efficacy of the new concept. But these promises of effectiveness are based on poor historical analogies and flawed concepts of war. While ASB serves as an effective operational concept in solving the A2/AD problem, it fails as a strategic concept because it fails to effectively deter China, lends itself to vertical escalation, exacerbates the security dilemma hindering engagement, and puts the United States on the wrong side of an economic cost equation. These weaknesses put the United States at risk, or at least leave it suboptimally positioned. While most Americans hope that conflicts will be won easily and at low cost, ASB simply does not deliver on these promises. Those in the security community owe it to the American public to scrutinize any defense concept that pledges to deter potential enemies. ASB makes these claims but fails to deliver its full promise. This is not to say that ASB should not continue to be developed as a concept—it is hard to argue with the idea of any two services learning to be more interoperable. But ASB should be downgraded from the primary focus of military action in the Pacific in favor of a much more robust strategy of engagement and provision of A2/AD technologies to the surrounding states.

ENDNOTES - CHAPTER 17

1. These definitions are taken from the May 2013 Air-Sea Battle Concept document released by the Air-Sea Battle Office, available from *www.defense.gov/pubs/ASB-ConceptImplementation-Summary-May-2013.pdf*. Anti-Access (A2) is an action intended to slow deployment of friendly forces into a theater or cause forces to operate from distances farther from the locus of conflict than they would otherwise prefer. A2 affects movement to a theater. Area denial (AD) is an action intended to impede friendly operations within areas where an adversary cannot or will not prevent access. AD affects maneuver within a theater.

2. Andrew Krepinevich, "Strategy in a Time of Austerity," *Foreign Affairs*, November 1, 2012, available from *www.foreign affairs.com/articles/138362/andrew-f-krepinevich-jr/strategy-in-a-time-of-austerity*.

3. See, e.g., Jan Van Tol *et al.*, *AirSea Battle: A Point-of-Departure Operational Concept*, Washington, DC: Center for Strategic and Budgetary Assessments, 2010, in which the Chinese PLA appears in the second sentence of the executive summary.

4. Aaron L. Friedberg, "Bucking Beijing," *Foreign Affairs*, August 18, 2012, available from *www.foreignaffairs.com/articles/138032/aaron-l-friedberg/bucking-beijing*.

5. Greg Jaffe, "US Model for Future War fans tensions with China and inside Pentagon," *The Washington Post*, August 1, 2012, available from *www.washingtonpost.com/world/national-security/us-model-for-a-future-war-fans-tensions-with-china-and-inside-pentagon/2012/08/01/gJQAC6F8PX_story.html*.

6. Stephen Glain, "The Pentagon's New China War Plan," *Salon.com*, August 13, 2011, available from, *www.salon.com/2011/08/13/sino_us_stephen_glain*.

7. *Quadrenial Defense Review Report*, Washington, DC: U.S. Department of Defense, 2010, pp. 32-33, available from *www.comw. org/qdr/fulltext/1002QDR2010.pdf*. The quoted passage continues:

> The concept will address how air and naval forces will integrate capabilities across all operational domains — air, sea, land, space, and cyberspace — to counter growing challenges to U.S. freedom of action. As it matures, the concept will also help guide the development of future capabilities needed for effective power projection operations.

8. Hillary Clinton, "America's Pacific Century," *Foreign Policy*, November 2011, available from *www.foreignpolicy.com/ articles/2011/10/11/americas_pacific_century*.

9. *Ibid.*

10. Jan Van Tol, Mark Gunzinger, Andrew Krepinevich, Jim Thomas, "AirSea Battle: A Point-of-Departure Operational Concept," Washington, DC: Center for Strategic and Budgetary Assessments, April 2010.

11. Joint Operational Access Concept (JOAC), Version 1.0, Washington, DC: U.S. Department of Defense, January 17, 2012.

12. *Air-Sea Battle: Service Collaboration to Address Anti-Access & Area Denial Challenges*, Washington, DC: Department of Defense, May 2013.

13. Marcus Weisgerber, "Annual DoD Report Claims Steady Chinese Military Expansion," *Defense News*, May 6, 2013.

14. While the CSBA ASB authors maintain that ASB should not be viewed solely through the lens of the defense of Taiwan (p. xi), they also spend a great deal of time on the vulnerability of Taiwan (see, e.g., pp. 11, 13, 20, 30, 37, 72).

15. Jan Van Tol *et al.*, p. xv.

16. *Ibid.*

17. *Ibid.*

18. *Ibid.*

19. *Ibid.*

20. *Air-Sea Battle: Service Collaboration to Address Anti-Access & Area Denial Challenges*, p. 4.

21. *Ibid.*

22. *Ibid.*

23. Shambaugh, p. 298.

24. Richard Clarke, "All US Electronics from China could be infected," *Defense Tech*, available from *defensetech.org/2012/03/29/richard-clarke-all-u-s-electronics-from-china-could-be-infected/*.

25. Ross Babbage, "Australia Needs Strategic Rethink on Submarines," *The Diplomat.com*, May 20, 2013, available from *the diplomat.com/flashpoints-blog/2013/05/20/australia-needs-strategic-rethink-on-submarines/*.

26. Ben Schreer, "Australia and AirSea Battle: Not Sold Yet," *The Diplomat.com*, April 22, 2013, available from *thediplomat.com/flashpoints-blog/2013/04/22/australia-and-airsea-battle-not-sold-yet*.

27. *Ibid.*

28. Thomas C. Schelling, *Arms and Influence*, New Haven: Yale University Press, 1966, p. 34.

29. Robert Jervis, "Cooperation under the Security Dilemma," *World Politics*, Vol. 30, No. 2, 1978, pp. 167-214. Copyright 1978 by Cambridge University Press.

30. *Ibid.*

31. Jaffe.

32. "China's Missiles," *The Economist* Online, December 6, 2010, available from *www.economist.com/blogs/dailychart/2010/12/chinese_missile_ranges*.

33. Andrew Krepinevich, "China's 'Finlandization' Strategy in the Pacific," *The Wall Street Journal*, September 11, 2010.

CHAPTER 18

BACK TO REALITY:
WHY LANDPOWER TRUMPS IN THE
NATIONAL REBALANCE TOWARD ASIA

Robert Chamberlain

This chapter appeared previously in *Armed Forces Journal*, May 1, 2013. The author gratefully acknowledges permission to republish.

The American Army is an organization in search of a strategic purpose. American conventional involvement in the war in Afghanistan is drawing to a close, the security establishment has rejected armed nation-building as a viable national strategy, and the projection of military power seems to take the form of drones and air support to local proxies. Simultaneously, the withdrawal from land wars in the Middle East and the prioritization of East Asia has led to a decline of the doctrinal focus the organization has spent a decade refining — counterinsurgency, or COIN — and the concomitant rise of the new strategy du jour, Air-Sea Battle. In this brave new world, it is not clear what Landpower does and, thus, what the Army is good for.

As a service with a limited presence in the air and on the sea, this is all a little nerve-wracking. How does an organization that projects Landpower contribute usefully to an off-shore doctrine and a defense focus on the waters around the Chinese coast? It has been suggested that the Army advertise itself as the only solution to state collapse, capable of rushing in to manage the consequences of a North Korean implosion. Others argue the Army should maintain its

COIN focus and commitment to stability operations. Still more turn their focus to the special operations forces (of which the Army provides 60 percent). My assessment is not nearly so modest: If Asia is the central theater in which American national objectives will be challenged in the coming decade, then Landpower is the key to decoupling economic and military competition in the region, and the Army is the best organization to lead a defense strategy that supports peace, stability and growth.

The current obsession with the rise of China and the active debate about its implications for the world and the appropriate Western response have afflicted the American foreign policy establishment with an acute case of cognitive dissonance. On the one hand, China's growing military capacity and willingness to employ force or threats of force to resolve regional disputes is alarming and may indicate an armed confrontation is in the offing. On the other, China's active participation in the global economy, substantial financial interests across the region, and heavy investments in the United States may indicate that it is essentially a status quo power more interested in wealth than conquest. The truth almost certainly lies somewhere in the middle, and, thus, the appropriate American strategy is to prepare for war while encouraging trade. The challenge, then, is to ensure that the pursuit of one goal does not inhibit the other.

The grand strategic solution to this challenge is "containment-lite." In this approach, America seeks out smaller regional states threatened by China's growing power and facilitates their balancing strategies by offering a much less threatening alternative than simply bandwagoning behind China's regional aspirations. Thereby, American power in Asia is pooled with smaller states, and incipient Chinese militarism is checked. However, unlike the Cold War, Chinese membership in regional organizations is encouraged, expanding Chinese trade is welcomed, and Chinese economic growth is applauded. The goal is to raise the cost of militarizing international disputes such that the only rational Chinese alternative is to seek pacific resolution through the tools of economic or diplomatic power.

This solution is not without controversy. In "Asia's New Age of Instability," Michael Wesley suggests that smaller states in the region cannot pay their share militarily against China, larger states are not interested in a partnership with the West, and the American public is uninterested in costly foreign wars in defense of a local ally. By contrast, I argue that small states will contribute progressively more as the Chinese threat emerges, that larger states will respond to growing threats nearby by considering alliances that previously would have been unthinkable, and that the "rally round the flag" effect makes U.S. intervention credible in domestic political terms. But I will set those debates aside and ask the reader to assume that it is possible to form new alliances in the region, and that public opinion is no barrier to short- to medium-term American military action. Instead, I wish to consider what tools of American power best facilitate "containment-lite," which requires that they must demonstrate military resolve without communicating aggressive intentions.

LANDPOWER—THE BEST DEFENSE

Before addressing the specific Landpower polices that would best advance American interests in East Asia, I will discuss the strategic ends within containment-lite that military means and ways must provide. The whole purpose of the strategy is to encourage China's peaceful rise, underwrite regional stability, and firmly delink military and economic modes of competition and dispute. The military contribution to these goals must therefore balance martial and diplomatic logics; the path to military superiority in the region could lead to strategic failure if it induces Chinese militarism, arms races, and a *fait accompli* crisis strategy. Instead, American military power should operate according to a defensive realist logic — increasing the security of allies without threatening China directly. Supported, but not dominated, by Air-Sea Battle, it must be able to allocate forces in such a way as to signal resolve and diffuse regional crises by removing the credible threat of Chinese military action against smaller states. Air and sea power cannot accomplish these missions alone — the linchpin of a successful American defense strategy in Asia is its use of Landpower.

The most obvious advantage of Landpower among the islands and peninsulas of East Asia is its heavily defensive character. Unlike Central Europe during the Cold War, where vast armored forces threatened the interests of each superpower and prudent defensive measures were indistinguishable from growing offensive capability, land theaters in Asia are separated from one another by vast bodies of water. This is a truly excellent situation from the U.S. perspective, since it means that land conflict can be localized — U.S. forces in Korea do not threaten China with the specter of rapid military defeat, nor would American reinforcements to allies in Southeast Asia or elsewhere in the region. In fact, we have multiple 20th-century examples of local wars in Asia staying relatively local, despite superpower involvement. Thus, the deployment of an American brigade to assist in the defense of an ally signals resolve and contributes military capacity without threatening China directly in a way that the deployment of a carrier task force or an air wing simply cannot.

Landpower is uniquely advantageous for a strategy of containment-lite, due to its ability to achieve regional stability without increasing Chinese insecurity. However, the American Landpower strategy in Asia must encompass much more than the rapid deployment of combat units into crises. Landpower must address the full spectrum of regional defense needs, which require careful cultivation of defense partnerships and capabilities in order to match the right force with each emerging contingency. The use of Landpower in Asia must also inform American doctrine and procurement strategies, as the Army returns to its conventional mission while expanding other capabilities. The chief of staff of the Army refers to these three elements as Win, Shape, and Prevent, respectively. Together, they form the three components of America's strategic solution.

THE SPECTRUM OF LANDPOWER

It is hard to think about Landpower without the boom of a cannon, the rumble of a tank, or the endless rows of soldiers on parade. But the full conventional capability of the United States is only one aspect of Landpower, and one that should be imagined alongside the shuffling of paper, the snapping of clipboards, and a small headquarters element winding their way through an airport. Landpower strategy must shape the security environment prior to the arrival of conventional forces, which could either facilitate victory or perhaps even forestall a conflict altogether.

The most limited form of Landpower engagement is back-channel coordination. In concert with other American diplomatic initiatives, this approach enables concerned regional powers with which the United States has no formal relationship to lay the groundwork for future engagement. It is the time for staff officers to have confidential discussions about future anticipated defense needs, how the recipient power understands U.S. policy objectives, and how American Landpower could help check Chinese militarism. This is also an opportunity to establish interoperable systems and procedures that will prove invaluable as American Landpower involvement moves up the scale.

A more overt tool of Landpower is foreign military sales, military aid packages, and technology transfers. These require virtually no uniformed presence or formalized relationship, but still facilitate the spread of military resources that can check Chinese adventurism. Moreover, to the extent that the Chinese threat is a function of air power or theater ballistic missiles, military systems of a purely defensive nature can be exported.

Further down the spectrum is the explicit integration of contingency planning between the United States and the local ally. This requires careful consideration of disembarkation points for U.S. reinforcements, their planned contribution, the command relationships of the forces in the field and all the myriad other details that create battlefield friction. In addition to personnel from the embassy, this might also entail the rotation of headquarters elements through joint war-game exercises.

Next are the types of conventional army interactions that are normally associated with Landpower: major joint exercises, rotating units, or even a permanent presence. These sorts of actions are easily understood and retain the desirable stabilizing properties of Landpower, but are also rather expensive. In the contemporary budgetary environment, it is imperative to maximize the cost-effectiveness of American defense initiatives. By preparing the ground through early shaping operations and staff integration, the United States will retain the flexibility to move forces quickly throughout the region while avoiding the costs of keeping units permanently on station.

PROCUREMENT AND POSTURE

In addition to a shift in defense strategy that prioritizes the stabilizing effects of Landpower over the inherently threatening alternatives discussed later, it will also be necessary to build a Landpower capacity that is designed to address both Pacific geography and Chinese capabilities. This represents both a return to the modern Army's conventional roots and a significant evolution in how it understands its role.

The Chinese regional military threat is primarily conventional and must be checked by conventional capabilities. While it would be foolhardy for the U.S. military to completely forget the lessons of the past decade and refuse to prepare units for COIN and stability operations, it would be equally myopic to decide that these operations ought to be an organizational priority in years to come. When China has used offensive military force to assert its political will, it has not been a particularly subtle affair in terms of either manpower or effect. Thus, a doctrine and equipment set that is built around small platoons running around the battlefield in up-armored humvees and mine resistant ambush protected military vehicles (MRAPs) is a recipe for disaster. The People's Liberation Army (PLA) will not be defeated by COIN and if America wishes to lend credible assistance to its allies, it will need to do so in terms of a conventional capability, supported by adequate training and equipment, that can defeat the PLA on conventional terms. The beauty of Landpower, however, is that the ability to defeat an expeditionary force from China that advances down one of the growing number of paved arteries that connect the region's industrial centers does not necessarily entail the ability to advance deep into Chinese territory and threaten China itself. Unlike air and sea power, the force can be tailored to meet the requirements of a limited war and return the system to stability.

However, many American allies in the region and many countries potentially threatened by Chinese power are islands. If China chooses to employ military threats against these states, the threat would almost certainly take the form of sea, air, or missile attack. Traditionally, these have been the purview of our vast and powerful Navy and Air Force. But the trouble with relying on these services is that keeping enough air and sea power in the region to sink the Chinese navy or cripple the Chinese missile fleet is an inherently threatening and destabilizing force posture.

I propose that, rather than relying on our ability to achieve dominance in the air and on the sea to thwart potential Chinese military adventurism, America develop a land-based anti-access/area-denial (A2/AD) capability of its own. This entails the expansion of theater missile defense initiatives, further development of the U.S. air defense capability, and investment in land-based anti-ship systems. All these capabilities, with the exception of some elements of missile defense, are currently met in Air-Sea Battle by the Air Force and the Navy. That means what the U.S. perceives as defending its allies, the Chinese could legitimately perceive as an expansion of power in the region. By contrast, land-based A2/AD systems are purely defensive. Once the attacker has been defeated (the planes driven off, the missiles shot down, the ships sunk, etc.), the system has no further capability. For example, a joint strike fighter could shoot down incoming aircraft and then be rearmed to attack ground targets. The same is simply not true for land-based air defense.

ALTERNATIVES TO LANDPOWER

One approach to regional defense which has captured the imagination of American policymakers in the aftermath of the Libyan revolution is to supply American firepower to local allies through the use of precision strikes guided by small special operations teams. In a conventional scenario, this approach would have our allies fight on their land, while we contributed firepower and technological capability from air and sea.

This is the Rumsfeldian dream reborn—the low-cost policy option that leverages American technical know-how and the ultimate expression of the "send a bullet, not a man" philosophy of casualty-aversion. The tools for implementing this vision are myriad: strike aircraft deployed from bases in the region or carrier groups, missiles launched from destroyers and submarines, or even long-range bombers flying from Diego Garcia or Missouri.

The issues with using this approach in Asia are two-fold. First, this particular strategy has never been tried in the face of a robust air-defense network. It is one thing to bomb Taliban loyalists and Libyan pick-up trucks. It is quite another to attack a military with the full suite of air-defense options—from shoulder-launched missiles to integrated radar systems—at its disposal. As the Israel Defense Forces learned to their dismay in 1973, the assumption that the skies will remain open is a dangerous one indeed. Second, this option is enormously destabilizing. Specifically, it will encourage militarizing and winning any dispute as quickly as possible. I will elaborate this point further.

Consider, for example, the lessons of Libya from the perspective of the target of U.S. bombing. One obvious policy alternative open to American targets is to give in to U.S. demands, but another more appealing alternative exists: One could simply win as quickly as possible. American firepower is immense, but it is not all-powerful. If one can win the ground campaign quickly and decisively, then one has the ability to disperse one's forces, absorb some casualties, and wait for the Americans to give up and leave or try to introduce ground forces of their own. But, of course, the initial American reliance on air power will likely entail the loss of uncontested ports of entry. Thus, the target has the advantage of opposing an amphibious assault using modern weapons, which holds out the prospect of massive losses to the United States. Given the increased cost of reversing the military outcome, the United States is more likely to simply accept the new status quo and move on. Therefore, you, as the target, have every incentive to go as quickly as possible in order to present America and its allies with a *fait accompli*.

The solution to this problem, from an off-shore firepower perspective, is simply to place more firepower in the area in order to compound the difficulties an aggressor would face in achieving a quick victory. Of course, more firepower would simply encourage the aggressor to move that much quicker, thus requiring more firepower, and so on. This is a classic conflict spiral, which has the twin disadvantages of being costly and destabilizing. It will increase Chinese militarism and fail to control American defense outlays, which is to say that it utterly fails to achieve the overall strategic goal of delinking military and economic disputes, fostering stability and discouraging militarism.

AIR-SEA BATTLE: THE NEW CONVENTIONAL WISDOM

Air-Sea Battle, the doctrine being created by the Navy and Air Force to support the rebalance toward Asia, offers a different approach. In "Air Sea Battle: Promoting Stability in an Era of Uncertainty" and "Air-Sea Battle: Clearing the Fog," the service proponents of this doctrine argue that projecting American power in the region will require the ability to get there in the first place. With the growing Chinese investment in A2/AD technologies, there is serious concern about America's ability to project power credibly. In order to ensure that the U.S. military can remain a viable instrument of national policy in Asia, this doctrine proposes to integrate air and sea power in such a way that American forces can arrive safely in the region and undertake whatever missions are necessary.

To that end, Air-Sea Battle requires that A2/AD systems are attacked simultaneously and in-depth by all available means. It is not enough to simply shoot down incoming ballistic missiles—the United States will also attack their launch platforms, the radars that guide them, the facilities that power the radars, the computers that make it all work, etc. This would seem to necessitate attacks against the Chinese mainland, which raises two important possibilities for the evolution of this doctrine.

In one evolution, which I will call "Offensive Air-Sea Battle," proponents of firepower are able to successfully make the case that, as long as one is going to attack China to facilitate the further introduction of forces into the region, one might just as easily use this capability to deter Chinese militarism altogether. If China is a rational actor, then using offshore firepower to threaten Chinese assets raises the costs of military action by China, thus encouraging them to seek alternative means by which to achieve their national goals. Landpower becomes a costly redundancy, and the optimal solution for U.S. regional defense needs is simply to invest further in the ships and aircraft that can project power against Chinese forces and industry.

From a Chinese perspective, this is obviously extraordinarily threatening. Even implicit threats of force against Chinese cities would have to be met with a robust counterthreat to valued American assets. On the low end, this could mean a naval buildup and an investment in missile capabilities to threaten U.S. bases throughout the region. On the high end, it could mean an expansion of the Chinese nuclear arsenal and a more aggressive nuclear readiness posture. In any event, the emergence of a new arms race and increasing military tensions would represent a significant failure of U.S. policy. While this policy is not currently under open consideration, history has shown repeatedly that the siren song of air-power-based compellence has an almost irresistible attraction for policymakers.

The other evolution, which is the current trend in Air-Sea Battle among the services, is what I call "Defensive Air-Sea Battle." In the defensive approach, Air-Sea Battle is not meant to compel anyone to do anything. It merely overcomes A2/AD barriers and allows American forces to arrive safely in theater. This is all well and good, but it raises two additional issues. First, how much air-sea capability is enough? Second, what is the American land contingent meant to be doing upon arrival?

First, in purely military terms, more is almost always better. As long as one can sustain a force logistically, then, all else being equal, greater numbers often lead to faster victories, lower casualties and a wider margin of error in dealing with unanticipated developments. However, in the larger strategic sense, more power can sometimes lead to less security. This is because of the ever-present "security dilemma," in which an increase in one state's military capability threatens another, thus inducing the second state to expand its own capability in response. Even if both states have benign intentions and seek only their own survival, they nonetheless end up spending progressively more on arms without ever enhancing their own safety. In fact, the system may become less secure, as each state becomes increasingly well-armed and prepared for war.

A twist on the security dilemma proposed in the political science literature is that if a military system had only defensive purposes, it would be less threatening. Conversely, if a system had only offensive purposes, it would certainly induce a robust response. Further, if one could tell defensive from offensive technologies, the system would be more stable, but if the two were indistinguishable, then a security dilemma would occur because one state's defensive preparations would look like a potential threat to another and vice versa.

The problem with the two possible evolutions of Air-Sea Battle identified here is that the offensive cannot be distinguished from the defensive. If disrupting Chinese A2/AD capabilities requires a simultaneous attack that involves strikes against the Chinese mainland, then, by definition, a greater investment in Air-Sea Battle represents a greater ability to attack China. The policy implication, then, is that not only must Defensive Air-Sea Battle remain doctrinally modest, but the associated procurement and deployment strategy must remain modest as well. It does no good to commit doctrinally to limited aims if doing so entails a massive arms increase and triggers the strategic outcome (militarization and instability) the doctrine was meant to avoid.

The second issue with Defensive Air-Sea Battle is that it really is not a strategy at all. It is a handy operational template that pre-coordinates the necessary assets to facilitate the projection of American power into East Asia in the face of enemy A2/AD capabilities. This is all well and good, but it is hardly an acceptable basis for American regional defense strategy. How America ought to deploy its power in order to delink military and economic competition, encourage the peaceful rise of China, and foster Asian regional stability remains an open question, one which can only be addressed by the prudent development and employment of Landpower.

RETURNING TO REALISM

After a decade of nation-building and revisionist adventures, America seems to be returning to a realist foreign policy. Prudence is once again the supreme virtue, security and stability the guiding lights. The hinterlands in the arc of instability, where transnational terrorism networks go to regroup, are the purview of special operations and drones; the bulk of American military power is being refocused on missions of central national importance. Chief among these is ensuring the peace and prosperity of East Asia. With the renewed focus that the "rebalance toward Asia" implies must come new thinking. Dominance in the air and on the sea may demonstrate the extent of American power, but it also creates a zero-sum security environment. In the world of Air-Sea Battle, America and China may find themselves locked in a security competition that serves the interest of neither state.

By contrast, Landpower represents a flexible tool that is uniquely suited to the Asian security environment. The Navy remains the essential guarantor of global commerce and the freedom of the seas, and the Air Force gives policymakers an unparalleled set of global strike options. But only the Army and Marines can provide a security commitment to America's partners in Asia that does not simultaneously threaten China itself. Landpower is the only avenue by which America can enhance regional security and stability, deter Chinese militarism and encourage Chinese commitment to the global status quo. It is Landpower, and Landpower alone, that can bring America's Asia policy back to reality.

CHAPTER 19

PREVENT, SHAPE, WIN IN CONTEXT:
THE CENTRAL REGION

Isaiah Wilson III

The author is indebted to his U.S. Central Command and U.S.
Africa Command colleagues. Some of the concepts and figures discussed and included in this chapter are representative
of concepts and concept (graphical) designs reflected in the
2013 *U.S. Central Command Theater Strategy*, September 2013.
That withstanding, the concepts and propositions presented
in this chapter reflect the author's views and opinions alone,
and do not represent official U.S. Central Command, Joint Staff,
Department of Defense, nor U.S. Government policy, more
generally.

The United States is now approaching a grand-
strategic inflection point.[1] Domestic and international
transitions will both challenge and create great opportunities for U.S. Central Command, which serves as
the fulcrum of U.S. vital national interests—interests
that lie at the heart of U.S. global power.

The U.S. Central Command (USCENTCOM) operating environment currently includes 20 countries.
Among them are nascent democracies recovering from
years of fighting, fragile nations attempting to regain
control of ungoverned space, and government leaders cautiously assessing our actions (and those of our
adversaries) to map their future security framework.
For the foreseeable future, three of the Nation's four
formally-stated missions—defense of the Homeland,
counterproliferation of weapons of mass destruction
(WMD), and ensuring the free flow of resources—will
remain anchored to the Central Region.

The geography of the USCENTCOM areas of responsibility (AOR) is a lynchpin of the global economy and includes critical international sea lines of communication (SLOCs), including the maritime chokepoints of the Suez Canal, Strait of Hormuz, and the Bab al-Mandeb Strait. With over 550 million people, 18 languages, hundreds of dialects, and 22 separate ethnic groups, the demographics in the AOR create an opportunity for friction and rivalry. The region includes both the wealthiest and most impoverished of the world's Muslim-majority states; abundant petroleum and natural gas reserves; an aspiring nuclear power and known state-sponsors of terrorism; former Soviet Union client states; prolific criminal networks trafficking in narcotics, weapons, and persons; and a wide variety of violent extremist organizations (VEOs). (See Figure 19-1.)

These conditions are further impacted, "compounded," by underlying currents of growing Sunni-Shia sectarian divide, a rising struggle between radical and moderate forms of government and styles of governance, endemic economic disparity, and an equally growing and worrisome age gap, exacerbated by an enlarging youth population—over 40 percent of the region is between 15-49 years of age. The region has never been peaceful and enduring U.S. national vital interests have repeatedly required deft, vigorous U.S. involvement in specific affairs. The intersection of these trends—geography, demographics, and political-military conflicts—will challenge the equilibrium of the regional balance of power for the coming decades.

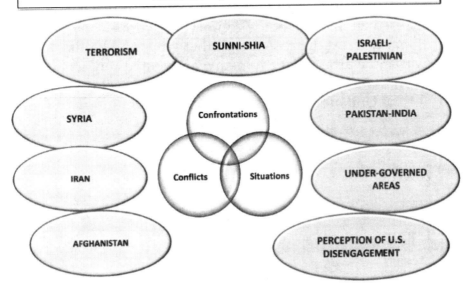

Figure 19-1. The Strategic Environment of the Central Region.

Given these security "atmospherics," USCENT-COM's challenge is to constantly assess its regional priorities to ensure that we do not create a "say-do gap" that could embolden adversaries and weaken the bonds of trust and confidence the United States has built through decades of investing in partner capacity.

PREVENT, SHAPE, WIN IN CONTEXT: THE MIDDLE EAST/CENTRAL REGION

The U.S. Army, as part of the Joint Force, has started to explore the potential for militarily effective and fiscally responsible uses of Landpower through what it calls the "Prevent-Shape-Win" (PSW) strategic solution. PSW is a new construct designed to explain the various roles of the Army. It is, at bottom, an attempt to break an old paradigm where Army leaders only focused on one end of the conflict spectrum—conventional war—at the cost of the other types and kinds of war and warfare that could have prevented conflict or even shaped the environment in more favorable terms for the United States. (See Figure 19-2.)

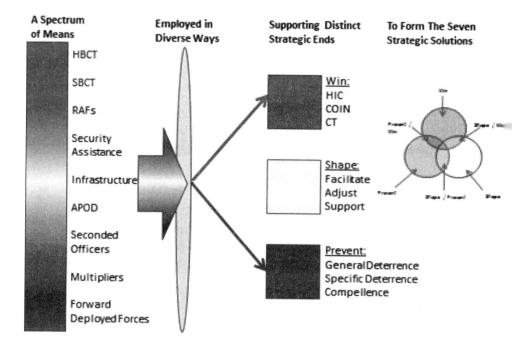

I would like to acknowledge the contributions of Rob Chamberlain, Joe Da Silva, and Cara Clarke in development of this concept design, as part of our work in 2013 leading the CSA's Prevent-Shape Group, as part of the CSA's Unified Quest Army Futures Wargame.

Figure 19-2. Prevent, Shape, Win.

The U.S. Army and Joint Forces Capstone Concepts use Prevent to describe **force generation** (the capacity to conduct war), **deterrence** (preventing an adversary from taking an action they would otherwise take), and **compellence** (inducing an adversary to do something they do not want to do).[2] Effective compellent and deterrent forces contribute to the larger preventive end, as they signal long-term resolve and the **willingness** to pay high costs (without having necessarily to pay them). The goal should be to place enough boots on the ground to suggest that more boots could soon arrive; the goal should not be to minimize the U.S. regional footprint and the potential costs of deployment for their own sake, as both courses may be counterproductive with a view to compellence and therefore ultimately with a view to cost-cutting as well. Sound and effective prevention is an effective way to shape the behavior of near-peer rivals **and** to address the "swamps" that breed extremism, insurgency, and terrorism. The best way to drain swamps is to prevent them from filling in the first place; as they say, **an ounce of prevention is worth a pound of cure**.

The "Shape" component of "Prevent-Shape-Win" includes strategies that mold the environment in which U.S. troops operate and create positive perceptions of America abroad. These strategies require the right forces to be placed at the decisive points on the globe in order to conduct successful deterrence and compellence and thus **facilitate** Prevent and Win requirements; they aim to **adjust** the strategic calculations of allies and adversaries by building the strength of our partners through a variety of means, from foreign military sales to direct reinforcement, and by demonstrating to our adversaries our preparedness and resolve. They are designed to **support** whole-of-government initiatives as an important part of our national diplomatic and homeland security strategies.[3] As each of these shaping strategies is highly context-specific, the forces designed to carry them out must be agile and adaptive — tailored, scalable, and task-organized to accomplish their specific strategic objectives.

There are several key and critical challenges companioning a Prevent-Shape-Win strategic approach, two of particular importance:

1. **The Challenge of Coercion**: Coercive diplomacy, where the threat of force is used to prevent undesired behavior (deterrence) or cause compliance (compellence), requires both capability **and** credibility to be effective. It is not enough to have forces available; the target state must **believe** that force will be used for as long as is necessary to alter its behavior. Moreover, the threat must be specific enough that the target believes it can be avoided through behavior modification — tailored deterrence causes compliance, imprecise deterrence causes reaction.

2. **The Challenge of Commitment**: Whether adjusting allies' or adversaries' calculations of U.S. strategic commitment to a region, facilitating Prevent or Win activities, or supporting whole-of-government efforts, the armed forces must do the following: provide tailored capabilities, demonstrate an enduring presence that will be there in a crisis, and meet interlocutors on their own terms. It will not work to show up with a lot of the wrong assets. It will not work to have a big, expensive, transient capability that is too big to risk. It will not work to make our partners speak our language about our concerns. **We have to meet people where they are to succeed**. (See Figure 19-3.)

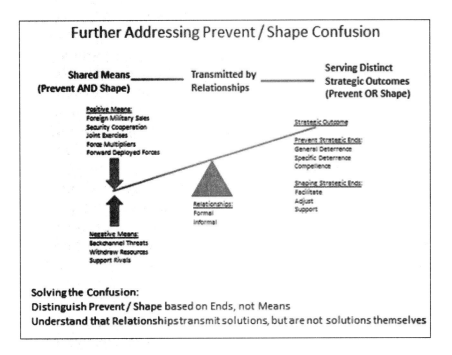

Figure 19-3. Relationships Turn Means
into Outcomes.

I would like to acknowledge the contributions of Rob Chamberlain, Joe Da Silva, and Cara Clarke in development of this concept design, as part of our work in 2013 leading the CSA's Prevent-Shape Group, as part of the CSA's Unified Quest Army Futures Wargame.

Figure 19-3. Relationships Turn Means
into Outcomes.

In fact, it is because of these two critical challenges or shortcomings endemic to Prevent and Shape strategies, as well as others, that maintaining a robust, credible, and present physical force capable of lethal compellence (i.e., warfighting) is fundamental to PSW as a "winning" strategic solution. While Prevent and Shape approaches are long-term investments that can and do yield significant effective-cost "dividends," maintaining a clear-and-present force at-the-ready, postured at the appropriate locations to strike at the right timing, if and when required, is the essential insurance policy to these long-term investments. If and when deterrence fails, a nation's capacity to generate and direct force in powerful ways is paramount.

USCENTCOM'S "MANAGE-PREVENT-SHAPE" THEATER STRATEGY

To provide security, stability, and prosperity across the Central Region, USCENTCOM manages current ongoing conflicts while shaping those conditions that prevent confrontations from becoming future conflicts. The USCENTCOM Theater Strategy focuses on six resource-informed ends: improve and increase regional stability and security, advancing U.S. vital national interests across the Central Region; deter regional adversaries; marginalize and erode the influences of those VEOs that have the capability to threaten U.S. national interests, working with regional partners in their efforts to actively counter regional VEOs and mitigate conditions that promote extremism; counter the proliferation, acquisition, and use of WMD that threatens U.S. vital interests; support U.S. ambassadors and the diplomatic corps in the formation and execution of AOR Country Team Mission initiatives and programs; and enhance and responsively deploy partner capacity to respond to regional challenges.[4]

Through a near, mid, and long-term theater strategy, USCENTCOM works closely with regional and international partners to promote cooperation among nations, respond to crises, deter or defeat state and nonstate aggression, and support Department of State efforts to develop economic growth and responsible governance. In the near and mid-term, USCENTCOM utilizes the Theater Campaign Plan (TCP) to achieve its desired military objectives. While its long-term objectives will most likely extend beyond the current TCP, the conditions the Command established now will benefit those that follow.

Manage.[5]

Although the element of "manage" exceeds near-term and mid-term objectives, managing conflicts is the cornerstone of the USCENTCOM TCP and ongoing operations. Under this effort, USCENTCOM supports nascent democracies emerging from either combat operations or internal revolution (i.e., Arab Spring). Principally by working "by, with, and through" regional partners, the mission is to deny VEOs and adversaries attempting to take advantage of these fragile democracies and exploit ungoverned spaces.

Prevent.[6]

Actions, activities, and operations to prevent confrontations and situations from becoming conflicts requires USCENTCOM to partner with Department of State, other U.S. Government agencies, as well as planning and working with allies and regional partner nation-states. These actions are intended to bridge the gap between near-term objectives and long-term shaping efforts. The goal of "prevent" is to bolster fragile nations in order to keep them from slipping into a conflict.

Shape.[7]

Shaping underlying currents to influence the future is paramount to prevention of future conflicts. Shaping efforts cross the entire theater-strategic framework (near-mid-long term actions). Building partner capacity (BPC), conducting regional exercises, and developing a regional security architecture not only supports U.S. efforts to deter adversaries but also creates opportunities to share ideas that cross cultural and geographic divides. These strategies require the right forces to be placed at decisive points within the Central Region theater in order to conduct successful deterrence and compellence and thus facilitate Prevent and Win requirements. Through Shape activities, USCENTCOM aims to adjust the strategic calculations of allies and adversaries by building the strength of our partners through a variety of means, from foreign military sales to direct reinforcement, and by demonstrating to our adversaries our preparedness and resolve; and they are designed in such ways that support whole-of-government and multilateral initiatives as an important part of our national diplomatic and homeland security strategies. USCENTCOM, through its Theater Strategy and Theater Campaign Plan (TCP), seeks to manage long-range shaping activities increasingly through a "by-with-through," conditions-based BPC collective approach, with a forward-presence posture of a minimum compliment of maximum-effectiveness U.S. forces forward-postured in-theater for reassurance of U.S. durable commitments both for friendly nations and partners in the region, as well as reassurance of U.S. capability and resolve for our adversaries upon which they can adjust and moderate their strategic calculations.

CRITICAL CAPABILITIES AND CAPACITY FOR ENABLING "EFFECTIVE" MANAGE-PREVENT-SHAPE WINNING STRATEGY

There are two aspects of the current and future global security environment that are of particular importance to the USCENTCOM AOR: First, there is the dangerous convergence of otherwise separate threats (e.g., VEOs; Syria Crisis; Iran) in such a way as to require the execution of two or more contingency or war plans near-simultaneously. Second, there is rising fiscal austerity and defense budget stringency. Through these times of complex, compound security dilemmas and resource austerity, USCENTCOM seeks opportunities to increase regional and international participation in U.S. security efforts (i.e., "by-with-through"). The past two-plus decades of investments in materiel support to regional friends and partners, as well as relationship-building efforts throughout the Central Region have proven very profitable investments, yielding what is today a relatively mature, yet still maturing, USCENTCOM durable presence built around the following three theater-spanning foundational capabilities and capacities:

Forward Headquarters.

Robust headquartering forward in Qatar, Bahrain, and Kuwait, along with USCENTCOM Forward-Jordan (CF-J) joint-combined headquarters provides "hub" architectures allowing for effective integration of regional partners, as well as allies from beyond the region for possible coalitional contingency operations. This presence also provides an enduring, durable U.S. presence, which in and of itself serves to reassure friends and allies, as well as adversaries, of U.S. resolve. Forward headquarters signal U.S. commitment not only to its own unilateral interests, but to regional partner security interests, while demonstrating robust U.S. physical force capability and capacity.

Robust, Emergent Regional Partnerships.

Over the past decade, USCENTCOM has accelerated its "Build Partners/Build Partner Capacity" shaping efforts, partnering with regional nations in operations in Iraq, Afghanistan, and Libya (the latter now a formal part of the U.S. Africa Command AOR). This period of time has witnessed unprecedented support for regional maritime air defense exercises. Also, exercises such as the International Mine Counter Measure exercise have united over 40 nations from six continents in defense of the region. Through these types of mature/maturing collective regional partnership activities, the United States is able to set and shape the conditions across the Central Region that will one day afford the Nation with a way to "build down" its own forces committed to security efforts in the region by-with-through a "building-up" of regional countries' capabilities and capacities to advance security, stability, and prosperity across the region.

USCENTCOM's military forward presence and military-to-military relations have led to a number of "big wins" over the past few years, building off of over at least 3 decades of dedicated foreign assistance and security assistance investments. Over the past 2 years, USCENTCOM has made significant gains with Gulf Cooperation Country (GCC) partners on establishment of bilateral defense plans against Iranian aggression. In the area of counterpiracy, through U.S.-

regional partner combined operations, piracy activity has been steadily trending downward since 2011, with 52 hijackings in 2009 trending downward to 7 hijackings in 2012, and zero hijackings as of November 2013. Arguably, two of the most powerful expressions of effective long-ranging Shaping through BPC investments and activities can be seen in USCENTCOM's International Mine Counter Measure Exercises (IMCMEX) and the Combined Air Operations Center (CAOC). With respect to IMCMEX, USCENTCOM has executed two successful exercises over the last 2 years, with over 40 participating regional and foreign allied countries. IMCMEX increases U.S. and partner nation unilateral and combined abilities in supporting and executing coalition mine interdiction warfare operations by improving maritime operational and tactical capabilities; force readiness; command, control, communications, computers, and intelligence; and by exercising tactical planning and execution. At least 20 years of military-to-military engagements with GCC partners have yielded a relatively mature Integrated Air and Missile Defense (IAMD)/Ballistic Missile Defense (BMD) collective theater defense capability. The Air Forces Central Gulf CAOC, which is manned by all GCC air forces, U.S. and U.K. air forces, is a hallmark coalition enabler centered on BMD/IAMD integration, with this Gulf CAOC providing the potential for GCC countries to shoulder an increasingly greater portion of the collective regional defense burden (operational and financial support).

These are only a few examples of the "big returns" that can come from a long-range "dollar-cost averaging" by-with-through regional partners approach to prevent and shape civilian-military activities. With the reality of emerging, increasingly ambiguous, and compounding security threats and the added complication of defense budget stringency, such by-with-through indirect approaches can help achieve an adequate risk-mitigating gap-spanning plan and approach. The anchor of this kind of approach lies in robust BPC investments and durable U.S. forward presence. Presence equals relationships. Relationships build and buy trust. Trust with truly capable regional partners buys the U.S. influence. However, it must be understood that the cornerstone to such a strategic approach is **strategic patience** and a **tolerance of ambiguity**. There are big penalties for early withdrawals from Prevent and Shape initiatives. But conversely, like an individual retirement account investment, with patience, these kinds of investments can yield grand returns if allowed to mature. Through stable and patient development of partners and capacities in other nations and organizations, as well as talent and a credible incentive structure in our own, the United States achieves and can continue to achieve **large dividends over the long term**. The search for year-to-year return on investment is illusory. These projects develop over years, and a full cost-benefit analysis is often possible only after a decade or more of effort.

STABLE REGIONAL ARCHITECTURES SUPPORTIVE OF REBALANCING OF FORCES AND FORCE POSTURE

As the United States inevitably and unavoidably rebalances its forces in the face of growing fiscal austerity, it will need to find ways to build, man, train, equip, maintain, and finance theater-spanning headquarters that can provide command-and-control, and act as sustaining "hubs" capable of effectively and rapidly receiving strategically-deployed joint and combined forces, while integrating these forces into effective Combined-Joint force packages readied for mission operations throughout the entire region.[8] The capabilities that are critical for ensuring a durable presence in the Central Region and that provide the cornerstone of an effective regional defense/security architecture include: physical military forces capable of responding to crises (i.e., counterterrorism/counter-violent extremist organizations [VEO] operations; non-combatant evacuation operations [NEO]; humanitarian assistance [HA]; counterpiracy operations; personal recovery [PR], etc.); scalable command and control (C2) infrastructure and personnel (including security cooperation operations [SCO]-type command and control missions); forces capable of securing infrastructure and personnel; base and port access footprints (i.e., APOD/SPOD/prepositioned stocks/lines of communications, sustainment, and supply; senior headquarters-forward (i.e., component commands); forces to execute security assistance and security cooperation activities (e.g., train-and-equip, train-advise-assist, train-the-trainer operations); intelligence, surveillance, and reconnaissance (ISR); and special operations forces (SOF) mission activities.

In light of U.S. defense force reductions (i.e., "build downs") and increasing defense budget cuts, all U.S. Armed Services are exploring and investing in some form of "regional alignment" of forces in support of a tilt in U.S. defense strategy more toward continental U.S.-basing of U.S. forces and an on-call forward-deployment rather than forward-presence strategic force posture. Regional architectures become all the more essential in light of this shift in U.S. strategic deployment and posture planning.

Leveraging security assistance and cooperation is the key to the Manage-Prevent-Shape strategic solution, and maintaining a durable regional defense/security capability architecture (i.e., right forces plus the right posture) is the critical enabling capacity for that strategic solution. Building systems that address the needs of a specific deterrent in a specific theater (such as land-based missile defense or anti-access/area denial in Asia) is expensive. But the United States need not bear that expense alone—through a variety of means (foreign military sales, foreign military financing, co-production) partners can contribute to the development of capabilities that support U.S. strategic objectives.

Given that "strategy always wears a dollar sign,"[9] we must continue to define and work toward achievement of our regional strategic goals with a pragmatic optimism tempering aspirations, our own and those of our regional friends and partners, with fiscal realities. That said, austere times are times of penury but also of promise as well, creating the kinds of environmental conditions ripe for great transformational change. Lest we forget: there was a similar set of conditions as we emerged from the Cold War in the early-1990s. Two wars (Cold War and Gulf War I) were then winding down; the economy crawled sluggishly out of a global recession; and U.S. Armed Forces experienced a commensurate building down of U.S. Armed Forces and intended rebalances from previous regions of major focus. This set of conditions generated a 20+-year evolution and maturation of the USCENTCOM AOR, both in terms of physical regional architectures and, most importantly, in terms of building the capacity of regional partners to generate their own force designs and systems. This current moment of compounding security challenges married with austerity could serve, as it did more than 20 years ago, as the next 2-decade long great transformation. In short, current conditions present certain perils for sure but unique promise as well. We must proceed with guarded optimism—but optimism nonetheless.

ENDNOTES - CHAPTER 19

1. For a more extended description of the United States' grand-strategic transition, see Isaiah Wilson III, "Beyond COIN," *The American Interest*, Vol. 9, No. 1, Autumn 2013, pp. 5-11.

2. *U.S. Army Capstone Concept*, Washington, DC: U.S. Army Training and Doctrine Command, December 2012.

3. *Ibid.*

4. Excerpt from *USCENTCOM Theater Strategy*, UNCLASSI-FIED, Washington, DC: Department of Defense, September 2013.

5. By "Manage" we mean: 1) "to deal with skillfully and efficiently; 2) to look after, long-term, and make decisions about; 3) to meet one's day-to-day needs." See *Merriam-Webster Dictionary*.

6. "Prevent" is a descriptive that encompasses a combination of force generation (i.e., the physical capabilities and capacities to conduct war), deterrence—both general and specific (i.e., preventing an adversary from taking an action they would otherwise take; causing an adversary to reconsider their strategic calculations), and compellence (i.e., inducing an adversary to do something they do not want to do with the promise of a capacity and will to use physical force, and in a timely fashion).

7. The "Shape" component of the manage-prevent-shape strategic solution includes strategies that mold the environment in which U.S. troops, unilaterally and/or multilaterally, operate and create positive perceptions of America abroad.

8. In military vernacular, combined, joint, reception-staging-onward movement and integration, or CJRSO&I.

9. Bernard Brodie, *Strategy in the Missile Age*, Santa Monica, CA: RAND Corporation, January 15, 1959.

CHAPTER 20

STRATEGY AND LANDPOWER ON THE CONTINENT OF AFRICA

John Baskerville

In the October 25, 2013, installment of *LiveatState*, The U.S. Department of State's web chat program for international journalists, Commander of United States Africa Command (AFRICOM) General David M. Rodriguez and Assistant Secretary of State for African Affairs Linda Thomas-Greenfield engaged journalists from throughout the continent on U.S. foreign policy and security cooperation in Sub-Saharan Africa.[1] After fielding several terrorism-related questions, the most recent of which referenced terrorist activities in Mali and Niger, Rodriguez asserted that "the solution to terrorism in the region is a long-term, broad, whole-of-government approach by all our partners, as well as all the international community."[2] He explained that terrorism is "not solved just by military operations," but is ultimately contingent upon "economic development," "improvement in governance," and "rule of law and law enforcement."[3] He characterized these factors as capacities that the Department of Defense (DoD), the Department of State, and the interagency help build in African nations. Three key themes underpin Rodriguez's statements: 1) the inextricable link between governance, development, opportunity, and security issues on the continent; 2) the necessity of a whole-of-government approach to complex security issues; and 3) the notion that the ultimate objective for the United States is to enable its African partners to confront these security issues.

However, as straightforward as these ideas may appear at first blush, they are intertwined with some of the more perplexing issues in contemporary discussions of U.S. grand strategy. These ideas suggest that issues of governance, development, security, and extremist ideology in far reaches of the globe are intimately linked to one another and to the security of U.S. citizens and interests, both at home and abroad. Rodriguez's ideas also suggest how U.S. policymakers might implement effective, large-scale, whole-of government, and multinational approaches to complex security issues such as organizing and establishing measures of effectiveness for prevent and shape operations. For students of Landpower, specifically, these ideas require thinking through the mix and division of labor between various types of land forces (reserve and active component forces, special operations and conventional forces) and exploring "innovative, low-cost, small footprint approaches" to security objectives.[4] Through a brief analysis of U.S interests in the AFRICOM area of responsibility, AFRICOM's strategy in support of those interests, and the role of land forces in AFRICOM's strategy, this chapter seeks to inform the greater discussion on U.S. grand strategy and the future of Landpower.

THE ENDS AND WAYS OF A COMPREHENSIVE STRATEGY

AFRICOM's 2013 posture statement identifies countering terrorism as DoD's priority mission in Africa and countering violent extremist organizations as the first among the Command's priorities.[5] This mission is a fitting starting point for considering the objectives of a comprehensive U.S. strategy in Africa, for the breadth of the challenge leaves none of the enduring U.S. interests untouched.[6] As evidenced by the September 2012 attack in Benghazi and the January 2013 attack on a British oil facility in Algeria, extremist organizations pose a direct threat to the security of the United States, its citizens, and its allies.[7] Extremist organizations are intricately tied to poor governance and the lack of opportunity, security, stability, and peace — sometimes as inhibitors, sometimes as indicators, sometimes as by-products.[8] As a result, the *end* of countering violent extremist organizations demands **ways** and **means** borne of effective and innovative integration of all instruments of power.

Ends.

AFRICOM defines U.S. vital national security interests in Africa as:

> protecting the security of the global economic system, preventing catastrophic attacks on the homeland, developing secure and reliable partners, protecting American citizens abroad, and protecting and advancing universal values.[9]

In support of these interests, AFRICOM aims its strategy at deterring and defeating near-term threats to U.S. interests, along with:

> building long-term partnerships that support and enable the objectives outlined in the U.S. Strategy Toward Sub-Saharan Africa: strengthening democratic institutions; spurring economic growth, advancing trade and investment; advancing peace and security; and promoting opportunity and development.[10]

Ways.

One of AFRICOM's guiding principles is that:

> over the long run, it will be Africans who will best be able to address African security challenges, and US-AFRICOM most effectively advances U.S. security interests through focused security engagement with African partners.[11]

This guiding principle, along with U.S. strategic defense guidance on "low-cost, small-footprint approaches," helps shape the activities AFRICOM undertakes in support of its objectives.[12] In AFRICOM's theater strategy and regional campaign plans, one observes a spectrum of relatively small-scale activities — referred to as operations, exercises, and security cooperation engagements. They are often situated within a larger Joint Interagency Intergovernmental Multinational framework, aimed at enabling African partners to shape a secure, peaceful, and prosperous regional order. Within this framework, U.S. military forces train, assist, advise, and mentor African military forces. U.S. forces undertake these tasks across a broad level of engagement, from bilateral to sub-regional and regional engagements, and from the small-unit to the institutional level. Of course, discovering and killing or capturing violent extremists is essential to U.S. strategy as well, but it does not represent the most prevalent use of land forces across the continent.[13]

STRATEGIC LANDPOWER: JOINING ENDS AND MEANS

In the Introduction to the May 2013 white paper entitled "Strategic Landpower: Winning the Clash of Wills," U.S. Army Chief of Staff General Raymond Odierno, U.S. Marine Corps Commandant General James Amos, and Commander, U.S. Special Operations Command Admiral William McRaven assert that their "three organizations intersect in the land domain among people."[14] These leaders extol the virtues of Landpower "at war," as well as "short of war."[15] In the "short of war" section, they speak of "interdependent teams of conventional and special operations forces" conducting activities that "preclude and deter conflict through shaping operations that leverage partners and populations to enhance local and regional stability."[16] This characterization of strategic Landpower, predicated on building the capacity of "local forces . . . while maintaining a low-cost, small footprint presence" aligns cleanly with the majority of AFRICOM's operations, exercises, and security cooperation engagements.[17] Within these engagements, one can also note the intersection of conventional forces and special operations forces breaking down the conventional wisdom that special operations forces operate in the realm of human interaction, whereas conventional forces focus on "combined arms maneuver, with less regard for the impact of human interaction."[18] The notion of Landpower breaks down the divisions separating Army, Marines, and Special Operations — and AFRICOM demonstrates the resulting unity of effort with particular clarity.

In practice, AFRICOM's (short of war) land-based activities, largely aimed at preventing conflict and shaping the operating environment, take the form of engagements led by U.S. Army Africa, Marine Corps Forces Africa, U.S. Special Operations Command Africa, Combined Joint Task Force-Horn of Africa, National Guard forces as part of AFRICOM's State Partnership Program, and 2nd Brigade Combat Team, 1st Infantry Division, AFRICOM's Regionally Aligned Brigade.[19] In these activities, rarely, if ever, does one see a perfectly clean split, dividing certain types of forces into certain set realms. Rather, one observes "interdependent teams" of forces: Marines leading a cadre of Marine and Army National Guard forces in Liberia; Conventional Forces and Army National Guard Special Operations Forces working in conjunction with one another in Mali; a Civil Affairs unit from Combined Joint Task Force-Horn of Africa working alongside the U.S. Agency for International Development and an Ethiopian nongovernmental organization. The three events (one operation, one exercise, and one security cooperation engagement) described give a brief glimpse of what AFRICOM's (short of war) activities look like in practice.

- Operation ONWARD LIBERTY. In this ongoing operation, Marine Corps Forces Africa have taken the lead in establishing a cadre of approximately 50 personnel from the ranks of the U.S. Marines, Michigan's Army National Guard, and the U.S. Air Force to serve as advisors and mentors to counterparts from the Armed Forces of Liberia. Their objective of restructuring the Armed Forces of Liberia, to include "rebuilding of the army from the ground up," stems from the peace agreement that ended the Liberian Civil War in 2003.[20]

- Exercise Atlas Accord. In the 2012 iteration of the annual exercise, which took place in Mali, U.S. Army conventional forces partnered with members of the 19th Special Forces Group (Army National Guard) to engage with troops from six African nations on retrieval and delivery of resupply materials and humanitarian aid, along with pathfinder operations to find and mark suitable drop zones. The focus of the exercise was to help build capacity for receiving and distributing aid and supplies to the population when a natural disaster or other disruptive event has made access to these necessities difficult or impossible.[21]
- In the fall of 2013, over a 10-week period, 21 Military Police personnel from 2nd Brigade, 1st Infantry Division, AFRICOM's Regionally Aligned Brigade, executed a **security cooperation engagement** in which they trained Ugandan forces on route security, riot control, marksmanship, first aid and combatives in preparation for an African Union Mission in Somalia (AMISOM) deployment. The focus of the engagement was to "prepare the Ugandan Military Police to plan, execute, and sustain counterterrorism operations against Al-Shabaab and other al-Qaeda affiliates in Somalia."[22]

Initial Success and Enduring Challenges.

In a December 2012 address at George Washington University, General Carter Ham, then-commander of AFRICOM, noted the success of the African Union-led, U.S. and international community-supported mission against Al-Shabaab that had pushed the group "mostly" out of the capital, Mogadishu, and the port city of Kismayo.[23] In the larger framework of AFRICOM's model for activities, this successful collaboration was especially poignant. From the standpoint of building partner capacity, relatively small-scale engagements had enabled U.S. military mentors and advisers to improve the capabilities of regional AMISOM forces through training in skills, such as intelligence analysis and countering improvised explosive devices. From the standpoint of effective whole-of-government collaboration, AFRICOM closely coordinated with the Department of State for its activities and received funding for these engagements through the Department of State Global Peace Operations Initiative's Africa Contingency Operations Training and Assistance (ACOTA) program.[24]

Yet, in this same address, Ham also took a moment to acknowledge the persistent threat Al-Shabaab poses, to include the potential to launch future attacks within Uganda and Kenya to undermine these states' will to continue to take the fight to the group. Indeed, when Rodriguez appeared on *LiveatState* in the fall of 2013, it had been just over a month since Al-Shabaab had launched a deadly attack on the Westgate Mall in Nairobi. So, as much as AFRICOM's activities provide a potential example for the successful employment of strategic Landpower in a prevent and shape construct, their work against groups who continuously transform, have no regard for borders and exploit seams, and who viciously target "will," demonstrates the precarious nature of the human domain. The Chiefs of the Land Forces describe the complex challenges Landpower confronts in this way:

The threat of hybrid warfare, involving multiple entities; the increasing ability of non-state actors to destabilize entire regions and challenge national forces; the complexity of rules of engagement that constrain one side and enable the other to operate with near impunity 'amongst the people' . . . the increasing pace and mutability of human interactions across boundaries, through virtual connectivity, to form, act, dissolve, and reform in pursuit of hostile purposes.[25]

Working in such a complex and potentially volatile environment, while relying on interagency and regional partners, raises numerous questions for those willing to grapple with the concept of strategic Landpower. With regard to building partner capacity and working with willing and able partners in the region, one must think about the following dynamics:

- How do the various populations conceptualize what the United States deems as "violent extremist organizations," and what makes their narratives resonate or fall on deaf ears?
- As the United States equips, trains, advises, and mentors armed elements, how do the populations think of armed forces and militias and the use of violence?
- How do the governments and other political actors in the region view extremist organizations, and what are the relationships between these organizations and various political stakeholders and powerbrokers, especially in the wake of ongoing disruptive events, such as the Arab Spring?
- How does the United States articulate threats and security interests such that its activities resonate as mutually beneficial global public goods, as opposed to activities that support narrow, selfish interests?[26]

With regards to working within an interagency framework, one must confront the following questions:

- How can DoD and its interagency partners synchronize and pace operations such that individual armed units do not outpace larger defense institutions, threatening the viability, credibility, and professionalism of the armed forces? How can individual armed units be kept from outpacing legal, law enforcement, and governing structures, threatening representative, civilian-led governance?[27]
- How can DoD stay open and flexible enough in its thinking to broaden its conceptualization of threat, while at the same staying sharp enough in its kinetic operations to deal effectively with imminent, tangible, physical threats?
- How can DoD and the Department of State break down barriers and close seams that exist across geographic combatant command boundaries and across regional bureaus?

CONCLUSION

During the past decade-plus of conflict, the U.S. Army has faced numerous types of asymmetric threats from adversaries seeking to evade U.S. Army overmatch capabilities on the battlefield. The Army responded by developing rapid and adaptive processes to counter and defeat these new threats. However, with the coming reduction of Army personnel and funding, there is significant risk of the erosion of the capabilities and knowledge gained over the course of these operations. How can the Army best institutionalize the lessons learned over the past decade, or should the Army make the deliberate decision to relearn these capabilities in future conflict?[28]

"Army Imperatives" section of the
2013-14 Key Strategic Issues List

This quote addresses lessons from the past; however, a range of paradigm shifts make it a relevant backdrop for thinking about AFRICOM's current focus and strategy. The overarching shift is a move away from thinking of asymmetric threats strictly during conflict and on the battlefield to thinking of asymmetric threats in a framework of **prevention** and **shaping** across both physical and cognitive domains. Within that framework, "U.S. Army overmatch capabilities" become "strategic Landpower" efforts, sometimes kinetic and lethal, but often aimed at building partner capacity to confront challenges. Traditional notions of fighting on a "battlefield" transition to understanding and interacting with dynamics of ungoverned spaces, the Internet, traditional trade routes, urban centers, and any of a number of unlimited spaces where narratives of violence may take root and give rise to action. Defeat, while still including kinetic kill and capture operations, now includes activities targeting governance, development, security, and information, aimed at making small, long-term, difficult-to-measure progress against ideology and conditions that would make segments of the population vulnerable to that ideology.

Any way one views it, the threat is still there. The fact that the United States is, for now, pulling large numbers of forces and significant formations from the battlefield does not diminish that broader reality. However, in a paradigm in which low-cost, small-footprint forces play a significant role in building partner capacity to shape the environment and prevent conflict, AFRICOM's activities present an opportunity to innovate, experiment, learn about challenges, and institutionalize effective interagency and multi-national approaches — not necessarily under fire, but while leveraging the important lessons learned over the past decade on the battlefield.

ENDNOTES - CHAPTER 20

1. TRANSCRIPT: General Rodriguez on Security Cooperation in Sub-Saharan Africa, available from *www.africom.mil/Newsroom/ Transcript/11406/general-rodriguez-on-security-cooperation-in-sub-saharan-africa.*

2. *Ibid.*

3. *Ibid.*

4. For additional discussion on the mix and division of labor between reserve and active component forces and special operations and conventional forces, see 2013-14 *Key Strategic Issues List*, John F. Troxell, ed., Carlisle, PA: Strategic Studies Institute, U.S. Army War College, pp. 1, 6, available from *strategicstudiesinstitute. army.mil/pubs/display.cfm?pubID=1183&CFID=45323327&CFTOK EN=5876a31ca87eb40f-038133A9-ABA4-DBE3-68137FF1E05C1E04;* and *Sustaining U.S. Global Leadership: Priorities for 21st Century Defense*, Washington, DC: DoD, January 2012, p. 3, available from *www.defense.gov/news/defense_strategic_guidance.pdf.* For "innovative, low-cost, small footprint approaches," see Sustaining U.S. Global Leadership.

5. Statement of General Carter Ham before the Senate Armed Services Committee, Washington, DC, March 7, 2013, p. 5, available from *www.africom.mil/Newsroom/Transcript/10566/transcript-africom-transcom-commanders-testify-before-senate-armed-services-committee.* These statements are commonly referred to as "posture statements."

6. For enduring U.S. interests, see *National Security Strategy*, Washington, DC: The White House, May, 2010, p. 7, available from *www.whitehouse.gov/sites/default/files/rss_viewer/national_security_strategy.pdf*.

American interests are enduring. They are: The security of the United States, its citizens, and U.S. allies and partners; A strong, innovative, and growing U.S. economy in an open international economic system that promotes opportunity and prosperity; Respect for universal values at home and around the world; and An international order advanced by U.S. leadership that promotes peace, security, and opportunity through stronger cooperation to meet global challenges.

7. Statement of General Ham before the Senate Armed Services Committee, p. 3.

8. For further discussion on the link between extremist organizations, instability, and poor governance, see Charles W. Hooper, "Going Farther by Going Together: Building Partner Capacity in Africa," *Joint Forces Quarterly*, Issue 67, 4th Quarter 2012, p. 9, available from *www.africom.mil/NEWSROOM/Article/10105/going-farther-by-going-together-building-partner-c*.

Africa's security challenges are daunting: terrorism and growing violent extremist organizations, piracy, and the illicit trafficking of arms, narcotics, and people. Poverty and corruption in many regions contribute to an insidious cycle of instability, conflict, environmental degradation, and disease that erodes Africans' confidence in national institutions and governing capacity. This, in turn, creates the conditions for a wide range of transnational security threats that can threaten America's homeland and its regional interests.

9. Statement of General Ham before the Senate Armed Services Committee, p. 5.

10. *Ibid.*, p. 6.

11. Hooper, p. 9.

12. *Sustaining U.S. Global Leadership*, p. 3.

13. "Redefining America's Military Leadership," *The National Military Strategy of the United States of America*, Washington, DC: DoD, 2011, p. 6, available from *www.army.mil/info/references/docs/ NMS%20FEB%202011.pdf*. The strategy outlines that the United States "will be prepared to find, capture, or kill violent extremists wherever they reside."

14. "Strategic Landpower: Winning the Clash of Wills," Washington, DC: U.S. Army Training and Doctrine Command, available from *www.tradoc.army.mil/FrontPageContent/Docs/Strategic%20Landpower%20White%20Paper.pdf*. The introduction to the "white paper" is signed by Raymond T. Odierno, GEN USA; Chief of Staff, James F. Amos, Gen, USMC, Commandant; and William H. McRaven, ADM, USN, Commanding. The authors define "strategic landpower" as "the application of Landpower toward achieving overarching national or multinational (alliance or coalition) security objectives and guidance for a given military campaign or operation."

15. *Ibid.*

16. *Ibid.*

17. *Ibid.*

18. Troxell, p. 1.

19. As noted, 2nd Brigade Combat Team, 1st Infantry Division is AFRICOM's regionally aligned force. Numerous sources discuss the concept of regionally aligned forces. See, for instance, *Army Strategic Planning Guidance 2013*, Washington, DC: U.S. Department of the Army, available from *usarmy.vo.llnwd.net/e2/ rv5_downloads/info/references/army_strategic_planning_guidance.pdf*. In Hooper, "Going Farther by Going Together," p. 13, the author states the following with regards to USAFRICOM:

> The RAF (regionally aligned force) concept is an innovative approach consistent with USAFRICOM's emphasis on operating with small teams and maintaining a light footprint. Security cooperation engagements will be conducted primar-

ily by small tailored units from within an aligned brigade. This alignment over time will allow staff and subordinate units to foster enduring security relationships and develop expanded regional knowledge as well as an understanding of our partners' unique security requirements.

20. Operation ONWARD LIBERTY, available from *www.africom.mil/what-we-do/operations/ool*.

21. *Atlas Accord*, available from *www.africom.mil/what-we-do/exercises/atlas-accord*.

22. Rich Bartell, "Ugandans Train for Future AMISOM Mission," available from *www.africom.mil/Newsroom/Article/11409/ugandans-train-for-future-amisom-mission*.

23. TRANSCRIPT: General Carter Ham Discusses Security Challenges, Opportunities at George Washington University, available from *www.africom.mil/NEWSROOM/Transcript/10170/transcript-general-ham-discusses-security-challeng*.

24. Statement of General Ham before the Senate Armed Services Committee, p. 14.

25. "Strategic Landpower: Winning the Clash of Wills."

26. Daniel W. Drezner, "Does Obama Have a Grand Strategy: Why we need Doctrines in Uncertain Times," *Foreign Affairs*, Vol. 90, No. 4, July-August 2011, p. 65.

27. In security sector reform, the need for coordination and synchronization of activities across government agencies is a recurring theme. See, for instance, *U.S. Security Sector Assistance Policy*, Washington, DC: The White House, available from *www.whitehouse.gov/the-press-office/2013/04/05/fact-sheet-us-security-sector-assistance-policy*. Also see Troxell, p. 18. This observation is also based on conversations with several military and civilian professionals with extensive experience in security assistance and security sector reform.

28. Troxell, p. 2.

CHAPTER 21

ADJUSTING THE PARADIGM: HUMAN SECURITY AS A STRATEGIC APPROACH TOWARD STABILITY, COUNTERTERRORISM, AND MILITARY EFFECTIVENESS

Andrew Gallo and Cindy Jebb

This work reflects the views of the authors and not the views of the U.S. Government, Department of Defense, the U.S. Army, or West Point. The authors would like to thank several scholars in the Department of Social Sciences to include the Combating Terrorism Center, especially Michael Meese, Reid Sawyer, Liam Collins, Nelly Lahoud, Arie Perliger, Gabe Koehler-Derrick, Alex Gallo, and Don Rassler, as well as P. H. Liotta, Angelica Martinez, Assaf Moghadam, and Mark Crow. All have discussed portions of this chapter especially as Cindy Jebb prepared several speeches and talks regarding this topic. This chapter builds from and contains major portions of Jebb and Gallo, "Adjusting the Paradigm: A Human Security Framework for Combating Terrorism," Chap. 16, Mary Martin and Taylor Owen, eds., *Handbook of Human Security*, New York: Routledge Press, 2013, pp. 210-222.

In his last speech at the United States Military Academy at West Point, New York, as the Secretary of Defense in February 2011, Robert M. Gates warned the Corps of Cadets that, while we cannot know with absolute certainty what the future of warfare will hold, we know that it will be exceedingly complex, unpredictable, and unstructured. Matter-of-fact, he asserted:

When it comes to predicting the nature and location of our next military engagement . . . our record has been perfect. We have never once gotten it right, from

387

the Mayaguez to Grenada, Panama, Somalia, the Balkans, Haiti, Kuwait, Iraq, and more—we had no idea a year before any of these missions that we would be so engaged.[1]

Given the dynamic nature of the environment in an era of complex local, regional, and global change, it is helpful to consider a new paradigm with a set of guiding principles that the U.S. military might leverage in its operations. Specifically, a human security framework provides a multidimensional and comprehensive approach that offers decisionmakers a practical set of options to achieve realistic outcomes.

Before we examine security, there are some macro-level truths that we must first acknowledge. First, Carl von Clausewitz's basic premise—that war is a continuation of politics by other means—is a useful foundation upon which we can build.[2] This enduring principle ought to be a touchstone as the United States searches for a paradigm that will help guide national security in a dangerous world. Second, we believe that Secretary Gates aptly describes the current complex reality:

> In recent years the lines separating war, peace, diplomacy, and development have become more blurred, and no longer fit the neat organizational charts of the 20th century. All the various elements and stakeholders working in the international arena—military and civilian, government and private—have learned to stretch outside their comfort zone to work together and achieve results.[3]

For the U.S. military, this reality means that it must be prepared to operate effectively across a range of operations, many of which will consist of a complicated mixture of lethal and nonlethal actions designed to affect not only military conditions, but also political, economic, social, and other conditions within a given operational area.[4] Moreover, there must be an equally understood common purpose at all levels and across the continuum. The military must not only synchronize its own actions, it must also effectively strive for unity of effort toward achieving a common goal with civilian organizations and non-U.S. military organizations in the operational area. The nonlinear, fast-changing nature of security environments requires that all leaders embrace the reality of these complex operations.

Past approaches have limited our ability to effectively anticipate, understand, and operate in these complex environments. In fact, such approaches have constrained our ability to understand the problem, and in many cases reduced our thinking to binary dyads, such as we-they; us-them; peacekeeping-counterterrorism; and military-nonmilitary.[5] While the world appears much simpler when viewed in such a binary manner, it causes security professionals to understate or miss the important contextual dynamics necessary for accurately assessing problems and capitalizing on opportunities.

Military leaders must not only be able to solve nuanced, unstructured problems, they must also be able to identify new problem sets; and this is increasingly more challenging. In regards to terrorism, it is not sufficient to just understand the structure of al-Qaeda (AQ); one must also understand its growing complexity—how it is morphing, influencing, and connecting to other groups and individuals globally, regionally, and locally. Many of these types of challenges require a multidimensional approach, with the military in a supporting role. Subsequently, military leaders must be open to forming new teams that reflect diverse perspectives and approaches whatever the operation, guided by a common purpose and a unity of effort.

There are two major questions that permeate this paradigm shift. First, how do we nurture strategic thinking? This does not necessarily mean "how do we produce strategists?" Rather, it asks how we develop strategic thinking that is holistic, critical, creative, systematic, empathetic, and forward-leaning.[6] This challenge applies not only to the military, but also across the government, the private sector, and among host-nation and allied partners. Second, how do we make sure that we do not lose the hard-earned lessons of the past decade? For the United States, it is unfortunate that the U.S. Army had to relearn counterinsurgency after the U.S. experience in the Vietnam War. Now that military operations have wound down in Iraq and we are leaving Afghanistan, how do we ensure that we do not lose critically important lessons learned?[7] Within this context, the purpose of this chapter is to share some thoughts on a potential way forward for the military, specifically the U.S. Army.

The problem of terrorism was the initial driving factor for our military engagements over the last decade.[8] Bruce Hoffman, in a discussion at West Point shared that, while terrorist organizations are dangerous, the real danger is the political movements that they can spark. The Princeton Project refers to terrorism as a "global insurgency with a criminal core ..." that should be addressed by a "counter-insurgency that utilizes a range of tools. ..."[9] These two views are important for two major reasons. First, they suggest that terrorism is not merely a military problem, but one that must be addressed primarily with nonmilitary means. Second, they highlight the crisis of legitimacy found in many parts of the world where people are also suffering from grave human insecurities.

RETHINKING SECURITY: TOWARD
A HUMAN SECURITY FRAMEWORK

The first step to understanding legitimacy is to consider security from the individual's point of view. This human security perspective opens up the security aperture in important ways.[10] When the United Nations (UN) presents aggregate data such as one billion people who lack access to clean water, two billion people who lack access to clean sanitation, three million people who die from water related diseases annually, 14 million people (including 6 million children) who die from hunger annually, and 30 million people in Africa alone who have HIV/AIDS, it primarily describes and reflects myriad human insecurities and the increasing global gap between the haves and the have-nots.[11]

While there are some commonalities among underdeveloped regions, they are far from all alike. One commonality, however, is that many of these transnational forces are directly harmful to people, do not recognize borders, and are particularly harmful to susceptible regions that are already suffering. Human security is a concept that both describes these conditions and provides an approach to better understand their effects. The UN recognized this approach in a 1994 document:

> The concept of security has far too long been interpreted narrowly: as security of territory from external aggression, or as protection of national interests in foreign policy or as global security from the threat of nuclear holocaust. It has been related to nation-states more than people. . . . Forgotten were the legitimate concerns of ordinary people who sought security in

their daily lives. For many of them, security symbolized protection from the threat of disease, hunger, unemployment, crime [or terrorism], social conflict, political repression and environmental hazards. With the dark shadows of the Cold War receding, one can see that many conflicts are within nations rather than between nations.[12]

Clearly, not all areas face the same insecurities.[13] As we have witnessed, these insecurities frequently have diffuse global effects, such as migrations, reverberations in Diaspora communities, environmental impacts, and even the exportation of terrorism.[14] The human security paradigm should remind strategists that they must approach issues holistically and empathetically; this painstaking analysis, patience, and tenacity is imperative to reach a set of realistic, achievable outcomes that are the result of understanding the problem, possible opportunities, and the identification of trade-offs and risks.

An effective human security framework and a set of guiding principles must be oriented to achieving realistic outcomes. While these outcomes will likely vary in time and place, failing to establish realistic, achievable ends will result in unfocused policies and the eventual loss of political will. It is often understood that a primary national interest is fostering a stable world order. Our national security strategies suggest that encouraging democracy would in fact lessen the prevalence of terrorism.[15] It is what we hope for in Iraq and Afghanistan.

What would reducing the prevalence of terrorism and stabilizing the world order entail? Ralf Dahrendorf explains stability as the sum of two key components: effectiveness and legitimacy:

Effectiveness . . . means that governments have to be able to do things which they claim they can do . . . they have to work. Legitimacy, on the other hand, is a moral concept. . . . A government is legitimate if what it does is right both in the sense of complying with certain fundamental principles, and in that of being in line with prevailing cultural values.[16]

Legitimacy is rooted in the people, not imposed. This central concept suggests that achieving stability requires tireless efforts, perseverance, and tenacity. Small changes over time will make a difference. The United States and the international community must demonstrate strategic patience, while learning how to better tap nonmilitary capital in ways that will make a difference. For the United States, this may require restructuring and properly resourcing its interagency process, so that the United States may effectively leverage all aspects of its power, such as diplomatic, economic, financial, agricultural, and commercial influences. Monitoring progress will be difficult but essential as policymakers, politicians, academics, business, nongovernmental organizations, and military leaders forge an adaptable way ahead.

Tony Blair suggests that the first step in determining whether to intervene anywhere is to diagnose the problem.[17] Key to this process is to understand and value the **local** perspective. To diagnose the problem effectively, one must understand that often there is a "conflict eco-system" at play.[18] If you do not understand that eco-system, affecting change in one area may produce unwanted change in another. The dynamic terrorist threat exists in such an eco-system.[19] Therefore, it is important to rethink security — for whom, from whom, by whom, and with what means to understand better this eco-system.[20]

The human security framework sheds light on the importance of the local perspective. For example, while international terrorism may be a U.S. priority, terrorism may not be the most pressing security problem for the host nation or its people. In many areas, there are far more pressing issues that affect daily survival. Moreover, a foreign force's presence in a country itself changes the security environment. The infrastructure, whether it is new roads, bridges, or electric grids, that the military provides enables the population, but also the adversary. Our actions may inadvertently create winners and losers. Even just moving vehicles may disrupt activities. Clearly, the simple acts of showing respect, reciprocity, and trust are extremely important at the individual engagement level. Even acts of kindness can seem cruel in a country occupied by so-called liberators. Empathic understanding is crucial.

This complex, uncertain, and unstructured environment presents a challenging landscape to assess progress. Many times progress does not occur in a linear fashion, and an overreaction may exacerbate the situation. For example, as a country democratizes and a terrorist group sees the window of opportunity closing, there may actually be a spike in violence. For Spain during the late-1970s and early-1980s, this was the case with the Basque National Liberation Movement (ETA). Spain's continuing adherence to democratic principles allowed it to contain and marginalize ETA, while furthering the state's legitimacy.[21]

It is also extremely difficult to assess adversaries like AQ because it requires hard and continuous study as the object of study constantly changes. A Combating Terrorism Center publication suggests the importance of assessing AQ across five dimensions: in terms of its power to destroy, power to inspire, power to humiliate, power to command, and power to unify.[22] Moreover, it is difficult to distinguish among bandits, terrorists, smugglers, thugs, and perhaps other illicit actors who support people's livelihoods. Yet, by not distinguishing among them, there is grave risk of applying a strategy that might exacerbate the problem, misunderstand risks, or engage the wrong people.

Of course, when we look only for threats, we miss opportunities. Often, providing opportunities for others creates opportunities for ourselves. General David Petraeus identified money as even more effective than ammunition in the campaigns in Iraq and Afghanistan.[23] This new dimension of military activity — expeditionary economics — suggests that grave human insecurity in many areas is a result of very little effective economic activity. The military has some tools that may help it act as the paramedic before the civilian experts are able to assist with long-term economic development.[24] Having said this, it is important to take the time to identify what economy does exist. What is currently being produced? How is it produced? And who benefits? There may be existing businesses, and perhaps even local entrepreneurs, that could be supported.[25] Military strategists must learn to map the political landscape, taking note of both formal and informal leaders, in order to recognize the power structures that may help to alleviate human insecurities.

Many practitioners and scholars rightfully ask why the West helps the rest when local or non-Western answers can be found. In fact, Petraeus' first observation in the article cited earlier concerns the importance of empowering the local people. He quotes T. E. Lawrence: "Do not try to do too much with your own hands."[26] Collaboration between international and local communities is important to build local stakeholders on projects that are jointly planned and relevant. While the United States and its allies want and ought to help states counter terrorism, this help cannot be at the expense of the local people, and it cannot allow real grievances to be ignored.[27]

In decisions to empower local forces, as in all strategic decisions, there are trade-offs that must be acknowledged. Let us consider two here. First, states must balance liberty and security. The temptation during wartime is to shift so much toward security that governments and societies no longer reflect the values that define and guide them. Strengthening local forces sometimes produces gains in security at the expense of losses in other values (including liberty) that Western societies hold dear. Striking the right balance in a world faced with dire transnational security issues is challenging. There is also a trade-off between urgent and legitimate action. When urgent action must be taken, it is easiest to operate unilaterally, but unilateral action is frequently considered illegitimate. Moreover, insurgents and terrorists try to provoke governments to take harsh retaliatory measures through violent actions. The trade-off between urgency and legitimacy, then, must also be carefully weighed.

Of course, the adversary faces its own trade-offs and makes choices that we must understand, although it is difficult for us to do so. Martha Crenshaw distinguishes between terrorists who have an effect in the security environment and those who succeed in producing their desired outcome. To evaluate a terrorist group's effect, one must observe outcomes alone, but to assess the group's success one must understand its intentions.[28] Similarly, the international community must distinguish between having an effect and succeeding; the two are not necessarily the same thing since a quick win in the short term might undermine a long-term strategic goal.

Traditionally, we apply military solutions to security problems, especially when we have a narrow view of security. As the old saying goes, when all problems are viewed as nails, there is no need to use anything but a hammer. As noted earlier, the majority of security challenges do not fall cleanly in the traditional kinetic category. The human security framework highlights this reality by shedding light on the transnational, multifaceted, and multidimensional nature of the security environment. As we rightly apply a human security lens and "see" more comprehensively the multidimensional nature of security challenges, it is imperative that we reassess the roles and missions of militaries. Specifically, if war is a continuation of policy through other means, as Clausewitz reminds us, then how do we bring to bear an integrated approach across all dimensions of power, while realizing that the nonlinear and complex nature of the security environment requires overlapping jurisdictions of responsibility?

No one nation can address the challenges that face all of humanity. The human security approach calls for the sharing of intelligence, knowledge, and perspective in order to facilitate an integrated strategy in support of policy. As discussed earlier, one of the challenges is to identify early the indicators of terrorism, insurgency, or opportunity. The earlier, the better to detect and take appropriate action. This is very difficult, but in order to shape the future, one must be open to different possibilities by not only sharing information, but applying different perspectives on the issues. Moreover, collaboration between international and local communities is important to build local stakeholders on projects that are jointly planned and relevant.

We are not suggesting that the international community must embark on a full-out nation-building effort everywhere there is terrorism. Quite the contrary. If terrorism is deemed a national and international security threat, there are combinations of kinetic and nonkinetic approaches that can address the terrorists kinetically, while simultaneously holding state leaders accountable and addressing the human insecurities in society. By fully diagnosing the problem in context and partnering among agencies internal to the U.S. Government, local stakeholders, and the international community, a more cost-effective early approach is better than waiting until open conflict and war occur at great costs. In other words, we offer a rethinking of the tools to address what has been recognized as a security environment that presents primarily nonmilitary challenges. While the military must accept its role in this nontraditional context, it is time that the United States and the international community capitalize on the enormous but not yet fully tapped nonmilitary elements of power that reside in the U.S. Government, society, and international community.

This rethinking is in line with the recent literature regarding future roles and missions of the military and specifically the Army. In the 2012 *Army Strategic Planning Guidance*, Secretary of the Army John M. McHugh and Chief of Staff of the Army General Raymond T. Odierno emphasized that the Army must be "an indispensible partner and provider of a full range of capabilities to Combatant Commanders in a Joint, Interagency, Intergovernmental, and Multi-national (JIIM) environment."[29] In order to do so, these senior leaders provide a **prevent, shape, and win** framework supported by a regionally aligned force that will help secure populations while assisting our allies' security forces. Such missions emphasize the development of "mutual understanding" between the United States and its allies. Understanding security from the individual's point of view by focusing on the concerns of ordinary people must be an integral component of a security model in today's operational environment.

GUIDING PRINCIPLES

From this discussion, we offer guiding principles that inform strategic direction. We deliberately do not offer a highly-detailed, cookie-cutter approach; the security environment demands otherwise. However, the human security lens offers some guiding principles that could best help inform not only decisions on whether to intervene but how to intervene with a better understanding of realistic outcomes. In fact, while these guiding principles hold whether they are in place at the highest levels of government or at the small military unit level, they are mostly aimed at the U.S. military.

Diagnose the Problem.

The human security lens raises the right questions not only to best understand the changing dynamic of a terrorist organization, but the context in which it is operating, to include the regime and its leaders, as well as all the environmental factors that affect human survival and dignity.

Identify Opportunities.

The human security approach highlights the economic, political, religious, and societal landscape to include informal leaders. This process leads to empowering local stakeholders, to include women.

Collaboratively Determine Achievable Outcomes.

While achieving national interests, the United States and the international community must view outcomes empathetically and in partnership with local stakeholders. In other words, there must be an empathetic understanding of the sources of legitimacy and the varied levels of state effectiveness. It is too easy to impose our own views on such matters. Moreover, as the security environment changes, we must be willing to reassess outcomes.

Acknowledge that Assessments Are Hard.

Assessments are critical, but we must also acknowledge their difficulty. Quantitative assessments do not adequately describe progress, given the nonlinear nature of complex situations; at worst, reliance on the wrong quantitative indicator can serve to incentivize behavior that worsens the problem at hand. It is important that assessment criteria be established collaboratively to establish partnerships among local stakeholders more firmly to best achieve both legitimacy and effectiveness.

Understand Trade-offs and Manage Risk.

The human security paradigm highlights trade-offs, especially if there are losers and winners involved in certain decisions. There may be trade-offs between short- and long-term gains and between unilateral and collaborative action. The important point is to acknowledge those trade-offs and seek to better understand the risks involved, both to ensure informed decisions and to better prepare for second and third order effects.

Be Ready for Full-Spectrum Operations.

The military must be ready for full spectrum operations in any situation. Even within a short span of distance, one local area may require immediate kinetic operations, while an adjoining area may require a nonkinetic approach. Given the short- and long-term uncertainties, the best hedge for now, and in the future, is competence across the full spectrum. It is this imperative that we focus on in the last guiding principles, which describe aspects of our profession.

Be Self-Aware.

The actions a military takes, even with the best intentions, may have adverse effects, especially if those actions include occupying another country. Units and service members affect the security environment; adversaries adapt; over time the local populations can become weary.

Value Human Capital.

Full spectrum competence under complex and uncertain conditions requires a diverse set of talents. As the U.S. military engages in talent management, it must ensure that the professional requirements of its members align with the personnel bureaucracy that manages recruitment, retention, employment, and development.[30]

Continually Professionalize Ourselves and Assist with Professionalizing Other Militaries.

The military must ensure that its members continue to have the experiences, education, and training required to face complex challenges successfully today and in the future. The positive impact that the U.S. military has had professionalizing other militaries should not be underestimated. Build upon the interagency and coalition partnering that has occurred over the last decade; educate and train alongside these partners.

Prepare Future Leaders Both at Home and Abroad.

The challenges facing future leaders require strategic thinkers who embrace the warrior ethos and are guided by moral-ethical principles. In short, the United States and its allies require leaders of character. This point may seem self-evident, but it is worth stating explicitly in the midst of budget stringency. The current programs at the Service Academies, War Colleges, and Reserve Officers' Training Corps (ROTC) educate and develop the U.S. officer corps, but their international programs also achieve tremendous effects around the world.[31]

Let us revisit the concept of strategic thinking introduced earlier. In a recent *Foreign Affairs* piece, General (Ret.) Stanley McChrystal observed:

> "In Iraq, when we first started, the question was, 'Where is the enemy?' . . . As we got smarter, we started to ask, 'Who is the enemy?' . . . And then . . . we asked, 'What's the enemy doing or trying to do?' And it wasn't until we got further along that we said, 'Why are they the enemy?'[32]

As Secretary Gates explained at a talk at West Point, we cannot expect our officers to succeed in these environments unless we provide them with the right experiences, education, and incentives.[33] There is too much at stake to do any less.

ENDNOTES - CHAPTER 21

1. Robert M. Gates, Speech to the United States Military Academy, February 25, 2011, available from *www.defense.gov/speeches/speech.aspx?speechid=1539*.

2. Carl von Clausewitz, Michael Eliot Howard and Peter Paret, eds. and trans., *On War*, Princeton, NJ: Princeton University Press, 1989, p. 87.

3. Robert Gates, Washington, DC, July 15, 2008, as cited in Mark Crow, "Senior Conference XLVI, Bridging the Cultural Divide: NGO-Military Relations in Complex Environments," Senior Conference Paper, West Point, NY, May 28-30, 2009.

4. Army doctrine refers to these operations as "full-spectrum operations." See *Field Manual 5-0, The Operations Process*, Washington, DC: Department of Defense, March 26, 2010.

5. See Azza Karam, "Transnational Political Islam and the USA: An Introduction," Azza Karam, ed., *Transnational Political Islam: Religion, Ideology and Power*, London, United Kingdom (UK): Pluto Press, 2004, p. 2.

6. Gregory D. Foster, "Teaching Strategic Thinking to Strategic Leaders," *The World & I Online*, November 2005, online edition. Also see Gregory D. Foster, "Research, Writing, and the Mind of the Strategist," *Joint Forces Quarterly*, Spring 1996.

7. Operations in Iraq and Afghanistan have wound down as of this writing; however, the authors acknowledge that changes in these two areas may slow or reverse this process.

8. For a full discussion on the definition of terrorism, see Cindy R. Jebb, P. H. Liotta, Thomas Sherlock, and Ruth Beitler, *The Fight for Legitimacy: Democracy vs. Terrorism*, Westport, CT: Praeger Security International, 2006, pp. 3-5.

9. See *Ibid.*, pp. 3-7, for a discussion on perceptions and definitions of terrorism. Bruce Hoffman's definition is from Bruce Hoffman, Lecture at West Point, April 2004; the Princeton Project reference comes from G. John Ikenberry and Anne-Marie Slaughter, *Forging a World of Liberty under Law: U.S. National Security in the 21st Century*, Princeton, NJ: The Woodrow Wilson School of Public and International Affairs, Princeton University, September 27, 2006, p. 9.

10. Note that this section is modified from Cindy R. Jebb, Laurel J. Hummel, Luis Rios, and Madelfia Abb, "Human and Environmental Security in the Sahel: A Modest Strategy for Success," P. H. Liotta *et. al.*, *Environmental Change and Human Security*, The Netherlands: Springer Books, 2008, pp. 343-353.

11. "Part One: Towards a New Security Consensus," *Report of the High-Level Panel on Threats, Challenges, and Change to the Secretary General*, New York: United Nations, p. 17, available from *unrol.org/files/gaA.59.565_En.pdf.* as cited in Jebb *et al.*, "Human and Environmental Security," p. 346.

12. United Nations Development Program (UNDP) Report, 1994, pp. 3, 22-23, as quoted by P. H. Liotta, *The Uncertain Certainty*, Lanham, MD: Lexington, 2004, pp. 4-5.

13. The UNDP lists the following categories of insecurity: economic, food, health, environmental, personal, community, and political. UNDP, UN Development Report, Chap. 2, "New Dimensions of Human Security," pp. 22-25 as cited in P. H. Liotta

and Taylor Owen, "Sense and Symbolism: Europe Takes on Human Security," *Parameters*, Vol. 36, No. 3, Autumn 2006, p. 90.

14. Also see Tedd Gurr, "Why Minorities Rebel: Explaining Ethnopolitical Protest and Rebellion," *Minorities and Risk: A Global View of Ethnopolitical Conflicts*, Washington, DC: United States Institute of Peace, October 1997, pp. 123-138; and Robert Kaplan, "The Coming Anarchy," *The Atlantic Monthly*, Vol. 273, Issue 2, February 1994, pp. 44-76.

15. Jebb *et al.*, *The Fight for Legitimacy*, p. 6.

16. Ralf Dahrendorf, "On the Governability of Democracies," Roy C. Macridis and Bernard Brown, eds., *Comparative Politics: Notes and Readings*, Pacific Grove, CA: Brooks/Cole Publishing Company, 1990, pp. 285-286. Also see Jebb *et al.*, *The Fight for Legitimacy*, p. 7.

17. Tony Blair, "Doctrine of the International Community," Speech delivered to the Chicago Economic Club, April 22, 1999.

18. David Kilcullen, "Counterinsurgency Redux," *Small Wars Journal*, available from *www.smallwarsjournal.com/documents/kilcullen1.pdf.*

19. David Kilcullen addresses the many differences between the classical insurgent and the modern insurgent, calling attention to the complex "conflict eco-system" that harbours numerous insurgent groups. See Kilcullen, p. 9-10.

20. This notion of security was discussed by P. H. Liotta in a presentation at West Point, NY, January 11, 2011.

21. For more on this case, see Cindy R. Jebb, "The Fight for Legitimacy: Liberal Democracy Versus Terrorism," *The Journal of Conflict Studies*, Vol. XXIII, No. 1, Spring 2003, pp. 126-152.

22. "Al-Qa'ida's Five Aspects of Power," Combating Terrorism Center, *CTC Sentinel*, Vol. 2, No. 1, January 2009, p. 1.

23. David H. Petraeus, "Learning Counterinsurgency: Observations from Soldiering in Iraq," *Military Review*, January-February 2006, p. 4.

24. Jeff Peterson and Mark Crow, Senior Conference Paper, West Point, NY, 2011.

25. See Mark Crow, "Economics and Counterinsurgency," Briefing to 10th Mountain Division, March 2011.

26. Petraeus, p. 3.

27. Interestingly, the UNDP's Arab Development Report cited the Arab world as suffering from three deficits: "the freedom deficit; the women's empowerment deficit; and the human capabilities/ knowledge deficit relative to income." Women's empowerment should not be an after-thought, but rather it is essential to addressing human insecurities and moving societies forward. *The Arab Human Development Report 2002: Creating Opportunities for Future Generations*, New York: United Nation's Human Development Programme, p. 27.

28. Martha Crenshaw, "Terrorism in the Algerian War," *Terrorism in Context*. University Park, PA: The Pennsylvania State University Press, 2001, p. 475.

29. *2012 Army Strategic Planning Guidance*, Washington, DC: Department of Defense, p. 4.

30. See Talent Management Series beginning with Casey Wardynski, David S. Lyle, and Michael Colarusso, *Towards a U.S. Army Officer Corps Strategy for Success: A Proposed Human Capital Model Focused Upon Talent*, Carlisle, PA: Strategic Studies Institute, U.S. Army War College, April 2009.

31. *Ibid.*

32. Gideon Rose, "Generation Kill: A Conversation with Stanley McChrystal, *Foreign Affairs*, Vol. 92, No. 2, March-April, 2013, p. 6.

33. Secretary of Defense Robert M Gates speech delivered February 25, 2011 to the Corps of Cadets at West Point, New York.

CHAPTER 22

LANDPOWER IN THE CYBER DOMAIN

Suzanne C. Nielsen

The views expressed in this chapter are those of the author and do not purport to reflect the position of the United States Military Academy, the Department of the Army, or the Department of Defense.

As this volume goes to press, the author notes that Secretary of the Army John McHugh approved the creation of a Cyber Branch within the Army on September 1, 2014. This chapter, which was written prior to this development, remains useful to thinking about the desirable characteristics of this branch and the supporting changes within the Army that are needed if this innovation is to succeed.

In addition to the need to adapt to ensure that Landpower remains relevant in meeting the country's security needs, the senior leaders of today's Army face a fundamentally new challenge. They must develop forces capable of operating and defending military networks in a contested cyber environment and conducting full-spectrum cyberspace operations in the service of the national interest. While instituting change in military organizations is never easy or quick, meeting this new imperative poses a special combination of challenges that adds to the usual difficulties.

This chapter seeks to provide useful context for this new mission, while briefly outlining what mission accomplishment may require. First, it puts the problem in perspective by tracing the need for military cyber force development back to changes in the strategic environment. Second, it acknowledges that military innovation is necessary but not sufficient; it must occur in the context of supporting developments across the interagency in order to be fully successful. Third, it surveys existing propositions about how change occurs in military organizations, and explores their implications in light of the need to build military forces capable of meeting the demands of military cyberspace operations. Finally, it concludes with a brief survey of changes within the U.S. Army to date. Though the Army has made progress, its efforts fall short of true innovation. It has not yet developed cyber personnel or organizations designed to approach military cyberspace operations as a fundamentally new way of war.

A STRUCTURAL CHANGE IN THE SECURITY ENVIRONMENT

Over the last several decades, the United States and other economically and technologically advanced countries have become dependent on cyberspace. In an amazingly short period of time, the Internet has gone from being a venue for collaboration among a small circle of trusted users to a place where individuals and organizations around the world communicate and obtain information, make and store wealth, operate critical infrastructure, and perform vital national security functions. Even Americans who do not own a computer cannot avoid dependence on cyberspace, given that their personal information, economic activities, communications, and the essential services on which they rely have reflections in or depend on cyberspace.

For society as a whole, one need look no further than the U.S. financial system to get a sense of how significant cyberspace has become. A disruption to the New York Stock Exchange that had its origins in cyberspace would be significant; a fundamental loss of confidence in the system would have grave consequences for U.S. and global economies with difficult-to-forecast ripple effects across society, government, and the international system.

The growing dependence of critical societal functions on cyberspace has not yet been accompanied by commensurate efforts to secure that space. This situation is made all the more dangerous by the existence of a wide array of malicious actors with increasingly dangerous capabilities. Those who seek to protect networks or other cyberspace resources are generally at a structural disadvantage, given that security has often taken a back seat to other goals such as functionality in system and architecture design. The vulnerabilities that do exist are subject to being exploited by diverse threat actors who range from individual hackers, to criminal groups, to states. Their activities include intrusion, theft, disruption, and even destruction. This destruction could occur through the deployment of malware designed to destroy information technologies, or the use of cyberspace to manipulate industrial control systems that regulate the operation of systems essential to critical infrastructure or other industrial processes in physical space. An example of the latter was the Stuxnet worm, discovered in June 2010, which damaged a number of uranium enrichment centrifuges in Iran. Though such incidents have a dramatic impact, other activities like the widespread theft of intellectual property from American universities and companies could have implications that are of even greater significance for the long-term prosperity and security of the country.

The dependence of modern societies on a cyberspace that is fundamentally insecure constitutes a significant transformation in the strategic environment in which the United States advances and protects its national interests. To date, however, the U.S. Government and private sector have barely begun to grapple with the full implications of this transformation. One could find fault with individual leaders or organizations across the public and private sectors for a slow rate of progress, but it is useful to recognize the inherent difficulties involved.

Since a full enumeration of the difficulties in securing cyberspace would require more space than is appropriate here, this section will describe just three examples for illustrative purposes. First, cyberspace is relatively unique in that internationally-agreed upon protocols allow users to operate as if international borders did not exist. Geography is not completely irrelevant, since sovereignty can still be exerted over cyber infrastructure that is physically located within a particular country. Nevertheless, borders are much less salient for a variety of reasons, including the insignificance of physical distance; the speed at which cyberspace operates; and the difficulty of attributing a cyber activity to the responsible actor. Second, cyberspace is intrinsically a multi-stakeholder domain in which private sector actors play a leading role. In the United States, for example, the private sector builds most cyberspace resources, owns and operates cyber infrastructure, and provides the vast majority of the essential services upon which the functioning of society relies. As they conduct these activities, private sector entities respond to market incentives; in the aggregate, their activities may not produce a level of risk that is acceptable to society as a whole. Government actions to address this situation through regulations or the establishment of standards are highly contentious and politically charged. As a third issue, tradeoffs between security and the privacy and civil liberties of individual citizens seem stark, which complicates efforts by the U.S. Government to improve cyber security. It is undoubtedly possible to improve cyber security while simultaneously protecting civil liberties and privacy, but technical complexity increases the difficulty of explaining such initiatives. In addition, it is likely that many Americans do not fully understand the risks to their welfare and privacy that exist in the status quo, which leads to weak public support for new policies.

THE ARMY'S NEEDED CONTRIBUTION TO INTERAGENCY CHANGE

Efforts to advance and protect U.S. national interests in this new strategic environment are not primarily the responsibility of the Department of Defense (DoD), but DoD and the military services have a role to play. The relatively borderless nature of cyberspace poses a challenge, given that U.S. laws and the structure of the government were developed to deal with a world in which distinctions between foreign and domestic were clear, relevant, and useful. To mitigate the risks that dependence on cyberspace creates, departments and agencies will have to leverage their unique authorities while engaged in an intense form of operational collaboration that does not come naturally.

To see why strong interagency partnerships are necessary, consider a scenario in which an adversary state actor uses foreign and domestic cyber infrastructure to disrupt the operations of critical infrastructure.

As a result of its responsibilities and legal authorities, the Federal Bureau of Investigation (FBI) within the Department of Justice has the lead with regard to law enforcement and domestic counterintelligence activities. It therefore has a necessary role in any effort to address the malicious use of cyber infrastructure within the United States. The Department of Homeland Security (DHS) will also need to leverage its authorities and capabilities to protect the private sector by establishing standards and orchestrating requests for technical support. In the scenario already described, DHS has a vital role to play in lessening the vulnerability of critical infrastructure and in consequence management. The intelligence community is a third important player, as it is the essential provider of intelligence on foreign threats and indications and warning. In the previous scenario, the intelligence community would be a source of information about foreign intentions and capabilities that would lead to better defenses; ideally, the intelligence community could also provide real-time information that would allow an attack to be stopped before succeeding. Finally, the DoD has a critical role to play in defending the country from foreign threats, when ordered to do so, through military activities abroad or through defense support to civil authorities. As Secretary of Defense Chuck Hagel has made clear, the responsibility of the DoD to defend the country extends to the cyber domain.[1] This could include the use of military forces in cyberspace to defeat an attack.

It is within this strategic context that the development of Army cyber forces should be assessed. The establishment of Cyber Command in 2010 reflected an appreciation that the military needed to unify its approach to cyberspace operations. It also reflected a decision to take a fundamentally joint approach. Rather than assign a particular military service the responsibility for cyberspace—a role that the U.S. Air Force sought unsuccessfully—cyberspace operations are similar to other military operations in that they will be conducted by joint force commanders. The military services must train, equip, and provide forces to these commanders. Though its creation was a critical step forward, U.S. Cyber Command is a small headquarters of less than 1,000 people. The forces that will provide the capability and capacity the military needs to operate in cyberspace must be built by the military services.

INNOVATION AND ARMY CYBER FORCE DEVELOPMENT

When thinking about military change, it is useful to start by recognizing that innovations that lead to the more effective or efficient performance of military tasks cannot be taken for granted. Like all large organizations, military services seek to coordinate the efforts of a large number of people to perform collective tasks. To make this possible, they are designed for stability rather than change. The organizations, processes, and incentive structures that foster this stability can also create vested interests and an organizational culture that favor the status quo.[2] In addition, the armed services are government bureaucracies whose leaders operate in an environment of constraints. Whereas executives in the private sector have discretion over basic choices such as what their organizations will produce, executives in government cannot entirely set their own goals and have limited ability to allocate resources such as a labor and capital in the

413

manner they see fit. Government executives have an incentive to define their organization's jurisdiction and to seek ways to reduce the costs of maintaining that turf. As political scientist James Wilson points out, "In a government agency, maintenance requires obtaining not only capital (appropriations) and labor (personnel) but in addition political support."[3] Substantial change usually requires the management of diverse internal and external constituencies, as well as stakeholders and overseers across the executive and legislative branches. Finally, change in military organizations can be plagued with uncertainty. In peacetime, militaries can try to assess effectiveness through wargaming or simulation, but the real test is likely to occur in the high-stakes environment of combat when lives are on the line.[4] This may tend to produce a natural conservatism when it comes to decisionmaking about change.

In the face of these substantial challenges, some have argued that change in military organizations is likely to occur only under special circumstances: when demanded by a political leader from outside the organization; in response to a major organizational failure; or in response to budget constraints.[5] Key obstacles to the first source of change include the difficulty busy political leaders face in acquiring adequate knowledge to drive reform and in ensuring that reforms are carried out. Organizational failure, the second source of change, does not always enable those responsible for change to see how to perform better. As security studies scholar Stephen Rosen has pointed out, failure could simply lead to more failure.[6] Finally, a lack of resources will not necessarily produce improvements; organizations may simply become less capable. In sum, while these three situations may sometimes contribute to positive change, there is nothing within them that makes organizational improvements inevitable.

As Wilson points out, change in government seems to be a highly contingent process about which no general theory exists. However, it is possible to make some valuable, limited generalizations. Following Wilson's definition of innovation as consisting of a change in core tasks, Rosen defines military innovation as "a change in one of the primary combat arms of a service in the way it fights or alternatively, as the creation of a new combat arm."[7] Rosen argues that innovation requires the development of a new "theory of victory," promising career paths for specialists in the new way of war, and organizations in which these specialists can be employed. In sum, "peacetime military innovation occurs when respected senior military leaders formulate a strategy for innovation that has both intellectual and organizational components."[8]

A second type of change in military organizations is reform, defined as "an improvement in or the creation of a significant new program or policy that is intended to correct an identified deficiency."[9] A reform does not necessarily require a new theory of victory or a change in core tasks. However, it does require institutionalization. Like innovation, the role of leaders within military organizations can be critical since meaningful change requires deliberate effort over a substantial period of time. To have impact, the implementation of reform should occur in an integrated fashion across doctrine, training practices, personnel policies, organizations, equipment, and leader development programs. An example is the transformation of the U.S. Army between the Vietnam War and the 1991 War in the Persian Gulf. Though it did not change its core task, it became much more operationally and tactically effective through a program of integrated reforms in a number of areas. The implementation of this kind of holistic change is generally possible only when these changes are underpinned by sound analytical work and implemented by an organizational entity with broad authority over the development of the entire organization.

Both these forms of military change are relevant to the development of needed cyber capabilities within the U.S. Army today. Rosen's conception of innovation is applicable to thinking about the creation of cyber forces. These forces would need to draw on expertise fostered through the development of new career pathways and employed in new organizational constructs. New cyber units would also have in common with the traditional combat arms of infantry, armor, and field artillery the capability to deliver effects. The idea of reform is also useful in thinking about the integration of cyber capabilities across the force. All U.S. Army formations depend upon assured access to communications and information technology for the accomplishment of their missions. Commanders and staffs across the Army will need to be able to integrate cyber capabilities into their military operations, while all users of cyber resources have a role in contributing to their effective operation and defense.

Another important factor that may impact the prospects for innovation or reform is organizational culture. As pointed out by defense analyst Carl Builder, members of the military services tend to have particularly strong collective values and worldviews reinforced through long years of service. The material interests of the services and the self-worth of individuals within them may become intertwined in a complex fashion, shaping how the services see the tasks that are appropriate to them as well as threats.[10] Several scholars, to include Elizabeth Kier in her study of armies in the interwar period and Andrew Krepinevich in his study of the U.S. Army in Vietnam, have argued that organizational culture can make armies resistant to change.[11] It should be noted that organizational culture need not always operate in this manner. Military historian Williamson Murray, for example, argues that the German Army in the interwar period had a "culture of critical examination" that was conducive to learning and to change.[12] However, these three scholars are likely to agree that organizational culture matters and should be examined for the likely impediments or impetus to change that it creates.

While Wilson may be right that there is no single, general theory capable of accounting for change in government bureaucracies, the literature surveyed does suggest some useful questions:

- Do senior leaders within the Army embrace the need to develop cyber forces and to integrate cyber capabilities across the force?
- Is there a new career pathway for specialists in military cyberspace operations?
- Is there a single organizational entity responsible for ensuring an integrated approach to cyber force development?
- How does Army culture create opportunities or obstacles to the development of cyber forces and the integration of cyber capabilities across the force?

At this point, answers to these questions are preliminary since the development of cyber forces within the U.S. armed forces is in its early stages. Nevertheless, attempting to answer these questions is useful in assessing the Army's progress to date as well as prospects for future change.

CHALLENGES ASSOCIATED WITH CREATING CYBER CAPABILITIES IN THE MILITARY SERVICES

Before addressing these questions, however, there are four aspects of military cyberspace operations that should be discussed since they shape the context and impetus for change. First, due to the highly classified nature of threat activity, a general lack of experience with the consequences of adversary action, and a broad unfamiliarity with the range of potential effects that cyber forces can produce, there is lingering uncertainty about both the necessity to change and the potential value added of cyber forces.

Second, it should be acknowledged that the development of cyber forces must contend with service perspectives about core tasks. As mentioned, DoD is currently approaching cyberspace operations as a joint activity. This may facilitate progress; Army cyber forces may have a natural advantage in providing support to ground force commanders due to familiarity with their needs, and the same may also be true of the other services. However, the fact that military cyberspace operations are joint also means that no service views cyberspace operations as a core task. Instead, cyberspace operations may be viewed as an add-on, and potentially a draw on resources better devoted to capabilities at the center of a service's view of its contribution to the joint force. Cyber forces are not carrier task forces to the Navy, advanced fighters to the Air Force, or brigade combat teams to the Army. In an environment that is fiscally constrained, this could lead all services to neglect their development. A useful historical parallel might be the position of special operations forces within the military services. The sense that they were not adequately developed by the services eventually led Congress to intervene with the creation of Special Operations Command (SOCOM) and the granting of at least some role to SOCOM in shaping the development of capabilities.

Just as military cyberspace operations in the past have not been viewed by the Army as one of its core tasks, they also have not been viewed by any of the communities within the Army as its central function. The Army's Signal Corps historically has provided, operated, and sought to secure communications systems through a compliance-oriented approach. Unfortunately, a compliance-oriented approach to securing networks is no longer adequate given rapid advances in information technology as well as the increasing capabilities of threat actors. Instead of believing that adherence to set standards will result in adequate security, it is necessary to presume that all information systems and networks will remain vulnerable and to be proactive in countering threats. The Army's Military Intelligence Corps, on the other hand, has conducted intelligence operations in cyberspace and, when ordered, applied this same expertise to attack. The Military Intelligence Corps is therefore expert on network exploitation and the threat, but not on the operations, security, and defense of friendly networks. This situation leads to a fragmented and suboptimal approach to cyberspace operations, which would ideally be conducted by a single force that operates, defends, and attacks in an integrated manner.[13] In addition, because both the Signal and Military Intelligence communities view cyberspace operations as only one of their tasks, they may not emphasize investments toward accomplishment of the cyber mission.

A third aspect of military operations in cyberspace to consider is their transnational nature, which may lead to the need for different constructs and concepts than military operations in the physical domains. For example, regional combatant commanders are accustomed to control over all U.S. military forces in their geographic areas of responsibility. Given the interconnected nature of cyberspace, the speed of developments in that domain, and the insignificance of physical distance, it is not clear that concepts and doctrine developed for the physical domains will be appropriate. The actions of adversaries in cyberspace are not bound by geography, increasing the need to collaborate with other commands, interagency partners, or allies. In addition, given that cyberspace is a multi-stakeholder environment, policy considerations and requirements for interagency deconfliction may drive a need for centralized decisionmaking that exceeds what is commonly required for traditional military operations.

Finally, there are aspects of military cyberspace operations that run counter to some aspects of service culture. In the case of the Army, the talents and character traits needed for cyberspace operations are unlikely to match fully the characteristics that the Army has traditionally sought in its soldiers, demanding a new model for attracting, retaining, training, employing, and promoting the right people for this new mission. In addition, military operations in cyberspace require highly specialized training and experience which can be fully developed and utilized only over a substantial period of time. This poses a challenge to the Army's bias toward the development of generalists who gain broad experience through relatively short periods of service in diverse duty positions. Finally, though some on-the-ground support may always be necessary, the Army may need to accept that operations conducted remotely may be more effective.

THE ARMY'S PROGRESS TO DATE

Though the Army has made progress in its development of cyber capabilities, significant challenges remain. To provide greater resolution, it is useful to provide preliminary answers to the questions raised earlier.

Do senior leaders within the Army embrace the need to develop cyber forces and to integrate cyber capabilities across the force? The answer to this question would appear to be "yes." On numerous occasions, Chief of Staff of the Army General Raymond Odierno has embraced the need to develop cyber forces within the Army and to enhance cyber capabilities across the Army's formations. However, while this rhetorical support is important, it is likely that senior leaders below the level of Odierno who are able to focus more specifically on cyber force development are probably needed to pioneer a new cyber force. It is not yet clear who these leaders will be, especially given the incentives that the branches of Signal Corps and Military Intelligence have to limit their investments in cyberspace operations.

Is there a new career pathway for specialists in military cyber operations? As discussed, if the Army does create new units with the core mission of conducting integrated cyberspace operations—across the missions to operate, defend, and attack—the key source communities are likely to be the Signal Corps and

Military Intelligence. To date, the Military Intelligence Corps has created one new enlisted military occupational specialty, and the Signal Corps has created one new warrant officer specialty. The Signal Corps has also discussed additional changes, to include changes to its officer corps. However, these changes are within the traditional areas of focus of these two communities: the Signal Corps operates and defends, and the Military Intelligence Corps exploits and attacks. New specialties capable of integrating across previously separate mission areas have yet to be created; within current branch structures, it seems unlikely this will happen. In addition, there are no new career pathways for the commissioned officers who will lead future cyber formations.

With regard to cyber force development, it is hard to overstate the significance of the absence of a career path for officers who want to specialize in this new combat specialty. Since cyberspace operations are not viewed as a core task by the involved communities, officers who work in this field may run the risk of being marginalized. Those who do work in this area are unable to remain dedicated to the cyber mission and have a successful career. Faced with this situation, some of the most experienced and talented emerging experts will choose to leave the service. Until there is a career pathway for the Army's cyber leaders, and an organizational structure within which they can be trained, utilized, and promoted, cyber force development in the Army will progress slowly—if at all.

Is there a single organizational entity responsible for ensuring an integrated approach to personnel policies, doctrine, training, leader development, and organizations? When it was first stood up as an operational command in 2010, Army Cyber Command was also given force proponency for the development of cyber capabilities. Though this sounds like the means to a unified approach, in reality force development remained fragmented. As branches of the Army, Signal and Military Intelligence continued to operate distinct force development processes. There were separate and distinct approaches to personnel, doctrine, training, leader development, and organizations across the missions that together constitute cyberspace operations. In addition, the U.S. Army Training and Doctrine Command (TRADOC) retained other functions relevant to cyber force development.

In addition to having responsibility for force proponency that was arguably unmatched by its authorities, Army Cyber Command also had limited authority as an operational entity. It could exercise operational control over what the U.S. Army Network Command (Signal) and U.S. Army Intelligence and Security Command (Military Intelligence) labeled "cyber," which gave these organizations the incentive to limit explicit commitments to cyberspace operations.

The Army has recently made progress in this area, though it has preserved a degree of separation between the Signal Corps and Military Intelligence Community. The progress was a recent decision by the Army Chief of Staff to return cyber force development responsibilities to TRADOC, which was originally designed to be the force development integrator across the Army. However, the Army also created the new Cyber Center of Excellence (the term used by the Army for its branch centers and schools) out of the former Signal Center of Excellence. It is not yet clear whether this Cyber Center of Excellence will eventually be able to integrate cyber force development across all relevant missions.

Cyber force development in the Army remains at a nascent stage. Doctrine remains to be written, career paths are yet to be established, organizations that blend the needed expertise of the Signal and Military Intelligence communities below the level of Army Cyber Command are yet to be created, and robust training and certification for cyber units and for leaders and operators across the force are in the early stages of being established. Where changes have been made, they have fallen short of making cyberspace operations a new core task for any of the relevant communities within the Army, and the Army as a whole is just beginning to gain an appreciation of how the new strategic environment should shape its operations across the physical and cyber domains.

How does current Army culture create opportunities for and/or obstacles to the development of cyber forces and the integration of cyber capabilities across the force? As the wars in Iraq and Afghanistan are drawing to a close, the Army is focused on recapturing the basic, tactical competencies for high-intensity conflict that have degraded during the decade since September 11, 2001. For example, one of the Army's major leader development initiatives has been to re-emphasize the role of the observer-controller in the combat training centers as a critical developmental opportunity for company grade officers. While this initiative may be constructive, the priority placed on it does not necessarily reflect a culture that is eager to embrace cyber personnel with unique characteristics who engage in long periods of service in highly-specialized organizations and who may operate most effectively when located remotely from the close fight. The Army may be able to accommodate multiple sets of career expectations — one for those engaged in traditional, ground combat roles and another for those who fight in cyberspace — but that remains to be seen. The pressure to prize the former over the latter could be even more intense as the Army faces a reduction in force structure and stringent fiscal constraints.

CONCLUSION

The creation of cyber forces within today's military services poses many challenges. In this regard, the Army is not unique; the challenges manifest themselves in varying ways across all the services. In fact, these challenges may be so great that the only real solution may become the creation of a completely new service that has military cyberspace operations as its core task from the very beginning. Until this happens, however, what the services do will matter. Can they succeed at the admittedly difficult task of military innovation? Or, instead, are the challenges too great? Concerned observers are left hoping that the United States does not have a cyber war on its hands before it has the military forces it will need to fight it.

ENDNOTES - CHAPTER 22

1. See, for example, Secretary Chuck Hagel's speech at the University of Nebraska, June 19, 2013, in which he stated: "DoD has a responsibility to defend our nation, and that extends to cyberspace," available from *www.defense.gov/transcripts/transcript. aspx?transcriptid=5260.*

2. There are numerous studies that make these points, to include: Graham Allison and Phillip Zelikow, *Essence of Decision,* 2nd Ed., New York Addison-Wesley Educational Publishers, 1999; Morton H. Halperin, *Bureaucratic Politics and Foreign Policy,* Washington, DC: The Brookings Institution, 1978; Carl Builder, *The Masks of War: American Military Styles in Strategy and Analysis,*

Baltimore, MD: The Johns Hopkins University Press, 1989; and Richard A. Stubbing with Richard A. Mendel, *The Defense Game: An Insider Explores the Astonishing Realities of America's Defense Establishment*, New York: Harper & Row Publishers, 1986.

3. James Q. Wilson, *Bureaucracy: What Government Agencies Do and Why They Do It*, New York: Basic Books, Inc., 1989, p. 181.

4. Stephen Peter Rosen, *Winning the Next War*, Ithaca, NY: Cornell University Press, 1991, pp. 8, 69-71; Williamson Murray, "Innovation: Past and Future," in *Military Innovation in the Interwar Period*, Williamson Murray and Allan Millett, eds., Cambridge, UK: Cambridge University Press, 1996, p. 301.

5. For the expectation that military organizations will stagnate when left on their own, see Barry R. Posen, *The Sources of Military Doctrine*, Ithaca, NY: Cornell University Press, 1984.

6. Rosen, pp. 8-9.

7. *Ibid.*, p. 7.

8. *Ibid.*, pp. 7, 20-21.

9. This discussion draws on Suzanne C. Nielsen, "Preparing for War: The Dynamics of Peacetime Military Change," Ph.D. Diss. Harvard University, 2003, especially Chap. 1. This definition is from p. 16.

10. Builder, p. 6.

11. See Elizabeth Kier, *Imagining War: French and British Doctrine Between the Wars*, Princeton, NJ: Princeton University Press, 1997; and Andrew F. Krepinevich, Jr., *The Army and Vietnam*, Baltimore, MD: Johns Hopkins University Press, 1986.

12. Murray, "Innovation," pp. 312-318.

13. This section draws on Robert K. Ackerman, "Cyber Command Redefines the Art," *Signal*, June 1, 2013, available from *www.afcea.org/content/?q=node/11117*.

PART IV:

HUMAN CAPITAL

CHAPTER 23

THE HUMAN DOMAIN:
LEADER DEVELOPMENT

Nadia Schadlow

Today's complex world creates an environment that requires much more of our leaders. It is not enough to be technically and tactically proficient. We must be able to assess, understand, adapt, and yet still be decisive. We have to think through complex multidimensional problems, taking into account the diplomatic, economic, military, political, and cultural implications of every action. And we have to do all of this in an age of instantaneous global communication, an age in which the flow of information and its influence on the local and global audience is often just as important as military action in determining the outcome of operations.

General Raymond Odierno[1]

In Afghanistan and Iraq, some of the earliest lessons were that the consolidation of combat victories required an understanding of the human domain of the contested landscape in which U.S. troops were operating. Accounts of the wars, from soldiers to general officers, stressed that U.S. planning and preparation had not taken physical, cultural, and social environments adequately into account. The concept of the human domain seeks to account for these factors, and in so doing to connect tactical and operational battlefield actions to desired strategic outcomes.[2] It also helps to guide leader development, as the U.S. Army forms officers capable of operating in the contested political, economic, cultural, and social environments that 21st century warfare entails.

THE HUMAN DOMAIN

The human domain concept holds that "although trained in the controlled application of combat power, [Army soldiers] quickly became fluent in the controlled application of national power."[3] The Army is developing the concept of the human domain and introducing it to soldiers on several levels. At the **strategic level**, the Strategic Landpower initiative, led by the Army Chief of Staff, the Marine Corps Commandant, and the Commanding General of U.S. Special Operations command (SOCOM) describes the human domain concept.[4] The Strategic Landpower initiative is an effort to "study the application of Landpower to achieve national objectives" and to convey the idea that we must "think beyond the battlefield and consider what else is required to turn joint tactical victories into strategic success." The concept describes war as "inarguably the toughest of physical challenges, and that we therefore tend to focus on the clash and lose sight of the will" and that as a result, more attention needs to be paid to those contextual factors that influence people's perceptions and actions, "be they government and military leaders or groups within a population."[5]

A recent discussion of the strategic Landpower concept by commander of SOCOM Lieutenant General Charles Cleveland and Special Forces officer Lieutenant Colonel Stuart Farris (who served six tours in Afghanistan as a member of the 3rd Special Forces Group [Airborne]), compares that concept to the earlier development of Air-Land Battle.[6] Air-Land Battle emerged in response to the threat posed by the Soviet military and the recognition that an attrition based strategy would not be suitable for dealing with the Soviet threat. In today's context, the strategic Land-power concept emerged in response to the likelihood that enemies would continue to pursue asymmetric advantages against the United States, through unconventional, irregular, and hybrid means. As a result, Cleveland and Ferris argue that forces will be required to understand populations within the operational context and take actions to influence human behavior to achieve desired outcomes. Overall, they observe that combat power in the form of superior weapon systems and new technologies may lead to tactical successes but that strategic success will require a more complete understanding of the human domain.

Also at the strategic level, the human domain concept is being reinforced through the Army's development and implementation of **regionally aligned forces**. Regionally aligned units are organized for specific mission sets and regional conditions. By aligning unit headquarters and rotational units to combatant commands and tailoring combatant training centers and exercises to plan for likely contingencies, it is hoped that units will be given the focus and time to gain the expertise and cultural awareness required to meet regional requirements more rapidly and effectively. In March 2013, the 2nd Brigade Combat Team, 1st Infantry Division (2/1ID) was designated to support U.S. Africa Command's security cooperation and partnering requirements. Teams of soldiers from the brigade will deploy to multiple African countries to engage in partnering and training events and to support bilateral and multinational military exercises. Over the next few years, the Army will establish the alignment of I Corps to U.S. Pacific Command, III Corps to U.S. Central Command, and XVIII Corps to the Global

Response Force. In addition the Army will align divisions to U.S. Southern Command, U.S. Northern Command, U.S. European Command, and U.S. Africa Command and will later align brigades to support theater requirements. Of significance vis-à-vis these regional alignments is that in the past, although the Army aligned Corps and even brigades to certain areas, they did so for operational war plans and not for shaping operations during peacetime.

These efforts reflect dual acknowledgement of the importance of how local and regional political and cultural factors will shape U.S. outcomes and the importance of prioritizing leader development topics for mission accomplishment. Regionally aligned forces will require soldiers to study, in detail, the places they are likely to deploy to, which, according to commander of the Army's Training and Doctrine Command (TRADOC) General Robert Cone, must be an intellectual commitment. Moreover, there will tactical and operational benefits: in preparing for regional deployments, units will begin experimenting with the right mix of cultural, language, and tactical training during the pre-deployment period. Soldiers will develop a greater appreciation for working with foreign militaries and developing capabilities that may be required in future conflicts; officers will develop a better appreciation for drivers of instability in regions and how (and how not) to build capabilities and capacity with partnered units.

At the **tactical** and **operational** levels, the human domain concept is being advanced through two important areas of training and education which have been directly informed by experiences in Iraq and Afghanistan: mission command and wide area security operations. First, the political, cultural, and social issues that comprise the human domain are being introduced through the U.S. Army's broader focus on mission command. Mission command is the U.S. military's principle of empowering junior officers to exercise independent judgment in the absence of real-time guidance from above. In Iraq and Afghanistan, enormous decisionmaking authorities devolved to lower levels and the current effort to advance mission command seeks to inculcate this reality of modern combat.

Mission command comprises more than the human domain, but it is through the mission command concept that issues related to this domain are being brought to soldiers' attention. With the new awareness of the human domain, mission command now encourages leaders at all levels to understand the principle of influencing people in the local area as well as winning kinetic battles. Contemporary discussions about mission command identify the requirement that the "commander must understand the problem, envision the end state, and visualize the nature and design of the operation."[7]

Success will require an understanding of the political, social, and cultural environment in which a unit operates. Throughout the recent wars, small units conducted decentralized operations across wide areas. Operations, led by young officers, involved continuous interactions between friendly forces, enemy organizations, and civilians. Small units were directly affected by the need to plan for and operate among the reconstruction requirements of local populations. Since each engagement with the enemy carried political, social, and cultural consequences, soldiers at the tactical level had to deal with local politics.[8] While there are ongoing debates about the nature of future war and the degree to which it will involve protracted on the ground deployments, most engagements involving U.S. Army troops will require the skills associated with mission command and the human domain.

Wide area security is a core operational concept through which the human domain idea is also being introduced to Army leaders. The 2009 *Army Capstone Concept*, the more recent 2012 *Capstone* document, and *Army Doctrine Publication (ADP) 3-0, Unified Land Operations*, articulate the wide area security concept. Wide area security is the ability to deny the enemy positions of advantage, to consolidate gains and to protect populations, forces, activities and infrastructure in an area of operations. It involves the ability to respond to the evolving character of a conflict by developing the situation through action and by continuously assessing of tactical, operational, strategic, and political contexts in order to defeat the enemy and support allies. Years of fighting in Afghanistan and Iraq highlighted the need for military forces to defeat identifiable enemy forces **and** to establish area security over wide areas of operations to facilitate the wide range of activities necessary to achieve political objectives.[9] While future contingencies may look different than those that unfolded during the recent wars, wide area security recognizes that solders must operate through the full spectrum of war and that conflict is not linear — it requires attention to the human domain as well as combat throughout an operation. This requires organizations, soldiers, and leaders who can understand and adapt to the complexity and uncertainty of future armed conflict.[10]

The challenge of training and education is to balance instruction in the enduring features of war with the modern changes to its character. Carl von Clausewitz captured this point elegantly when he wrote, "very few of the manifestation in war can be ascribed to new inventions or new departures in ideas. They result mainly from the transformation of society and new social conditions."[11] The Army's introduction of the human domain concept is important not because it discovered something new, but because it recognizes an enduring characteristic of war and sets forth the need to develop leaders to meet this requirement. As one former brigade commander pointed out in a recent issue of *Military Review*, leader development is not the outcome of a series of classes or the product of a sequence of assignments; nor is it the job of one person or organization. Rather, leader development is a continuous process in which, ideally, lessons from one experience inform other experiences.[12] The subject of the human domain, which incorporates a range of factors that shape operational and strategic outcomes, lends itself to this approach to education and development.

RECOMMENDATIONS

The earlier discussion identifies many of the positive steps the Army is taking to introduce and institutionalize the human domain concept. Nonetheless, some additional considerations and improvements might be considered going forward. First, we should consider why the term "political" was omitted from the description of the human domain in the Strategic Landpower concept. Politics — the relationships among people and groups competing for power and seeking to advance ideas — will impact almost any conceivable U.S. engagement in pre-conflict and conflict contingencies. Politics is a term that is not adequately captured by the document's existing references to "social" or "cultural." An absence of the word politics from discussions about the human domain suggests that knowledge about political relationships and tensions and objectives in a particular region would not be a core part of leader development. This would be shortsighted. Leader development programs related to the human domain must, necessarily, focus on preparing soldiers for the political considerations that they will face in any deployment to any theater around the world.

Second, to operate more effectively in the land domain while fully accounting for the human aspects of conflict and war, the Army requires an additional warfighting function. Currently, it has six warfighting functions: mission command, movement and maneuver, intelligence, fires, sustainment, and protection. A warfighting function is a group of tasks and systems (people, organizations, information, and processes) united by a common purpose that commanders use to accomplish missions and training objectives. Army forces use the warfighting functions to generate combat power. All warfighting functions possess scalable capabilities to mass lethal and nonlethal effects. The Army's warfighting functions link directly to the joint functions.[13]

A seventh warfighting function would capture the tasks and systems that provide the lethal and nonlethal capabilities to assess, shape, deter, and influence the decisions and behavior of a people, its security forces, and its government. Such a function would provide the foundation for training, education, and leader development in the human domain area and would help to institutionalize the human domain concept.[14] Army leaders have debated the idea of adding a seventh warfighting function since (at least) the spring of 2012, when TRADOC leaders met at the U.S. Army War College as part of the Army's ongoing campaign of learning. The issue is still being discussed. The Army should make a definitive decision to add this seventh warfighting function. Doing so would send a clear signal to soldiers that political, cultural, and social considerations impact combat outcomes just as other warfighting functions such as fires, mission command, and protection.

Capturing the human domain idea within a new warfighting function would be a pivotal shift for the Army. It would be the decisive way to affirm that these political activities are central to war, to winning, and that they have always been so. Moreover, since the warfighting functions do not change as often as other Army concepts or doctrines, it would embed the idea of the human domain more permanently into the Army's identity. In addition, historically, the Army's attempts to institutionalize some of the ideas behind the human domain concept have almost always taken place outside the regular Army: first by creating a civil affairs reserve structure after World War II and then by shifting most activities related to the social, political, economic and cultural spheres to the special forces. The Strategic Landpower concept, which features the human domain, was signed separately by the commanding general of SOCOM. Yet the human domain requirement exists throughout the full spectrum of war; it impacts the whole conventional force and a war fighting function that acknowledges this would accurately capture both recent and historical Army experiences.

Third, as the Army considers what it must do to organizations, soldiers, and leaders who can understand and adapt to the complexity and uncertainty of future armed conflict, it must make it clearer to both soldiers and civilians how the personnel system is changing to allow for the incorporation of these challenges. The new doctrine on the Army Profession establishes "political-cultural" expertise as one of the four fields of expertise for all Army professionals.[15] This is important because it identifies the issue as an Army-wide goal (i.e., not a goal for the special forces alone). But analyzing and producing the associated doctrine, organization, training, materiel, leadership and education, personnel, and facilities (referred to as DOTMLPF) will be a concrete and necessary next step toward institutionalizing the human domain (and strategic Landpower) concept.[16]

The Army's human resources structure will determine whether and how the human domain is adopted into the mindset of future leaders. Formal doctrine and the world's finest training cannot transform strategic thinking if the personnel system is agnostic or hostile. In addition, while many strategic statements exist that emphasize the need to change priorities in the way the Army organizes, mans, trains, equips, and sustains to "ensure that it is an agile, responsive, tailorable force capable of responding to any mission, anywhere, anytime" the practical matter is whether leaders that embrace the human domain are able to thrive through assignment and promotions in the coming years. The Army's 2013 *Strategic Guidance* acknowledges that unit training and leader development are critical to prepare for operations in a complex environment.[17] Political, social, and cultural considerations of the regions in which Army forces will operate and deploy will be a critical component of unit training and leader development. The problems posed by these political and cultural drivers will challenge Army leaders at all levels.

One Army major who completed a detailed study of officer development observed that Army senior leaders identified the need for a new type of officer, a multi-skilled leader, often dubbed the "pentathlete," who could meet the challenges of the modern battlefield as a function of his maturity, experience, education, and formal training. The study noted however, that U.S. Army officers faced a career path marked by up or out promotions, short tours leading and commanding soldiers, and few opportunities to seek advanced degrees in residence. Officers weather the other second and third order effects of an outdated 20-year retirement plan that does not optimize the resources dedicated to building a highly effective officer corps.[18]

There remains considerable anecdotal and survey evidence from junior leaders that the existing human resources system continues to reward orthodox career paths. A more flexible personnel system might be essential to identify the Army's most creative and insightful officers and empower commanders to engage them successfully. Will the Army personnel system adapt to reward less conventional career paths oriented toward the human domain?

ENDNOTES - CHAPTER 23

1. General Raymond Odierno, Interview, *Joint Forces Quarterly*, Issue 55, 4th Quarter, 2009.

2. Strategic Landpower Task Force paper, May 2013, signed by USA Chief of Staff General Raymond Odierno, Commandant, U.S. Marine Corps General James Amos, and Admiral William McRaven, available from *www.tradoc.army.mil/FrontPageContent/Docs/Strategic%20Landpower%20White%20Paper.pdf*.

3. Major General Peter W. Chiarelli and Major Patrick R. Michaelis, "Winning the Peace: The Requirement for Full Spectrum Operations," *Military Review*, July-August 2005, p. 4.

4. See Strategic Landpower Task Force paper.

5. *Ibid*.

6. See "Toward Strategic Land Power," *Army*, July 2013, pp. 20-23.

7. Chairman of the Joint Chiefs of Staff General Martin Dempsey, Mission Command White Paper, April 2012, p. 4, available from *www.jcs.mil/content/files/2012-04/042312114128_CJCS_Mission_Command_White_Paper_2012_a.pdf*.

8. See *TRADOC Pamphlet 525-3-0, Army Capstone Concept 2009*, Washington, DC: U.S. Army Training and Doctrine Command, for discussion of this. See also Brigadier General Herbert McMaster, "Centralization vs. Decentralization: Preparing for and Practicing Mission Command in Counterinsurgency Operations," *Lessons for a Long War: How America can Win on New Battlefields*, Thomas Donnelly and Frederick Kagan, eds., Washington, DC: American Enterprise Institute (AEI) Press, May 2010, pp. 64-92.

9. *Ibid*., p. 13.

10. *TRADOC Pamphlet 525-3-0*.

11. Carl von Clausewitz, Michael Howard and Peter Paret, eds. and trans., *On War*, Book VI, Princeton, NJ: Princeton University Press, 1976, pp. 45-46.

12. Colonel Doug Crissman, "Improving the Leader Development Experience in US Army Units," *Military Review*, May-June 2013, p. 7.

13. These descriptions are in *Army Doctrine Reference Publication (ADRP) 3-0, Unified Land Operations*, Washington, DC: Department of the Army HQ, May 2012, p. 3-2, available from *armypubs.army.mil/doctrine/DR_pubs/dr_a/pdf/adrp3_0.pdf*.

14. See *Army Capstone Concept*, Washington, DC: U.S. Department of the Army, December 2012. While this concept was discussed in that document, most recent discussions and debates (as of the summer of 2013) may be downplaying the seventh warfighting function idea.

15. Chap. 3, available from *armypubs.army.mil/doctrine/ADRP_1.html*.

16. Cleveland, p. 23.

17. *Army Strategic Planning Guidance*, Washington, DC: U.S. Department of the Army, 2013, available from *usarmy.vo.llnwd.net/e2/rv5_downloads/info/references/army_strategic_planning_guidance.pdf*.

18. Major William D. Linn, II, *Officer Development: A Contemporary Roadmap*, Ft. Leavenworth, KS: School of Advanced Military Studies, Academic Year 2008, available from *www.dtic.mil/cgi-bin/GetTRDoc?AD=ada485472*.

CHAPTER 24

FROM SWORDS TO PLOUGHSHARES: VETERANS AFFAIRS AND U.S. GRAND STRATEGY

Daniel M. Gade

For it's Tommy this, an' Tommy that, an' "Chuck him out, the brute!"
But it's "Saviour of 'is country" when the guns begin to shoot;
An' it's Tommy this, an' Tommy that, an' anything you please;
An' Tommy ain't a bloomin' fool—you bet that Tommy sees!

Rudyard Kipling, "Tommy," 1892

There is no question, as this volume makes clear, that Landpower is a key part of power projection and of achieving our grand strategic aims. All too often, however, our nation's focus is on the strategic imperative of making plowshares into lethal swords, and not the moral imperative of turning the swords back into plowshares after their mission ends. This is not a new phenomenon: the members of the famous Bonus Army that gathered in Washington, DC, in 1932 were attempting to cash in on promised benefits that were not due them until the end of 1945, and the Civil War Veterans on both sides were generally treated with something like benign neglect by the society they returned to after their service ended.[1] Within the last generation, the treatment of Veterans after the Vietnam War was particularly shabby. Our society has seemingly addressed this problem: spending at the

Department of Veterans Affairs has nearly tripled over the last decade, and thousands of large and small Veterans groups exist to serve Veterans.[2] Arguably, however, the pendulum has now swung too far in one direction. The current system of Veterans' care smothers them under a paternalistic blanket, stifling personal growth, employment, and social opportunity. Our warriors — our swords — are not being returned to society as productive plowshares; but instead are allowed to rust, their skills and their potential wasted.

This "rust" is all around us: unemployment among young Veterans is nearly twice that of their age-group peers, even though Veterans as a whole are more educated and healthier than average citizens, and leave the service with valuable job skills and discipline.[3] Veterans commit suicide at a much higher rate than their civilian peers, and anecdotal stories about drug and alcohol abuse, domestic violence, and other indicators of poor reintegration are legion.[4] In short, our society's efforts to reintegrate Veterans after service are failing, and there is a better way.

THE PROBLEM

The Veterans disability compensation system is in crisis. It encourages almost one out of every two retiring service members to call themselves disabled.[5] It habituates millions of talented young men and women to think of themselves as broken and dependent upon others for support for the rest of their lives. Today's disability system actually interferes with healthy reintegration of Veterans. It tells injured service members all the things they cannot do. It literally trains them to highlight their incapacities rather than their capacities. It is built on outdated medical criteria, emphasizes disability, discourages mainstreaming, and impairs independence and self-reliance.

Beyond these destructive effects at the individual level, the system has become unbearably expensive. Disability payments to Iraq-Afghanistan Veterans alone are now on a path to cost taxpayers $425 billion over the next 40 years, and that is a conservative estimate.[6] Disability and medical care together are projected to be nearly a trillion dollars over that timeframe.[7] Today's disability payments are untaxed, rise with inflation, are not tied to income level, have no work requirement, and do not even require the recipient to seek treatment for his or her disabilities. The system creates the perfect incentive for Veterans to invest time and effort in proving to the government that they cannot overcome or make accommodations for their injuries. It literally buys learned helplessness and dependence.

Work and self-reliance are among the very most important elements in long-term human flourishing and happiness. Work not only puts us on a path to economic independence but also lends a sense of accomplishment and self-worth, creates a social network that pulls us out of isolation and self absorption, and gives dignity to our daily routine. People who do not work for their own living are more depressed, more solitary, less healthy, and poorer. Soldiers who leave the spirited, mission-oriented, team work of military service and fall into the isolation of the mailbox economy — living off of disability checks, consigned to their couch at home — are particularly likely to lose their sense of purpose.

A SOLUTION: THE RECOVERY TRACK

What if, rather than trickling a lifelong entitlement of payments to Veterans, sapping their initiative and self image, we instead invested heavily up front in retraining them to succeed at their dream job and participate fully in their communities, such that their injuries would not interfere.[8] With new social attitudes toward disability, some remarkable modern technology, widespread computer enhancements of work, and many legal protections and physical accommodations growing out of laws like the Americans with Disabilities Act, persons with a disability in the United States have wider horizons than at any time in human history and many options for satisfying work.

Instead of maintaining the current, broken disability compensation system with its built-in work disincentives, the government should try a more promising alternative. In return for surrendering their lifetime entitlement to disability checks, government and private industry would pour medical, rehabilitative, educational, and training resources into them over a much shorter period — perhaps 1 to 4 years, depending on the goal of the rehabilitation and the conditions of the individual Veteran. These investments could include everything from trauma therapy to computer instruction to personalized occupational training.

For the first time, Veterans would have a choice. They could either stick to the old system of monthly checks that discourage work and independence. Or they could avail themselves of intensive resources focused on maximizing their strengths and personal potential. This alternative recovery track would begin with an extensive battery of diagnostic evaluations to determine physical and mental health, innate aptitudes, interests, and personality traits, and what accommodations might be necessary for social, professional, and recreational life. Based on these results, a personalized educational and therapeutic course would be offered to the Veteran.

While Veterans already have health coverage and in theory some training options, in practice, few high-quality programs exist. Private and not-for-profit projects like the Shepherd Center's SHARE Program, the University of California-Los Angeles' Operation Mend, Welcome Back Veterans' Home Base Programs, and dozens of other top-notch rehab providers would be used to transition Veterans to an exciting new level of competence and independence.

Beyond healing injuries, this track would ensure that participants have all of the adaptive equipment they need at home, and in their places of school and work to ensure they live full and independent lives. The Veterans Administration and charitable organizations like Habitat for Humanity provide these unevenly now, mostly for the home, but individuals are largely left on their own to coordinate accommodations at schools and places of work.

Perhaps most importantly, this program would work with Veterans to set and achieve new education and career goals. Service members exiting the military with a disability must simultaneously get used to a completely different work world and altered personal abilities. In a period of uncertainty, it can seem easier just to accept guaranteed disability payments and forget about making the transition to independence. The new track would attack the root of the problem — helping Veterans figure out where their aptitudes, interests, and opportunities lie now that their military careers are over. This proposed recovery track would connect Veterans with the right training and education for their career goals, and ensure that they complete their degrees or vocational training without wasted time or resources.

Finally, this recovery track would provide supported work opportunities for Veterans, easing their transition into rewarding family-supporting careers. Programs such as Workforce Opportunity Services and the National Organization on Disability have already addressed some of these needs with small cohorts.

This new recovery track would provide the non-profit partners with funding, quality control, and evaluation services, and provide every Veteran with resources, case-management, and personal coaching. This potent combination would lift and energize many Veterans who are currently lost in the shuffle and languishing, their talents lost to their families and to society as well. Graduates of this program would enjoy higher incomes and higher quality of life.

Not every Veteran will be ideal for this program. On one end of the spectrum, there are small numbers of Veterans who are so catastrophically injured that independent living, much less self-sustaining employment, will be impossible. These are appropriate candidates for lifelong disability pensions. On the other end of the spectrum, Veterans with minor disabilities do not require intensive rehabilitation to achieve their full potential as civilians. But most of the surge in disability payments since 2002 comes from Veterans with moderate disabilities rated at between 30 percent and 60 percent. These are prime candidates for front-loaded rehabilitation instead of lifelong pensioning.

There will be strong interest among Veterans in this voluntary track. Few young men and women want to languish on entitlement payments. The challenge of rising to a major personal remake will appeal to many September 11, 2001-era Veterans. There are successful models available that would guide implementation. The Netherlands instituted a civilian disability reform that places first priority on reemployment, and incentivizes both individuals and employers to find accommodations for previous work, or invest in retraining for new jobs.[9] The Canadian military employs a lump-sum mechanism to better encourage injured Veterans to return to work.[10]

As for costs and financing under the current disability system, the average annual compensation for a typical Veteran newly entering the system was about $8,000 per year.[11] Over the next 4 decades, each of these individuals will collect hundreds of thousands of dollars from their fellow citizens in the form of disability payments. Even worse, billions of dollars of economic activity that they would have generated will be lost forever.

This trial will actually save taxpayer money while dramatically improving Veteran outcomes by spending just a portion of that sum in an intensive, front-loaded fashion. For the equivalent of perhaps 5 to 8 years of average payments, a typical participant could be put on the road to a much better life, without a lifelong entanglement in the government disability system.

This alternative system would include funding for a careful evaluation on the professional and health outcomes of Veterans in the pilot program compared against a control group receiving standard Veterans disability compensation, and also against a third group receiving simple lump-sum payments. With documented success, this program would be positioned for rapid adoption and expansion by the Department of Veterans Affairs. The ultimate benefits of this pilot program could be enormous — for participants and the treasury alike. Total government spending in this country on disability compensation is about $262 billion in 2013, between Social Security Disability Insurance, VA Disability Compensation and Pensions, and Supplemental Security Income.[12] That includes Veterans, those compensated through our Social Security System, and others. If even 10 or 20 percent of recipients volunteer for an alternative of front-loaded training resulting in work success and independent life, the 40-year difference in improved personal outcomes and reduced government spending would be enormous. Literally hundreds of thousands of lives will be touched and hundreds of billions of dollars saved.

CONCLUSION

Today's disability programs are well intentioned but unsustainable; they cause much human misery and seriously damage government finances. The Recovery Track would remedy both of those problems. Because this reform's heavy upfront investments for a limited time would ultimately be repaid by eliminated lifetime costs down the road, the program could be a pioneer in using Social Impact Bonds, or the so-called pay-for-success grant model which offers private investors a chance to finance reforms in return for a portion of any long-term savings.[13] Pay-for-success grants and Social Impact Bonds have excited many social entrepreneurs, but it can be difficult to find a social dysfunction where there is a sufficiently large, potentially productive population, and a substantial yet reversible set of costs such that the resulting savings could attract market investors. Veteran disability payments represent a perfect opportunity for bringing this new tool to bear, so that private resources can be wielded to repair public problems.

This plan does not immediately end the current disability compensation system, despite its well-documented flaws. The interest groups that thrive on the current system are too well-entrenched and invested in the current plan for that to be a realistic goal. Instead, this plan offers injured Veterans a new choice, on a voluntary basis, in how they will recover and set themselves up for success after their service. This plan treats injured Veterans with the same rights and respect we now accord other people with disabilities, and allows them a chance to flourish on their own two feet rather than become permanent wards of the state.

The country has a Grand Strategic imperative to protect itself and its interests abroad. Generating and utilizing military force requires that citizens be made into soldiers and used as tools of the State. It is obvious that some of the soldiers used in this manner will be killed or maimed, and that many will require lifetime medical care and pensions. However, the use of Landpower cannot and should not be held hostage to the fact that the legacy costs of wars are so high. Out of control Veterans' benefits increase the financial costs of strategic engagement and impair our ability to shape the world when needed by military force. It is incumbent upon those who claim to be Grand Strategists to consider the issues raised in this chapter, not as a separate and distinct, but as an integral part of the Landpower equation. Poorly designed post-service reintegration policies harm our Grand Strategic interests in two major ways: first, they dramatically increase the direct costs of the use of military force, perhaps even to the point where the ability of a democratic society to use that force may be crippled or at least hampered. Second, as the poem which opened this chapter points out, "An' Tommy ain't a bloomin' fool — you bet that Tommy sees!" The society also sees what "Tommy" sees, and citizens will be unwilling to join the military if they continue to see malaise and widespread problems with Veterans' care. There is no Landpower without soldiers.

ENDNOTES - CHAPTER 24

1. Following the Department of Veterans Affairs, we capitalize "Veteran" and its derivitives.

2. Thomas Meyer, *Serving Those Who Served*, The Philanthropy Roundtable, Washington, DC, 2013, p. 187.

3. Meredith Kleykamp, "Unemployment, Earnings, and Enrollment among Post 9/11 Veterans," *Social Science Research*, Vol. 42, No. 3, May 2013.

4. Richard J. McNally and B. Christopher Frueh, "Why Are Iraq and Afghanistan War Veterans Seeking PTSD Disability Compensation at Unprecedented Rates?" *Journal of Anxiety Disorders*, Vol. 27, Issue 5, June 2013, pp. 520-526; Farhana Hossain, Peter Baird, and Rachel Pardoe, "Improving Employment Outcomes and Community Integration for Veterans with Disabilities," Working Paper, New York: Manpower Demonstration Research Corporation, available from SSRN, *ssrn.com/abstract=2273578* or *dx.doi.org/10.2139/ssrn.2273578*.

5. The precise proportion is 45 percent at present. See *costsofwar.org/sites/default/files/articles/52/attachments/Bilmes Veterans Costs.pdf*.

6. See Linda Bilmes, "The Financial Legacy of Iraq and Afghanistan: How Wartime Spending Decision Will Constrain

Future National Security Budgets," Cambridge, MA: Harvard University, available from *research.hks.harvard.edu/publications/ workingpapers/citation.aspx?PubId=8956&type=WPN*.

7. *Ibid.*

8. See Richard Burkhauser and Mary C. Daly, *The Declining Work and Welfare of People with Disabilities*, Washington, DC: American Enterprise Institute, September 2011, available from *www. aei.org/publication/the-declining-work-and-welfare-of-people-with-disabilities/*; and David Autor, Mark Duggan, and David Lyle, *Battle Scars? The Puzzling Decline in Employment and Rise in Disability Receipt among Vietnam Era Veterans*, Cambridge, MA: Massachusetts Institute of Technology, May 2011, available from *economics. mit.edu/files/6391*.

9. Burkhauser and Daly.

10. Elizabeth Schaefer and Eric W. Christensen, "Lump Sum Alternatives to Current Veterans' Disability Compensation," Alexandria, VA: CNA Corporation, 2006, available from *www.cna.org/ sites/default/files/research/d0014443.a3.pdf*.

11. This figure is calculated from VA statistics on the average level of disability of Veterans newly entering the system.

12. This figure includes $51B in Veterans' payments, $145B in SSDI payments, and about $60B in SSI, available from *www.ssa. gov/budget/FY14Files/2014BO.pdf*.

13. Jeffrey Liebman, "Social Impact Bonds," Report, Washington, DC: Center for American Progress, February 9, 2011, available from *www.americanprogress.org/issues/open-government/ report/2011/02/09/9050/social-impact-bonds/*.

CHAPTER 25

CONCLUSIONS

Joseph Da Silva and Cindy Jebb

Perhaps the Army is a hammer, but that hammer does not just drive nails to destroy but also to build.

> Cadet Nate Davison,
> West Point Class of 2014
> "MX 400: Officership"

We open with one of our cadet's discussion points in the capstone course for 4th-year cadets at West Point, NY. We co-teach "MX400: Officership," a course that provides an overarching examination of our profession and helps crystallize in cadets the strategic thinking they have acquired through their liberal arts and sciences education. As with this compendium, MX400 does not offer cadets a playbook or a definitive solution; rather, it offers a strategic approach toward understanding roles and missions, while providing guiding principles to members of the profession of arms. It captures French General and strategist André Beaufre's perspective from 1965: "The word strategy may be used often enough, but the science and art of strategy have become museum pieces. . . . Strategy . . . is a method of thought."[1] At the end of the day, an Army in transition will depend on the talents and character of its leaders and soldiers and their ability to secure effectively the nation's interests, implement policy, and win the nation's wars while securing the peace.

Even as we work to nurture habits of mind that foster strategic thinking, it is important to acknowledge that too often our biases and narrowed perspectives hinder real strategic thinking. Gregory Foster describes strategic thinking as encompassing critical, systematic, holistic, creative, and, we would add, empathetic thinking. Strategic thinking is accompanied by self-awareness, and it enables leaders to look around corners to anticipate second and third order effects.[2] Moreover, this kind of thinking complements a strategic framework that necessarily focuses on the nation's security interests and its diplomatic, informational, military, and economic means. Strategic thinking also considers constraints—including fiscal limitations, perceived and/or real war weariness, and lack of political will—as well as the risks involved with any course of action, given the internal and external security environment.[3] Adding to the complexity is the realization that within our own country and among allies and friends, it is difficult to sustain a foreign policy consensus in the midst of a dynamic, complex, and global conflict ecosystem.[4]

For two reasons, we examine these strategic issues with cadets who will soon be second lieutenants: first, strategic thinking must start early and be nurtured through a lifetime. Strategic thinking does not automatically happen when officers arrive at the U.S. Army War College as senior officers. Second, if we are truly embedding the mission command ethos within our profession, then we must develop leaders of character who will be able to address the unknown challenges that lie around the corner.

The Army now faces numerous challenges. Clearly, the Army is working toward understanding its roles and missions now and in the future, as well as the force structure and human capital that it will require. There is consensus on several key points. First, the Chief of Staff of the Army provides an important starting point with his articulation of a **prevent, shape,** and **win** strategic framework supported by a regionally aligned force. Second, there is consensus that we cannot lose the hard-fought lessons of the past decade-plus of war. Of course, the challenge of capitalizing on lessons learned is understanding which lessons ought to be brought forward and which lessons are unique to a particular set of circumstances. Third, we have to approach the uncertain future with humility while thinking strategically. At the very least, we have to think through all phases to include winning the peace. This imperative translates to working jointly at the lowest levels but also continuing our partnering with whole-of-government and society (nongovernmental organizations, international governmental organizations, and local government). All are required to deter, attack, defend, and win the peace; in all of these functions, the Army plays a prominent role.[5]

When the Army shifted its focus during the post-Vietnam era to the Soviet threat, it lost its institutional memory of counterinsurgency and other forms of warfare. The Army also did not pay attention to developments in other parts of the world, where second and third order effects are now just being realized. For example, our support of the *mujahedeen* in the 1980s, with the aim of fighting the Soviets, helped to globalize a radical form of Islamic insurgency. Moreover, what were once thought to be nontraditional threats cannot now be ignored by serious strategists: climate change, disease, refugee flows, land scarcity, and terrorism. Each represents a vulnerability that can expand from states to regions and from regional to global proportions.

The Army's strategic posture must be nested within the nation's grand strategy and should focus on other states, as well as nonstate actors. Nevertheless, by focusing on Asia, the Persian Gulf, and Europe, the United States may miss emerging threats elsewhere. With the diffusion of technology and the rise of nonstate actors, the nation may leave itself vulnerable if it does not help to shape dynamics and conditions in other parts of the world before they become direct threats. Even as the United States prepares for potential state rivals in the Pacific, U.S. leaders must consider how their actions may be perceived by their allies and adversaries since what they consider defensive in nature may inadvertently signal offensive intentions.[6]

ACKNOWLEDGING ASSUMPTIONS

As the Army's understanding of its role in U.S. grand strategy advances, it is important to identify sources of bias. Highlighting the assumptions one uses to develop theory, strategy, and policy helps one to understand differing perspectives and lays the foundation for rigorous study and testing of competing ideas. The job of military professionals is to provide sound military advice grounded in time-tested facts and challenged assumptions. When unchallenged assumptions structure strategic debate, military professionals should be the first to question them.

Let us consider four assumptions rightly recognized in contemporary debates, to include the preceding chapters, over U.S. Landpower and grand strategy:[7]

1. The United States will not fight any wars in the near future.

2. **If** the United States is forced to fight a war, it can rely on its technological comparative advantage.

3. Given that budget constraints will force reductions in military spending and that these reductions entail acceptance of some strategic risk, it is safer to accept risk by greatly reducing the size of the Army rather than other services.

4. The United States will avoid conflicts similar to Afghanistan and Iraq by building the Army to fight only conventional, rather than unconventional, wars to prevent future policymakers from repeating their predecessors' mistakes.

As each of these claims is influential but unproven, it is important to examine them critically. We will discuss each in turn.

Assumption #1: The United States will not fight wars in the near future.

The first assumption is not always publicly stated, but it can be inferred by the roles and missions assigned to the component forces. The budgetary process, consisting of an iterative exchange between Congress and the Department of Defense, determines the size and shape of the Army.[8] As of this writing, the most recent budget has decided that end strength (or total manpower) for the Army will be 450,000 by Fiscal Year (FY)2015, from a high of 560,000 in FY2012. Without a clear and articulate narrative for Landpower in the 21st century, this end strength seems likely to continue to decrease, leaving the nation exposed to considerable risk in the event of another war.[9]

There seem to be two primary drivers for the assumption that the United States will not fight wars in the near future: war-weary public sentiment and the belief that whatever conflicts the United States engages in will not be land wars.[10] Polls of the American public reveal their war-weariness. A 2014 survey conducted by the Pew Research Center and the Council on Foreign Relations (CFR) found that 52 percent of Americans believed that the "United States should mind its own business in the world," and a record 80 percent believed the United States should focus on domestic problems over international issues.[11] In many ways, these viewpoints are unsurprising. Americans have watched countless men and women return home dead or wounded from wars many do not understand, fought in countries that seem not to welcome the presence of U.S. troops. In addition, since 2008, the choices between domestic and international issues have grown starker, as the opportunity cost of sending soldiers overseas is seen in terms of domestic spending on programs such as infrastructure, jobs, health, education, or other internal investments. Americans do not want to hear about more war. The experiences in Afghanistan and Iraq serve as a warning of the perils of intervention.

While at least one of the first two wars of the 21st century is seen as a war of choice, however, there is no guarantee that the next war will allow a choice. Nonparticipation might not be an option if land forces are necessary to defend national interests. Policymakers must also consider ongoing roles and missions that support national interests such as grand area access, hemispheric policing, the containment and neutralization of remote projectable threats, and the mitigation of humanitarian crises. When these interests are threatened, it is unlikely that Landpower will continue to seem as irrelevant to their promotion as it currently does.[12] Public sentiment reflects this point as well. In the same survey conducted by Pew and CFR,

56 percent of Americans disagreed with the idea that America should remain isolationist.[13] Public sentiment is divided between war-weariness and resolution to maintain international engagement. Americans are neither myopic nor naïve, but they do deserve clear, logical, and sound arguments for the use of military force in the future.

Assumption #2: The United States can rely on technology to win its wars.

While Americans may be divided about the role of America in the world, they are not ambivalent about their faith in technology. Many believe the United States can rely on its comparative technological advantage to win the wars of the future. This viewpoint should not come as a surprise as one of the most powerful images to come out of the global war on terror is that of the armed predator drone patrolling the skies and dropping ordnance on unsuspecting terrorists. Drones, robots, and cyber capture the imagination of most Americans, particularly as they project a view of future warfare tailored to the American advantage.

Without a doubt, American technology has helped to cement the U.S. military as the premier fighting force in the world, but it has also hidden some inconvenient truths about the nature of conflict and war. Theories that rest in the destructive force of technology fail to understand this fundamental and eternal truth: war is a human endeavor.[14] Force is only effective when it produces the change in human behavior that it was initially summoned to change; then and only then can it be deemed military power.[15] Technology-based strategies or concepts that do not consider all the elements of national power — both military and nonmilitary — will ultimately fall short of their goals.

As we move into the future, technology will continue to play a large part in providing for our security as a means to accomplish strategic ends; however, technology alone does not win wars. Certainly, technology can augment other elements of American power—including Landpower. Simple faith in advanced technology, combined with the hope that war will not recur soon, risks U.S. national security.

Assumption #3: Reducing the size of the Army quickly saves cost with minimal risk.

The third assumption rests on the idea that it takes much longer to build a Navy than it does an Army. If this were so, downsizing the Army would be an acceptable risk if, in fact, we could quickly raise an educated, well-trained, and disciplined Army. It is true that it takes a considerable amount of time to build a naval ship—5 years, for instance, in the case of a *Virginia*-class nuclear powered submarine. It is also true that during World War I and World War II, the United States put millions in uniform in a short time. It seems easier to build an Army than to construct a Navy; as a result, the case for a large Navy rather than a large Army seems strong.[16]

This argument is misleading, however. An army that is well-trained and effective takes as much time to build as a strong navy—more, in certain cases. The preceding narrative of the U.S. experience in major wars fails to note the performance of the U.S. Army in the opening battles of these major conflicts. History was not kind to these armies. From the experiences of the American Expeditionary Forces in the opening days of World War I, to the battle of Kasserine Pass in World War II, or the failed and infamous

Task Force Smith in Korea, the Army paid deferred costs in human lives. In the edited volume, *America's First Battles*, various authors discuss the first battles of America's first nine wars from 1776 to 1965. The lessons are striking. The United States lost five of the nine first battles—Long Island, Queenston, Bull Run, Kasserine, and Osan. Even more striking is that the battles that were won—San Juan, Cantigny, Buna, and Ia Drang—were won at a very high cost in human lives.[17] Preparation, training, and education are the costs of building a capable Army. When these costs go unpaid in peacetime, they are deferred until the war begins and then exacted in human lives due to inexperience. This deferred cost was often overlooked in budget discussions of the past, and it continues to be overlooked today.

How long does it take to build an expert in the management of violence? How long does it take to build a brigade combat team filled with quality sergeants steeped in Army doctrine? How long does it take to educate, train, and inspire a quality lieutenant, and to build and sustain the institutions (such as West Point) devoted to this task? Building a quality Army unit is about more than wielding steel; it is about developing thoughtful leaders of character who can reason logically, think strategically, lead formations, and develop cohesive teams through tough training, shared sacrifice, and common purpose. Cost must be measured not only in dollars and cents, but in the time it takes to rebuild a quality fighting force after deactivating it. History has taught us a sobering lesson: when we do not invest properly in peacetime to build the quality force we need in war, then costs are measured in the blood of America's sons and daughters.

Assumption #4: An Army built only for conventional war prevents adventurism in unconventional wars.

The final assumption focuses on the Army and its internal divisions. As the force begins to transition from 13 years of war, different camps have arisen within the Army to debate the future of the force. Many within the Army argue that the wars in Afghanistan and Iraq were mistakes that should not be repeated, and the only way to avoid these wars in the future is to construct an Army that is designed to fight only conventional conflicts. An Army designed only for conventional fights will limit the options of future policymakers.[18] Similar arguments were made after the Vietnam war, when the Army organized around the Soviet conventional threat in Europe and then maintained this force structure even after the Cold War. The Army did not just focus on conventional threats; it discounted counterinsurgency wars as aberrations never to be fought again. Lieutenant General William DePuy, the first commander of the Army's U.S. Training and Doctrine Command (TRADOC), put the point plainly, "U.S. combat forces were not and are not the preferred or proper instrument for counterinsurgency operations amongst the people."[19] Reflecting this strong dislike for counterinsurgency strategy, DePuy endeavored to purge the Army educational system of a majority of related courses and texts. From 1972 to 1976, both the Armor School and the Artillery School largely discontinued courses on counterinsurgency. At the same time, the Intelligence School cut counterinsurgency down to only 4 hours in its Officer Basic Course, and the U.S. Command and Staff College also steadily diminished academic hours for it. Since many of the Army leaders also wanted to lessen the focus on counterinsurgency, DePuy was largely successful in this endeavor, even when many of the faculty at the Army's educational institutions objected.[20]

As threats in the 1990s — Bosnia, Kosovo, and Haiti, for instance — demonstrated the need for different capabilities and schools of thought, the Army, nonetheless, largely maintained its focus on its Cold War force structure. We saw similar problems as the Army planned and executed both the Iraq and Afghanistan wars, where planning did not include "phase four," or any serious thought into post-war reconstruction. This refusal to recognize the role of the Army in post-war reconstruction helped to exacerbate already-tenuous situations.

One can argue that today the United States does not face a clear conventional threat. Uncertainty is the dominant view of the future. In the face of uncertainty, flexibility and adaptability will be keys to success. Indeed, the only true defense against an uncertain security environment is an educated force with adaptive formations. As we move forward, it is important to remember that the threat and the environment will decide how we will have to fight. The true failures in Afghanistan and Iraq were not in formations but in the inability of the people **in** the formations to deal with the post-war environment and win the peace. The Army should not prepare never to do these missions again, but to ensure that its people understand them when we do.

As the country continues to look for efficiencies within the DoD, the Army will most likely pay the bill for cost cutting because of the previously stated assumptions: the nation will not fight any wars in the near term; it can rely on technology; reducing the

Army quickly cuts costs with little risk; and an Army built for conventional war can preclude unconventional missions. These assumptions require rigorous study and debate, however. It is important that Army leaders help to frame the discussion about the future of the U.S. military more accurately.

CONTEXT: A UNIQUE PERIOD IN HISTORY . . . OR IS IT?

A common maxim among military historians is that military defeat is the best teacher for an Army.[21] The basic idea is that in defeat an Army can look at itself candidly and see past institutional interests, identify deficiencies, and implement reforms. Historically, that has not proven true in every case. Edward Drea notes that:

> The way an Army interprets defeat in relation to its military tradition, and not the defeat itself, will determine, in large measure, the impact an unsuccessful military campaign will have on that institution.[22]

Drea's observation is enlightening, yet it does not go far enough. Military institutions process **all** events, both defeat and victory, in relation to their military tradition. As the U.S. Army looks to the past to inform its future, it must ensure that it draws the right lessons—not just those that fall in line with preconceived views.

Today's U. S. Army finds itself at a difficult yet familiar crossroads. After most major conflicts, the U.S. Army has faced a number of challenges: constrained budgets driving personnel strength, unclear strategic guidance, internal debates about force structure and mission focus, and, of course, questionable domestic will for the commitment of troops in foreign interventions. The Army now finds itself once again challenged in terms of its relevance, size, shape, and ultimately the future of its organizational DNA. While these challenges seem historically cyclical, the security environment, fiscal, and bureaucratic realities today call for fresh thinking as well.

How has the U.S. Army responded to previous periods of budget austerity? By and large, it has focused on investments in human capital, on the understanding that well-trained and educated leaders would ensure appropriate and prudent transitions once austerity ended and budgets increased.[23] The Army has also tried to maintain expansibility while distributing resources equally among its commands, as seen in the interwar period between World Wars I and II.[24] Insofar as these policies have succeeded previously, perhaps they can help to guide today's Army leaders.

Nevertheless, today's situation presents new challenges. The Army seems to be competing with more groups than ever before for dominance over expertise in the land domain. In the past, the Army competed with the Marines over various mission sets, but today the National Guard (Guard) and Special Operations Command (SOCOM) present new competition. SOCOM has come to challenge the Army for functions such as training foreign militaries and even some direct action missions. In addition, the wars in Iraq and Afghanistan have forced greater use of the Guard and Reserve. Today, the Guard advocates for its budget apart from the regular Army; the Guard's preferences are at times at odds with Army estimates, ideas, and force structures. New understandings and cooperative agreements must be developed going forward to make this relationship among the Army, Guard, Reserve, and SOCOM an enduring and fruitful one for all organizations. These Landpower organizations complement one another and make U.S. Landpower effective across a wide range of mission sets.

These four organizations coexist in a symbiotic relationship. The Marines provide a small and necessary mobile force that can react quickly around the world, while relying on the strategic depth and staying power of the regular Army to sustain operations or build upon initial gains. The Guard and Reserve provide the strategic depth and logistics needed by the regular Army, while relying on training, education, and institutional support from the regular Army. SOCOM relies on the Army to train, develop, and lend quality officers, noncommissioned officers (NCOs), and Soldiers to the various SOCOM units; in many cases, the Army builds on the battlefield effects of these SOCOM units. Within these complementary relationships, the Army is the primary sustainment force, human capital developer, and dominant deterrent. However, without the Marines, Guard and Reserve, and Special Operations, the Army could not play the role that it does, nor could these organizations produce the results they do without the symbiotic relationships that exist among the components of U.S. Landpower.

CONCLUSION: HARNESSING THE DIVIDEND BY MANAGING TALENT

The past 13 years have seen much debate about the logic, efficacy, and feasibility of the missions in Iraq and Afghanistan. Many see these wars as a needless waste and a loss of national blood and treasure. Without a doubt, much was spent and many great Americans were lost in these wars, but we honor them best not by ignoring the past but by allowing these events to inform our path forward. As we draw down in the Middle East and return home, the Army coming back is much more experienced, battle-hardened, and adaptive.

The people in our force, with their broad experience and talents, make up an invaluable investment. Harnessing the returns on this investment will be the key to ensuring that the Army of the future is prepared to meet a complex security environment. As the Army transforms within this environment, it will be even more critical that its members sustain their professional identity vis-à-vis a daunting, albeit necessary, bureaucracy.[25] The Army must focus its attention on its human capital since the Army's people will be essential to strategic adaptation in support of the country's security interests.

Human capital is the Army's strategic hedge. This hedge is necessary if we are to have a resilient Army that can anticipate problem sets, solve problems, and take decisive action across a range of roles and missions. We offer the Army's talent management model as a way to guide the recruitment, development, employment, and retention of human capital. The evaluation and promotion system should align with these activities as well. The key to understanding the need for talent management is recognizing that the world has moved beyond the industrial era, and the people who comprise our government are not interchangeable. We all have unique talents that need to be recognized and valued and therefore recruited, developed, employed, and retained.[26]

There are several transformations occurring within the Army that provide important opportunities to implement talent management. For example, the Army is opening up all combat roles to women and taking a serious approach to sexual harassment and assault within its ranks. To know that gender will no longer constrain accessibility, we can reevaluate with renewed focus what talents are indeed required for particular branches and assignments.

We offer the following principles as some of the key lessons gathered over the course of this project and discussions with various scholars and practitioners.

1. Continue to train as a member of the Joint, Interagency, Intergovernmental, and Multinational team and understand how the Army contributes to the Joint Force.

2. Understand the Army's role as a deterrent to prevent war against the homeland, friends, and allies.

3. Be prepared to shape the environment through all phases to include phase four: post-war reconstruction.

4. Engage political leaders so they understand opportunity costs and risks.

5. Approach the security environment and its challenges with the humility to ensure we properly diagnose the problem and do not rely on flawed or untested assumptions.

6. It is much harder and requires **more** resources to hold and secure an objective than to initially take it.

7. Educate, educate, and educate. Investment in the education of our Soldiers and officers, more than any platform or machine, has generated dividends over the history of our Army.

While this is not an all-inclusive list, we do hope that it provides a starting point for future discussion.

We opened the chapter with a quotation from one of our cadets. In doing so, we highlight that the decisions we make now impact the lives of the young officers and Soldiers who have chosen to serve. They are the nation's strategic hedge; in an uncertain, complex, and dangerous world, the nation counts on those who comprise this hedge.

As we close this volume, we hope that this is not seen as a book of answers but rather a point of departure for further discussion, debate, and inquiry. Not everyone will agree with all of the ideas presented here, but we hope that all agree that the venture is worthwhile. We encourage others to continue the research and push this thinking forward. Let us move forward deliberately and thoughtfully, with the courage to collect the lessons we learned, the energy to enact the changes we need, the wisdom to challenge the untested ideas of the day, and the humility to admit our mistakes.

No one truly knows where, how, or when the Army will be used in the future. Predictions of these events are tenuous at best. But we can know one thing for certain. As General (Ret.) Frederick M. Franks, Jr., remarked to cadets in the opening days of MX 400:

> Sometime after graduation, and I cannot predict when, our Nation will look to you to accomplish a mission of extreme difficulty and importance, and one that only you and your soldiers can do. I do not know the conditions nor part of the world, nor even how long after graduation, but I know you will be on the spot to deliver mission accomplished at least cost to the soldiers our Nation has entrusted to your command. You must be ready for that and have your soldiers ready. You must begin to get ready for that here as cadets just as you are doing today. This is why you are here.[27]

At some point in the future, the nation will turn to the Army to accomplish a mission as difficult and important as those in our history. Regardless of the mission, we must be ready and able to accomplish it with the least cost to our Soldiers. Keeping this in mind, we hope that others will follow this volume's endeavor to tackle large questions and push discussion so that when that day comes, when the call is given, and our mission is received—we are ready. Too much is at stake to do any less.

ENDNOTES - CHAPTER 25

1. Hew Strachan, "The Lost Meaning of Strategy," *Survival*, Vol. 47, No. 3, Autumn 2005, pp. 33-54, especially p. 44.

2. Gregory Foster writes extensively on strategic thinking. See Gregory D. Foster, "Teaching Strategic Thinking to Strategic Leaders," *The World & I Online*, November 2005, online edition. Also see Gregory D. Foster, "Research, Writing, and the Mind of the Strategist," *Joint Forces Quarterly*, Spring 1996, as also cited in Gallo and Jebb, Chapter 21 in this volume.

3. See *The Art of Strategy and Force Planning in Strategy and Force Planning*, 3rd Ed., Newport, RI: Naval War College, p. 20 for a more detailed examination on the strategic framework.

4. David Kilcullen, "Three Pillars of Counterinsurgency," Remarks delivered at the U.S. Government Counterinsurgency Conference, Washington, DC, September 28, 2006, available from *www.au.af.mil/au/awc/awcgate/uscoin/3pillars_of_counterinsurgency.pdf*.

5. Huba Wass de Czege discusses the functions of attack, deter, defend, and pacify in, "The Military Power to Deter, Defend, Enforce, and Pacify," Chap. 5 in this volume.

6. See Robert Chamberlain, "Back to Reality: Why Land Power Trumps in the National Rebalance Toward Asia," Chap. 18 in this volume.

7. See Michael J. Meese, "The Army in Times of Austerity," Chap. 10 in this volume, regarding adopting national strategy as Army doctrine.

8. See Kerry Schindler, "Translating Strategic Ends into Means," Chap. 11 in this volume.

9. See David Barno and Nora Bensahel, "New Challenges for the U.S. Army," Chap. 12 in this volume.

10. "U.S. Public Positive About America's Global Economic Engagement, While Support for International Intervention Slips, Finds New Pew Research-CFR Poll," news release, Washington, DC: Council on Foreign Relations, December 3, 2013, available from *www.cfr.org/united-states/us-public-positive-americas-global-eco nomic-engagement-while-support-international-intervention-slips-finds-new-pew-research-cfr-poll/p31988*.

11. *Ibid.*

12. See Scott Silverstone, "American Grand Strategy and the Future of Landpower in Historic Context," Chap. 3 in this volume.

13. "U.S. Public Positive About America's Global Economic Engagement, While Support for International Intervention Slips, Finds New Pew Research-CFR Poll."

14. See Huba Wass de Czege, "The Military Power to Deter, Defend, Enforce, and Pacify," Chap. 5 in this volume.

15. On the distinction between force and power, see Isaiah Wilson, "Reconsidering American Power," Chap. 4 in this volume.

16. Elisabeth Bumiller, "Romney's Proposal for More Military Ships Draws Skepticism," *The New York Times*, October 20, 2012, available from *www.nytimes.com/2012/10/21/us/ politics/romney-plan-for-more-military-ships-is-called-unrealistic. html?pagewanted=all&_r=0*.

17. Charles E. Heller and William A. Soft, eds., *America's First Battles, 1776-1965*, Lawrence, KS: University of Kansas Press, 1986.

18. See Elisabeth Bumiller, "West Point is Divided on a War Doctrine's Fate," *The New York Times*, May 27, 2012, available

from _www.nytimes.com/2012/05/28/world/at-west-point-asking-if-a-war-doctrine-was-worth-it.html?pagewanted=all&_r=0._

19. William E. DePuy, _Selected Paper of William E. DePuy,_ compiled by Richard M. Swain, Donald L. Gilmore and Carolyn D. Conway, eds., Fort Leavenworth, KS: Combat Studies Institute, U.S. Army Command and General Staff College, 1994, p. 373.

20. Donald B. Vought, "Preparing for the wrong war?" _Military Review,_ Vol. 57, No. 5, May 1977, pp. 19–34.

21. Conrad C. Crane, _Avoiding Vietnam: The U.S. Army's Response to Defeat in Southeastern Asia,_ Carlisle, PA: Strategic Studies Institute, U.S. Army War College, September 2002, p. 2.

22. Edward J. Drea, _In the Service of the Emperor: Essays on the Imperial Japanese Army,_ Lincoln, NE: University of Nebraska Press, 1998, p. 13.

23. See Conrad Crane, "Maintaining and Modernizing the Force in Periods of Reduced Resources," Chap. 9 in this volume.

24. See Michael Meese, "The Army in Times of Austerity," Chap. 10 in this volume.

25. For the tension between bureaucratic and professional identities, see Don M. Snider, _Once Again, the Challenge to the U.S. Army During a Defense Reduction: To Remain a Military Profession,_ Vol 4, Professional Military Ethics Monograph Series, Carlisle, PA: Strategic Studies Institute, U.S. Army War College, and Center for the Army Professional Ethic, February 2012, p. 1.

26. For a full discussion of human capital and the role of accession, development, employment, and retention in talent management, see Casey Wardynski, David Lyle, and Michael Colarusso, _Towards a U.S. Army Officer Corps Strategy for Success: A Proposed Human Capital Model Focused Upon Talent,_ Carlisle, PA: Strategic Studies Institute, U.S. Army War College, 2010.

27. Frederick M. Franks, Jr., "Address to 'MX 400: Officership'," West Point, NY: U.S. Military Academy, August 27, 2013.

ABOUT THE CONTRIBUTORS

DAVID W. BARNO is a Senior Fellow and Co-Director of the Responsible Defense Program at the Center for a New American Security, Washington, DC.

JOHN BASKERVILLE is an Academy Professor of Arabic in the Department of Foreign Languages at West Point, NY.

JORDAN BECKER is a recent Assistant Professor of International Relations in the Department of Social Sciences at West Point, NY.

NORA BENSAHEL is a Senior Fellow and Co-Director of the Responsible Defense Program at the Center for a New American Security, Washington, DC.

MATTHEW CAVANAUGH is an Instructor in the Department of Strategic Studies at West Point, NY.

ROBERT CHAMBERLAIN is an Assistant Professor of International Relations in the Department of Social Sciences at West Point, NY.

CONRAD CRANE is Chief of Historical Services for the U.S. Army Heritage and Education Center, Carlisle, PA.

JOSEPH DA SILVA is a recent instructor of International Relations in the Department of Social Sciences at the United States Military Academy at West Point, NY.

DANIEL M. GADE is a recent Assistant Professor of American politics, policy, and strategy in the Department of Social Sciences at West Point, NY.

ANDREW GALLO, a recent Assistant Professor of American politics, policy, and strategy in the Department of Social Sciences at West Point, currently serves as a brigade S-3 (operations) in the 3rd Cavalry Regiment at Fort Hood, TX.

CINDY JEBB is Professor and Department Head in the Department of Social Sciences at West Point, NY.

SETH A. JOHNSTON is an Assistant Professor of International Relations in the Department of Social Sciences at West Point, NY.

HUGH LIEBERT is an Assistant Professor of American politics in the Department of Social Sciences at the United States Military Academy at West Point, NY.

DOUGLAS MACGREGOR is Executive Vice President of Burke-Macgregor Group, LLC, Reston, VA.

JOHN MEARSHEIMER is the R. Wendell Harrison Distinguished Service Professor of Political Science and the co-director of the Program on International Security Policy at the University of Chicago, Chicago, IL.

MICHAEL J. MEESE is the Chief Operating Officer at The American Armed Forces Mutual Aid Association, Fort Meyer, VA.

SUZANNE C. NIELSEN is Professor and Deputy Head in the Department of Social Sciences at West Point, NY.

DOUGLAS OLLIVANT is a partner and Senior Vice President for Strategy at Mantid International, LLC.

RICHARD ROSECRANCE is Adjunct Professor of Public Policy at Harvard's John F. Kennedy School of Government, Research Professor of Political Science at the University of California, and Senior Fellow in the Belfer Center for Science and International Affairs, Cambridge, MA.

NADIA SCHADLOW is a Senior Program Officer in the International Security and Foreign Policy Program of The Smith Richardson Foundation, Westport, CT.

KERRY J. SCHINDLER is Branch Chief, Programs Branch (Team TAA), in the HQ Department of the Army G-37 Force Integration and Management Division, Washington, DC.

SCOTT A. SILVERSTONE is a Professor of International Relations in the Department of Social Sciences at West Point, NY.

HUBA WASS DE CZEGE is the Founder and First Director of The School of Advanced Military Studies, Ft Leavenworth, KS.

ALBERT S. WILLNER is a Principal Research Scientist in the China Studies Division at the Center for Naval Analyses, a nonprofit corporation, in Arlington, VA.

ISAIAH WILSON III is a Professor of Political Science and former director of the American Politics, Policy, and Strategy Program in the Department of Social Sciences at the United States Military Academy at West Point, NY. He currently serves as a staff officer in the U.S. Central Command.